Sustainable Economy
Corporate, Social and Environmental Responsibility

Sustainable Economy
Corporate, Social and Environmental Responsibility

Raymond W Y Kao
Ryerson University & McMaster University, Canada

World Scientific

NEW JERSEY · LONDON · SINGAPORE · BEIJING · SHANGHAI · HONG KONG · TAIPEI · CHENNAI

Published by

World Scientific Publishing Co. Pte. Ltd.
5 Toh Tuck Link, Singapore 596224
USA office: 27 Warren Street, Suite 401-402, Hackensack, NJ 07601
UK office: 57 Shelton Street, Covent Garden, London WC2H 9HE

British Library Cataloguing-in-Publication Data
A catalogue record for this book is available from the British Library.

SUSTAINABLE ECONOMY
Corporate, Social and Environmental Responsibility

Copyright © 2010 by World Scientific Publishing Co. Pte. Ltd.

All rights reserved. This book, or parts thereof, may not be reproduced in any form or by any means, electronic or mechanical, including photocopying, recording or any information storage and retrieval system now known or to be invented, without written permission from the Publisher.

For photocopying of material in this volume, please pay a copying fee through the Copyright Clearance Center, Inc., 222 Rosewood Drive, Danvers, MA 01923, USA. In this case permission to photocopy is not required from the publisher.

ISBN-13 978-981-4277-63-1
ISBN-10 981-4277-63-0

CONTENTS

	CONTRIBUTORS	xiii
	INTRODUCTION *Raymond W. Y. Kao*	1
	A Feasible Economic Paradigm	1
	Have We Put Back Equivalent Value for What We Have Taken?	1
	Profit, True or False?	2
	Can We Rely on Government for Re-distribution?	3
	It is All About Making Changes	3
	A Candle of Hope	4
I.	**CORPORATE SOCIAL RESPONSIBILITY AND DEVELOPMENT**	**7**
1.	CORPORATE SOCIAL RESPONSIBILITY *Raymond W. Y. Kao and Rowland R. Kao*	9
	Is the "Increase of Profit" the Sole Corporate Social Responsibility?	9
	Historical Perspectives on Business Social Responsibility	10
	The Issue of Corporate Profit	12
	The Challenge of Corporate Profit and Social Inequality	14
2.	ON THE DIALECTICS OF SUSTAINED (CAPITALIST) DEVELOPMENT "FROM WITHIN" *J. Hanns Pichler*	35
	A "Theory" Against the Mainstream	37
	Toward Entrepreneurially Driven "Capitalism"	39

	Uncovering the Subtlety of Implied "Dialectics"	41
	Legacy and Topical Relevance in Today's Perspective	42
	References	44
3.	**FOSTERING SUSTAINABILITY IN FAMILY FIRMS**	53
	Alan L. Carsrud and Malin Brännback	
	Introduction	53
	Overview of the Field of Family Business	54
	Succession, Conflict and Sustainability	55
	Complexity of Family Business: Eight Factors	56
	Values, Entrepreneurship and Family Firms	56
	Conflict, Succession and Ownership	58
	Drivers of Family Firm Sustainability	58
	Sustaining for the Generations	64
	Sustainability: Managing Change Process	65
	Conclusion	66
	References	67
II.	**THE CHALLENGE**	**71**
4.	**POVERTY: A SOCIAL DISGRACE AND DILEMMA**	73
	Franco Gandolfi and Philip A. Neck	
	Introduction	74
	Definitions of Poverty	74
	Rationale for Treating Poverty as a Priority Subject	77
	Scope and Scale of Poverty	78
	Possible Causes of Inequality and Poverty	83
	Effects of Poverty	90
	Implications for Change	93
	Poverty Reduction/Alleviation	95
	Conclusion	104
	References	104

5.	SUSTAINABILITY AND HEALTH CARE *Catherine Popadiuk*	107
	The Effects of Globalization on Health	108
	The Impact of Globalization on the Health of Seemingly Disparate Groups	111
	Exploitation of the Health of Vulnerable Populations in the Modern Era	115
	From Human Organs to Human Research Subjects	117
	Strategies for Sustainable Health Care	125
	The Brazilian Response to the AIDS/HIV Crises: A Model of Sustainable Decision-Making	125
	Sustainability in the Pharmaceutical Industry: Health for the Industry or the World	129
6	MINIMIZATION OF RESOURCE DRAINS AND ENVIRONMENTAL DAMAGE *Peter Hing*	135
	PART I. DEVELOPMENT OF SUSTAINABLE LIGHTING FROM GASEOUS DISCHARGE	136
	Introduction	136
	How Radiation is Generated	141
	The Development of Compact Fluorescent Lamps	144
	The Development of Phosphors	146
	Conversion UV to Visible Using Phosphors	149
	Compact Fluorescent Lamps (CFLs)	152
	Energy Conservation and Sustainable Development in Lighting	153
	Advanced Ceramics and Composites for High Intensity Discharge Lamps	154
	Development of Alumina to Translucency	156
	Ceramic-Metal (Cermets) Composites for High Intensity Discharge Lamps	162
	Development of Glass Ceramic Sealing Materials for the Ceramic Halide Lamps	167

Development of Compact White Light High Pressure Sodium Lamps — 168
Development of Seals for the Ceramic Metal Halide (CMH) Lamps — 168
Materials Systems Investigated to Produce Refractory and Metal Halide Resistant Glass Seals — 171
Conclusions — 172

PART II. DEVELOPMENT OF SUSTAINABLE SOLID STATE LIGHTING — 173

Introduction — 173
Organic Light Emitting Diodes (OLEDs) — 178
Basic Principle of Solid State Lamps Obtained from Light Emitting Diodes — 179
Materials Used for LEDs — 184
Internal Efficiency of LEDs — 188
Various Colors of LED and White LEDs — 195
Discussion — 198
Conclusion — 199

PART III. SUSTAINABLE DISPERSED COMBINED MICRO POWER AND HEAT GENERATION — 201

Introduction — 202
Review of Fuel Cell Technologies — 208
Thermodynamic Efficiency and EMF of Fuel Cells — 210
Types of Fuel Cells — 213
Design of Solid Oxide Fuel Cells — 221
Reactions Occurring at the Interfaces of the Anode, Cathode and Electrolyte — 224
Current Development of Intermediate Temperature Solid Oxide Fuel Cells (ITSOFCs) — 226
Current Status of Research in Solid Oxide Fuel Cells Worldwide — 226
Research Carried Out by the Author and His Group — 228
Discussion — 229
Summary — 234

7. BUILDING A SUSTAINABLE FUTURE FOR OURSELVES 237
   AND OUR COMMON HOME
   Mirian Vilela

   Incorporating Ethical Reflections in Our Daily Lives and 239
     Decisions
   Integrated Approach to Decision Making and Planning 244
   Participatory Governance as a Way to Ensure an Integrated 249
     Approach to Decisions

III. ENTREPRENEURSHIP EDUCATION 265

8. SUSTAINABILITY AND ENTREPRENEURSHIP 267
   EDUCATION AT THE UNIVERSITY LEVEL
   Lloyd W. Fernald

   Introduction 267
   Current Global Business Sustainability Practices 270
   Entrepreneurship Education 273
   Conclusions 285
   References 287

9. FROM ENTREPRENEURSHIP TO 291
   STEWARDSHIP-BASED ECONOMICS
   Raymond W. Y. Kao, Rowland R. Kao and Kenneth R. Kao

   Entrepreneurship 291
   Defining Entrepreneurship, Past, Present and Future 301
   Evolution of Entrepreneurial Thought 302
   Entrepreneurism 304
   Stewardship-Based Economics 306

IV. ENTREPRENEURSHIP AND SMALL VENTURE 311
   DEVELOPMENT FOR SUSTAINABILITY

10. SMALL IS STILL BEAUTIFUL AND SUSTAINABLE 313
    Wee-Liang Tan

    Schumacher — Advocate of the Small and Creative 313
    Still Relevant Today 314

Smallness and Entrepreneurship	316
Implications for Entrepreneurship Education — The Gaps that Remain	320
Conclusion	329
References	330

11. INNOVATION AND ENTERPRISE SUSTAINABILITY   333
Gary Oster

Introduction	333
Innovation Based on Fresh Ideas	334
The Source of Innovative Ideas	335
Constraints to Workplace Innovation	337
Encouraging Successful Corporate Innovation	339
Concluding Thoughts	347
References	348

12. TOWARD SUSTAINABLE ECONOMIC DEVELOPMENT: AN EXPERIMENT IN WEST AFRICA   353
Leo Paul Dana

Introduction	353
Ghana and Togo, West Africa	357
A Short History	358
Extent of Entrepreneurial Activity	361
Recommendation	371

13. LANDSCAPE ENTREPRENEURSHIP: LESSONS FROM THE MONT SAINT HILAIRE NATURE CENTRE   377
Emmanuel Raufflet, Maria Tengö, Marc-André Guertin, Kafui Dansou and Louis Jacques Filion

Introduction	377
From Classic to Social Entrepreneurship	379
Case Study: The Mont Saint Hilaire Nature Centre	382
The Nature Centre as Landscape Entrepreneur: Four Perspectives	392

Lessons for Landscape Entrepreneurship	411
Conclusion	415
References	418

14. THE CANDLE OF HOPE   421
    Raymond W. Y. Kao

INDEX   425

CONTRIBUTORS

Malin Brännback
Chair of International Business
Department of Business Studies, Åbo Akademi University
Henriksgatan 7, FIN-20500 Åbo, Finland

Alan L. Carsrud
Loretta Rogers Chair of Entrepreneurship Research
Professor of Entrepreneurship and Strategy
Ted Rogers School of Management, Ryerson University
350 Victoria Street, Toronto, Ontario M5B 2K3, Canada

Leo Paul Dana
University of Canterbury, New Zealand
GSCM — Montpellier Business School, France

Kafui Dansou
Department of Management, HEC Montréal
Édifice Côte-Sainte-Catherine
3000, chemin de la Côte-Sainte-Catherine
Montréal (Québec), Canada H3T 2A7

Lloyd W. Fernald
Professor Emeritus, University of Central Florida
Orlando, FL 32816, USA

Louis Jacques Filion
Rogers-J.A. Bombardier Chair of Entrepreneurship
HEC Montréal
3000, chemin de la Côte Sainte-Catherine
Montréal (Québec), Canada H3T 2A7

Franco Gandolfi
Director, MBA/EMBA Programs
Professor of Management, Regent University
School of Global Leadership and Entrepreneurship
1333 Regent University Drive, Suite 102
Virginia Beach, VA 23464-5048, USA

Marc-André Guertin
Environment Coordinator, City of Granby
87, rue Principale, Granby (Québec), Canada, J2G 2T8

Peter Hing
Associate Professor of Physics
Faculty of Science (FOS)
Universiti Brunei Darussalam (UBD)
Jalan Tungku Link, Gadong
BE1410, Brunei Darussalam

Kenneth R. Kao
Biomedical Science Professor, School of Medicine
Memorial University of Newfoundland, Canada

Raymond W. Y. Kao
Professor Emeritus, Ryerson University
Adjunct Professor of Entrepreneurism, McMaster University
Quality Assessor, Post Secondary Education Assessment Board
Ministry of Training, Colleges and Universities
Government of Ontario, Canada

Rowland R. Kao
Professor of Mathematical Population Biology and
 Wellcome Trust Senior Research Fellow
Boyd Orr Centre for Population and Ecosystem Health
University of Glasgow, Glasgow, UK

Philip A. Neck
Graduate College of Management, Southern Cross University
Tweed Gold Coast Campus, Cnr Wharf and Brett Street
New South Wales, 2485, Australia

Gary Oster
Associate Professor of Innovation and Entrepreneurship
Regent University, School of Global Leadership and Entrepreneurship
1333 Regent University Drive, Suite 102
Virginia Beach, VA 23464-4236, USA

J. Hanns Pichler
President, Austrian Institute for SME Research
Professor Emeritus, University of Economics and Business
Augasse 2-6, A-1090, Vienna, Austria

Catherine Popadiuk
Associate Professor, Department of Women's Health
Memorial University, 300 Prince Philip Dr.
St. John's, NL, Canada A1B 3V6

Emmanuel Raufflet
Associate Professor, Department of Management, HEC Montréal
3000, chemin de la Côte-Sainte-Catherine
Montréal (Québec), Canada H3T 2A7

Wee-Liang Tan
Lee Kong Chian School of Business
Singapore Management University
50 Stamford Road, #05-01
Singapore 178899

Maria Tengö
Department of Geography, McGill University
805 Sherbrooke Street West
Montreal, Quebec, Canada H3A 2K6

Mirian Vilela
Executive Director, Earth Charter International Secretariat and
  Earth Charter Center for Education for Sustainable
  Development at the University for Peace
Professor, University for Peace
P.O. Box 138 — 6100, San Jose, Costa Rica

INTRODUCTION

Raymond W. Y. Kao

A Feasible Economic Paradigm

On 27 November 2007 on CBC radio, David Suzuki had a message for all of us. He said that we need "a feasible economic paradigm" to deal with the problem of sustainability.

Such a "feasible economic paradigm" is one that cannot rely on the market economy. Economic doctrine has been developed entirely on the basis of the challenges of production and exchange with little regard for the matter of distribution. The main distributive responsibility lies with the exchange system in the market place, via a networking mechanism of governing, that which we (usually favorably) refer to as the market economy, with profit as the mainstream incentive.

Under the umbrella of the profit-driven market economy, we have learnt how to take from nature, the environment and people without coming to the realization as a society and as a civilization, that if humanity is to continue in this manner, it needs a sustainable economy. The problem is simple enough to appreciate — we know how to take, but we do not wish to, and perhaps do not even know how to, give back.

Have We Put Back Equivalent Value for What We Have Taken?

Grassroots movements have politicized the environmental concerns of today and for the future, but consumers still rely on massive energy consumption and resource-sapping products to maintain the high quality of living to which they have become accustomed by attractive marketing techniques. What is needed is a global, yet personal mechanism of accounting that engenders human needs, the constraints on natural resource and environmental concerns. It is by no means a new story, but sadly a very old one with often catastrophic results. The world will come closer to the solution of equitable distribution when the personal incentive for all individuals to "give back" takes precedence over the incentive to "take from" the environment, and others. Relying on the market systems to put back what we have taken, when it is too often assumed that it is our unalienable right to make a profit if it is within our power to do so, is extremely difficult for this author at least to believe. Individuals must make a personal choice to assume responsibility for the stewardship of the remarkable life on this wonderful planet.

Profit, True or False?

What is generally considered to be "profit" consists, in large part, of the unaccounted costs to people, resources and the environment, in addition to the currently accounted for costs required to bring a product or service to the consumer. The continued practice of denying these extra, undisclosed components will result in an inevitable, eventually irreversible drain on our non-renewable resources unless innovation and creativity surpass consumption. The pressing issue of poverty will remain a significant challenge for a very long time. While the plight of the poor has improved in many places, especially in the so-called "developed nations," many still live often unseen, tragic lives blighted by poverty, and throughout much of the globe abject poverty is often the norm, accompanied by an average age of mortality that would be considered tragic in developed countries. Where is the system of justice to provide these individuals with the basic requirements of life? The Market system relies on "blind" justice for distribution, and the end result is the limitless accumulation of profit for some, acquired from the undeclared costs to humanity and the natural environment. Such a process, if allowed to continue unchecked, leads to continued destitution for those out of reach of the "justice" available only to those playing the market game. So if we cannot depend on a profit-chasing economy to provide a fair and equitable distribution system, can we rely on governments?

Can We Rely on Government for Re-distribution?

A perfect government would ensure a fair and equitable distribution of resources, but as no system is perfect, no government has ever succeeded in achieving this. Karl Marx and his followers and successors overturned the distributive system of many countries, most importantly, Russia, and we are all aware of the results. China, under the leadership of its Governing Party, has made great economic progress in the post-Mao era. Some might point to its production of at least 15 new billionaires (American dollars) in a recent two-year period as a sign of its success, yet, for all its claims of socialism, China has yet to contend with the problem of child beggars in the streets of its major cities. And yet the accusing finger of poverty can be pointed in many other directions as well. Where is the justification for the US to spend over US$600 billion in an unjustified war in a foreign country like Iraq, when that war has done little or nothing to improve the lives of the Iraqis, and cost perhaps hundreds of thousands of human lives without first addressing poverty and environment damage at home?

One might argue that in a democratic nation, it is up to the citizens of that nation to engage in the political process to prevent a recurrence of the unjustified blunders that end up causing more harm than good. For individuals to take part meaningfully in the decision-making processes of their country requires education, and in the US, for instance, a residence — property ownership in effect, to register to vote, leaving the homeless perpetually disenfranchised from the process. To be a candidate for a political office without money is out of the question. Where does election money come from? The environment, resources and poor people have no money to support candidates who would be concerned about their issues. Only those who have money can further their schemes to get money to support their candidates. Leaders of other forms of governments more conveniently use their position of military strength to eliminate those who question them or create symbolic laws to get what they want.

It is All About Making Changes

It was in Belfast, Ireland, when I was invited to a posh country club for a steak dinner. The waiter asked me: "How would like your steak? Well done? Medium? Or rare?" I answered: "Done well." The difference between well done and done well is simple: the former one is that the steak will be fully cooked. "Done well," is an assurance from the chef that the steak will be prepared to suit the expectations of the best. This may mean so little to what I intend to put forth, only a simple reality which means we can make a change with no great effort, but that would make a great difference.

In a similar sense, the aim we have is not to promote capitalism or communism, socialism or libertarianism, Catholicism or Buddhism or atheism, or any of the myriad other philosophies that humankind has produced, promoted, fought for and died for. What we aim for is to create a better world for the future, for all our children, and our children's children. How we do so, is less important than that we do so. In short, how do we want to conduct our stewardship of the world? We want it done well.

A Candle of Hope

This book brings together an impressive list of international experts, all of whom share the goal of a brighter future for our descendants and ourselves. All contributors draw on their experience and expertise to discuss the obstacles and opportunities that will contribute to formulating feasible solutions towards a sustainable economy for humanity.

For my own part, I concur with David Suzuki, to say that a *feasible economic paradigm* is one that must change our mindset to realize that we are all part of the Earth, but that we don't "own" it. It is there for us as well as for the future. A healthy environment is integral to any sustainable economic solution. We must learn to share in the fruits of labor of those who have contributed their lives to make a better life for us, while restoring what Nature needs to survive and continue to serve all living beings on the planet Earth. To reiterate the message printed on the cover of "Entrepreneurism":

We are here to serve you, your children, and their children's children. When they are here, we will serve them the same way we serve you.

To achieve these lofty goals, it is a necessity to change our mindset from what we who have become so used to the primacy of the market economy, are so accustomed to. The term "Profit" should never be part of our thinking, since there really is no such thing as profit, unless our costing system is able to recognize all costs including the cost of human efforts above and beyond their minimal wage compensation, repayment of environmental and nature's contribution and restoration of resources above and under the ground. Although accounting professionals have skillfully replaced "Profit" by "Financial Income," they have not replaced what is in people's minds. "Residual" must become the reality. The allocation of residual is the decision of those who have stewardship responsibility and accountability. Full disclosure is required for comparability and reporting purposes. We need to fully recognize that there is an unaccounted cost to everything, and it is not possible to "get something from nothing."

Is this difficult? Of course it is. Changing the world always is. However, I leave you to read the collected wisdom contained in this book, with the following thought in mind. "A Candle of Hope" was a holiday greeting message sent to me by Catherine Jiong Gu (a student of mine). It was a pictorial e-card with four candles, of which only the fourth candle was lit. The first candle represented Peace, the second Love, and the third Confidence, As long as the fourth candle, representing Hope remained lit, the possibility of restoring light to each of the other candles existed. Likewise, while most realize it is impossible to replace the market economy, we at least consider the possibility of a better solution as a candle of Hope.

The End of a Beginning

I. CORPORATE SOCIAL RESPONSIBILITY AND DEVELOPMENT

1
CORPORATE SOCIAL RESPONSIBILITY

Raymond W. Y. Kao and Rowland R. Kao

Is the "Increase of Profit" the Sole Corporate Social Responsibility?

"Trust" is a simple word that is critical to the conduct of business and governance. The downfall of Nationalist China was as much due to a collapse in the confidence of the people in Chiang Kai-shek's economic policy as due to defeat at the hands of the communist revolutionaries. On the front lines, disillusioned soldiers refused to fight the Red Army. Rather, led by their generals and officers, they turned their backs on the Nationalist Government. Today, we are witness to an economic crisis of global proportions, in which the loss of trust in the banking system, has made all the efforts of governments around the world to support the banks and large corporations (such as with the US$70 billion going to the large American automakers) come to naught. The attainment of trust is a result of earning trust, and thus is intimately tied to social responsibility. Yet the late Milton Friedman said that *"The social responsibility of business is to increase profit."*[1] Profit maximization does not earn the public trust. He also asked "Can a building have moral opinions? Can a building have social responsibility? If a building can't have responsibility

---

[1] Friedman, M. (1970). The social responsibility of business is to increase its profits, *New York Times Magazine*, 13 September 1970.

what does it mean to say that a corporation can't? A corporation is simply an artificial legal structure. It doesn't have any, it's neither moral nor immoral. It's simply what it is. But the people who are engaged in it, be it the stockholders, the executives, or the employees, they all have moral responsibilities."[2] In one sense, this is true enough; if one were to ask a person on the street where to find a corporation, if they were to give any advice, they are likely to point to a building. However, Friedman's second point, that a corporation is a legal person is more important. Offenders of the law, whether natural or legal, are punishable under the law. If the legal entity is found guilty of violating the law, it will be subject to a court judgment, and for example be subject to a fine, or even lose its right to function in the market place. Just as for a "natural" person, the death sentence is the most severe punishment available under the law (though of course banned in many countries), similarly, for a legal entity, the lifting of a corporate charter, and dissolution may occur. Of course, a corporation can only "act" through the medium of its officers. The real question, then, is whether or not there is a moral ethos to which corporations should subscribe and which corporate officers' performance is measured against, above and beyond legal requirements?

Another view of a corporation is that it is an entity representing a body of people functioning in the market place as stewards, with resources entrusted to the entity that will earn a sufficient rate of return to their investment. Traditionally, only those who invested "money" into the entity directly would be considered as having a stake in the corporation. However, this view is really a distortion of the true role and function of a business entity, which has a much wider role in the market system of the market economy.

Historical Perspectives on Business Social Responsibility

Considerations of business social responsibility are not just a recent matter. Long before corporate social responsibility became a concern in

---

[2] From the transcript of an interview with Milton Friedman for "The Corporation," by Mark Achbar, Jennifer Abbott and Joel Bakan, http://www.thecorporation.com.

society, Confucius had already incorporated it into his teaching with the following words of wisdom:

> "*Communal responsibility first before profit.*"
> "*In the presence of profit, think about societal interest.*"[3]

Indeed, the importance of corporate social responsibility has been in the thoughts of many of the most important classical and neo-classical economic thinkers. For example, Adam Smith said that "*... Every individual endeavors to employ his capital so that its produce may be of greatest value. He generally neither intends to promote the public interest, nor knows how much he is promoting it. He intends only his own security, only his own gain. And he is in this led by an invisible hand to promote an end which is no part of his intention. By pursuing his own interest he frequently promotes that of society more effectively than if he really intended to promote it.*"[4] Similarly, from John Stuart Mill: "*... The cause of profit ... is that labor produces a surplus. As the wages of the labor are the remuneration of the labor, so the profits of the capitalist are properly ... the remuneration of abstinence.*"[5] More recently, in *The General Theory of Employment, Interest and Money*, John Maynard Keynes noted the vital need to establish some central controls in matters which are now left in the hands of the individual's initiative. For example, the state will have to exercise a guiding influence on matters of consumption of limited or vital resources through tax schemes, and fix the rate of interest on borrowing.[6]

Relating the operation of business entities to social responsibility has always been and continues to be a vital concern in the academic world, but more importantly as an issue rooted in business and the government as well. Unrestricted earnings, and how these earnings were distributed have

---

[3] Jin, C. (1990). *Confucius' Business Management Philosophy*. Taipei: Sun Tun Publishing Co., p. 105 (in Chinese, translated by R.W.Y. Kao).
[4] Smith, A. (1776). *The Wealth of Nations*.
[5] Mill, J.S. (1920). *Principle of Political Economy*. London: Longmans, Green, p. 405.
[6] Keynes, J.M. (1965). *The General Theory of Employment, Interest and Money*. New York: Harcourt, Brace and World, Chap. 14.

always been a matter of importance even when they are legally derived, and especially when they are of large value; in the latter case, the question of "do they really deserve it?" is invariably asked.

The Issue of Corporate Profit

Profit is a controversial word. To most people, profit is what is earned through a transaction. For example, if I sold something that cost me $3, but receive $5, then I have made a profit of $2. Thus the perception of profit is one of gain. If it is an instant transaction, involving the trade of goods of equal subjective value to both parties without adding labor or any additional input to that something in trade, then, to consider the $2 difference of trade as profit is justifiable. This fits well with J.R. Hick's definition of profit:

> *We ought to define a man's income as the maximum value which he can consume during a week, and still expect to be as well off at the end of the week, as he was at the beginning.*[7]

This definition, while in many ways sensible, really only applies in the instance of barter trade, which is not much use in practice, since government and taxation have no role in barter. Of course, barter trade is mostly a thing of the past, though it still can be found in the grey market, beyond the realm of the tax collectors. Nevertheless, the basic concept, that profit is related to an amount left over, remains central to all other definitions. Whatever the definition, it is the pursuit of this left over profit that is almost undisputably held as the basis for the existence of corporations in business. Thus dealing with the issue of corporate social responsibility, above and beyond government intervention and legislation, is a crucial challenge for corporate decision makers, as well as those concerned about the state of social justice, and the future of humanity. However, what is often missed is the fundamental, underlying question of whether or not profit really exists, if we account for all costs acquired and, in accounting terms, expensed to earn the revenue or receipt after

---

[7] Hicks, J.R. (1950). *Value and Capital* (2nd Edn.). Oxford, p. 172.

restoring what's taken from the nature, and recognizing the sacrifices by all the parties involved?

Profit driven corporate practice on the basis of accounting practice and the issue of accounting bias

There is only one official way to determine corporate profit. It is done by accounting, based on generally accepted accounting conventions and governed essentially by two rudiments: Revenue and Costs. Following on from Hicks' definition, and still used in practice, **profit** is determined as being **revenue minus cost**, where "cost" is the amount of money or cash expended.[8] Such an expression of profit has been criticized many times as not reflecting economic reality, and therefore, instead of "Profit," "Financial Income" or "Accounting Income" is used.

The expression of accounting income does not support the issue of cost determination as prescribed based on accounting convention. What for example, is the value of a child? Is the value of a CEO's child the same as the value of a shop floor worker's child? If their value is fundamentally the same, how can we compare the sacrifices of the CEO and the shop worker without accounting for the effect on those children? There are even more difficult issues if we go beyond the immediate costs associated with human sacrifice, to the role and value of the Earth itself. What is the true cost associated with the development over millions of years of the Earth's reserves of oil and natural gas, when they can never be restored by human intervention? We can and do include the cost of exploration and exploitation, but what about the cost to the Earth?

The inequalities of accounting are not confined to the problem of quantification. Quantities must be universally comparable, both nationally, and internationally in order to have any meaning in the modern "global village." Yet in the capitalist society, we can also legitimately ask what is the cost or value of war, in particular where the victors claim that their victory is to be to the benefit of both protagonists? If we consider the Iraq War of 2003 and the resultant ongoing occupation, as of the end of 2008, there were over

---

[8] Grady, P. (1965). Inventory of generally accepted accounting principles for business enterprise. New York: American Institute of Certified Public Accountants.

4200 US service men and women killed while serving in Iraq, and at a minimum tens of thousands of Iraqi civilians also killed directly as a result of the invasion and occupation since 2003, with some estimates ranging up to well over half a million.[9] At least one estimate for the prosecution of the war by the US is over US$3 trillion,[10] more than enough to offset the US$700 billion bailout fund to save the American economy in the recent recession. How does one determine if there is any "profit" in the entire process? Insofar as the accounting point-of-view matters, this is perhaps impossible to determine. Whether or not the Iraqi "beneficiaries" feel they've received good value for the invasion is also a difficult matter, however, recently, when President Bush flew to Iraq and meeting the press, he was greeted by the challenges "This is a gift from the Iraqis; this is a farewell kiss, you dog" and "This is from the widows, the orphans and those who were killed in Iraq!" as one of the reporters in the crowd first threw one shoe and then the other at the visiting dignitary (a thrown shoe is a severe insult in Iraqi culture).[11] While such an incident cannot be taken as representative of all the Iraqi people, nevertheless it begs the question: is there any way that a balance sheet and income or loss statement for this war can be structured in accordance with generally accepted accounting principles?

The Challenge of Corporate Profit and Social Inequality

The fact is that corporate profit and social responsibility are inevitably closely related. The effort to recognize social responsibility must result in social costs such as unpaid labor surplus value, environmental damage and non-renewable resources being incorporated into accounting practice. For example, workers may be underpaid by 10% of the value they contribute. In this case, if labor cost as per accounting record accounted for as $12,000,000, then adding in the 10%, $12,000,000 + $1,200,000 = $13,200,000 should be

---

[9] http://news.bbc.co.uk/1/hi/in_depth/629/629/7036068.stm.
[10] Stiglitz, J. and Bilmes, L. (2008). The three trillion dollar war, *The Times*, 23 February 2008, viewed online at http://www.timesonline.co.uk/tol/comment/columnists/guest_contributors/article3419840.ece.
[11] Myers, S.L. and Rubin, A.J. (2008). Iraqi journalist hurls shoes at Bush and denounces him on TV as a "dog," *New York Times*, 14 December 2008, viewed online at http://www.nytimes.com/2008/12/15/world/middleeast/15prexy.html.

Table 1 Cost and unpaid sacrifice added to profit (all figures are in US$ and are for illustration purposes only; they do not reflect any actual corporate figures)

Item	Accountable Cost	Added to Profit
Labor cost	12,000,000	1,200,000
Executive remuneration	9,000,000	0
Innovation and creation	4,000,000	400,000
Resources renewable	5,000,000	200,000
Resources non-renewable	20,000,000	15,000,000
Environment contribution		200,000
Total	50,000,000	17,000,000

paid to workers. As it happens, these unrecognized costs result in a surplus of $1,200,000 tabulated in the earned account or profit (see Table 1). The same principle applies to environmental damage and draining of undeniable resources.

There is a thin line between failing corporate social responsibility and corporate crime

(a) *Is social responsibility a waste?*

The profit-driven corporate mentality of the people who are responsible for the operation walks a thin line between social responsibility and corporate crime. Some of those corporate crimes could induce government or legal action, and if found guilty, result in heavy financial penalties (see for example the documentary film "The Corporation," http://www.thecorporation.com). For those who have been found guilty of causing danger to the public interest, either knowingly or through irresponsibility, this may result in personal charges as well.

We must assume that the majority of corporations are not complicit in criminal activities, but there are also some that would have done so and are both undiscovered and uncharged. More common is the case where significant damage to stakeholders is incurred, without legal implications. Whether it be the payment of legal but sub-subsistence wages to workers in developing countries, the excessive and wasteful use of packaging or the proliferation of paper advertising, and other wasteful media, these are legal but commonly criticized as excessively exploitative of natural and human resources. The automobile industry is seen by some as one of the worse offenders to social responsibility. However, we must seek alternatives. Corporations are a powerful engine for change (can anyone imagine what life would be like in many countries today without the personal automobile?), both good and bad, but we have ready examples of where their lack of social responsibility has led to financial disaster, the widening of the rich/poor gap, environmental damage, and environmental change and waste of non-renewable resources. Would we really like this to be perpetuated? If not, we must seek alternatives.

Now what would happen to the $17,000,000? If the company's finance department would present the balance sheet as well. rather than stating that there were additional costs to be added into the operating statement, instead the board might declare the extra $17,000,000 to be allocated as follows:

Executive Bonus	$9,000,000
Dividend	1,000.000
Retained Earnings	7,000,000
Total	$17,000,000

The significance of this transaction is that, while all shareholders needs are accounted for, there is no direct financial reflection of corporate social responsibility; no recognition is made by contributions other than shareholders. This includes silent contributors such as: (1) the labor value — their contribution to the worth after barely above poverty level of wages, (2) no return of what has been taken from Nature, (3) environmental damage, and (4) general societal contribution. In this sense, Friedman is right — in the absence of any direct, financial recognition of the role of such stakeholders, the concept of corporate social responsibility is so nebulous as to be essentially meaningless.

(b) *Corporate social responsibility and global economic crisis*

History is littered with stories of financial booms and busts, and economic catastrophes, from the "Tulip mania" in the Netherlands in the early 1600s and the "South Sea Bubble" in England in the 1720s to the Great Depression of the 1920s and the current Global Recession that some say signals the end of Wall Street trading as we know it. What possibly makes the current crisis different, is that it reflects a more global society, in which spatial distance shrinks to nothing for the electronic trader, and transactions involving billions of dollars can occur in the blink of an eye. That there is much good in this there is little doubt, but we must also recognize the problems that it engenders as well — in particular, the effectively limitless accumulation of wealth in the hands of the few, and the extent of the catastrophe when those few overreach themselves. Two aspects of modern economics that have recently changed have been the role of credit in personal financing, the role of the banks and the way mortgage lending is handled. While concentrating on the US, these are problems that to varying degrees affect many countries in the world.

(i) *Causes of the financial crisis part 1:*
    changing attitudes to personal finances and the credit card

Greed is a human trait that is a significant force behind progress, and a strong motivation factor for the pursuit of corporate profit maximization. In reality, the pursuit of greater profit could extend beyond a margin that can be harmful, and affect the market as a whole.

It could be argued that without a relaxation in our view of personal debt, the financial meltdown of 2008 would not have happened. It can be argued that this has been at least partially driven by the vast expansion in the level of personal credit available, and in particular, in the attitude towards credit engendered by the ubiquity of the personal credit card. While the modern credit card has been in existence for some decades (the first to use the concept of a single card to pay for transactions with different merchants was the Diner's Club card, initiated in 1950), it is only in the past quarter century or so that a pattern of consumer spending based on the credit card has become so universally established.

Issuing financial institutions grant credit to consumers with minimum proof necessary, but with interest rates approaching in some cases, 30% per annum. Combining convenience with easy access to credit, including targeting of young college and university students, and the attraction of an initial month's credit without interest payments, credit cards have become the commonly accepted medium for shopping, dining, and traveling. In the UK, unpaid balances for personal credit cards totaled £55.7 billion as of October 2008,[12] while in the US, "revolving credit" that includes credit cards was at US$962 billion as of May 2008,[13] though as a result of the economic recession, there has been some decline in "revolving credit."[14] This easy credit is supported by the extraordinarily high rates of interest, effectively giving a free ride to those who pay off their cards every month (and thus are usually better off), at the expense of poorer and less experienced users paying monthly interest. Consumer's credit expansion has certainly boosted banks and financial institutions profit expectation. The velocity of monetary spending is increasing at an accelerating rate. With credit card balances in the US rising by 75% since 1999, over a period in which real income growth and real wages have increased by 4%, many view the credit card situation as a crisis waiting to happen.[15] Over this time, the interest rates that credit card companies charge have not been universally legislated against, nor has the advertising and incentives campaigns aimed at the young and impressionable.[16] Yet, there is evidence that individuals can become addicted to credit in much the same way they can become addicted to gambling.[17] Second, if this is the case, and credit

---

[12] Butterworth, M. and Wallop, H. (2008). Credit card borrowing reaches record levels as consumers turn to plastic, *Daily Telegraph*, 30 October 2008, viewed online at http://www.telegraph.co.uk/finance/personalfinance/3279955/Credit-card-borrowing-reaches-record-levels-as-consumers-turn-to-plastic.html.

[13] Korkki, P. (2008). Watching that balance grow …and grow, *New York Times*, 13 July 2008, viewed online at http://www.nytimes.com/2008/07/13/business/13count.html.

[14] *Thomson Financial News*, 8 January 2008. US ECON: November Consumer Credit Falls by Record $7.94 Bln, viewed online at http://www.forbes.com/afxnewslimited/feeds/afx/2009/01/08/afx5897114.html.

[15] Dell, K. (2008). With defaults rising, is a credit-card crisis looming?, *Time Magazine*, 14 November 2008, viewed online at http://www.time.com/time/business/article/0,8599, 1859224,00.html.

[16] Palmer, K. and Brandon, E. (2007). Pushing credit on the college crowd, *US News and World Report*, posted 24 December 2007.

[17] Lowenstein, G. (2008). Lottery tickets and credit cards: The dangers of an irrational brain, *Scientific American*, 11 September 2008.

card companies are aware of it, what steps should they be taking to avoid targeting those who might be most vulnerable to such addictions?

(ii) *Causes of the financial crisis part 2: easy mortgage loans on housing*

The easy attitude towards debt, exemplified and possibly engendered by credit cards, received a shattering blow in the 2008 financial crisis. The fall of Wall Street that lay at the center of it, has been the source of a downfall of trust in the market economy, and in the financial institutions that stood behind it. It is a clarion call for corporate awareness of social responsibility, and for the brakes to be put on the drive for "profit" and more "profit." The immediate cause of the financial crisis was high risk lending associated with home mortgage loans. Housing mortgages have a long history. Once upon a time a home loan was strongly tied to the mortgage taker's ability to repay the loan; the loan would be secured on the property, but the security would only be secondary. Full closure of the mortgage would give the mortgage holder the right to recover the mortgager's investment, but this would be avoided at all costs, due to the impact on the minds' of people of seeing homes being foreclosed on. The sense of bad times ahead can trigger a crisis in trust on overall economy. It is this fact that further shakes the base of financial security. This has largely changed — the approval of mortgages that represent a higher and higher proportion of an individual's income reflects increased reliance on rising property prices rather than the ability of the individual to pay, and inevitably is reflected in increased vulnerability of many individuals to economic reverses, both personal and once more widespread.

The modern money market relies on rapid transactions between institutions, facilitated by the explosion in information and communications technology over the last few decades. Merely at the push of a button, there goes the money, and equally so, information in market reports (via fastest media facilities) can instantly change the perceived value of a corporation's worth, at least in part based on investors' expectations.

At the first level of credit, granting agencies can secure a contract that would charge an extreme high rate of interest (perhaps after an initial low interest "honeymoon period"), and these might then be repackaged and resold to other financial institutions. This process can continue, with each institution selling the debts onwards until at the very end, there are extremely large financial institutions underpinning the entire chain. In good times, this chain of financing works peacefully with a few foreclosures, referrals to collection agencies or declarations of personal bankruptcy by the initial borrowers. Every institution within the financing scheme works on a cashflow basis. If any part of the chain breaks, it affects the complete chain, and like multiple balloons sitting close to bursting, if one pops then the rest will as well.

(iii) *Causes of the financial crisis part 3: the lost of trust and confidence — we don't believe any more*

The market economy is the subject of endless analysis by top level mathematicians and economic theorists, governed by the hard data of well measured indicators, and constantly monitored by countless financial institutions. And yet, despite all the analysis and rational thought behind the strategies and maneuverings of businesses large and small, what the function of the market economy comes down to is largely a matter of trust. Corporate social responsibility must take into account its responsibility to shareholders and indeed, to stakeholders. More often than not, it is the majority shareholders' games that runs the corporations, with little or no real input from the small or individual shareholder. And yet it is also true that without the explicit goodwill of the shareholder (explicit because it requires conscious investment on the shareholders behalf) and the implicit "goodwill" of the stakeholders (by definition, a stakeholder is someone with a stake in the corporation), the corporation cannot exist. Yet some corporations have clear mission statements, to only serve their shareholders to protect their investments and generate a profit. While much of the media headlines are taken up by the fall of the "great," it is the little stories that often appear in the middle pages of the newspaper that are the real tragedy of the boom and bust economy. The average or small investors, and the home owners losing their houses are the real victims.

Over the past few years, there have been several profile cases where corporate executives were found guilty of fudging the books for their personal interests: Audacious Ebbers and Sullivan steered World.com to world-class profits, but the company misreported expenses by

US$3.8 billion.[18] In Canada, the Nortel Corporation was once known as a market leader in telecommunications. In 2005, a report alleged that its ex-CEO Frank Dunn and key executives improperly shifted loss provisions to achieve 2002–2003 financial targets and trigger bonuses. On 3 February 2005, the company made claims for former executives to return various corporate bonuses: Frank Dunn US$4.86 million, Douglas Beatty US$1.75 million and Michael Gollogly US$665,554.[19]

While charges of corruption were not made against the initiators of the 2008 crisis, it is true that corruption on a large scale, was symptomatic of the "anything for profit" culture that led to the downfall of institutions such as Freddie Mac and Fanny Mae, Lehmann Brothers, Northern Rock and others.

The Wall Street breakdown, financial crisis and economic downturn are symptoms of the lack of social responsibility of corporations, continuing the drive for profit with no concern for people, the environment and resources, and undermining the basis of trust that must lie at the bottom of every financial system. The bailouts engineered by governments around the world, and other government actions to ease the financial burdens and risks on individuals should help to ease the pressure in the money market, but it does not; all that happens is that economic indicators go down, down, and farther down and companies around the world fail as the spending of individuals (mostly non-shareholders in any corporation) dries up. Is there any more evidence needed that the market economy as we operate needs the trust of not only shareholders but stakeholders as well?

It seems to be a long time in the past, but the fall of the Chinese Nationalist Government is an example from the senior author's own experience, of how the downfall of a government occurs largely through mistrust of its monetary policy and economic measures.[20]

During the last stages of the Second World War, the Nationalist Chinese Government had no way to support its currency value and hyperinflation occurred, although the US government attempted to rescue the situation in

---

[18] *Time Magazine*, 5 July 2002, p. 11.
[19] *Toronto Star*, 3 February 2005.
[20] This account is largely based on the author's personal experience, however see also Ji, Z. (2003). *A History of Modern Shanghai Banking*. London: M. E. Sharpe, pp. 220–239.

1942 by issuing a US$500 million loan that included US$200 million in gold bullion to the Chinese government. As a result, tons of gold bullion were put on sale at the Agricultural (or Farmers') Bank of China in Chungking in order to reduce the amount of currency in circulation. The price of the gold was initially fixed, however this soon changed as speculation became rife. Crucially, those in the know were able to make vast amounts of money on speculation, and was soon accompanied by a number of scandals involving insider trading and corrupt buying. With vast differences in the fixed price and what would be paid on the black market, in no time at all, people lined up all the way outside of the bank, buying in total billions of dollars worth of gold. And soon there was no gold available for sale, even though the price had risen sky high. The end of the war with Japan was soon followed by the outbreak of civil war with the communists, resulting in further massive military spending and soon large populations of refugees, depleting local resources in "safe" areas, and resulting in hoarding of commodities and wild monetary speculation. Out of desperation, the bank, with the permission of the Central Bank, issued a new paper currency, the "gold yuan," bearing nominal quantities of gold (like a currency using gold as standard). This did not go well at first, however the bank then redeemed some of those notes (not all of them, because the gold shipment was not large enough to redeem all the "Gold Notes" at the same time), which resulted in note holders putting their own notes on sale in the market. Price fluctuated widely on gold notes, resulting in similar fluctuations in the price of all goods and services, to an extent that no one seemed to believe the normal bank notes any more. The prices of all commodities shot up like ballistic missiles into the sky, and monthly pay cheques came as a big bundle. In view of the amount of counting required, financial institutions would use large numbers of small children at the back of the counter, counting bills in terms of tenth thousands, then bundled up with stickers marked as $10000 or $5000. How much were these bundles worth? Perhaps no more than a bottle of Coca Cola from the small traders seated outside the bank. The end result was that the economy of the Republic of China in Nanking was governed by a force created by a market system called "the rate of inflation," as simple counting could not function in and serve the market, and in the end the money had to be weighted to determine its value at that time. Between August 1948 and May 1949, the price of rice had increased by

19 million times.[21] The net result was to destroy any support the Nationalist Government had from the middle classes who, under more stable circumstances, would have had the most to lose from a Communist regime, while a relatively rich few benefited in the short term, by taking advantage of the uncertainty where the risks would have been too great for those with fewer resources. In the end, Chiang Kai-Shek removed the entire gold reserve from Shanghai to Taiwan, signaling the complete collapse of the system and effectively marking the end of Nationalist Mainland China (though attempts to resuscitate the dead regime continued for some months thereafter).

While in many ways this situation seems distant from our own, the disasters were largely caused by individuals who exploited the system, sometimes illegally but often legally, to make huge profits while undermining the confidence of the average individual. The similar loss of confidence in banks today, while not a result of the same forces that occurred in Nationalist China, can nevertheless be traced back to the near mindless accumulation of "profit" by the few. So long as we are only hindered by what is "legally" allowed, there will always be exploitable loopholes in any system, and as the global economy becomes more integrated, the resilience to exploitation of these loopholes and resultant catastrophes is drastically lessened. We must rethink and reshape how we can promote one of the most important commitments in the market economy — that corporations must assume their social responsibility as the number one stewardship responsibility before striving for more profit, greater profit.

When the economy is in crisis, and in full recession, lowering interest rates and government bailouts of troubled corporations are ineffective methods, which may further the dissatisfaction of those affected by the recession. All these measures can be viewed as supporting the rich, while making the poor poorer, as was the case in Nationalist China.

(iv) *The emerging economic power, how China views corporate social responsibility*

Immediately after the conclusion of the 29th Olympic Games in Beijing, the Government of China, via its Ministry of International Trade, issued a

---

[21] Ji, Z. (2003). A History of Modern Shanghai Banking. London: M.E. Sharpe, p. 239.

draft soliciting opinions in respect to foreign investors, corporate social responsibility for their invested corporations. In short it reads as follows (translated from Chinese by the senior author):

One: Purpose

For the purpose of continuing economic development and growth, in connection with the Chinese counterparts, work in harmony exemplifying how corporate social responsibility helps to promote cooperation, to attain both corporate growth and society welfare, environmental health, as a reference to guide foreign investment. The purpose of this document intended to guide foreign investors investing in China.

Two: Corporate Social Responsibility in Brief

The fundamentals of corporate social responsibility include shareholders rights and responsibilities. Essentially it includes the assumption of economic, societal and environmental responsibility. For the reason of continuing development and growth. Corporate decision makers must care for corporate employees, consumers, business partners, societal and governmental related interests, promote societal harmony, assume social responsibility, recognize the totality of inter-relationship of promoting social harmony, favorable productive environment, be responsible for and appreciate the interrelationship of environment, economical, societal and preservation of favorable environment in their totality.

In all, corporate social responsibility is a three-tier system. First, abide by the law and commercial ethics. Second, seek economic value of the enterprise, and attain to fulfill the objective of long term equilibrium. And third, attaining societal benefit as corporate essential obligation. These are fundamentals of corporate social responsibility regardless of the entity.

Three: Ethics, and the Basics of Corporate Social Responsibility

Respect and protect shareholders' right, improve corporate completive ability, level of earning and legal rights.

Observe commercial ethics, against corruption.

Fairness in competition.

Continuing to create and innovate.

Protecting intellectual property rights.

Respect employee's rights, with no discrimination, protect their rights of expression, equal promotion opportunity, safety, among other things, provide a healthy, clean and safe environment, caring for their health and training need.

With consumers, corporation need to exercise discipline to provide them with honest service, no cheating, lying deception of any kind, respect their right and sort procedures to deal with disputes, promote effective communication. Help them where and when necessary.

Act with Chinese partners, recognize their rights, help with research and development efforts, help and assist them where and when necessary, help them to assume social responsibility.

Encourage cooperative spirit, extend such spirit to meaningful cooperation and effective work on corporate responsibility with others in the market.

Help where necessary to fulfill the mission of community centers, assist where and when necessary to preserve cleanness and healthy environment, and proper measure to enter and withdraw the association.

For charitable and public welfare and community service organizations, participate and/or assist in their work, encourage corporate personnel to become involved and assist such community welfare organizations. Must not in the name of charity, deceive the public or any individual.

Stay away from meaningless and wasteful competition, set example for efficiency and effectiveness, with a high standard of work, quality products promoting technical excellence and resources preservation.

Act with respect and care for the environment.

Four: Corporate Social Responsibility Support Ethics

There is no set format or guide for implementation. Essentially, corporations need to judge and implement the guide according to circumstances, initiating action as needed.

Establish high levels of corporate social responsibility and if possible, organizational mechanisms into the operational system.

Establish an environmental protection administration.

Develop the apparatus to define needed responsibility and measure progress.

Establish a network with those involved both inside and outside of the corporate entity.

Establish a needed information network with other corporations.

Develop entities for sharing of information and to learn from one another for improvement where and when necessary.

Assume a leadership role to assist others in their effort to assume corporate social responsibility.

Establishing corporate social responsibility apparatus for implementation.

The adoption of this credo (or at least its proclamation) by the Chinese government is only a recent happening, and as yet it is still in its initiation stage. Only time will tell if these brave words are matched by the necessarily braver deeds. However, it does lead us to consideration of corporate social responsibility in a number of basic areas:

(i) exploitation of labor value;
(ii) taking advantage of silent partners contribution, such as taking non-resources not to provide adequate return, but transfer into an "Earning" account for privileged distribution;
(iii) ignoring and damaging the environment, and erode its health; and
(iv) having no regard for the need for future humanity.

In order for this assumption of greater corporate responsibility to take place, "profit" must be redefined, on the basis of economic realities rather than relying on, and derive through the accounting process and efforts to have a re-distribution scheme in the market economy. By referring to China's *Corporate Social Responsibility Draft Guide*, and taking into consideration the author's earlier work, we use a simple example in connection with an early illustration provided by the American Accounting Association in its *Statement of Basic Accounting Theory* (1970). The following model illustrated in page 86 of that text represents current accounting practice:

Statement of Retained Earnings
XYZ Company
Year ended 31 December 1966

Retained Earnings 31 December 1965	$400,000
Net Income	530,000
	$930,000
Dividend	230,000
Retained Earnings 31 December 1966	$700,000 (1)

If an operating statement is made today, it would show, if based on the above model:

XYZ Company
Operating Statement
for the operating period of year 2008

Revenue	$110,000,000
Operating Cost	50,000,000
Profit	$60,000,000
Income Tax	30,000,000
Net (Retained Earnings)	$30,000,000

Consider now the following revised statement:

Profit Analysis for XYZ Company

Total	$30,000,000
Less: Silent Contributors. Contribution	17,000,000
Entitlement Profit	13,000,000
Income Tax	6,000,000
Retained Earning	$7,000,000

If the contribution from silent partners is recognized and it is not paid for, it would land in the company's liability account. However, to establish such claim, it needs material evidence. If not, it will not be recognized. The income tax will be calculated on $13,000,000, instead of on $30,000,000. The company will have paid its income tax, and the financial report audited is considered to be in accordance with the general accepted principle. The chairman of the board will then, with a big smile and with a clear conscience, be able to stand before the shareholders and say: "Thank God, we have had a good year." However, considering the natural resources taken from the ground; how is it possible to account for losses which will take millions of years to be replaced?

As it currently stands, quantification of non-renewable resources via accounting statements will not be considered generally acceptable. What the company can then do for the distribution is to show the extra gain of increase in assets with an accounting entry made to settle this matter for all:

Dr. Executive Bonus		$9,000,000
Dividend		1,000,000
Special Reserve		7,000,000
	Cr. Cash or Other Assets	$17,000,000

Nothing is illegal. Previously, the consequence of the normal form of corporate practice shows a lack of social responsibility and takes advantage of the silent business supporters. With "normal practice," the damage can be a serious matter to society, perhaps not now, but for generations to come. Of course, as with all such matters, the problems are essentially man made. We can do good for humanity and the environment, act fairly and responsibly with respect to resources, and in particular, be more innovative and creative, both for self-interest and the common good. Then, through a collective effort we can live in a world both for mankind and for Nature.

The XYZ Company Operating Statement would be structured based on "Residual"[22] instead of "Profit" or "Accounting Income" but, proposed on the basis of corporate residual for re-distribution to reflect its social responsibility, therefore, its operating statement will be:

Operating Statement*
for the operating period of year 2008

Revenue	$110,000,000
Operating Cost	50,000,000
Operating Residual	$60,000,000
Income Tax	30,000,000
Net Residual (for re-distribution)	$30,000,000

Recognize Corporate Social Responsibility

Net Residual for Re-distribution:		
Labor's Contribution	5,000,000	
Resources Replenishment	5,000,000	
Community Support	5,000,000	
Environmental Damage Repair	2,000,000	
Provision for Innovation	1,000,000	
Executive Additional Sacrifice		
For Corporate Interest	1,000,000	
Un-allocate Contingent	6,000,000	$30,000,000

---

[22] For reference on "Residual," see Kao, R.W.Y. (2007). *Stewardship-Based Economics*. Singapore: World Scientific, pp. 184 and 185.

The above financial information is for demonstration purposes only, as so-called corporate profit must be reconsidered. Unwarranted "profit" must not end up in corporate executives' pocket, rather under proper accounting it must be re-distributed to other stakeholders or contributors. This form of re-distribution system must become a part of the market economy function, and the decision for the re-distribution needs to be placed on, and as a function of corporate decision makers, not imposed by the government. In the senior author's *Stewardship-based Economics*, it is suggested that an additional class of corporate law can be established, involving two classes of corporate structures, the normal limited liability company and the social entity corporation — the latter having no special tax benefits, with the government still taxing recipients who will receive a corporate residual distribution benefit. By this mechanism, transparency of social responsibility will be upheld, and the "moral behavior" of the corporation will not be dependent on the personal morality of the CEO and directors (always susceptible to failure when the underlying culture and values demand the maximization of profit), but will be inherent in the "DNA" of the corporation, and a part of its very life's blood.

When the Nationalist Chinese Government failed to control inflation, people lost confidence in the currency; consequently people often relied on barter or warehouse receipts for trading, though of course warehouse receipts lost their value once the backing of the receipt value is lost. Rice was the most important commodity because of its role as the foundation of the people's diet. When confidence in the official currency approached zero, warehouse receipts for sacks of rice became a *de facto* currency. However, when the warehouse doors were opened, there was sometimes nothing there — the rats had eaten everything. Trusting corporations without guidance by appropriate levels of social responsibility will be like trusting the rats with the warehouse.

Appendix: An example of corporate greed for profit, and failure to assume its social responsibility resulting in a government intervention.

The following news release from the Government of Newfoundland and Labrador in respect to corporate social responsibility.

The following statement was issued by the Honorable Danny Williams, Premier of Newfoundland and Labrador. It was also read in the House of Assembly:

Province Introduces Legislation Regarding Abitibi Bowater

I stand today to inform my honorable colleagues and the people of the province of a very important piece of legislation our government will introduce today in this legislature.

This piece of legislation is very simply about trees and water — the most basic of all natural resources. Natural resources that rightfully belong to the people of Newfoundland and Labrador. Indeed, our province is home to an abundance of natural resources; some of which have not been properly managed or protected in the past.

However, this government stands for something different. We stand for the protection, preservation and fair and proper development of all our natural resources. This certainly includes those related to the forestry industry.

We all know that the pulp and paper industry has faced tremendous challenges in the past few years. The people of Stephenville felt this first-hand when Abitibi Bowater closed their mill a couple of years ago. And I am proud to say that the people of that region were resilient and strong in the face of that adversity and survived and thrived.

Today, our people in Grand Falls-Windsor and surrounding region are facing the same fate. Abitibi Bowater has announced that after a century of operations, they will be closing their doors on 28 March 2009.

I would like to quote from a letter dated 24 March 1903, from Mayson Beeton, President of the Anglo-Newfoundland Development Company Limited — the predecessor to Abitibi — to the Right Honorable Sir Robert Bond. He said, "I have come to this colony for the purpose of ascertaining whether there are available any timber lands and water powers suitable for the creation of pulp, paper and lumber mills of the capacity we want for the supply requirements at home."

Furthermore, Section 3 of the 1905 Charter Lease states, "The Lessee shall be entitled (so far as the Government can, consistently with any grants heretofore made and actually subsisting grant the same) to have, use and enjoy for its milling and logging business all streams, lakes, watercourses, springs or water in, upon under or intersecting the demised premises, and all water power or powers in and upon Exploits River down to and excluding Bishops Falls and particularly, but not by way of limitation, the entire water power of Grand Falls on said Exploits River...."

These statements lay out the clear indication of the purpose and being of the company in this province.

This company has been granted some very generous terms in the past, in order to ensure they continue operations in this province. Now, through their decision to close their operations, they have effectively told the province that they are no longer willing to stand by their commitments. Abitibi has reneged on the bargain struck between it and the province over the industrial development of the province's timber and water resources for the benefit of the residents of the province.

Having said that, we cannot as a government allow a company that no longer operates in this province to maintain ownership of our resources. We will not give away our valuable timber and water resources to a company that does not honor its historic commitments on industrial development of our timber resources.

For 100 years, Abitibi and its predecessors have enjoyed the privilege of Newfoundland and Labrador's natural resources. It simply makes sense that if Abitibi are not going to continue the operation of a pulp and paper mill and renege on their commitment to our province they will no longer have access to our natural resources.

We will, therefore, today introduce a bill to ensure these valuable natural resources are returned to their rightful owners — the people of Newfoundland and Labrador.

There are numerous charters and licensing agreements which allow Abitibi to operate in this province and those relevant to the natural resources of Newfoundland and Labrador will be repatriated to the province.

The Provincial Government will also be taking control of the power plants of Abitibi as without these power plants the hydro power would be wasted. Nalcor Energy will now manage this asset. Abitibi may be compensated for any power related infrastructure assets which the Provincial Government takes control of.

It is not our intention to adversely affect the business interests of lenders or independent business partners of Abitibi in Newfoundland and Labrador and we will be discussing this matter with lenders and partners in the days ahead.

While the Government of Newfoundland and Labrador will now own and control these assets, we will allow Abitibi full use of them until 31 March 2009 so that the mill can remain in operation as indicated by the company.

Once Abitibi ceases operations in Grand Falls-Windsor our government task force which is already fully operational will continue to work for the best interests of the people of the region.

I have complete confidence in the resilient people of Grand Falls-Windsor and the surrounding area and the viability of the community, and our government is committed to stand by them through this transitional period.

2
ON THE DIALECTICS OF SUSTAINED (CAPITALIST) DEVELOPMENT "FROM WITHIN"

J. Hanns Pichler

Underlying hypotheses and observations, Schumpeter states in the early German edition of his seminal *Theory of Economic Development* (1912),[1] were not invented or merely fictitious, but taken and gleaned from economic reality in contrast to — then — prevailing equilibrium oriented and essentially "static" views of interpreting the market based capitalist process as "conditioned by given circumstances" (as he subtitled the very first chapter). Thus, the telling motto right on the title page of the first edition: "Hypotheses non fingo." (As such never appearing again in any later issues, including the English translation of 1934; see Annexes 1 and 2.)

From hindsight one might be left wondering as to what, in fact, makes Schumpeter's early conceived vision of the leadership role of the entrepreneur in "economic life" still so very topical, if not to say outright indispensable for explaining the dynamics of the "capitalist" system. In recognizing role and importance of entrepreneurially driven innovation with related forces of "creative destruction" as intrinsically market based

---

[1] Newly edited and reprinted with an "Introduction" by J. Roepke and O. Stiller (2006). References and quotations in the following are being identified, respectively: if relating to the earlier German editions (in particular, the first or second) as *Theorie* followed by year; if relating to the English version as *Theory* (1934 or reprints). Quotations translated from the German editions being either omitted or referred to only passim in the 1934 English version, are marked "transl. J.H.P."

phenomena, Schumpeterian notions indeed seem to have gained new momentum in today's economic debate for the very understanding of entrepreneurial by driven systems, including competitive entrepreneurial behavior with emphasis also on related entrepreneurship education.[2] All that against a bibliographical background of his "Theory" which — intermittently nearly forgotten, widely misread or misinterpreted — took fully 14 years until its second, in parts radically revised and modified edition in 1926.[3]

Schumpeter explicitly voices his irritation in the foreword to the second edition that readers of the earlier version obviously "mistook" the book as a kind of "history" of economic development in line with the — methodologically more descriptive — German "Historical Schools" to which, nonetheless, the very flow and partly rather verbose style of the original text undoubtedly shows a certain affinity. In restating and emphasizing the theoretical thrust of his argument, the somewhat lengthy subtitle[4] was added from the second edition onwards (and retained also in the English translation) to bring home the very essence together with substantial revisions to the core second chapter on "The Fundamental Phenomenon of Economic Development."[5]

In the context of such revisions Schumpeter, in our view, perpetrated two "sins": Firstly, by trying to schematize, thereby narrowing down and kind of "sterilizing," in the second chapter the very role of the

---

[2] Witness the numerous university chairs and programs on "entrepreneurship" having sprung up, and still expanding, over the past decades. Cf. more recently also Thomas K. McCraw (2007) with extensive references to Schumpeter's "Legacy"; or the relevance of innovative elements and factors in the context of the New (endogenous) Growth Theory (cf. P.M. Romer *et al.*, 1990), as well as distinct Schumpeterian traits in the relatively new discipline of "Evolutionary Economics."

[3] As essentially the basis for the subsequent English translation, published 1934 at Harvard after the third and fourth — both largely unchanged — German printings (1931, 1934).

[4] In German: "Eine Untersuchung über Unternehmergewinn, Kapital, Kredit, Zins und den Konjunkturzyklus"; in English: "An Inquiry into Profits, Capital, Credit, Interest and the Business Cycle" ("Profits" to be understood entrepreneurial or "private").

[5] In German: "Das Grundphaenomen der Wirtschaftlichen Entwicklung" (*Theorie* 1912, 103–198; 1926, 88–139; *Theory* 1934, 57–94).

entrepreneur to the meanwhile famous, again and again being referred to, "five cases" in "the carrying out of new combinations";[6] as such conveying a rather bloodless, sort of descriptive "listing" of implied entrepreneurial traits and "characteristics" lending itself to a rather limited, yet tempting interpretation as a sort of proxy for defining the "Schumpeterian entrepreneur," quite in contrast to the full blooded picture so vividly painted in the original version refraining from such schematization. Secondly, by omitting the entire seventh chapter (from 1926 onward),[7] wherein Schumpeter tried to put his vision and overall conceptualization in a systemic context by way of a "holistic" topping off in form of a socio-economic synopsis to the expositions in the preceding chapters. It seems a pity that, especially the English reader, remains deprived of a possibly still more comprehensive and deeper understanding of the very thrust of the Schumpeterian message even if, admittedly, this chapter (of nearly 90 pages in the German original) might appear less rigorously argued.

A "Theory" Against the Mainstream

In order to fully appreciate the very boldness of Schumpeter's message, his "Theory" needs to be viewed in light of the prevailing mainstream of economic thought at time of its first publication. Classics and Neoclassics, notably of the Viennese marginal ("Grenznutzen") tradition with Eugen v. Boehm-Bawerk and Friedrich v. Wieser as principal advisers to Schumpeter's habilitation at the Vienna University,[8] clearly were dominating the discipline's common body of knowledge; and so was Marx' quite different, non-market based ("socialist") interpretation

---

[6] *Theorie* 1926, 100f.; Theory 1934, 66, by contrast to the German version not explicitly being "listed," but less conspicuously integrated in the text as such (see Annex 3).

[7] In German: "Das Gesamtbild der Volkswirtschaft" ("Overall View of the Economy," transl. J.H.P.), *Theorie* 1912, 463–548.

[8] Based on his first book, entitled: "Das Wesen und der Hauptinhalt der theoretischen Nationaloekonomie," Leipzig 1908 ("The Nature and Content of Theoretical Economics"), repeatedly also being referred to (as "Wesen" for short) in Schumpeter's subsequent *Theorie*.

of the economic process, all of which Schumpeter was well familiar with, while more specifically having been exposed, of course, to neoclassical thinking in the Viennese academic "style." His habilitation thesis as mentioned, submitted in 1908, indeed was devoted to a theoretical treatment and discussion of the "state of the art" at the time, including a rather shrewd reception and re-interpretation of Walrasian equilibrium as an exposition of "pure economics" on essentially static grounds.[9]

These scientific environs and ingredients are important to note as points of departure in Schumpeter's own "Theory," wherein his critical stand against the prevailing "mainstream" finds ample expression right in the first chapter[10] by pointing at the intrinsically static, "circular flow"-type view of "economic life" and voicing his discontent over the obvious deficiency of such theorizing to adequately capture and explain the underlying dynamics of the market based "capitalist" process. By contrast, he explicitly commends Marx as — with his (dialectic) methodology — being able to indeed grasp the intrinsically dynamic nature of "economic development."[11]

---

[9] Cf. Walras, L.: "Elements d'economie politique pure ou theorie de la richesse sociale," Lausanne 1874–77; English translation by Jaffe, W.: "Elements of Pure Economics," Homewood, Ill.-London 1954.

[10] Entitled "The Circular Flow of Economic Life as Conditioned by Given Circumstances," *Theory* 1934, 3, 56; in German: "Der Kreislauf der Wirtschaft in seiner Bedingtheit durch gegebene verhaeltnisse," *Theorie* 1912, 1–102. Already the "Physiocrates," Schumpeter argues, in grasping "the fact of circular flow ... ipso facto describe a static economy ... And this remained the objective of pure economics to our days." Also with A. Smith, "wherever his arguments rest on firm ground, his view is essentially static ... Wherever he speaks of progress, he never explains this on the basis of economic processes in themselves ..." (*Theorie* 1912, 92ff., transl. J.H.P.)

[11] "The only major attempt toward the problem of development is the one of Karl Marx... He strived to treat the development of economic life itself on basis of economic theory. His accumulation, his immiserization, his crisis theories follow from pure economic reasoning ... aiming at the evolution of economic life as such ... not just its circular flow ..." (Theorie 1912, 98; transl. J.H.P.) And if he "had not been more than a purveyor of phraseology, he would be dead by now. Mankind is not grateful for that sort of service and forgets quickly the names of the people who write the librettos for its political operas." (Schumpeter, 1942, 5.)

To mention as of specific relevance in this very context is Eugen v. Boehm Bawerk's profoundly neoclassical — and pointedly anti-Marxian — "The Positive Theory of Capital"[12] as for Schumpeter yet another bone of contention and point of critical departure since, despite its erudite theoretical reasoning, again resting on essentially "static" grounds and, therefore, bound to miss the intrinsic nature of "capitalist" dynamics. (For an ingenious early re-interpretation of "The Positive Theory" with Boehm-Bawerk's subtle theorizing on the "roundaboutness" of capitalist accumulation by his contemporary Swedish economist Knut Wicksell see graphical illustration, Annex 4.)[13]

It is against such background and dissatisfaction with mainstream "circular flow" concepts as prevailing then, that Schumpeter's own "Theory" evolved and took shape: as a theoretical — and in its endeavor similar to Boehm Bawerk's preceding, albeit "static" — attempt to, for his part, provide a non-Marxian dynamic interpretation of capitalist "development" driven by its inherent systemic forces "from within."[14]

We shall try in the following to pinpoint — against such background — what seems to emerge as a kind of "hidden agenda" behind Schumpeter's vision rendering it such lasting a legacy for interpreting capitalist development and its dynamics.

Toward Entrepreneurially Driven "Capitalism"

In taking a profoundly critical stand against mainstream "statics," Schumpeter in his "Theory" endeavors to depict market based (long term) "economic development" as an ever-changing — and as such never toward

---

[12] Translated with a "Preface" by W. Smart, London-New York 1891. German original: "Positive Theorie des Kapitales" (1889), as Vol. 2 of "Kapital and Kapitalzins"; a centerpiece til today of neoclassical capital theory, which propelled its author to international fame. Boehm-Bawerk by the way, as Schumpeter states himself, never really approved of his "Theory" (cf. *Theorie* 1926, "Vorwort").

[13] Cf. Wicksell, K. (1893).

[14] "By development, therefore, we shall understand only such changes in economic life as ... arise by its own initiative, from within." (*Theory* 1934, 63.) "Development in our sense is then defined by the carrying out of new combinations." (*Ibid.*, 66; with the "five points" to follow, see Annex 3.)

equilibrium tending — process of "economic life" generally. This, in fact, constitutes the all pervading thrust of his argument; and indeed no one — apart from Marx in his systemic theorizing — has done so before in a similarly rigorous fashion which, no doubt, lends such seminal and lasting fascination to his "Theory."

The essence of capitalist dynamics, in Schumpeter's view, thus boils down to a continuous pursuit of "carrying out ... new combinations"[15] as an entrepreneurially driven process which proves "that economic life never is static; it lies in the very nature of development."[16] The question then arises: who is "carrying out," what stands for the "new" and how are "new combinations" being carried through?

Schumpeter's straightforward answer to that is: the entrepreneur, being depicted and singled out in the very "Schumpeterian" meaning (or "in our sense" as he repeatedly emphasizes). In any given economic moment or situation, so his argument, there exist "numerous possibilities for new combinations," yet only a small group has the drive and takes "leadership" to, in fact, carrying them through, while "most do not see them."[17] Thus, "... the carrying out of new combinations is a special function ... of people who are much less numerous than all those who have the 'objective' possibility of doing it. Therefore, ... entrepreneurs are a special type, and their behavior ... the motive power of a great number of significant phenomena."[18] Hence it is, with Schumpeter, the entrepreneur — and only he — who "'leads' the means of production into new channels ... drawing other producers ... after him," thereby rendering "a service, the full appreciation of which ... is not so easily understood by the public at large."[19]

---

[15] *Theory* 1934, 66.

[16] *Theorie* 1912, 162 (transl. J.H.P.).

[17] *Theorie* 1912, 162 (transl. J.H.P.).

[18] *Theory* 1934, 81f.

[19] *Ibid.*, 89; yet, such "leadership in particular ... must be distinguished from 'invention.' As long as they (inventions, J.H.P.) are not carried into practice, inventions are economically irrelevant." (*Ibid.*, 88). However: "In as much as the carrying out of new combinations constitutes form and substance of development, so much so is the leader's initiative its driving force." Alas, not all are "equally far sighted and energetic ..." (*Theorie* 1912, 162, footnote; transl. J.H.P.)

From there it follows, "the most typical incorporation of future value creating potentials is a new enterprise ...," and the "specific type" as characteristic for "a special class of economically active individuals has taken on a name of its own, namely *entrepreneur*."[20] The entrepreneur as the driving or "leading" force in economic life, be it as "business founder"[21] or as "creative innovator" who through "anti-hedonist"[22] activity and initiatives creates future values. "They (these values, J.H.P.) correlate with new combinations, ... new combinations translated in value terms ... the shadows of things to come ...."[23]

In carrying out new combinations, the entrepreneur, firstly, singles out from a "multitude of various moments ... the related right decision ... which is given to few people only with specific capabilities, and secondly, carries them through. These are the characteristics of our entrepreneur, of our man of action. They are inseparable and of equal importance. And the result is economic development, progress";[24] development or progress being triggered by "our type" of (Schumpeterian) entrepreneur.

Uncovering the Subtlety of Implied "Dialectics"

The role of the Schumpeterian entrepreneur, as inseparably being geared to the very essence of "economic development," thus resembles a kind of "hidden" form of what might be called Schumpeterian "*dialectics*" for interpreting the dynamics of capitalist development from a (non-Marxist) systemic perspective.

---

[20] *Theorie* 1912, 170f. (transl. J.H.P.); or somewhat more barren in the English version later on: "The carrying out of new combinations we call 'enterprise'; the individuals whose function it is to carry them out we call 'entrepreneurs'." (*Theory* 1934, 74).

[21] In merciless Schumpeterian understanding: If a business founder merely continues to manage his "enterprise ... in simply a static way, he ceases to be an entrepreneur!" His very nature "is linked to creating (to combining, J.H.P.) something new." (*Theorie* 1912, 174, footnote; transl. J.H.P.)

[22] *Theory* 1934, 94; the entrepreneur as — in a "non-hedonist" way — ever being absorbed by "the joy of creating, of getting things done, or of just exercising ... ingenuity." (*Theory* 1934, 93.)

[23] *Theorie* 1912, 170 (transl. J.H.P.).

[24] *Theorie* 1912, 177 (transl. J.H.P.).

The market system itself, under "given circumstances," thereby constituting the *thesis*; the entrepreneur in the Schumpeterian sense as the driving (also the "creatively destructive") force being the *antithesis* to the system, ever striving to "outcompete" given circumstances by way of new combinations and thus — temporarily at least — trying to be or to become a kind of "monopolist";[25] finally, the *synthesis* of such a scenario to be seen in prevailing market forces tending forever to catch up with, to "compete down" temporarily dominating entrepreneurial initiatives provoking, by force of such process, entrepreneurial creativity yet anew in trying to tackle or outmaneuver the system "from within" and, as such, quite distinct from Marxist "dialectics."

The entrepreneur in such a scenario takes on the role of unsettling "disequilibrator," as an ever-disturbing element to static or "circular flow" tendencies toward equilibrium in the very sense of "creative destruction"; as a movens of forever challenging the system "conditioned by given circumstances,"[26] of constantly trying to trick competitive market constraints and forces through innovative "new combinations" providing thus the intrinsic drive for (Schumpeterian) "economic development."

Different from Marx, different also from the classical-neoclassical and as such essentially "static" concepts, Schumpeter in his "Theory" boldly presents an alternative (non-Marxist) interpretation of the "capitalist" process with the entrepreneur taking centerstage. It is this very boldness too, which in good measure seems to account for the lasting relevance, if not to say fascination of his "Theory" up till now (shortly, by the way, to celebrate the 100th anniversary since its first printing).

Legacy and Topical Relevance in Today's Perspective

By provocatively casting the entrepreneur — traditionally being considered the "epitomy" of capitalism itself — as sort of villain or "antithesis"

---

[25] Since, with Schumpeter, "perfect competition" temporarily always having been "suspended whenever anything new is being induced ... ," thereby providing "the fundamental impulse that sets and keeps the capitalist engine in motion." (Schumpeter, 1942, 104f.)

[26] Cf. heading of the very first chapter of the "Theory" (in German: "... Bedingtheit durch gegebene Verhaeltnisse"; *Theorie*, both 1912 and 1926).

to the market system with its "mainstream" proclaimed tendencies toward (static) equilibrium, amply testifies to the originality of Schumpeter's own theorizing. Thereby depicting the specific role of the entrepreneur under systems-related aspects further implies that the very same ("capitalist") system essentially derives its inherent strength and dynamics from ever self-renewing entrepreneurial drive and initiatives; dynamics and strength, in the end, for sustained reproduction of the system as such out of its own forces, or "from within."

Notwithstanding Schumpeter's later skepticism under changed economic conditions in the face of World War II whether entrepreneurially led capitalism indeed may "survive,"[27] we today can witness a sheer global revival of Schumpeter's early vision: be it in form of a new and growing awareness of the need for entrepreneurial initiatives, values and attitudes as crucial for sustainable development and more broadly based welfare; be it in recognizing the specific relevance of "entrepreneurship education," or the importance of diversified entrepreneurially based small and medium sized business structures; be it in the context of fostering business start-ups combined with venture capital financing and concomitant tendencies toward privatization worldwide (including related emphasis on economies "of scope" rather than just one-sidedly "of scale")[28] — this all relates to the very notion of Schumpeterian "entrepreneurship" as being reflected in entrepreneurially driven initiatives, creativity and "leadership." Leadership that in any market based system stands for structural diversification, for sustained viability and capabilities of success and sheer systemic "survival" under competitive conditions.[29]

From a contemporary perspective, relevance and importance of Schumpeter's vision nowadays seems to be demonstrated vividly in the

---

[27] Cf. his famous "Capitalism, Socialism and Democracy" (1942) and numerous related references; it is in this his later work (not in his "Theory") wherein Schumpeter explicitly coins the popular and much cited phrase of "creative destruction" (later on back-translated into German as "schoepferische Zerstoerung").
[28] Cf. Aiginger and Tichy (1984).
[29] Cf. Heertje (1981); Heertje and Perlman (1993); Heilbroner (1993); Scherer (1992); Scherer and Perlman (1992).

ongoing — and partly still painful — restructuring from formerly centrally planned to market oriented systems in Central and Eastern Europe. A transformation whereby the final verdict over success or failure in large measure hinges on how effectively these economies are capable to build and rebuild their over decades ruthlessly weakened, if not outright ruined entrepreneurially based business structures as a prerequisite for economic dynamics and sustained development in an increasingly competitive environment with more and more diversified markets.[30]

More than ever, as it seems, can under today's regional as indeed worldwide challenges Schumpeter's erstwhile vision serve as a valuable guide, as a kind of compass with a view to policy formulation for entrepreneurially conducive framework conditions, or more bluntly still: for creating conditions wherein entrepreneurial initiatives, creativity and leadership in the very Schumpeterian meaning can thrive and adequately are being rewarded. To conclude on that note in Schumpeter's own words: "Look around — and you will see, things really are like that."[31] Or in conformity to his early motto again: "Hypotheses non fingo."[32]

References

Aiginger, K. and Tichy, G. (1984). *Die Groesse der Kleinen. Die Ueberraschenden Erfolge kleiner and mittlerer Unternehmungen in den Achtziger Jahren*, Vienna.

Allen, R.L. (1991). *Opening Doors. The Life and Work of Joseph Schumpeter*, 2 volumes, New Brunswick.

Anderson, B.M. (1915). Schumpeter's Dynamic Economics, *Political Science Quarterly*, Vol. 30, December.

Backhaus, J.G. (ed.) (2003). *Joseph Alois Schumpeter. Entrepreneurship, Style and Vision*, Boston.

---

[30] Cf. Becker and Knudsen (2002); Backhaus (2003); Giersch (1984 and 1987); Scherer (1999); Shionoya and Perlman (1994).

[31] *Theorie* 1934, "Vorwort" (Preface) to fourth German printing (transl. J. H. P.).

[32] See Annex 1; as kind of an invitation to scientifically "creative destruction" Schumpeter, by the way, sums up the preface to the first edition wishing for himself "nothing more that this work as soon as possible be rendered obsolete and forgotten." (Transl. J.H.P.) — And this invitation, after now almost 100 years, apparently still holds.

Becker, M.C. and Knudsen, T. (2002). Schumpeter 1911. Farsighted Visions on Econonomic Development, *American Journal of Economics and Sociology*, Vol. 61, April.

Boehm, S. (ed.) (1987). *Joseph A. Schumpeter. Beitraege zur Sozialoekonomik*, Vienna.

Boehm-Bawerk, E.v. (1921). *Positive Theorie des Kapitales* (Innsbruck 1889), 4th printing, ed. by Wieser, F.v., Jena 1921 (= Vol. 2 of "Kapital und Kapitalzins").

Bottomore, T. (1992). *Between Marginalism and Marxism. The Economic Sociology of J.A. Schumpeter*, New York.

Chandler, A.D. Jr. (1997). *The Visible Hand. The Managerial Revolution in American Business*, Cambridge, Massachusetts.

Id. (1990) *Scale and Scope. The Dynamics of Industrial Capitalism*, Cambridge, Massachusetts.

Clark, J.B. (1912). Theorie der wirtschaftlichen Entwicklung, *American Economic Review*, Vol. 2, Nr. 4 (review).

Clemence, R.V. (ed.) (1951). *Joseph A. Schumpeter. Essays on Entrepreneurs, Innovations, Business Cycles and the Evolution of Capitalism*, Cambridge, Massachusetts.

Dopfer, K. (1994). *The Phenomenon of Economic Change. Neoclassical vs. Schumpeterian Approaches*, in Magnusson, L. (ed.), Boston-Dordrecht-London.

Ebner, A. (2003). *The Institutional Analysis of Entrepreneurship. Historist Aspects of Schumpeter's Development Theory*, in Backhaus, J.G. (ed.), Boston.

Elliott, J.E. (1983). Schumpeter and the Theory of Capitalist Economic Development, *Journal of Economic Behavior and Organisation*, Vol. 4, December.

Fagerberg, J. (2003). Schumpeter and the Revival of Evolutionary Economics. An appraisal of the literature, *Journal of Evolutionary Economics*, Vol. 13, Nr. 2.

Giersch, H. (1984). The Age of Schumpeter, *American Economic Review*, Vol. 74, May.

Id. (1987). Economic Policies in the Age of Schumpeter, *European Economic Review*, Vol. 31, February/March.

Haberler, G. (1981). *Schumpeter's Capitalism, Socialism and Democracy. After Forty Years*, in Okada, M. (ed.), Kyoto (also in Heertje, New York).

Harris, S.E. (ed.) (1951). *Schumpeter. Social Scientist*, Cambridge, Massachusetts.

Hedtke, U. and Swedberg, R. (eds.) (2000). *Joseph Alois Schumpeter. Briefe/Letters*, Tuebingen.

Heertje, A. (ed.) (1981). *Schumpeter's Vision. Capitalism, Socialism and Democracy after 40 Years*, New York.

Heertje, A. and Perlman, M. (eds.) (1990). *Evolving Technology and Market Structure. Studies in Schumpeterian Economics*, Ann Arbor (3rd printing 1993).

Heilbroner, R.L. (1981). Was Schumpeter right? *Social Research*, Vol. 48, Nr. 3.

Id. (1993). Was Schumpeter right after all? *Journal of Economic Perspectives*, Vol. 7, Summer.

Klausinger, H. (1993). *Schumpeter und die Grosse Depression. Theorie-Diagnose-Politik*, Diskussionsbeitraege, Institut fuer Volkswirtschaftslehre der Universitaet Hohenheim, Nr. 78.

Kurz, H.D. (2005): *Joseph A. Schumpeter. Ein Sozialoekonom zwischen Marx und Walras*, Marburg.

Id. (2006). *Schumpeter on Innovations and Profits. The Classical Heritage*, Paper, Conference on "Neo-Schumpeterian Economics: An Agenda for the 21st Century," Trest (mimeo).

Langlois, R. (1998). Schumpeter and Personal Capitalism, in Eliasson, G. and Green, C. (eds.), *Microfoundations of Economic Growth. A Schumpeterian Perspective*, Ann Arbor.

Magnusson, L. (ed.) (1994). *Evolutionary and Neo-Schumpeterian Approaches to Economics*, Boston-Dordrecht-London.

McCrae, R.C. (1913). Schumpeter's Economic System, *Quarterly Journal of Economics*, Vol. 27, Nr. 3.

McCraw, T.K. (2007). *Prophet of Innovation. Joseph Schumpeter and Creative Destruction*, Cambridge, Massachusetts–London.

Mokyr, J. (1990). *The Lever of Riches. Technological Creativity and Economic Progress*, New York.

Mugler, J. (1990). Entrepreneurship and the Theory of the Firm, in Donckels, R. and Miettinen, A. (eds.), *New Findings and Perspectives in Entrepreneurship*, Aldershot.

Id. (2002). Strategic development of SMEs in Turbulent Environments, in Piasecki, B. (ed.), *Entrepreneurship and Small Business Development in the 21st Century*, Lodz.

Nelson, R. and Winter, S.G. (1982). *An Evolutionary Theory of the Firm*, Cambridge, Massachusetts.

Nicholas, T. (2003). Why Schumpeter was Right. Innovation, Market Power, and Creative Destruction in 1920s America, *Journal of Economic History*, Vol. 63, December.

Perelman, M. (1995). Retrospectives. Schumpeter, David Wells and Creative Destruction, *Journal of Economic Perspectives*, Vol. 9, Nr. 3.

Roepke, J. (2002). *Der lernende Unternehmer. Zur Konstruktion und Evolution unternehmerischen Bewusstseins*, Marburg.

Roepke, J. and Stiller, O. (eds.) (2006). *Joseph Schumpeter. Theorie der Wirtschaftlichen Entwicklung*. Nachdruck der 1. Auflage von 1912, ergaenzt um eine Einfuehrung, Berlin.

Romer, P.M. (1990). Endogenous Technological Change, *Journal of Political Economy*, Vol. 98, Nr. 5.

Scherer, F.M. (1984). *Innovation and Growth. Schumpeterian Perspectives*, Cambridge, Massachusetts.

Id. (1992). Schumpeter and Plausible Capitalism, *Journal of Economic Literature*, Vol. XXX, September.

Id. (1999). *New Perspectives on Economic Growth and Technological Innovation*, Washington D.C.

Scherer, F.M. and Perlman, M. (eds.) (1992). *Entrepreneurship, Technological Innovation and Economic Growth. Studies in the Schumpeterian Tradition*, Ann Arbor.

Schmidt, K.-H. (1987). *Vorlaeufer und Anfaenge von Schumpeters Theorien der wirtschaftlichen Entwicklung*. Arbeitspapiere des Fachbereichs Wirtschaftswissenschaft, Neue Folge, Nr. 8, University Paderborn.

Schumpeter, J.A. (1908). *Das Wesen und der Hauptinhalt der theoretischen Nationaloekonomie*, Leipzig.

Id. (1912). *Theorie der wirtschaftlichen Entwicklung*, Leipzig.

Id. (1934). *The Theory of Economic Development. An Inquiry into Profits, Capital, Credit, Interest and the Business Cycle*. Translated by R. Opie, Cambridge, Massachusetts.

Id. (1942). *Capitalism, Socialism and Democracy*, New York; 5th edn. Introduction by T. Bottomore, London.

Id. (1946). Capitalism, *Encyclopedia Britannica*, London.

Id. (1949). Science and Ideology, *American Economic Review*, Vol. 39, March (=Presidential Address, December 1948).

Id. (1949). The Communist Manifesto in Sociology and Economics, *Journal of Political Economy*, Vol. 57, June; reprinted in Clemence, Cambridge, Massachusetts.

Id. (1949). *Economic Theory and Entrepreneurial History*, in Center for Research in Entrepreneurial History: *Change and Entrepreneur. Postulates and Patterns in Entrepreneurial History*, Cambridge, Massachusetts.

Id. (1991) *Comments on a Plan for the Study of Entrepreneurship*, reprinted in Swedberg, Princeton.

Seidl, C. (ed.) (1984). *Lectures on Schumpeterian Economics*, Berlin etc.

Shionoya, Y. and Perlman, M. (eds.) (1994). *Innovation in Technology, Industries and Institutions. Studies in Schumpeterian Perspectives*, Ann Arbor.

Stolper, W.F. (1991). The Theoretical Bases of Economic Policy. The Schumpeterian Perspective, *Journal of Evolutionary Economics*, Vol. 1, Nr. 3.

Id. (1994). *Joseph Alois Schumpeter. The Public Life of a Private Man*, Princeton.

Stolper, W.F. and Seidl, C. (eds.) (1985). *Joseph A. Schumpeter. Aufsaetze zur Wirtschaftspolitik*, Tuebingen.

Streissler, E.W. (1992). *The Influence of German and Austrian Economics on Joseph A. Schumpeter*, Paper, Conference of the International Joseph A. Schumpeter Society, Kyoto (mimeo).

Swedberg, R. (1991). *Joseph A. Schumpeter. His Life and Work*, Oxford.

Id. (1991). *Joseph A. Schumpeter. The Economics and Sociology of Capitalism*, Princeton.

Id. (1992). Schumpeter's Early Work, *Journal of Evolutionary Economics*, Vol. 2, Nr. 1.

Vecci, N. de (1995). *Entrepreneurs, Institutions and Economic Change. The Economic Thought of J.A. Schumpeter (1905–1925)*. Translated by A. Stone, Aldershot.

Wicksell, K. (1893). *Ueber Wert, Kapital and Rente nach den neueren nationaloekonomischen Theorien*, Jena; reprinted in London School of Economics Series Nr. 15, London (1933).

Id. (1997). Zur lehre von der Steuerinzidenz, Diss., Uppsala (1895); transl. as "Income Taxes and Duties," in Sandelin, B. (ed.), *Knut Wicksell. Selected Essays in Economics*, Vol. I., London-New York (esp. Part II, Appendix to Eugen v. Boehm-Bawerk).

Winter, S.G. (1984). Schumpeterian Competition in Alternative Technological Regimes, *Journal of Economic Behaviour and Organisation*, Vol. 5, Nr. 3–4.

Theorie der wirtschaftlichen Entwicklung

Von

Dr. Joseph Schumpeter.

Hypotheses non fingo.

Leipzig,
Verlag von Duncker & Humblot.
1912.

THE THEORY OF ECONOMIC DEVELOPMENT

An Inquiry into Profits, Capital, Credit, Interest, and the Business Cycle

JOSEPH A. SCHUMPETER

TRANSLATED BY
REDVERS OPIE

COPYRIGHT 1934
BY THE PRESIDENT AND FELLOWS OF HARVARD COLLEGE

FIRST PUBLISHED BY THE DEPARTMENT OF ECONOMICS
OF HARVARD UNIVERSITY AS VOLUME XLVI IN THE
HARVARD ECONOMIC STUDIES SERIES, 1934

SCHUMPETER's FAMOUS "FIVE CASES"
characterising entrepreneurially driven development
"by the carrying out of new combinations":

(I) The introduction of a new good – that is one with which consumers are not yet familiar – or of a new quality of a good. (2) The introduction of a new method of production, that is one not yet tested by experience in the branch of manufacture concerned, which need by no means be founded upon a discovery scientifically new, and can also exist in a new way of handling a commodity commercially. (3) The opening of a new market, that is a market into which the particular branch of manufacture of the country in question has not previously entered, whether or not this market has existed before. (4) The conquest of a new source of supply of raw materials or half-manufactured goods, again irrespective of whether this source already exists or whether it has first to be created. (5) The carrying out of the new organisation of any industry, like the creation of a monopoly position (for example through trustification) or the breaking up of a monopoly position.

("Theory" 1934, p. 66)

Boehm-Bawerk's "Roundabout Production"*
<in WICKSELL's re-interpretation> **

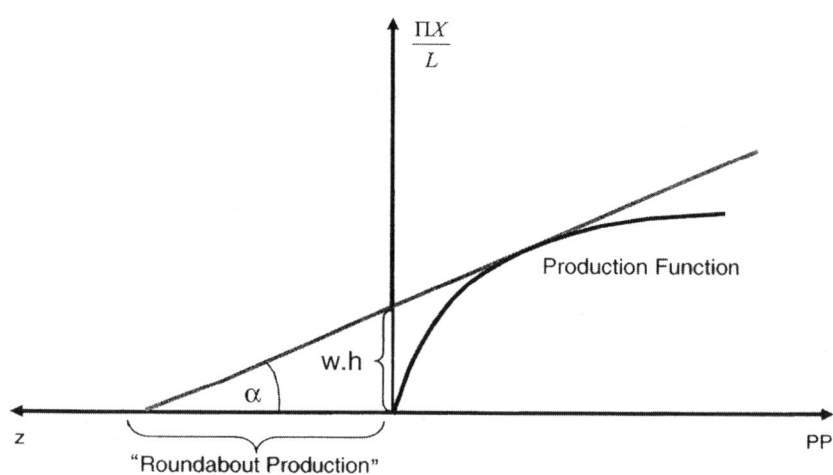

$\dfrac{\Pi X}{L}$ ····· Output : Employment (= Labour Productivity)

PP ····· ⌀ Production Period

z ····· "Roundabout Production" $\left(= \dfrac{2}{i} \right)$

3
FOSTERING SUSTAINABILITY IN FAMILY FIRMS

Alan L. Carsrud and Malin Brännback

Introduction

This chapter focuses on sustaining family owned and managed firms in an increasingly competitive global environment. The issue of sustainability of family firms has long been an area of interest (Neuberg and Lank, 1998; Ward, 2004). Family firms dominate the economies of most nations and range from the newest, or smallest, firms to the largest multinational, or oldest firm on the globe (Astrachan and Shanker, 2003). Over time, firms move beyond the start-up issues of opportunity recognition, planning and initiating a venture to the next levels which focus on sustainability, growth, and global competitiveness. Firms become more aware of a social system that existed within them from the start, *the entrepreneur and their family*. This social system is often reflected in the family firm by a striving for immortality on the part of founder and family using the mechanism of the firm. Often these firms reflect the desire of the founder and/or their family to create some form of legacy for future generations. Thus, the desire and goal for the sustainability of the family firm, via long term survival, are often parts of the "tacit" knowledge of firm (Brännback *et al.*, 2008). In this chapter we will try to show how family firms use this tacit knowledge to sustain themselves over long periods.

Overview of the Field of Family Business

At this point, a brief overview of the history of the field is appropriate (Sharma, 2004; Sharma *et al.*, 1996). The study of family business, from an academic standpoint, is often assumed to begin with the founding of the journal *Family Business Review* in 1987, although Hoy and Sharma (2006) in their excellent review of the history of the field, date it back to a dissertation by Grant Calder at Indiana University in 1953. Research on family firms has tended to focus on the leaders of such firms, usually male (Hall *et al.*, 2006; Steier, 2001; Poza and Messer, 2001). Typical of this orientation is the paper by Poza and Messer (2001) who discussed spousal leadership and continuity of the family firm with the implicit assumption the spouses were female, while the firm leaders were male, often first-born males. Clearly women can run family firms and research has started to address their leadership role (Cole, 1997; Hisrich and Fulop, 1997). This focus on demographic factors related to leaders reflects the fact that much of the family business field continues to lack any unifying theories. It remains focused on demographic analysis of characteristics rather than on predictive theories.

To help family firms be sustainable, researchers and consultants need to develop both good data, sound theories of the family firm, and apply them to real family firms. If the study of family business is to advance, researchers need to start adopting or developing definitions and theories that can gain legitimacy within the broader study of this social phenomenon. Much of what we know is from case studies, primarily of males, that are only loosely connected to theory. Some attempt to say they are adopting the methodology of "grounded theory" (Eisenhardt, 1989), but it is time to move beyond the current approaches. Despite 55 years of work, we still have much to learn if we are going to help family firms to survive, be sustainable, thrive and grow.

Research themes and definitions

Family business research is typically characterized by research themes such as succession, intergenerational conflict, and governance (Miller *et al.*, 2003; LeBreton-Miller *et al.*, 2004; Ward, 2004; Sonfield and

Lussier, 2004; Carney, 2007). Interestingly, these topics are also critical to sustainability of economic activity especially when considered from a family business perspective. While, the academic field of family business cannot agree on a definition of what constitutes a family business or even a family (Carsrud *et al.*, 1996; Sharma *et al.*, 1996; Chua *et al.*, 1999; Carsrud, 2006), in reality this seems less importance to family owned and managed firms. Their view is much more pragmatic: "… if we see ourselves as a family firm, we therefore are one." Often, however, families do not realize they are family firms until there is a family issue that brings that dimension into focus. That focus usually comes with issues of succession and conflict. However, family firms are not identical, clearly there are what one might consider traditional family firms, entrepreneurial firms where the founder is still in control, established owner/manager firms, and then family firms who are professionally managed. Carsrud *et al.* (1996) proposed 16 different classifications of family firms. Regardless of classification, different types of firms have different strategies.

Succession, Conflict and Sustainability

The defining event for business owning families is some form of family conflict or succession crisis. Either one will have consequences for the sustainability of the family firm, but it is succession that is clearly much more critical to the long term sustainability (Handler, 1990 and 1992; Rogers *et al.*, 1996). In fact, succession may be a source of conflict in itself. Certainly, the management of the family and the firm must change with the size, complexity, and diversity of the organization. Firms must also change when the sustainability of the business is threatened, which can also threaten the existence of the family. Hence, in this chapter sustainability takes a different meaning from *sustainable business*. Sustainability in family business context is here first and foremost seen as ensuring that the business survives succession. Thus sustainability means the sustainability of the family as well as the firm. If a family business also can be classified as a "green" business we have to speak of sustained sustainable business — and that is beyond the scope of this chapter.

Complexity of Family Business: Eight Factors

While one might describe the family firm as the "totem pole around which the family dances" it is a very complex entity around which they "dance." Several factors can be used to describe the complexity of the firm. This will be discussed in more depth later in this chapter. There are eight factors that impact the growth and sustainability of the family firm:

(1) succession, inheritance, and retirement (Handler, 1990 and 1992; Miller *et al.*, 2003; Garcia-Alvarez and Lopez-Sintas, 2006);
(2) strategic thinking, globalization, and innovation (Hall *et al.*, 2006);
(3) professionalization of management (Songini, 2006; Moores and Craig, 2006);
(4) governance of the family in the firm (Gallo, 1995; Gallo and Tomaselli, 2004; Cabrera-Suárez *et al.*, 2001);
(5) transfer of knowledge within the family firm (Brännback *et al.*, 2008; Trevinyo-Rodriguez and Tapies, 2006);
(6) governance of the firm (Astrachan *et al.*, 2004);
(7) managing conflict within the family firm (Kellermanns & Eddleston, 2006); and
(8) separating the family wealth from the family firm (Lyagoubi, 2006).

Values, Entrepreneurship and Family Firms

What many entrepreneurs fail to appreciate is that their new firm often morphs into a family owned and managed business with little forethought as to long term viability or how to manage the family aspect of the business. Individuals who start firms have unique values of their families that they bring to the firm. One of the great strengths of family firms is a strong tradition of shared moral and ethical values (Yan and Sorenson, 2006). It is often these shared values that are the basis for the legacy being created by the firm. These shared values also are examples of how family systems impact the business system.

Figure 1, based on Hoy and Verser (1994), demonstrates the intersections of three social systems: management, ownership systems, and family in a family firm. As the entrepreneur grows older their personal goals

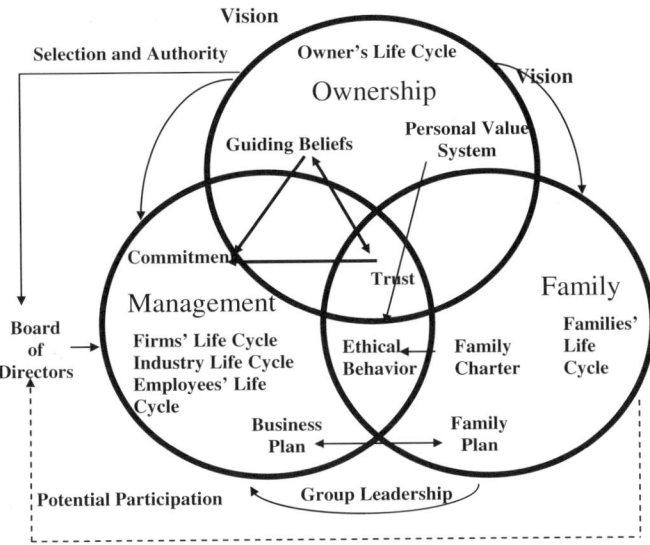

Fig. 1 The family firm.

change as does the firm's business goals. With these changes in goals, there are required changes in strategy. One of these changes is that entrepreneurs often have families, many of whom will join the venture in some capacity (Gersick *et al.*, 1997). In many family businesses, the differences in goals between the generations (founder versus offspring) become major issues in family succession and therefore impact sustainability.

Many family firms have to work at preserving and maintaining entrepreneurship as family firms get ossified at times and often will not innovate. Yet innovation is critical for long term sustainability in increasingly competitive global markets (Brännback and Carsrud, 2008). Most entrepreneurs and family business owners recognize that growth is usually good. They recognize that larger organizations typically have more resources, greater credibility, and more employees beyond just family members. However this growth requires realizing that it was easier to be nimble and change with new knowledge and innovations when a small venture. Thus, as a firm gets bigger they need to avoid rigidity of status quo nor the tyranny that some tacit knowledge brings in family firms. Striving to be "immortal" as a family firm does not mean "failure to adapt or change." A desire to leave a legacy may be a goal, but it alone will not guarantee sustainability.

Conflict, Succession and Ownership

One of the great management challenges of a family firm is avoiding the perils of conflict over roles, power, money, traditions, growth, and personalities. This is *frequently* frustrating to managers, family members, and employees. Too often it is an unsuccessful juggling act. This is because family firms literally begin when the entrepreneur starts a firm. If they use family funds, family as employees, or even have a family, their family members are involved even if the entrepreneur fails to be aware of that involvement. These conflicts increase as the firm moves from the "owner-manager" to a "partnership of siblings or spouses" and finally to a "consortium of cousins" (Rosenblatt *et al.*, 1985). This transition of ownership is compounded by changes in who constitutes the family over time (Ward, 2004). The role of ownership will be discussed in greater detail later in this chapter.

The resulting three-dimensional model of family business (Ownership, Family, and Business) as shown in Fig. 1 makes the management of the family business the bookend to the complexity and challenge of starting the firm. This figure shows just how complex family firms can be and demonstrate why sustainability is so difficult to achieve.

Drivers of Family Firm Sustainability

There are multiple drivers that impact the sustainability of the family firm. Several of these drivers are discussed in detail below.

Conservative orientation: beneficial and hazard

Studies have shown that family firms operate relatively conservatively, such that the orientation of their owners and/or managers is less profit and growth-oriented, and more risk-averse than their non-family firm counterparts (Donckels and Frohlich, 1991; Gallo, 1995). This has implications for both innovation within the firm and the potential downside to the financial well-being of the family which the firm supports. At the same time there is evidence that those in family firms believe in personal sacrifice for the long term sustainability of the firm which also includes a sense of personal responsibility and stewardship of the family firm (Khanin and Mahto, 2007). Gallo (1995) postulated that family firms are less open to outsiders because of trust, which in many cultures is associated primarily with family members or clans. Another way to perceive this inside versus outside is via identity or ownership. Consider a family owning a firm has not only physical ownership but also a "psychological ownership."

Family orientation has had other impacts. Family firms tend to reinforce the status quo, emphasizing shorter-range decision making. These family firms tend to be more centralized and are less likely to have formal training programs in place than non-family firms (Ellington *et al.*, 1996). However, Ward (2004) would disagree with that assessment. These results may well have been influenced by the society, culture, and economy in which these firms operated such as Catholic Spain in the case of the Gallo (1995) study. However, not all firms are innovation adverse or unable to develop long term strategies critical for sustainability.

Innovation, strategic orientation and sustainability

One of the biggest issues that face family firms is the lack of strategic planning for both the family and the firm (Carlock and Ward, 2001; Chrisman and Carsrud, 1989 and 1991). In a ten-year study of strategy and innovation in family firms, Moores and Craig (2006) failed to support previous studies of the strategic orientation of family firms in Australia. For example, their family firms considered innovation practises and strategy to be critically important. Their study also revealed interactions between innovative strategy and environmental uncertainty associated with technological change, and the scope and timeliness of information acquisition and use. They concluded that family firms manage and adjust to innovative strategy, do not select postures based on environment and innovative strategy, but adapt such postures over time. They suggest linkages between established family firms and innovation are stronger than previously assumed (Moores and Craig, 2006), a view supported by Ward (2004).

Sustainability as tacit knowledge

If families in business develop unique knowledge about their firm and its competitive environment then understand the un-written, but tacit knowledge held by members of these families is critical to the sustainability of the firm (Brännback et al., 2008; Cabrera-Suárez et al., 2001). Given the comparisons of family versus non-family firms, researchers suggest that a level complexity exists among behavior and performance variables for each that may be different. To really understand the tacit knowledge held by member of firms requires both rigorous research methodologies and operational definitions if such comparisons between family firms and non-family firms are to be useful (Gudmundson et al., 2003; Carsrud, 2006). Brännback et al. (2008) consider these reflections of the different tacit knowledge that families transmit between generations as unique knowledge about to how to operate the family firm that does not exist in non-family firms. The lack of adequate research on such tacit knowledge reflects the fact that family business research has been constrained in its scope because of the theoretical concepts examined and the complexity of the interaction of those concepts in reality. Here is clearly where Eisenhardt's (1989) call for grounded theory could be most useful.

Sustainability: managing family, firm and wealth

As entrepreneurs' personal goals change over time they may become less attached to the firm they started. They may want someone in the family to take over the firm or consider exiting the firm to capture the wealth accumulated there (Gersick et al., 1997). Likewise the assets needed, or investment required, for the firm to grow may be beyond what the entrepreneur and their family considers personally acceptable or available. Thus they may then consider selling the firm. While this reduces the need for the family to provide management succession it does create issue of wealth management and inheritance. In this case the legacy being created is wealth separate from the family's firm. Separating the family wealth from the family firm may necessitate selling the firm to family member, to management, and/or to others outside the firm.

Thus, what is a legacy changes from the wealth of owning a family firm to the wealth being managed by a family office or private banker. While it is not likely that most entrepreneurs will be involved in an Initial Public Offering (IPO), it does remain an option for some. Often family firms are merged or acquired for the assets that may be critical to the growth of another firm. Other options include liquidation or shrinking and regenerating the firm in a new direction to better fit the entrepreneur's personal goals (Carsrud and Brännback, 2007). Sustainability is not just for the firm, but also for the family.

A key to having a successful firm is to deal with the role of the family in the firm early and effectively as this will eliminate many of the less critical issues in the process. This is not to suggest that family not be involved, but that the entrepreneur plans this process as well. One way to do this is focusing on goal setting for both the family and the family in the firm. Is every one headed the same direction? This is the reason one needs individual "strategic" plans for family that are involved in the firm. It is very hard to have a functional family owned and managed business if the family is dysfunctional. To make the family firm successful it is important to understand of the complexity of the family enterprise.

Identity, ownership and sustainability

It is important to realize that there is a difference between "ownership" of a business and the "ownership" of the family. In family firms these are often confused (Khanin and Mahto, 2007). Ownership can mean the motivation to possess something, much like children wanting to possess toys as youths or the biggest house as an adult. Ownership can also mean control of physical space or territory as one has seen in the kingdoms of the Middle Ages. Ownership can also mean having possessions that have an instrumental function, such as allowing people to do other things. Clearly both Franklin Roosevelt and George W. Bush enjoyed the "ownership of wealth and a family name" which allowed them to ultimate claim the prize of being the President of the United States. Certainly in this definition of ownership one thinks of the family firm as the "totem pole" for the family, as the firm serves as a symbolic expression of who they are. That is the family's identity is the firm. This sense of ownership impacts one's sense of self-efficacy, self-identity, and having a place in society. Thus ownership of the family firm has broader implications than just ownership of wealth or an asset.

There are a number of other issues that face a family owned and managed firm as it continues to develop. One is that families grow often faster than the size and value of the firm. Rapid growth of family size has a diluting effect on potential managerial and ownership control. It is also true that what holds a family together often changes from bonding by biological-emotional and emotional ties to more bonding legal ownership by the third generation (Carsrud *et al.*, 1996). As family takes on more and more managerial roles (entrepreneurs often want to take care of their children and other family members) there are increasing barriers to promoting non-family to top managerial roles where outside expertise is needed. If family members want to join the firm then there are the issue of educating them for management positions and learning to treat them as employees not family (Gersick *et al.*, 1997; Ward, 2004; Carsrud, 2006).

Sustainability: planning for change over time

As mentioned above, as the firm grows the goals and objectives of the first generation may be very different from those of later generations (they do not realize the hard work it took to create the firm). This difference in goals can mean disgruntled shareholders, often minority shareholders, or individuals without the necessary skills and training to do their jobs properly (Handler, 1990 and 1992; Carsrud, 2006). There is also the changing nature of relationships between family members as they age and take on new social roles. Likewise there are changing relationships with employees and family as the firm grows and management becomes more distant from new employees. If building an effective management team was critical at the start-up stage, it is even more critical as the entrepreneur grows the firm into a family owned and managed business. Male entrepreneurs often forget that the female members of their family can be strong managers (Cole, 1997). Part of this reluctance reflects the changing roles for men and women in various cultures and ethnic groups (Cole, 1997; Hisrich and Fulop, 1997).

Long-term sustainability: inheritance and succession

For a family firm to outlast the first generation there is a need for a shared vision of the future of the family and the firm. Family owned and managed firms are the most complex because they have both the complexity of the business environment and the complexity of the family. Here once again leadership becomes critical. This leadership challenge is most obvious in dealing with the related issues of succession and inheritance (LeBreton-Miller *et al.*, 2004). Inheritance is the transmission of property or wealth while succession is the transmission of a particular position in a firm (Rogers *et al.*, 1996).

To deal with succession and inheritance there are in essence two sets of strategic decisions: eliminating personnel or potential leaders, and dividing existing assets or creating new assets (Rogers *et al.*, 1996). When one cannot find appropriate leadership within family members via succession then there are the challenges of bringing in outside management as leadership. Regardless there are the issues professionalizing family managers or board members in the family firm. Owners of family businesses traditionally resist bringing in outside managers or boards of directors because they do not want anyone telling them what to do or because they do not want to reveal company secrets. Entrepreneurs need to bring in outsiders in both management and boards if they are going to have sufficient human capital and social resources to grow (Carsrud and Brännback, 2007).

Sustainability: managing transitions

What has been attempted in the above discussion is to show the transitions the founding entrepreneur has to make if a firm is to be sustained over time. This requires understanding markets as well as the family (Moores and Mula, 2000). These concerns in the business arena move from the reliance on one person, to building a management team, to dealing with excessive attachment to the firm, learning let go, and finally successor development. In the arena of family the founding entrepreneur is dealing with attention to family, family resentment, building family competence, entry of in-laws, and sometimes teambuilding among siblings and children. In the ownership area the entrepreneur is obviously dealing with passing on control, and choosing an appropriate ownership model to avoid conflict over succession and inheritance (Rogers *et al.*, 1996). The entrepreneur is the one who is leading the business, but who is leading the family might be very different. In some cultures, those who lead the family are women, not men.

Building for the future

In the family arena the post-entrepreneurial family should be focused on building family competence, harmony, and teamwork. They must address historical roles and issues as well as a potentially growing difference in the cultures and backgrounds of the different family branches because of marriages. The family will have to manage issues of status and fairness as well as the acceptance of differences in family members and their personal goals and objectives including increasingly freedom of career choices. Communications in a multigenerational family are often difficult and indirect. As the firm grows, issues in the ownership realm shift to managing reinvestment, shareholder liquidity, and board representation. Firm governance in the immediate post-founder period is usually the parents in the family or a family controlled board. Over time, the nature of how the firm is governed and who is on the board will shift. Thus, managing growth transitions in family firms is not always easy (Tan and Fock, 2001; Ward, 2004).

Thus, in the generation after the founding entrepreneur the family owned and managed firm is now dealing with:

(1) building professional management and systems,
(2) escaping the founder's shadow,
(3) caretaking of the firm while recreating the "Founder's Dream,"
(4) redefining the leadership model, and
(5) developing the next generation of family members to lead the firm.

Sustaining for the Generations

For the family firm, keeping the entrepreneurial spirit alive is hardest in the period of the "cousin consortium" (Handler, 1990 and 1992). Here business issues are concerned with non-family leadership, aggressive reinvestment, and maintaining innovation (Carsrud and Brännback, 2007).

In the family area, the concerns are managing family scale and the potential conflict between different branches of the family. If there is going to be long term viability of the family owned and managed firm work, then there has to be a healthy relationship among siblings and the children of siblings (Gersick *et al.*, 1997). For the sustainability, there has to be a shared vision or dream about the family firm and its direction. This begins with the founding entrepreneur setting the vision. As the firm gets older, this requires a relatively similar approach or business philosophy to be developed as leadership is transferred to different generations. Individuals in the family and in the family firm must have the ability to capitalize on the unique talents of each person as well as their deep knowledge of a shared history of the firm (Brännback *et al.*, 2008). What sometimes is hard to keep in a family is the notion of a generosity of spirit or "one for all and all for one." Certainly there will be rivalry, but the issue is to make sure it is constructive managed (Gersick *et al.*, 1997; Rosenblatt *et al.*, 1985).

Sustainability: Managing Change Process

As the firm grows the family ownership is going to have to manage the change process (Ward, 2004). The reality is that there is nothing more difficult to do, nor more uncertain than trying to change an existing organization. The firm and family leadership need to manage change in a variety of areas. These include:

(1) what is being changed at the firm and in the family,
(2) the degree of change required of all participating,
(3) the timing for change: crisis or not,
(4) the anticipated resistance from family, from leadership, and from employees,
(5) the size of the firm,
(6) how spread out geographically the firm is, and
(7) the climate for change at the firm.

Major changes in any existing organization are fragile and difficult to implement, especially in an established family firm. Remember it takes time, energy, resources, and skills for change in even the most flexible organization to occur. It is important also to remember that what to change is related to how one is going to change it. Constant communications are necessary and essential. It helps if all involved with the firm (family and non-family) are committed to change, but patience is required. One must manage this change process. It is essential that family firm leadership has a compelling vision of the future which can serve as a new paradigm or a reframing of the existing situation in the firm. When discussing family business it should have been clear that organizations are a collection of open systems. Firms expand, contract and respond to various pressures, but hopefully are held together by dedicated behavior (Ward, 2004; Chrisman and Carsrud, 1989 and 1991).

Conclusion

In this chapter we have attempted to outline the critical issues that face family owned and managed firms if they are both to sustain the family as well as the firm. We have attempted in this chapter to show that certain critical issues impact the survivability and sustainability of the family firm. Family firms must deal with the issues of succession, inheritance, and retirement (Miller *et al.*, 2003; Garcia-Alvarez and Lopez-Sintas, 2006). They must constantly be engaged in strategic thinking, addressing globalization, and engaged in innovation (Hall *et al.*, 2006). They must foster professional management (Ward, 2004; Songini, 2006; Moores and Craig, 2006) as well as governance of both the family and the firm (Gallo and Tomaselli, 2004; Ward, 2004; Astrachan *et al.*, 2004).

Sustainability also means the transfer of knowledge, often tacit, within members of the family firm (Brännback *et al.*, 2008; Trevinyo-Rodriguez and Tapies, 2006). Critical to sustainability is to assure that there is personal sacrifice and the assumption of risk by members of the family, thus managing conflict within the family firm (Kellermanns and Eddleston, 2006). Finally it is critical to remember that sustainability is sustainability of the family, not just the firm and therefore at some point it is important to separate the family wealth from the family firm (Lyagoubi, 2006). This chapter should challenge those interested in the sustainability of family firms to understand the complexity of that task and the factors that will contribute to a family firm surviving beyond the founding entrepreneur.

Family business sustainability is an important part, a pillar of overall sustainable economy. To put it simply, the continuation of a family business is a function of overall sustainable economy, where the public is served by not only the present, but also all future generations thereafter.

References

Astrachan, J.H., Keyt, A., Lane, S. and McMillan, K.S. (2004). *The Loyola Guidelines for Family Business Boards*. Chicago: Loyola University-Chicago.

Astrachan, J.H. and Shanker, M.C. (2003). Family business' contribution to the U.S. economy: a closer look, *Family Business Review*, 16(3): 211–219.

Brännback, M. and Carsrud, A.L. (March 2008). A decade of do they see what we see? A nordic tale about perceptions of entrepreneurial opportunities, goals and growth, *Journal of Enterprising Culture*, 16(1): 55–89.

Brännback, M., Carsrud, A. and Schulte, W. (2008). Exploring the role of *Ba* in family business context, *VINE: Journal of Information and Knowledge Management Systems*, 38(1): 104–117.

Cabrera-Suárez, K., De Saa-Pérez, P. and García-Almeida, D. (2001). The succession process from a resource- and knowledge-based view of the family firms, *Family Business Review*, 14(1): 37–46.

Carlock, R.S. and Ward, J.L. (2001). *Strategic Planning for the Family Business: Parallel Planning to Unite the Family and Business*. London: Palgrave MacMillan.

Carney, M. (2007). Minority family business in emerging markets: organization forms and competitive advantage, *Family Business Review*, 20(4): 289–300.

Carsrud, A.L. (2006). Commentary: "Are we family and are we treated as family? Nonfamily employees' perceptions of justice in the family firm": It all depends on perceptions of family, fairness, equality, and justice, *Entrepreneurship: Theory and Practice*, pp. 855–860.

Carsrud, A.L. and Brännback, M. (2007). *Entrepreneurship*. Westport, Connecticut: Greenwood Press.

Carsrud, A.L., Perez, S.E. and Sachs, R. (1996). A multi-national study of a typology for family and closely-held firms, in *Proceedings of the 7th Annual Family Business Network Conference*. Edinburgh, Scotland, September.

Chrisman, J.J. and Carsrud, A.L. (1989). Outside contributions to business ventures development and change, *Journal of Organizational Change Management*, 2(3): 75–87.
Chrisman, J.J. and Carsrud, A.L. (1991). Outsider assistance needs of pre-venture and established small businesses: a comparison of minority and non-minority clients, *Entrepreneurship and Regional Development*, 3(3): 207–220.
Chua, J., Chrisman, J. and Sharma, P. (1999). Defining the family firm by behavior, *Entrepreneurship: Theory and Practice*, 23(4): 19–39.
Cole, P.M. (1997). Women in family business, *Family Business Review*, 10(4): 53–71.
Donckels, R. and Fröhlich, E. (1991). Are family businesses really different? European experiences from STRATOS, *Family Business Review*, 4(2): 149–160.
Eisenhardt, K.M. (1989). Building theories for case study research, *Academy of Management Review*, 14(4): 532–550.
Ellington, E., Jones, R. and Deane, R. (1996). TQM adoption practices in the family-owned business, *Family Business Review*, 9(1): 5–14.
Gallo, M. (1995). The role of family business and its distinctive characteristic behavior in industrial activity, *Family Business Review*, 8(2): 83–97.
Gallo, M.A. and Tomaselli, S. (2004). Family protocols in Spain: a survey of 10 years of experience, in *Proceedings of the Family Business Network and International Family Enterprise Research Academy Annual Conference*, Copenhagen, Denmark, September.
Garcia-Alvarez, E. and Lopez-Sintas, J. (2006). Founder-successor's transition: a model of coherent value transmission paths, in Poutziouris, P.Z., Smyrnios, K.X. and Kleine, S.B. (eds.), *Handbook of Research on Family Business*, Edward Elgar Pub., pp. 237–252.
Gersick, K.E., Davis, J.A., Hampton, M.M. and Lansberg, I. (1997). *Generation to Generation: Life Cycles of the Family Firm.* Boston, MA: Harvard Business School Press.
Gudmundson, D., Tower, C.B. and Hartman, E.A. (2003). Innovation in small businesses: culture and ownership structure do matter, *Journal of Developmental Entrepreneurship*, 8(1): 1–17.
Hall, A., Melin, L. and Nordqvist, M. (2006). Understanding strategizing in the family business context, in Poutziouris, P.Z., Smyrnios, K.X. and Kleine, S.B. (eds.), *Handbook of Research on Family Business*, Edwar Elgar Pub., pp. 253–268.
Handler, W. (1990). Succession in family firms, *Entrepreneurship Theory and Practice*, 15(1): 37–51.

Handler, W. (1992). Succession experience of the next generation, *Family Business Review*, 5(3): 283–307.

Hisrich, R.D. and Fulop, G. (1997). Women entrepreneurs in family business: the Hungarian case, *Family Business Review*, 10(3): 281–302.

Hoy, F. and Sharma, P. (2006). Navigating the family business education maze, in Poutziouris, P.Z., Smyrnios, K.X. and Kleine, S.B. (eds.), *Handbook of Research on Family Business*, Edward Elgar Pub., pp. 11–24.

Hoy, F. and Verser, T.S. (2001). Emerging business, emerging field: entrepreneurship and the family firm, *Entrepreneurship: Theory and Practice*, 19(1): 9–23.

Kellermanns, F.W. and Eddleston, K.A. (2006). Feuding families: the management of conflict in family firms, in Poutziouris, P.Z., Smyrnios, K.X. and Kleine, S.B. (eds.), *Handbook of Research on Family Business*, Edward Elgar Pub., pp. 358–370.

Khanin, D. and Mahto, R.V. (2007). The positive and negative aspects of family ownership in family firms: a psychological business ownership perspective. Paper presented at *Family Enterprise Research Conference*, Monterrey, Mexico, April.

LeBreton-Miller, I., Miller, D. and Steier, L.P. (2004). Towards an integrative model of effective FOB succession, *Entrepreneurship: Theory and Practice*, 28(4): 305–328.

Lyagoubi, M. (2006). Family firms and financial behavior: how family shareholder preferences influence firms' financing, in Poutziouris, P.Z., Smyrnios, K.X. and Kleine, S.B. (eds.), *Handbook of Research on Family Business*, Edward Elgar Pub., pp. 537–551.

Miller, D., Steier, L. and Le Breton-Miller, I. (2003). Lost in time: intergenerational succession, change, and failure in family business, *Journal of Business Venturing*, 18(4): 513–531.

Moores, K. and Craig, J. (2006). From vision to variables: a scorecard to continue the professionalization of a family firm, in Poutziouris, P.Z., Smyrnios, K.X. and Kleine, S.B. (eds.), *Handbook of Research on Family Business*, Edward Elgar Pub., pp. 196–214.

Moores, K. and Mula, J. (2000). The salience of market, bureaucratic and clan controls in the management of family firm transitions: some tentative Australian evidence, *Family Business Review*, 10(3): 221–237.

Neuberg, F. and Lank, A.G. (1998). *The Family Business: Its Governance for Sustainability*. London, UK: Macmillan.

Poza, E.J. and Messer, T. (2001). Spousal leadership and continuity in the family firm, *Family Business Review*, 14(1): 25–36.

Sharma, P. (2004). An overview of the field of family business studies: current status and directions for the future, *Family Business Review*, 17(1): 1–36.

Sharma, P., Chrisman, J.J. and Chua, J.H. (1996). *A Review and Annotated Bibliography of Family Business Studies*. Boston, Massachusetts: Kluwer Academic Publishers.

Songini, L. (2006). The professionalization of family firms: theory and practice, in Poutziouris, P.Z., Smyrnios, K.X. and Kleine, S.B. (eds.), *Handbook of Research on Family Business*, Edward Elgar Pub., pp. 269–297.

Sonfield, M.C. and Lussier, R.N. (2004). First-, second-, and third-generation family firms: a comparison, *Family Business Review*, 17(3): 189–202.

Steier, L. (2001). Next-generation entrepreneurs and succession: an exploratory study of modes and means of managing social capital, *Family Business Review*, 14(3): 259–276.

Rogers, E.D., Carsrud, A.L. and Krueger, N.F. (1996). Chiefdoms and family firm regimes: variations on the same anthropological theme, *Family Business Review*, 9(1): 15–28.

Rosenblatt, P.C., de Mik, L., Anderson, R.M. and Johnson, P.A. (1985). *The Family in Business*. San Francisco, CA: Jossey Bass.

Tan, W. and Fock, S.T. (2001). Coping with growth transitions: the case of Chinese family businesses in Singapore, *Family Business Review*, 16(2): 123–139.

Trevinyo-Rodriguez, R.N. and Tapies, J. (2006). Effective knowledge transfer in family firms, in Poutziouris, P.Z., Smyrnios, K.X. and Kleine, S.B. (eds.), *Handbook of Research on Family Business*, Edward Elgar Pub., pp. 342–357.

Ward, J.L. (2004). *Perpetuating the Family Business: 50 Lessons Learned from Long-Lasting, Successful Families in Business*. New York: Palgrave MacMillan.

Yan, J. and Sorenson, R. (2006). The effects of Confucian values on succession in family business, *Family Business Review*, 19(3): 235–250.

II. THE CHALLENGE

4
POVERTY: A SOCIAL DISGRACE AND DILEMMA

Franco Gandolfi and Philip A. Neck

"*Jesus said to them, you have the poor among you always*" — Matthew 26:11.

"*Since Eden: Inequality*" and "*Humanity does not live by GNP alone*" — Paul Samuelson, Nobel Prize in Economics, introducing the issue of quality of life and poverty to mainstream economics.

"*Essentially nothing can be done about inequality. The basic forces determining inequality are too strong and persistent to be affected by the state*" — Vilfredo Pareto, Italian sociologist and economist (1848–1923) promoter of the idea of an elite class of society and an architect of fascism.

"*Man is the only species that feels shame — or needs to*" — Mark Twain.

"*Poverty anywhere constitutes a danger to prosperity everywhere*" — The International Labour Organization's Philadelphia Declaration (1944).

"*The US has arrived at the point where poverty could be abolished easily and simply by a stroke of the pen*" — University of Michigan Survey — Income and Welfare in the United States (1962).

Introduction

This chapter examines the causes, problems, and consequences of poverty. Following an overview of definitions of poverty, the rationale for including the topic in an economics text is then introduced. Next, a brief analysis of the scale and scope of poverty in today's economic, social, and political world is discussed. The causes and effects of inequality and poverty are then argued in concert with implications concerning the consequences of chronically sustained poverty. Finally, possible means available to address the problems of poverty are then presented.

Definitions of Poverty

Poverty (also referred to as *penury*) is a persistent problem presenting political, economic, ethical/moral, spiritual, and physical challenges to all nations at all times. While most people understand, or think that they understand, the term poverty, the specific meaning that we attach to the word depends upon the underlying concept of poverty. In other words, it is of great importance to conceptualize the term in order to deeply appreciate and truly understand the meaning and significance of the term. One's choice of definition will, in turn, lead to parallel differences in the methods and measures used to estimate the numbers in poverty and gauge the depth of their impoverishment.

Poverty is a relatively broad concept denoting the lack of basic elements of the quality of life, including food, drinking water, clothing, and shelter. More broadly, poverty may also refer to the absence of "intangibles," such as the lack of opportunities to pursue meaningful employment, to engage in learning endeavors, and to enjoy social and community relationships. For the purpose of this chapter, poverty has been defined as: "The insufficiency of the material necessities of life." While poverty is generally considered involuntary, undesirable, and intolerable, the term "voluntary poverty" has appeared within predominately spiritual contexts, where it describes the virtuous renunciation of material goods, also known as simple living, downshifting, and voluntary simplicity. This paper exclusively focuses upon *involuntary poverty*. It is in this context that various dichotomies have emerged.

Absolute and relative poverty

Poverty may be expressed in *absolute* or *relative* terms. The former, absolute poverty, refers to a set standard which is consistent between countries over a certain period of time. Therefore, definitions based on an absolute concept of poverty allow a measured prevalence of change over time. As such, they require an absolute poverty line based on a survival criterion, such as a specified minimum daily caloric intake, the proportion of income spent on food, or the income level required to purchase a minimum basket of consumption goods. An example of an absolute poverty measurement would be the percentage of the population eating less than 2500 calories per day (for an adult male).

In contrast, relative poverty, defines income or resources in relation to the average and, thus, depicts poverty relative to some threshold. As such, it describes a person as poor in comparison to other members of their society. For example, relative poverty could be defined as a household income of less than 50% of a region's median income. Interestingly, if everyone's real income in an economy were to increase and the income distribution to stay the same, then relative poverty would also remain the same. Measures of relative poverty may be used as a surrogate for measuring inequality. Thus, if a society achieves more equality in its income distribution, then relative poverty will inevitably fall.

Moderate or extreme poverty

Poverty may also be expressed in *moderate* or *extreme* terms. Relative poverty can be expressed as "moderate poverty," which is a standard of living or level of income that is sufficient to meet basic needs, but significantly lower than the majority of the population under consideration. Extreme poverty, on the other hand, is the most severe form of poverty, where individuals are simply unable to meet basic needs for their own survival, including food, drinking water, clothing, shelter, sanitation, education, and healthcare.

The World Bank has characterized extreme poverty as living on US$1 or less per day. This figure has been adjusted for purchasing power parity (PPP), which eliminates differences in the costs of goods and services between countries. However, while this presents a more meaningful comparison, it is important to bear in mind that this amount has not been adjusted for inflation since the early 1990s rendering it almost irrelevant. The World Bank reported in 2001, that 1.1 billion people had consumption levels below the US$1 threshold (extreme poverty), while a staggering 2.7 billion people lived on less than US$2 a day (moderate poverty)!

When the United Nations (UN) created the *Universal Declaration of Human Rights* in 1948, signatories proclaimed that all people have the right to education, work, health, and well-being. It is clear that today millions around the world are too crippled by poverty to fulfill even these basic rights. Millions continue to go hungry every day. Scores of children never step inside a classroom. Families watch their loved ones die from preventable causes because they do not have access to adequate medical care. In essence, poverty may be considered the denial of the most basic human rights.

Extreme poverty is most prevalent in the so-called least developed countries (LDC's). These fourth-world countries exhibit the lowest socio-economic development indicators and Human Development Index (HDI) ratings of all countries in the world (United Nations, 2007). The eradication of extreme poverty and hunger by 2015 is part of the UN's Millennium Development Goals. The blueprint agreed to by all of the world's leading development institutions include eight goals, ranging from halving extreme poverty and providing universal primary education to halting the spread of HIV/AIDS by the target date of 2015. Regarding extreme poverty, the specific goals are defined as "reducing by half the proportion of people living on less than US$1 per day" and "reducing by half the proportion of people who suffer from hunger" (United Nations, 2008).

The 2007 World Bank "Global Economic Prospects" report predicts that in the year 2030, the number of individuals living on less than the equivalent of US$1 a day will fall to about 550 million worldwide. This represents a drop of almost 50% from the 2007 levels. However, while global economic growth has been relatively strong since the year 2000, much of Africa has shown and will probably continue to face difficulty keeping pace with the rest of the developing world. As a projected future consequence, Africa will likely be home to a larger proportion of the world's poorest people than it is today.

Finally, poverty also occurs in the most industrialized nations. The official determination of poverty in many developed countries is based on *relative income*. Thus, it has been argued that poverty-related statistics in those industrialized countries measure inequality rather than real material deprivation and hardship. For instance, in the European Union (EU) and the Organisation for Economic Co-operation and Development (OECD), the poverty line is based upon "economic distance" which is a level of income set at 50% of the median household income. In contrast and more arbitrarily, the poverty line in the US is based on the dollar costs of an "economy food plan" multiplied by a factor of three. The multiplier was created back in 1963/64 and is based on the assumption that food costs account for about one third of a household's total income. At the same time, the US measure excludes from income the value of non-cash benefits like food stamps, as well as the imputed rental value of owner-occupied housing. As such, comparisons across national lines are problematic because of variations in government funded programs, such as healthcare and childcare.

Rationale for Treating Poverty as a Priority Subject

The following background information should serve to provide a warrant for treating poverty as a subject requiring priority treatment in the field of economics, politics, and the humanities:

- almost half the world's population — nearly three billion people — lives on less than US$2 a day;
- the GDP (Gross Domestic Product) of the 41 most heavily indebted poor countries (567 million people) is smaller than the wealth of the world's seven richest people combined;
- nearly one billion people entered the 21st century unable to read a book or sign their names;
- less than 1% of what the world spent every year on weapons was needed to put every child into school by the year 2000, and yet it did not happen;
- a staggering one billion children live in poverty (one in two children in the world) — 640 million live without adequate shelter, 400 million

have no access to safe water, 270 million have no access to health services;
- 10.6 million children died in 2003 before they reached the age of five (equivalent to roughly 29,000 children per day);
- over 100 million primary school-age children cannot go to school;
- each year, more than eight million people around the world die because they are too poor to stay alive;
- over one billion people (one in six people around the world) live in extreme poverty, defined as living on less than US$1 a day; and
- more than 800 million people go hungry each day.

Based on definitions established by the World Bank, nearly three billion people (or almost half of the world's current population) are considered poor. Still, poverty is not merely a numbers game. It is about scores of men, women, and children enduring unimaginable obstacles that keep them from fulfilling their most basic human rights and achieving their individual potentials.

Consider the following: Around the world, between 27,000 and 30,000 children die from poverty-related conditions every day. That is equivalent to one child dying every three seconds, 20 children perishing every minute, a 2004 Asian Tsunami occurring almost every week, or 10–11 million children dying every year. More than 50 million children died between 2000 and 2005 alone. The silent killers are poverty and poverty related causes like easily preventable diseases and illnesses. In spite of the scale of this ongoing, daily catastrophe, poverty rarely manages to achieve, much less sustain, prime-time, headline coverage.

Scope and Scale of Poverty

The poverty scenario is not a pretty sight. No matter what sort of poverty measure is employed, its very nature, coverage, and gravity are untenable on humane, moral, economic, and political grounds. Unmistakably, the continuity of such conditions has to be viewed as simply shameful!

Global overview

To review the global alongside the domestic and national scenarios does not require a highly detailed statistical approach. Available data show that poverty prevails globally. When 20% of the world's population lives below the poverty line we are clearly not confined to some Third World phenomenon, although people in less developed and developing countries do undergo substantially more poverty than the rest of the world.

Interestingly, in Western industrialized countries poverty and affluence co-exist. For instance, the US has less than 6% of the world's population, possesses more than 25% of its GNP, yet nearly 15% live below the poverty line. In other industrialized countries poverty also exists where differences in income, wealth, and assets are growing more and more unequal. Thus, it can be alleged that poverty is a human, global, and universal phenomenon where the richest and most industrialized countries of the world also face the specter of poverty.

Is poverty a greater problem today than in the past? In other words, have the poor of today always been with us? Relatively dependable statistics are not easily available, but we can draw on comparable estimates. The International Economic Association compared the economic situation existing in today's Third World and the industrialized countries of today that obtained their status two centuries ago. At that time, most of the present developing countries were either "developed" countries of that era, or on par with others in respect of per capita income, capital stock position, participation in international trade, and general measures of financial substance. The situation in most of the Third World countries was either comparable or better. In India, a modern fast-growing country, data reveals that in the years prior to independence it was then the richest country in the world, and throughout the past century India's real per capita remained constant. Therefore, it is important to consider the causes of poverty and factors responsible for generating poverty — both current and historical — suggesting that a global perspective must be pursued.

Today's global capitalism is moving from a physical economy to one of financial economic expansion. It can be observed that, over the course of the last three decades, there has been enormous financial expansion not commensurate with the physical expansion of the economy. The financial mechanism of currency and derivatives dealings is neither value-adding nor creating real assets, but trading in claims on assets. This trading takes place at different levels with the outcome that financial expansion is taking place leading towards greater global financial instability, while enriching only a selected few. We now know that sole, reckless individuals are in a position to shake the economies of entire sovereign nations by manipulating their investments. This begs the question as to what type of distribution of wealth and power is taking place through this process? Also, what are its implications for Third World countries and the banking system as a whole?

The global debt issue is very much related to economic development, poverty alleviation, and the future economy of the world. Pricing is an important concern, particularly for primary commodities, mineral resources, and the products of the less developed and developing countries. Finally, the behavior and attitudes in raising protection by industrialized countries towards imports from these countries also need to be considered.

These issues have implications for Third World countries. How were the prices of primary commodities arbitrarily be kept low? For instance, the price of fossil fuels, one of the key resources, was maintained at the same levels from the 1920s to the 1970s while prices of all other commodities, primary or otherwise, increased. The oil price was deliberately kept at the same level. We need to ask how the buyers of these raw materials managed to control the whole system. Technically speaking, the total control over demand is touted as a monopsony. Consider the changes that have taken place in the prices and the terms of trade between the industrialized and the less developed countries and examine their implications for their relative economies. These are among the key areas most relevant to the global issue of alleviation of poverty. Add to these factors those of child labor, forced labor, and the suppression of human rights, and we have a new set of economic questions to take into account!

The design, manufacture, and marketing of sport shoes, which multinational corporations (MNCs) import from Third World countries, constitutes an interesting and compelling case. A pair of shoes, for instance, can be sold for well over US$100; the wholesale price is probably less than US$60, while the factory price is less than US$30 of which the actual labor cost is around US$3. Sadly, while globalization has produced enormous wealth for a few, relatively little wealth has been directed to the local laborers.

These issues have important global dimensions. During the last half-century, for example, most developing countries that could point to a rapid economic growth between the two world wars have subsequently failed to alleviate poverty. Even during the phases of economic development, spread over a few decades, there has been no bona fide alleviation of poverty at the grassroots. It appears that we can, or must, argue for a totally new approach to be adopted. To do so, means that the process of economic development will have to change its attitude towards people and human welfare by shifting the focus from wealth generation to human well-being; economics to move from becoming the purpose and the sole determinant to become a means for even-handed development. Until and unless a more humane, ethical, just, and people-oriented approach is adopted at the individual, community, societal, and global levels, no fundamentally positive change can or should be expected.

This will call for a shift from a one-dimensional economic approach to one that deliberately promotes a moral individual inspired by certain values and ideals seeking not merely satisfaction for their own welfare, but also the welfare of others. Such a transition will demand structural changes like the redistribution of wealth, income, and assets. Land reforms will need to be introduced and people need to be able to be in a position to decide their own economic future. Consequently, changes need to take place calling for judicial change at policy, structural, and institutional levels. Such a multi-faceted, comprehensive approach will need to be introduced to change the situation and establish a just and viable society.

Most importantly, there is some hope! Recent World Bank data shows that the percentage of the population living in households with consumption or income per person below the poverty line has decreased in each region of the world since 1990 (Table 1).

Table 1 Population below the poverty line

Region	1990 (%)	2002 (%)	2004 (%)
East Asia and Pacific	15.40	12.33	9.07
Europe and Central Asia	3.60	1.28	0.95
Latin America and the Caribbean	9.62	9.08	8.64
Middle East and North Africa	2.08	1.69	1.47
South Asia	35.04	33.44	30.84
Sub-Saharan Africa	46.07	42.63	41.09

Source: World Bank (2007) Polycalvet Poverty Data (Human Indicator regional tables).

There are various criticisms of these measurements. For instance, it is noted that: "although a clear trend decline in the percentage of people who are absolutely poor is evident, although with uneven progress across regions...the developing world outside China and India has seen little or no sustained progress in reducing the number of poor." At the same time, however, since the world's population has increased, if instead looking at the percentage living on less than US$1 per day, and if excluding China and India, then this percentage has decreased from 31.35% in 1981 to 20.70% in 2004.

Regional perspectives

In the US, an acknowledged bastion of capital success, as well as in Europe and elsewhere in the industrialized world, differences between the rich and the poor in terms of income, wealth, and assets are becoming larger. *The Guardian* reported that the US Federal Reserve Bank revealed that 1% of American households with US$2.3 million each own nearly 40% of country's wealth and the top 20% own more than 80%. Moreover, 1% of US households own nearly 40% of the country's wealth and the top 20% own more than 80% of the assets, indicating that Pareto's Principle (i.e. the ratio of four to one) declared in the 19th century is still alive and well. While the US is arguably the richest country of the world, its national debt was US$1 billion in 1901: that nation now has a domestic debt today over three and a half trillion dollars and is in budgetary deficit. One of the major causes is the interest payment on this domestic debt.

A developing country is characteristically identified by low levels of living, manifest in the form of low incomes (poverty), inadequate housing, poor health, limited or no access to education, along with high and rising levels of unemployment and underemployment. The 1960s and 1970s marked two decades of remarkable economic growth on a global scale. However, the 1980s was a "lost" decade as far as development was concerned with its economic downswing in most parts of the developing world. Other than parts of Asia, all other regions experienced deterioration in growth and diminished economic performance which led to increased poverty in the developing world and a widening inequality gap between the developing and the industrialized world.

Clearly, given the way poverty has been created in the Third World and the role that the transfer of resources has played over the last several centuries with its cumulative effect on the world economic situation today, these issues cannot be ignored when considering the global dimensions of poverty. At the same time, however, not all problems of poverty were created by the current industrialized countries.

There are very potent factors generating and aggravating poverty within the Third World countries themselves: the distribution of wealth and income, the control of political and economic power and resources, the stratification of society into groups, classes, and vested interests, the monopolization of power, and corruption and despotic regimes, have all played their part to contribute to the overall poverty plight. These factors make a "clarion call" for fundamental changes to be made where structural power equation is changed. Mere cash transfers and decorative social action programs will not materially change the situation. Developing countries are not living in isolation but are part of a global system.

Foreign aid and international transfers have shown to be imperfect acts of generosity of no value in ameliorating poverty. In real terms, there continues to be a reverse flow of resources (i.e. material, human, and physical capital) and brain-power from Third World countries to industrialized countries.

Possible Causes of Inequality and Poverty

In order to effectively alleviate inequality and eradicate poverty, it is of primary importance to determine the alleged causes. Unsurprisingly, a multitude of causes and factors have emerged in the literature. By definition, a cause contributes to the origin of a problem, whereas a factor contributes to its continuation after it already exists. In reality, the clean separation between causes and factors of problems does not exist. Thus, this chapter assumes that the two elements are indivisible. While many different elements have been cited to explain the causation and occurrence of poverty, there is no universally accepted explanation.

This section provides an overview of the main causes/factors that have been cited in discussing inequality and poverty. Some of the most salient aspects include:

Environmental factors

(1) Erosion — intensive farming often leads to a vicious cycle of exhaustion of soil fertility and decline of agricultural yields and hence increased poverty.
(2) Desertification and overgrazing — approximately 40% of the world's agricultural land is seriously degraded. In Africa, if current trends of soil degradation continue, the continent might be able to feed just 25% of its population by 2025, as cited by UNU's Ghana-based Institute for Natural Resources in Africa.
(3) Deforestation — as exemplified by the widespread rural poverty in China that began in the early 20th century and is attributed to non-sustainable tree harvesting.
(4) Natural factors — such as climate change or the environment.
(5) Geographic factors — including access to fertile land, fresh water, minerals, energy, and other natural resources. Natural features like mountains, deserts, navigable waterways, and coastlines aid or hinder communication. Historically, geography has prevented or slowed the spread of new technology to areas, such as the Americas and Sub-Saharan Africa. The climate also limits what crops and farm animals may be used on similarly fertile lands. On the other hand, research on the resource curse has found that countries with an abundance of natural resources have a propensity to create quick wealth from exports that tends to have less long-term prosperity than countries with less of these natural resources.
(6) Droughts and water crises.

Economic factors

(1) Unemployment.
(2) Increased farming for use in biofuels, along with world oil prices at more than US$100 a barrel, has pushed up the price of grain. Food riots have recently taken place in many countries across the world.

(3) Capital flight by which the wealthy in a society shift their assets to offshore tax havens deprives nations of revenue needed to break the vicious cycle of poverty.
(4) Weakly entrenched formal systems of title to private property are seen by writers such as Hernando de Soto as a limit to economic growth and therefore a cause of poverty.
(5) Unfair terms of trade, in particular, the very high subsidies to and protective tariffs for agriculture in the developed world. This drains the taxed money and increases the prices for the consumers in the developed world; decreases competition and efficiency; prevents exports by more competitive agricultural and other sectors in the developed world due to retaliatory trade barriers; and undermines the very type of industry in which the developing countries do have comparative advantages.
(6) Tax havens which tax their own citizens and companies but not those from other nations and refuse to disclose information necessary for foreign taxation. This enables large scale political corruption, tax evasion, and organized crime in the foreign nations.

Healthcare

(1) Poor access to affordable healthcare makes individuals less resilient to economic hardship and more vulnerable to poverty.
(2) Inadequate nutrition in childhood, itself an effect of poverty, undermines the ability of individuals to develop their full human capabilities and thus makes them more vulnerable to poverty. Lack of essential minerals such as iodine and iron can impair brain development. It is estimated that two billion people, one-third of the total global population, are affected by iodine deficiency, including 285 million six- to 12-year-old children. In developing countries, it is estimated that 40% of children aged four and under suffer from anemia because of insufficient iron in their diets.
(3) Diseases, specifically diseases of poverty, including AIDS, malaria, tuberculosis, and others afflict developing nations overwhelmingly. These diseases perpetuate poverty by diverting individual, community, and national health and economic resources from investment and productivity. Further, many tropical nations are affected by parasites

like malaria, schistosomiasis, and trypanosomiasis that are not present in temperate climates. The Tsetse fly makes it very difficult to use many animals in agriculture in afflicted regions.
(4) Clinical depression undermines the resilience of individuals and when not properly treated makes them vulnerable to poverty.
(5) Substance abuse, including alcoholism and drug abuse, when not properly treated undermines resilience and can consign people to vicious poverty cycles.

Governance

(1) Lacking democracy in poor countries: The records of social dimensions of development, access to drinking water, girls' literacy, and healthcare are starkly divergent. For example, compared to poor autocracies, poor democracies typically enjoy life expectancies that are nine years longer than poor autocracies, opportunities of finishing secondary school are 40% higher, and infant mortality rates are 25% lower. Also, agricultural yields are about 25% higher, on average, in poor democracies than in poor autocracies. This is an important fact, given that 70% of the population in poor countries is often rural. Poor democracies are not found to spend any more on their health and education sectors as a percentage of GDP than do poor autocracies, nor do they get higher levels of foreign assistance. They do not run up higher levels of budget deficits. They simply manage the resources that they have more effectively.
(2) The effectiveness of governments has a major impact on the delivery of socio-economic outcomes for poor populations.
(3) Weak rule of law can discourage investment and thus perpetuate poverty.
(4) Poor management of resource revenues — this may mean that rather than lifting countries out of poverty, revenues from such activities as oil production or gold mining actually leads to a resource curse.
(5) Failure by governments to provide essential infrastructure worsens poverty.
(6) Poor access to affordable education traps individuals and countries in cycles of poverty.

(7) High levels of corruption undermine efforts to make a sustainable impact on poverty. In Nigeria, for example, more than US$400 billion was stolen from the treasury by Nigeria's leaders between 1960 and 1999.

Demographics and social factors

(1) Overpopulation and lack of access to birth control methods. Note that population growth slows or even becomes negative as poverty is reduced due to the demographic transition.
(2) Crime, both white-collar and blue-collar crimes, including violent gangs and drug cartels.
(3) Historical factors, for example imperialism, colonialism and communism (at least 50 million children in Eastern Europe and the former Soviet Union live in poverty).
(4) The brain drain (i.e. human capital flight).
(5) The *"Matthew-effect"* is a phenomenon that is widely observed across advanced welfare states in that the middle classes tend to be the main beneficiaries of social benefits and services, even if these are primarily targeted at the poor.
(6) Cultural causes, which attribute poverty to common patterns of life are learned or shared within a community. For example, Max Weber argued that the Protestant work ethic contributed to economic growth during the industrial revolution.
(7) Wars, including civil wars and genocide.
(8) Discrimination of various kinds, such as age, gender, race, and caste discrimination.
(9) Individual beliefs, actions, and choices (for example, some homeless people opt to live on the streets rather than in a shelter for the perceived freedom it allows them).

While the above-listed overview provides a compartmentalized approach, others have come up with explanations combining the various, interrelated elements causing poverty and inequality.

(1) Differences in property wealth. The greatest disparities in income are due to differences in wealth ownership. Such differences might be

associated with good fortune in discovering natural resources or with productive innovation.
(2) Differences in personal ability. These may be inherited. Such inheritance may come from the environment as well as from genetic "hand-me-downs."
(3) Differences in education, training, and opportunities. This has been particularly noticeable in the emancipation of women in the industrialized countries.
(4) Class barriers of opportunity. There is empirical evidence that state expenditure on higher education goes to subsidize the middle classes rather than the urban and rural poor. Calculations show that families of students at universities and higher education institutions have incomes well above the median of the population at large and this relative scarcity of children or working-class families at universities can be found throughout the world.
(5) Differences in age and health. Even if people were all born alike and in the same environment, there would still be differences caused by bad health and lack of employment that is further exacerbated by lack of money.
(6) Environmental pollution. This provides a dramatic example of "externalities" that free market pricing cannot be expected to handle optimally. There is a case of public concern in zoning, effluent taxes, subsidies, and rules of the road.
(7) Physical resources are not inexhaustible. There are limits to growth and population.
(8) Pareto is associated with the view that inequality is a universal constant, unchangeable by policy that is not consonant with historical experience.
(9) Many different factors have been alleged to cause poverty. Some of the most frequently cited causes include corruption, state discrimination, crime, competition rather than cooperation, the abuse of public power, and the lack of social integration. Some individuals cite natural factors (e.g. climate, environment), historical factors (e.g. imperialism, colonialism), and war (e.g. civil war, genocide), while other writers emphasize global causes (e.g. trade, aid, debt) as well as national and domestic level deficiencies (e.g. public administration, financial management).

Evidently, no single factor can be held solely responsible for the catastrophic consequences of global inequality and poverty. It is extremely difficult to determine and address the root causes and to prepare contingency plans to deal with the associated problems. Historically speaking, the dramatic misery of mass poverty did not exist until the industrial revolution in the late 18th and early 19th centuries. Since that time, mass poverty has increased at an alarming rate affecting well-off countries and poorer nations alike where affluence and poverty frequently co-exist.

It has been alleged that the structural adjustment programs (SAP) prescribed by the International Monetary Fund (IMF) and the World Bank have deepened poverty in developing countries. SAP policy changes are conditions for obtaining new loans or receiving lower interest rates on existing loans. SAPs are created with the goal of reducing the borrowing country's fiscal imbalances. While the two Bretton Woods Institutions maintain that SAPs promote economic growth, generate income, and reduce debt, opponents claim that inevitable cutbacks in health, education, and other vital social services around the world have ensued as a result of internal and external structural changes. Governments of developing nations have also been required to open their economies in order to compete with each other and with more powerful and established industrialized nations. Critics say that to attract investment, poor countries enter a spiraling race to the bottom to see who can provide lower standards, reduced wages, and cheaper resources.

Finally, given the complexity of the concept, it comes as no surprise that many misconceptions regarding poverty have appeared in both the literature and the popular press. For instance:

- One common belief holds that poverty is caused by overpopulation. Some argue that if people affected by poverty would stop having children, then they could escape poverty.
- Another widely held belief is that poor people have made poor decisions that have led them to poverty. While some aspects may make sense on the surface, they are overly simplistic and unrealistic. Also, poverty is not necessarily the result of personal failings, nor it is solely a matter of income. What seems true, though, is that poverty is directly related to health, housing, education, and work opportunities.

Poverty causes a person's status to fall while it diminishes his or her involvement in the larger community.
- In the industrialized nations, where poverty also exists, beliefs about poverty are frequently based on stereotypes. For instance, people may think that poor individuals are generally lazy and dangerous. Alternatively, there may be a misconception that the majority of poor people are immigrants, ethnic minorities, criminals, and mentally retarded.
- It has been shown that people suffer from hunger not because of a lack of availability of food, or over-population, but because they are too poor to afford the food. In many ways, politics and economic conditions have led to poverty and dependency around the world. Thus, addressing world hunger implies addressing world poverty. If food production is further increased and provided to more people while the underlying causes of poverty are not addressed, hunger will still continue because people will not be able to purchase food.
- Even non-emergency food aid, which seems a noble cause at face value, has shown to be destructive since it under-sells local farmers and can ultimately affect the entire economy of a poor nation. If the poorer nations are not given the sufficient means to produce their own food and other existential items, then poverty and dependency are likely to continue.
- Finally, leaders from rich countries are often heard telling poor countries that aid and loans will only be given when they show they are stamping out corruption. While the eradication of corruption is of primary importance and definitely must occur, the rich countries themselves are often active in the largest forms of corruptive practices in those poor countries. Indeed, many economic policies that rich countries have prescribed have exacerbated the problem. Thus, corruption must be high on the priority lists of both developing and developed countries.

Effects of Poverty

Poverty is an exceptionally complicated social phenomenon. Having determined the causation of poverty, the effects of poverty may in fact also be the causes thereby creating a poverty cycle. Undeniably, the consequences of poverty are serious at best and disastrous at worst. Individuals living in poverty and lacking access to the basic elements of life inevitably suffer from hunger and, in the most severe cases, starvation and death. Statistics and facts on poverty are unpleasant, offensive, and humanly unacceptable. The following is a summary of poverty-related statistics.

- Half the world's population, that is three billion people, live on less than US$2 a day.
- One billion people (i.e. one in six people) live on less than US$1 a day (i.e. extreme poverty).
- One billion children, half the number of children in the world, live in poverty.
- 790 million people worldwide are chronically undernourished.
- 100 million primary-age children do not have access to education.
- 18 million people, or 50,000 individuals a day, die of poverty annually.
- Between 26,500 and 30,000 children die each day due to poverty.

Most disturbingly, according to the United Nations Children's Fund (UNICEF): "children die quietly in some of the poorest villages on earth, far removed from the scrutiny and the conscience of the world. Being meek and weak in life makes these dying multitudes even more invisible in death." Poverty-related problems have shown to generate considerable social, economic, political, and environmental effects for all individuals around the world. There is strong evidence suggesting that individuals living in poverty suffer from lower life expectancies, face the increased risk of homelessness, and are frequently involved with drug abuse, prostitution, and other criminal activities. Individuals living in poverty in the industrialized world have a tendency to suffer from social isolation and higher rates of suicide. Relatively low income levels, poor housing options, and a lack of employment opportunities for adults can create conditions where households need to depend on child labor. The absence of employment opportunities also leads to an increase in criminal activity through the informal economy. This has a tendency to discourage investment into the local economy, thereby further perpetuating the conditions of poverty.

Longitudinal research carried out by the Institute for Social and Economic Research (ISER) in Wales found strong correlations between poverty in childhood and overall well-being as adults. Thus, child poverty is likely to have the following long-term consequences.

(1) Children born into poverty are more likely to have a lower birth weight, high infant mortality, and poorer overall health than more affluent children.
(2) Poverty conditions, such as homelessness and chronic overcrowding, impact upon a child's mental, social, and physical development and well-being.
(3) Individuals living on low incomes are more likely to experience debt. Debt, in turn, is likely to lead to decreased levels of health, relationships, and quality of life.
(4) The correlations between poverty, social class, and poor educational experience and attainment have been clearly established. Poverty affects the likelihood of progressing through school and attaining formal professional qualifications. Poor children are also more likely to play truant and to be excluded from schools.
(5) Poor children frequently grow up in areas affected by crime and poor investments in infrastructure.
(6) Poverty impacts on opportunities to engage in social activities and to participate fully in their communities.

Low income and wealth levels generally undermine the local government's ability to levy taxes for public infrastructure adding further to the vicious cycle of connecting the causes and effects of poverty. Poor access to public services, infrastructure, health services, and education generally contribute to the perpetuation of poverty. Sadly, escaping the malaise of poverty has shown to be difficult. At its worst, poverty can become a self-perpetuating cycle. It is clear that individuals affected by poverty, for instance, are at an extreme disadvantage in the labor (job) market, while the lack of education and employment opportunities ensure continued poverty. The cycle of poverty repeats itself until the pattern of poverty is broken.

Finally, a relatively recent poverty-related phenomenon constitutes the feminization of poverty, which is the over-representation of women among the poor at a given moment. Popularized in the 1990s, the feminization of poverty includes single, divorced, and widowed women affected by poverty and is caused by a number of factors, including changes to family composition and family organization, as well as labor market inequalities. The majority of the three billion individuals living on US$2 or less are women and the gap between men and women caught up in the poverty trap is widening on a global scale.

Implications for Change

Globalization, the integration of national economies, political systems, and entire societies, has brought new challenges and opportunities for workers and trade unions. Analysts of global change speak of a competition between two visions of globalization, one that emphasizes market relations and seeks to maximize profits, and another that emphasizes democratic values and seeks to promote international cooperation prioritizing human well-being. In the latter view, markets are seen as just one aspect of society, and notions of human solidarity restrain market competition to curb its anti-social and unsustainable effects. Groups pursuing each of these contrasting visions of globalization advocate a system of international laws that will help bring about their preferred world order. The laws of markets and profitability are championed by transnational corporate owners within the institutional framework of the World Bank, the IMF, and the World Trade Organization (WTO), while the laws of democracy and human rights are most strongly defended by unions and other citizens' groups working primarily through the much weaker UN system.

Some contend that the global economy has systematically disempowered workers around the world. As such, the failure of global markets to meet the needs of large segments of the world's population is becoming increasingly difficult to ignore, and growing numbers are mobilizing in opposition to the dominant model of economic globalization. This development has created new possibilities for a revitalization of co-operatives and trade unions and a reversal of labor's downward trajectory calling on unions to fundamentally rethink their organizing models and reorient their attention to the difficult but necessary work of nurturing civil society and democracy. For their part, other social movements will need to increase their attention to the plight of workers and find ways to help empower individuals around the globe to be informed and engaged citizens of their nations.

In recent decades, several Asian countries have replicated the growth performance of the East Asian pioneers, such as Singapore and Malaysia. However, most have failed to replicate their performance in income distribution and poverty reduction. This occurred mainly because their growth pattern was not as nearly employment-intensive as in the case of the East Asian pioneers. The fastest growing Asian countries of today have low and declining elasticities of employment. This represents a major factor in weakening the impact of economic growth on the earnings of the poor and making growth less poverty-alleviating than it might have been otherwise. In other instances, the poor employment performance was, by and large, due to inadequate growth or growth bypassing the large sectors where poor workers were concentrated. A further lapse is the relative reduction in access to credit for small labor intensive enterprises in a period of macro-economic contraction. Notwithstanding the above issues, employment is powerfully influenced by macro-economic policies where higher economic growth would help overcome the problem. Too often, disproportionate degrees of macro-economic stabilization have reduced economic growth to rates that are simply too low to permit adequately high rates of employment growth even when employment intensities are high and intact.

Such a redefinition has found expression in two distinctly different strategies, the redistribution with growth and the basic needs strategies. The former strategy highlights the redistribution of economic opportunities in a more egalitarian direction, while the latter emphasizes the need for development to provide and guarantee a decent livelihood to the largest majority of the population. The basic needs to be met include adequate food, shelter, and clothing, as well as access to health facilities, education, and greater employment opportunities. Lack of fulfillment of these needs is both a symptom and a cause of absolute poverty. The opinions and attitudes of policy makers over the poverty issue have been oscillated between the adoption of growth-promoting policies and poverty-focused strategies. The former held sway in the 1950s and 1960s with the assumption about the trickle-down effects of growth on poverty, while the swing of the pendulum favored poverty-focused strategies in the 1970s.

The change was prompted by the notion of basic needs and the premium accorded to distributional objectives generally. The basic needs strategy, however, lost ground in the 1980s as the world moved into recession and the imperative of structural adjustment programs came to be acknowledged globally. The primary policy focus came to be on the achievement of sustainable economic growth, while the issues of distributional objectives and poverty alleviation dropped out of sight. In the 1990s, the issue of poverty alleviation was once again back in the international limelight and has continued into the present century.

Poverty Reduction/Alleviation

Poverty reduction, also called poverty alleviation, denotes any process seeking to reduce the level, magnitude, or severity of poverty amongst a group of individuals in a country. Poverty-reduction programs are commonly aimed at economic or non-economic poverty. Popular poverty-alleviation methods include education, economic development, and income redistribution; while others focus on removing social and legal barriers to earning and income growth among the poor. Some economists have stressed the importance of property rights as a potent tool of poverty reduction, whereas others view corruption in both government and non-government sectors as the chief culprit causing poverty.

The fight against poverty is usually considered a social-political goal in that many governments have established institutions dedicated to tackling poverty. A vigorously debated issue is the role of the government in poverty alleviation. For instance, should the government manage the economy and provide public services to tackle the problem of poverty? While there are various theories and schools of thought, it must be clear that, in order for them to be sustainable in the long run, poverty reduction programs ought to increase both the competitiveness of the economy and the viability of the state.

Back in 1962, a University of Michigan survey headed by Morgan, David, Cohen, and Brazer concluded that: "The US has arrived at the point where poverty could be abolished easily and simply by a stroke of the pen. To raise every individual and family in the nation now below a subsistence income to the subsistence level would cost less than 2% of the gross national product, less than 10% of tax revenues, and about one-fifth of the cost of national defense."

In a similar vein, according to the UN and its affiliated development experts, an end to extreme poverty can be achieved. Effectively tackling global poverty demands a multi-pronged approach, while it must be acknowledged that there is no single cure-all. Issues of poverty are many and complex. Thus, initiatives must address interwoven but distinct issues, such as children's rights, women's rights, epidemics (e.g. HIV/AIDS), access to clean water and sanitation, and the preservation of the world's natural resources.

The Millennium Development Goals (MDG), agreed to by the international community in the year 2000, represent an unprecedented opportunity for the world to usher in a new era of collaboration in fighting poverty. The eight goals and 21 targets set forth concrete objectives for significantly reducing extreme poverty and related ills by the year 2015. The year 2005 was also heralded as a milestone year in the fight against poverty giving it the moniker of "The Year of Development." While a great deal has been accomplished, there is still much work to be done. Based on current trends, most developing countries will fail to meet the majority of the MDG's by 2015. Many believe that achieving the MDGs must involve a real and measurable focus on the eighth goal, the development of a global partnership for development. As such, the notion of governments' working together with the larger civil society, multilateral institutions, and private sector entities would not just represent a fanciful idea, but constitute a most effective strategy to eliminate poverty forever.

While the eradication of extreme poverty and hunger by 2015 remains the overarching objective, the Sachs Report (headed by Dr. Jeffrey Sachs, world renowned macroeconomist and special advisor to UN Secretary-General Ban Ki-moon) proposes a series of "quick wins." Development experts see these interventions as being comparatively cheap, highly effective, containing very high potential for short-term impact, and applicable in most developing countries. Specifically, some of the quick wins are the following action points:

- directly assisting local entrepreneurs to grow their businesses and create jobs;

- accessing information on sexual and reproductive health;
- acting against domestic violence;
- appointing government scientific advisors in every country;
- de-worming school children in affected areas;
- introducing drugs for AIDS, tuberculosis, and malaria;
- eliminating school fees;
- ending user fees for basic healthcare in developing countries;
- providing free school meals for school children;
- legislating for women's rights, including rights to property;
- planting trees;
- providing soil nutrients to farmers in sub-Saharan Africa;
- providing mosquito nets;
- providing access to electricity, water, and sanitation;
- supporting breast-feeding;
- providing training programs for community health in rural areas; and
- upgrading slums, and providing land for public housing.

A number of concrete poverty alleviation proposals have appeared. Some of the most commonly cited aspects include the following categories.

Employment

Employment is recognized as the principal link through which economic growth permits the poor to overcome the problems associated with poverty. Analysis of policy measures demonstrates that any benefit to the poor emanating from economic growth depends on the type and extent of the growth that is generated. However, since not all economic growth creates employment, it becomes important to identify ways and means of increasing the intensity of employment of economic growth. Recent country studies contain detailed empirical analyses of trends in the employment intensity of economic growth and of factors that could explain the observed trends. These studies provide interesting insights into the reasons for low and declining employment outcomes of economic growth.

The main findings serve as an advocacy and dissemination tool that includes the following: The employment intensity of growth, defined as the rate at which employment grows when output grows by one percentage point, has not only been low but has been declining over some time in some of the fastest growing Asian countries, especially India and China, two of the countries at the top of the contemporary growth league. In many countries, inadequate output growth has been exacerbated when employment growth has been low despite high growth of output. Notable factors have been the transition towards a market-based competitive environment, introduction of economic reforms that lead to shedding excess labor, a shift in output towards less employment friendly sectors, policy environments favoring capital intensive sectors coupled with the adoption of more capital-using technologies, and, finally, lack of financing opportunities for small and medium-sized enterprises.

Moreover, the distribution of income has worsened in many countries implying that the rate of poverty reduction could have been higher if the income distribution remained unchanged. Employment performance is strongly influenced by macro-economic policies where higher economic growth could at least partially assist in addressing the problem of inadequate employment growth. In all countries reviewed, almost without exception, slow employment growth was associated with low employment intensity of growth.

Economic growth

The World Bank and its anti-poverty strategy focuses heavily on a reduction of poverty through the promotion of economic growth. Studies cited by the World Bank demonstrate that economic growth accompanied by progressive distributional change of income is fundamental for poverty reduction. At the same time, economic growth *per se* does not positively affect income/wealth equality and high income inequality prevents poverty reduction. World GDP per capita rapidly began to increase beginning with the Industrial Revolution. Accordingly, the World Bank argues that an overview of a multitude of studies has shown that:

- economic growth is fundamental for poverty reduction;
- economic growth *per se* does not affect inequality;
- economic growth accompanied by progressive distributional change is better than growth alone;

- high initial income inequality is a brake on poverty reduction;
- poverty itself is also likely to be a barrier for poverty reduction; and
- wealth inequality seems to predict lower future growth rates.

Market reforms (free market)

Free market reforms represent a powerful strategy for reducing poverty. The abandonment of collective farming in China, the cutting of government regulations in India, and the structural changes in Russia's economy all resulted in significant poverty reductions in the 20th century. At the same time, a strong government and significant investments into infrastructure, including railroads, roads, ports, and telecommunication, have shown to be vital. These "free market reforms" represent a potent strategy for reducing poverty. Considerable reductions in poverty have been reported in both India and China, where hundreds of millions of people grew out of poverty mostly as a result of the abandonment of collective farming in China and the cutting of government red tape in India. This was also critical in fostering their dramatic economic growth in the 1990s. However, UN economists argue that in order for the market reforms to work, good infrastructure is required, which in turn necessitates a strong state. This has been exemplified in both modern-day China's investing in railways, roads, and ports, and in various African countries developing rural telephony as part of their international strategy.

Developing countries face a range of obstacles to trading competitively on international markets. For instance, almost half of the budget of the European Union is directed to agricultural subsidies, which primarily benefit large, well-represented multinational agribusinesses. In 2005, Japan spent US$47 billion on subsidies to its agricultural sector denoting nearly four times the amount it gave in total foreign aid. The US gives US$3.9 billion annually in subsidies to its cotton sector, consisting of 25,000 growers. This constitutes three times more in subsidies than the entire USAID budget for Africa, although the US contributes a sum far larger through other agencies. Critics argue that agricultural subsidies in the industrialized world drain taxation revenue, increase the end-prices paid by consumers, and discourage efficiency improvements; while retaliatory trade barriers unfairly undermine the competitiveness of agricultural and other exports in those industries in which developing countries would otherwise have significant comparative advantages.

A now defunct theory for reducing poverty suggested that raising tariffs and import substitution leads to greater wealth by protecting the country from free trade. This theory, practiced between the 1950s and 1970s, failed to develop wealth. The theory assumes that a lack of trade barriers on incoming (often highly subsidized) goods from wealthier countries constitutes a driver of poverty. Most countries have some history of import substitution and direct government protection of and investment in local industries. The theory infers that reducing tariff receipts can lower a major source of government revenue and spending, while raising tariffs may improve the terms of trade for the poor. However, practice has shown that high tariffs lead to a stagnation of economic growth and development and the costs of the tariffs are borne most heavily on the poor.

Fair trade

Fair trade is a market-based approach aimed at eradicating global poverty. The movement advocates the payment of a "fair" price as well as implementation of social and environmental standards related to the production and exporting of goods. To date, this practice has been associated with trade in coffee, cocoa, tea, bananas, cotton, and honey. Fair trade promotes the sustainability of exports of goods from developing to mainly developed countries. The overall strategic intent is for marginalized producers to move from a position of vulnerability to economic self-sufficiency. Developing countries face a range of obstacles to trading competitively on global markets. For instance, industrialized nations, including the European Union, the US, and Japan, spend billions of dollars every year on agricultural subsidies protecting their own domestic industries and thereby increasing the end-prices paid by consumers and disadvantaging developing countries that would have comparative advantages.

Direct aid

Western governments regularly resort to helping individuals living in poverty directly through cash transfers. These short-term payments from the welfare states produce mixed results at best. Some of the more recent initiatives include "Direct Aid Iraq" and "Direct Aid to Darfuri Refugees." Direct aid is also provided by private charities. These not-for-profit and voluntary organizations encourage direct payment transfers to individuals living in absolute poverty. This set-up is commonly supported by charitable trusts and tax deduction arrangements provided by state governments. A government can directly help those in need through cash transfers as a short-term expedient. This has been applied with mixed results in most Western societies during the 20th century in what became known as the welfare state. Governments have made special payments to those most at risk, such as the elderly and people with disabilities.

Development aid

The majority of industrialized nations provide development aid to developing nations. Development aid (also called foreign aid and international aid) is financial support given by governmental and economic agencies to support the political, economic, and social development of developing nations. Development aid differs from humanitarian aid in that the former is aimed at eradicating poverty in the long run, while the latter endeavors to alleviate short-term suffering of individuals living in poverty. The UN target for development aid is 0.7% of the GDP of each respective country. Currently only a few nations (mainly Scandinavian countries) have achieved the target.

Other approaches

The Organization for Economic Co-operation and Development (OECD), which is made up of the world's most developed nations, has committed to providing development assistance to less developed countries through its Official Development Assistance (ODA) in the form of monetary donations.

A number of think-tanks and non-governmental organizations (NGO) have argued that Western monetary aid often serves only to increase poverty and social inequality. This may be because the aid is conditioned with the implementation of harmful economic policies in the recipient countries, because it is tied with the importing of products from the donor country over cheaper alternatives, or because foreign aid is seen as serving the interests of the donor more than the recipient. Critics also argue that some of the foreign aid is stolen by corrupt governments and officials, and that higher aid levels erode the quality of governance. Policy becomes much more oriented toward what will get more aid money than it does towards meeting the needs of the people. Victor Bout, one of the world's most notorious arms dealers, told the *New York Times* how he saw firsthand in Angola, Congo, and elsewhere: "how Western donations to impoverished countries lead to the destruction of social and ecological balance, mutual resentment and eventually war. Once countries give money, they control you." Supporters argue that these problems may be solved with better auditing of how the aid is used. Indeed, aid from NGOs may be more effective than governmental aid in that NGO aid may be more successful at reaching the poor and better controlled at the grassroots level.

In politics, the fight against poverty is usually regarded as a social goal and many governments have institutions or departments dedicated to tackling poverty. One of the main debates in the field of poverty reduction is around the question of how actively the state should manage the economy and provide public services to tackle the problem of poverty. In the 1990s, international development policies focused on a package of measures known and criticized as the "Washington Consensus." This involved a reduction in the scope of state activities, state intervention in the economy, and trade barriers, as well as opening economies to foreign investment. While most poverty reduction programs attempt to increase the competitiveness of the economy and the viability of the state, vigorous debate over these issues continues.

Improving the environment and access of the poor

Numerous other (sometimes contradictory) methods have been adopted to upgrade the situation of those individuals in poverty. These mechanisms include:

- subsidized housing development;
- education, especially that one directed at assisting the poor to produce food in underdeveloped countries;

- family planning to limit the numbers born into poverty and allow family incomes to better cover the existing family;
- subsidized healthcare;
- assistance in finding employment;
- subsidized employment;
- encouragement of political participation and community organizing;
- implementation of fair property rights laws;
- reduction of regulatory burden and bureaucratic oversight;
- reduction of taxation on income and capital; and
- reduction of government spending, including a reduction in borrowing and printing money.

Another method in helping to fight poverty is to have commodity exchanges that will supply necessary information about national and perhaps international markets to the poor. They would then know what products to sell, where to sell them, and how to maximize profitability. For example, in Ethiopia, remote farmers lacking this information, produce crops that may not generate the best profits. When they sell their products to a local trader, who then sells to another trader, and another, the cost of the food rises before it finally reaches the consumer in large cities. Economist Gabre-Madhin proposes warehouses where farmers could have constant updates of the latest market prices, making the farmer think nationally rather than locally. Each warehouse would have an independent neutral party that would test and grade the farmer's harvest, allowing traders in Addis Ababa, and potentially outside Ethiopia, to place bids on food, even if it is unseen. Thus, if the farmer gets five cents in one place he would get three times the price by selling it in another part of the country where there may be a drought.

Some experts argue for a radical change of the economic system. There are several proposals for a fundamental restructuring of existing economic relations, and many supporters argue that their ideas would reduce or even eliminate poverty if they were implemented. Proposals have been put forward by both left- and right-wing groups, including groups embracing socialism, communism, anarchism, libertarianism, binary economics, and participatory economics.

Finally, in his book *"The End of Poverty"*, economist Jeffrey Sachs laid out a plan to eradicate global poverty by the year 2025. Following his recommendations, international organizations need to work to help eradicate poverty worldwide with prescribed interventions in the areas of housing, food, education, basic health, agricultural inputs, safe drinking water, transportation, and communications.

Conclusion

Poverty and poverty-related issues can still be found on the agenda of virtually every conference when discussing themes dealing with economic development, employment, and growth. The international community represented by powerful and august bodies, such as the World Bank, the regional development banks (including the Inter-American Development Bank and the Asian Development Bank), the IMF, and others, as well as a raft of NGOs all acknowledge the grave consequences attributable to poverty. Sadly, the global problems have prevailed in spite of massive financial and non-financial injections and programs designed to alleviate and eradicate this social curse. Occasionally, one hears about the problems of the "exploitation of the poor." We suggest that the following comment might be borne in mind by heeding the response of one such "poor person" who confided to the authors that the *"problems of being exploited are but nothing, compared to the problems of not being exploited at all!."* On a final note, an elderly lady benefactor to a religious group, sponsoring assistance to developing countries, sincerely said that she hoped that donations such as hers were not part of a system *"where poor people in very rich countries give money to very rich people in very poor countries!."*

References

Ahmad, K. (2002). *Poverty in the World: Some Points to Ponder*, in Sahibzada, M.H. (Retrieved from www.gla.ac.uk/centres/cradall/docs/Botswana-papers/Fasokun.)

Bould, S. (1977). Rural poverty and economic development: lessons from the war on poverty, *The Journal of Applied Behavioral Science*, 13(4): 471–488.

Funk & Wagnalls New Encyclopedia — Volume 21 (Copyright MCMLXXI).

Global Economic Prospects (2007). *The World Bank Report*, Washington.

Henriques, M. (2008). *Personal Correspondence*. Geneva: Head Employment Department, ILO.

Human Development Report (HDR) (2006). New York: United Nations Development Program.

Human Development Report (HDR) (2007). New York: United Nations Development Program.

Jabes, J. (ed.) (2004). The role of public administration in alleviating poverty and improving governance, in *Selected Papers from the Launching Conference of the Network of Asia-Pacific Schools and Institutes of Public Administration and Governance (NAPSIPAG)*, Kuala Lumpur, Malaysia, 6–8 December 2004.

Lappé, F.M., Collins, J. and Rosset, P. (1998). *World Hunger: 12 Myths* (2nd Edn.). New York: Grove Press.

McTaggart, D., Findlay, C.V. and Parkin, M. (1992). *Economics*. Addison-Wesley Publishers Ltd.

Moore, D. (ed.) (2007). *The World Bank: Development, Poverty, Hegemony*. University of Kwazulu Natal Press.

Morgan, J.N., David, M.H., Cohen, W.J. and Brazer, H.E. (1962) *Income and Welfare in the United States*. New York: McGraw-Hill Book Company.

Oladeji, S.I. and Abiola, A.G. (July 2000). Poverty alleviation with economic growth strategy: prospects and challenges in contemporary Nigeria, *Journal of Social Development in Africa*, 15(2): 33–54 (archive.lib.msu.edu).

Poverty external links. (Retrieved from http://en.wikipedia.org/wiki/Poverty.)

* *World Bank Data and Analysis on Poverty and Economic Growth in South Asia*.
* *The Crime of Poverty* by Henry George.
* *Global Distribution of Poverty Global Poverty Datasets and Map Collection*.
* *Why Poor Countries are Poor*.
* *The End of Poverty — an Interview with Jeff Sachs*, Yale Economic Review.
* *Fighting Hunger and Poverty in Ethiopia* by Peter Middlebrook.
* *Poverty in the United States* by Isabel V. Sawhill. Concise Encyclopedia of Economics on Econlib.
* *Poverty* on the World Bank portal.
* *Poverty Eradication*, UN Division for Social Development.
* *Education is the Key to Reducing Poverty*, Omedia.
* *Causes of Poverty*, GlobalIssues.org.

* *The Freedom to be Frugal* by Molly Scott Cato.
* *PPHP: Global Poverty Forecast.*
* *Poverty in the UK and Beyond.*

Poverty and Pauperism (1913). *Catholic Encyclopedia*. New York: Robert Appleton Company.

Poverty Facts and Stats. (Retrieved from http://www.globalissues.org/TradeRelated/Facts.asp.)

Sachs, J. (2005). *The End of Poverty*. Washington: World Bank.

Samuelson, P.A. (1980). *Economics*, (11th edn.). New York: McGraw Hill Book Company.

Shah, A. (2008). *Causes of Poverty: Global Issues*. (Retrieved from http://www.globalissues.org/TradeRelated/Poverty.asp.org.)

Smith, J. (2006). Economic globalization and labor rights: towards global solidarity, *Notre Dame Jl Ethics and Public Policy, 861*.

Smith, J.W. (2000). *Economic Democracy: The Political Struggle of the 21st Century*, Institute for Economic Democracy. The Netherlands: Springer.

State of the World (February 1997). Issue 287, New Internationalist.

The State of the World's Children (1999). New York: UNICEF.

The State of the World's Children (2005). New York: UNICEF.

The Universal Declaration of Human Rights (1948).

The 2005 World Summit High-Level Plenary Meeting of the 60th Session of the General Assembly of the United Nations, New York.

World Bank (2007). *Polycalvet Poverty Data*. (Retrieved from http://en.wikipedia.org/wiki/Poverty.) (Data replicated using World Bank 2007 Human Indicator regional tables with default poverty line of US$32.74 per month at 1993 PPP.)

World Food Programme Emergency Report (2006). Issued by the United Nations, New York.

5
SUSTAINABILITY AND HEALTH CARE

Catherine Popadiuk

The World Health Organization (WHO) has defined "Health" as "a state of complete physical, mental and social well-being and not merely the absence of disease and infirmity."[1] The definition reflects the fact that health is not only for the individual, but is profoundly affected by factors in the community and environment surrounding the individual. Since this definition was stated in 1948, it has not been changed. The state of the world, however, has changed dramatically; particularly so over the last two decades following the fall of the Iron Curtain and the effects of enhanced globalization.

The world is evolving in all dimensions: political, economic, social, technological and ecological at an exponential pace as compared to centuries ago. The exciting and rapid advances in the fields of communication, technology, science and industry impact on every facet of human existence, especially, on the health of the individual, the community and the respective nation. In the words of Thomas Friedman, the world is becoming "flat": "the technological revolution that was leveling the global economic playing field and enabling so many more people around the world to compete, connect, and collaborate was ushering in a new phase of globalization that would have a huge impact on economics, politics, and military and social affairs."[2] We are now at a juncture in the human continuum to

---

[1] http://www.who.int/about/definition/en/print.html, accessed on 19 December 2008.
[2] Friedman, T.L. (2005). *The World is Flat. A Brief History of the Twenty First Century*, Farrar, Straus and Giroux.

achieve a fair and equitable state of being across the world. The question is: what will that new equilibrium of existence be? Will it be closer to the health achieved in the developed world such as the US, the Norwegian countries and Western Europe; or will the new steady state approach the diseased and impoverished levels of the developing world such as Africa, India and parts of Asia.

The Effects of Globalization on Health

The greatest impact on health care has come from safe living conditions, sanitation, and hygiene. These components include clean drinking water, access to adequate and nutritious food sources, and safe environments in which to live. Many developing countries have yet to achieve basic rudiments including health and the developed world may be relinquishing them in a quest for an even higher standard of living.

With access to medication, preventive, medical and surgical treatments for chronic and acute disease conditions, citizens of the developed world now have life expectancies well into the eighties and beyond.[3] Paradoxically, the next generation's life expectancy is expected to be less as obesity rates and chronic disease conditions associated with a more sedentary lifestyle overcome medical advancement.

The most unprecedented concern for the world today and generations to come is the impact of our existence on the earth itself. Since the advent of industrialization, developed countries have grappled with the deleterious effects on the environment and health. Legislation and regulations have been enacted addressing clean air and water, urban air pollution, industrial waste contamination, smog, ozone depletion, acid rain and litter.[4] Countries and continents such as China and India are now progressing through the effects of globalization dealing with these same concerns.[5]

---

[3] CIA — The World Factbook 2008 (https://www.cia.gov/library/publications/the-world-factbook/fields/2012.html) — Rank Order — Life Expectancy at Birth.

[4] Friedman, T.L. (2008). *Hot, Flat, and Crowded. Why We Need a Green Revolution — And How It Can Renew America*, Farrar, Straus, and Giroux, p. 33. Enforcement of the legislation and regulations is still an issue.

[5] Air pollution at the Beijing Olympics was a priority.

On a more macroscopic level, the Earth is being overwhelmed with the human thumbprint of our modern existence. By 2053, the UN estimates that there will be nine billion people on the planet — thanks to improvements in health care, disease eradication, and economic development. The majority of this increase from the present six billion people today will be in the developing countries. While the populations of developed countries were expected to decrease, immigration from developing countries will keep them stable. Rapidly expanding population growth will overwhelm infrastructures and cause a depletion of resources such as arable land, water and food, resulting in worsening deforestation, overfishing, and air and water pollution.[6] The 40% to 45% increase will occur in countries least able to sustain such growth, resulting in instability and extremism. These countries will have a large proportion of young people who are highly impressionable and susceptible to indoctrination of thought.

Scientists argue that greenhouse gas emissions are threatening to choke the society we know by the next few generations. Greenhouse gases are invisible pollutants that warm the earth by creating a thick blanket in the atmosphere. The emissions are composed of carbon dioxide (CO_2) and carbon monoxide (CO). Carbon dioxide is generated from vehicles, power plants burning coal, oil and gas, and burning of trees, plants and soil in forests. The deforestation in Indonesia and Brazil release more CO_2 than all the world's cars, trucks, ships and trains combined — 20% of all global gas emissions.[7] Methane emissions are even more potent — 21 times stronger than CO_2.[8] They result from rice farming, coal mining, petroleum drilling, animal defecation, solid waste landfill sites, and cattle belching. Scientists believe that the human contribution to greenhouse gases since industrialization is directly contributing to the deleterious effects now being seen in global warming.

In a quest for living conditions approaching that of the modern world, the "American Dream," newly developing populations entering the middle class are following the same steps of modernization over the

---

[6] Friedman, T.L. (2008), p. 26.
[7] *Ibid.* p. 33.
[8] *Ibid.* p. 35 quoted from " Science World" (21 January 2002).

last decade as developed countries began addressing a century ago. For example, China's economic and political might has seen a vast expansion in industry and wealth for the Chinese people. But as more citizens become members of a rapidly growing middle class, moving out of poverty levels, the effects of pollution and urban growth are taking effect. The country is grappling with a need for safeguards and limits to save the environment and the nation's health. The quest of the individual, however, to be on par with their developed world brethren, is difficult to control. Unless all societies on the earth recognize and participate in non-renewable energy conservation, the health of all will suffer as global temperatures continue to rise and the climate, geography, and life forms becomes irreversibly impacted.

As more populations join the "developed" way of life, there is a further need for energy sources with a majority still in the non-renewable form such as oil, gas and coal. Competition for limited goods is already having a rippling effect on the world economy and politic which is not sustainable. Andy Karsner, who in August 2008 resigned as the US Department of Energy's assistant secretary for energy efficiency and renewable energy summarized: "We built a really inefficient environment with the greatest efficiency ever known to man."[9]

One can apply this premise to the classic tale "The Tragedy of the Commons" by Hardin where freedom to the commons can bring destruction to all.[10] The story often takes place in a pasture shared by a number of livestock. The pasture is available to all but can only nourish a limited number of animals. The farmers bring their animals to graze but one farmer sees no harm in having an extra animal partake in the green grass and adds to the fold. In economic terms, the story is told in terms of profit margins and costs. The farmer bringing the extra animal considers the added benefit of a fattened animal for her proportion of cost, but in so doing, shortchanges the competitor farmers. Eventually and imperceptibly, further mutual exploitation continues until overgrazing, communicable disease and erosion destroy the entire pasture and economic ruin affects

---

[9] *Ibid.* p. 33.
[10] Hardin, G. (1968). The Tragedy of the Commons, *Science*, 162(3859): 1243–1248.

all but the one farmer. Hardin illustrates a critical flaw of freedom in the commons: everyone must agree to conserve the commons but any one individual or group can lead to its destruction. The fundamental resources for our human survival and health are the commons of the earth: the air, water, land and species surrounding us. The exponentially rapid industrialization of developing and developed countries around the world resulting from the expanded connectivity from globalization, is ripe for exploitation and destruction unless all countries unite and participate in limits to the commons; most notably, non-renewable products and energy resources.

The Impact of Globalization on the Health of Seemingly Disparate Groups

Unfortunately, the lessons that make the most impact and resonate greatest on us are those resulting from the worst disasters and circumstances. The world takes notice through monumental hardship. With the improvements in communication via the Internet and satellite, news can be transmitted almost instantly. But such was not available for the case on 26 April, 1986 with the Chernobyl nuclear power plant explosion in Pripyat, Ukraine. On the contrary, the Soviet Union attempted to downplay the extent of the disaster until the effects of the radiation were detected by Swedish nuclear surveillance alarms. Only then did the Soviet Union admit a catastrophic accident had occurred. The industrial explosion sent a plume of highly radioactive fallout into the atmosphere over an extensive geographic area. The fallout was 400 times greater than that released by the atomic bombing over Hiroshima. The plume drifted over extensive parts of the Western Soviet Union, Europe and Eastern North America. Large areas of the Ukraine, Belarus and Russia were badly contaminated, resulting in the evacuation and resettlement of over 336,000 people. According to a report by the Chernobyl forum led by the WHO and the International Atomic Energy Agency, this was the costliest disaster at the time, estimated at US$2 billion dollars. There were 56 direct deaths due to radiation exposure and there may be 4000 extra cancer deaths among 600,000 exposed people. The true impact may never be known. Rivers, lakes and reservoirs were exposed to the radiation and contaminated. The flora and fauna in a four square kilometer radius was decimated, called the "red forest." Until this day, the accident site is encased in concrete, a shrine of radioactivity. The accident was ultimately thought to be a result of flawed operations and designs. It left a lasting impact on all nations as to the harm we can do to our environment and health with the manmade products and industries we create.[11]

The magnitude of tragedy in Chernobyl was not unique. Not two years earlier, on 3 December 1984, an industrial disaster occurred in Bhopal, Madya Pradesh, India. It resulted in the immediate deaths of more than 3000 people and likely 8000 within two weeks of the explosion and an additional 8000 afterwards from gas related diseases. A Union Carbide subsidiary pesticide plant released 42 tonnes of methyl isocyanate gas, exposing this densely populated area of over 520,000 people to toxic gases. This is considered to be the world's worst industrial disaster. A number of factors contributed to the disaster: the use of hazardous materials instead of more costly less dangerous ones, storing chemicals in large tanks instead of smaller ones, poor maintenance of plant materials, and failure of several systems due to poor maintenance and regulations. At the center of the tragedy was the recognition for cost containment of products, processes and safeguards. Working conditions were dangerous due to cuts in equipment budgets and lax safety regulations. Previous warnings and accidents were ignored until this disaster. Ultimately the parties responsible were the United Carbide corporation, the Government of India as a partner, and to a lesser extent the government of Madya Pradesh.[12] The victims of this tragedy and their families have been shuffled through

---

[11] http://ngm.nationalgeographic.com/ngm/0604/feature1/*National Geographic* (April 2006). http://www.iaea.org/NewsCenter/Focus/Chernobyl/. In http://wikipedia.org/wiki/Chernobyl_disaster.

[12] Eckerman, I. (2001). *Chemical Industry and Public Health — Bhopal as an Example* (http://www.dnsy.se/_upload/lfm/2006/bhopal%20gas%20disaster.pdf) and Eckerman, I. (2004). *The Bhopal Saga — Causes and Consequences of the World's Largest Industrial Disaster* (http://www.eckerman.nu/default.cfm?page=The %20Bhopal%20Saga). India: Universities Press. In http://en.wikipedia.org/wiki/Bhopal_disaster.

decades of legal proceedings with small recompense for their lives. The lessons of Bhopal have reverberated across the world to prevent further cataclysmic destruction of life and health.

More recently, the world watched horrified, as terrorists attacked the World Trade Center in New York, USA, decimating the "Twin Towers" and killing thousands. One could ask, what does a terrorist attack have to do with a nation's health? But the results of this attack reverberated through the American citizens and across the world. If health is defined in terms of physical, psychological and social well-being, this attack has directly affected the nations psychological well-being and tolerance toward foreign interests. The resulting War in Iraq has impacted on the financial stability of the US and consequently countries intertwined in trade and foreign relationships. For example, business travel to the US fell by 10% between 2004 and 2005. According to the US travel industry, the US entry process "has created a climate of fear and frustration that is turning away foreign business and leisure travelers from visiting the US damaging Americans' image abroad."[13]

The heightened sensitivity toward travelers may have spared the US the effects of the frightening Severe Acute Respiratory Syndrome (SARS) epidemic felt around the world between November 2002 and July 2003. According to the WHO, there were 8096 known infected cases and 774 deaths worldwide. Within a few weeks in 2003, SARS spread from the Guangdong province of China to infect individuals in 37 countries across the world. The epidemic started in a farmer in Shunde Foshan, Guangdong, in November 2002. He died without an official diagnosis being made, nor precautions for infectivity taken. The Chinese government attempted to control an outbreak afterwards but did not notify the WHO of the outbreak and restricted media coverage and information. The lack of transparency resulted in the widespread dissemination of the disease across the world through travel of exposed individuals. Delays in communication through modern Internet channels with the WHO due to translation problems and the initial understatement of the problem,

---

[13] Friedman, T.L. (2008). p. 13

resulted in the worldwide near pandemic. The most highly affected countries were China, Hong Kong and Canada, with 5328, 1755 and 432 cases, respectively. The US, with ten times the population as Canada, had 27 cases.[14]

Despite the magnitude of the tragedy, the world rallied and united to identify and respond to the problem. Arguably, the outbreak could have been much worse had modern communications not been available to share information rapidly once identified. Paradoxically, modern air travel, helped spread the virus much faster than in decades past.

Similarly, although not as acutely deadly and dramatic, the crises impacting upon the health of individuals and countries are equally important. For example, as China rapidly builds its industrial infrastructure with the assistance of modern equipment and technology, the safeguards and regulations which took decades to create in developed nations, are lagging. Traces of the industrial chemical melamine in infant formula exported across the world are raising awareness for the importance of assuring safeguards and quality control standards to assure health.[15] The recall of 967,000 toys by Mattel due to lead paint concerns are forcing a swift lesson and implementation of product regulations that are new in the developing world's foray into manufacturing and production.[16]

These lessons are not unique to the developing world; health concerns are still being identified in the developed. For example, Maple Leaf foods in Canada had a recall of meat products in 2008 due to contamination of Listeria in the processing plants.

---

[14] WHO targets SARS "super spreaders" (http://www.cnn.com/2003/HEALTH/04/05/sars.vaccine.index.html), *CNN News*, 6 April 2003; Mawudeku, A. and Blench, M. (2005). *Global Public Health Intelligence Network*, mt-archive (http://www.mt-archive.info/MTS-2005-Mawudeku.pdf); Heymann, D.L. and Rodier, G. Global surveillance, national surveillance, and SARS, *Emerging Infectious Diseases — Medscape*, 10 February 2004 (http://www.medscape.com/viewarticle/467371) in http://en.wikipedia.org/wiki/Severe_acute_respiratory_syndrome.

[15] http://www.politicsandcurrentaffairs.co.uk/Forum/us-politics-forum/56881-chinese-poison-baby-formula.html and www.time.com/time/health/article/0,8599,1841757,00.html.

[16] http://www.nytimes.com/2007/08/02/business/02toy.html.

Exploitation of the Health of Vulnerable Populations in the Modern Era

In 2002, Dr Bhaget Makkar was disciplined by the British General Medical Council and banned from practice for trafficking living donor organs. Dr Makkar admitted to an undercover reporter in a taped interview that he could arrange for a living donor in the UK or India.[17] This case is unique in that Dr Makkar was apprehended and censured for these actions. But as transplantation medicine has advanced, the need for transplantable organs has skyrocketed. Living donor organs fair better than postmortem specimens and hence a subversive undercurrent of distorted supply and demand is being waged amidst the academic debate on the ethics and legality of the practice.

In many developed countries such as the US, Canada and Europe, a human organ or tissue is considered a gift which cannot be bought or sold for economic gain. The gift of a living donor organ is considered very special and altruistic and is not without risk to the donor. The capital market concepts of supply and demand are not to be incorporated into the equation. But harsh reality sets in when supply of the essential organs for medical treatments are not available to the needy and desperate recipients. As populations age and life expectancy increases in many developed countries, the demand for living donor organs rises in parallel. But for various reasons, from cultural and religious norms and taboos, to reticence on the part of donor patients due to risk or autonomous choice, the organs are not available. Hence, there is the need to explore other avenues outside the status quo in developed countries.

The kidney is the body part that accounts for the most "sales" of organs throughout the world. Waiting times for a suitable donor can be from two to three years in the US and UK, six to eight years in Singapore, and unknown durations in many countries that do not keep records such as the Gulf States and Asia. As there are no clear regulations surrounding organ "trafficking," the practice has flourished since the 1990s and arguably has been made easier through the communications and connectivity

---

[17] Rothman, S.M. and Rothman, D.L. The organ market, *The New York Review*, 23 October 2003, pp. 49–51. Cain, G. Asia's kidney bazaars, *Far Eastern Economic Review*, 6 January 2009, http://www.feer.com/economics/2009/january/Asias-Kidney-Bazaars.

afforded through Internet technologies. In the early 1990s, residents from the Gulf States procured their kidneys from India and Asian residents from India and China. Now the trade is international. India continues to be a popular source despite laws prohibiting the sale there. Buyers come from the US, Canada, and the UK. China also runs an elaborate and extensive transplant business although denies that its surgeons remove organs from executed prisoners. Chinese ex-patriots travel to China to purchase kidneys. The Philippines too has a large number of kidneys for sale and its hospitals actively try to sell them to Japanese recipients. Similarly, Estonia, Turkey and Moldova sell to Israelis, and Bulgaria and Romania sell to Israelis and other Eastern Europeans.[17]

The trafficking is not just the solitary organ, but the movement of the donor, recipient and sometimes the surgeons. Receiving organs from developing countries raises suspicions and is perceived as unpalatable, unethical and illegal. Instead, a "relative" traveling on a special visa to the hospital for a procedure, with no discussion of monetary compensation is considered acceptable. The hospital also has the opportunity to scrutinize the donor and assure no transmission of communicable diseases and deadly viruses.

Although Dr Makkar was disciplined for his role in the trafficking of humans for the purpose of organ donation and sale, it is uncommon to restrict, limit and punish the participants in this practice. Commerce of organs is prohibited by numerous national and international transplant societies and the World Medical Association (WMA), but enforcement of the rules is lacking. When China requested entry to the WMA, concern was expressed regarding its participation in human organ trafficking. To be allowed entry into the WMA, China promised to hold a conference on the ethics of organ transplantation to educate the physicians regarding ethical practices. The conference did not take place and it is unlikely that the practices changed. The WMA did not respond to enforce the request or limit China's participation in the WMA.[18]

Not surprisingly, the sale of organs can be very profitable and complex agreements to donate kidneys are made with families in exchange for medical care. For example, in Bangkok's Vachiraprukarn General Hospital,

---

[18] *Ibid.* p. 49.

a young pregnant woman was admitted to hospital in a coma following a car accident. The impoverished family agreed to let her be cared for there at no cost, in exchange for her kidneys if she died. Following her death, the family was given a monetary gift, $2500, to assist with funeral arrangements. The hospital profited ten times more, $25,000, for the two kidneys they transplanted. An inquiry was established in this case when it was alleged that the woman was not yet brain dead when her organs were harvested. The physician, Siroj, was accused of unethical medical conduct and indicted for murder, the first such case in Thailand.[19]

In contrast, in Manila, Philippines, kidneys are sold openly and legally. The practice is quite streamlined. Physicians go to the slums, perform blood and tissue tests on the men, and when a recipient is identified matching one of the screened men, he is identified through a "broker." The vulnerable poor are paid for the organs, but generally their living conditions and health deteriorate. The effects of surgery impact on their ability to do hard labor resulting in job loss and a worsening financial situation.[20]

At present, the exchange and sale of living donor organs has become highly efficient with the advancement in technology and communications; and correspondingly more exploitative of vulnerable impoverished populations. In the US, however, the American Medical Association posits a "futures market" for donor organs from brain dead recipients. Postmortem reimbursement and funeral expense tax credits would be incentives to donate.[21] The debate surrounding the globalization of living donor organ donation will rage on as the practice escalates and greater division is propagated between the poor and wealthy nations, only increasing the divide in their respective health status.

From Human Organs to Human Research Subjects

Before any new medical drug or treatment device is approved for a clinical indication in the general population, pharmaceutical and medical

---

[19] *Ibid.* p. 50.
[20] *Ibid.* p. 50.
[21] *Ibid.* p. 50.

device companies must go through rigorous pre-clinical and clinical trials to the satisfaction of national regulatory bodies. Prior to the 1990s, most clinical trials research took place in the US and Western Europe to fulfill the criteria for the local end user. To accelerate the clinical trials process, the US Federal Drug Agency, overseeing the world's largest and most lucrative drug market, opened clinical trials to include subjects from outside the US, essentially opening the borders for human subjects to participate in trials for drug development in the US. The US FDA contributed to the globalization of clinical trials. It played a key role in the International Conference on Harmonization (ICH) which eased the acceptability and transfer of clinical data from foreign sites to the FDA. Under the auspices of the ICH, the FDA allowed clinical trial data collected from test subjects in "non-traditional" research settings, to be used in US drug regulatory approvals.[22]

Following the ICH, participation in US sponsored research grew exponentially. According to FDA estimates, 4000 research subjects participated in clinical trials in 1995. By 1999, the number grew to 400,000. Subjects were recruited from countries where the drugs would likely not be made available at affordable cost to the patients, if at all. The recruited subjects thus would not benefit from the developed drugs although they would potentially get access to new treatments while on trial. Countries such as Argentina, Brazil, Hungary, Mexico, Poland, Russia and Thailand became "clinical trial research markets."[23]

The globalization of clinical trials is a recent phenomenon which has profoundly shaped the ways in which individuals in low-income settings can access medical treatments. Health care crises, the collapse of medical infrastructures, the lack of treatment access, and the relatively easy availability of research subjects are some of the factors moving commercial therapeutic drug research to Latin America, Eastern and Central Europe, Africa, India, and Africa among other places. Much has also changed in the last three decades from the scientific and regulatory perspectives to make the movement of human subjects' research to such areas both

---

[22] Petryna, A. (2005). Ethical variability: drug development and globalizing clinical trials, *American Ethnologist*, 32(2): 183–197.
[23] *Ibid.*

ethical and opportune.²⁴ For individuals who would never have access to new life saving or benefiting therapies, clinical trials offer hope, but at what price? Are the protections and regulations for human research subjects adequate?

In September 1999, the death of Jessie Gelsinger made headlines. This 18-year-old man had a rare genetic disorder of impaired ammonia metabolism due to ornithine transcarbamylase deficiency. He underwent a gene transfer experiment at the University of Pennsylvania Institute for Human Gene Therapy. Theoretically, the gene used to repair the deficiency is transferred to the patient's abnormal cells by an attenuated adenovirus. At the time of his participation, he was in good health and stable on a special diet and medications and was not in any jeopardy of imminent death or medical hardship. Within four days of his injection with adenovirus, he died in the intensive care unit, of multiple system failure. The principal researcher overseeing the trial had a substantial stake in Genovo, the private company that produced the gene altering virus. Genovo provided substantial funds to finance the research at the Human Gene Therapy Institute.²⁵ In this case, the former Dean of the University of Pennsylvania Medical School, Dr Wilson had patents on aspects of the gene therapy procedure and he subsequently admitted he would have received US$13.5 million from a biotechnology company in exchange for his shares in Genovo, had the trial succeeded.²⁶ Ultimately it was found that the trial did not have adequate safeguards and oversight, thus resulting in Jesse's death. Good judgment and due diligence were clouded over by greed and economic gain. Following the death of Gelsinger, a special committee of the Institute of Medicine concluded that the failure to protect him was "paradigmatic of failures in the system

---

[24] *Ibid.*
[25] Emanuel, E.J., Crouch, R.A., Arras, J.D., Moreno, J.D. and Grady, C (2003). *Ethical and Regulatory Aspects of Clinical Research: Readings and Commentary. Part VIII. The Behavior of Clinical Investigators: Conflicts of Interest.* Baltimore: John Hopkins University Press, pp. 369–374.
[26] Goldner, J.A. (2000). Dealing with conflict of interest in biomedical research: IRB oversight as the next best solution to the abolitionist approach, *Journal of Law, Medicine & Ethics,* 28: 379–404.

of protections itself." Included in these failures was insufficient control over conflicts of interest of investigators and institutions, and an inadequate review process.[27]

In a more recent case, TGN1412, an immunomodulatory drug developed to treat B cell chronic leukemia had its first human clinical trial on 13 March 2006. It resulted in catastrophic systemic organ failure in all six voluntary subjects. They were admitted to the ICU at Northwick Park Hospital in London, England. Although the subjects were all released from hospital by July, it is believed that they continue to beat risk of long term sequelae such as cancer. The drug was designated by the European Medicines Agency in March 2005 as an orphan medical product, the status granted to a drug that is necessary but prohibitively expensive or unprofitable to develop. It was developed by TeGenero Immuno Therapeutics, tested by Parexel and manufactured by Boehringer-Ingelheim. The Medicines and Healthcare Products Regulatory Agency issued a review and found no deficiencies in the way the trial was conducted. The regrettable adverse effects were due to an unpredicted biological action of the drug in humans. The fee paid to the volunteers was £2000, much higher than other trials that compensate trial subjects for time and invasiveness of the interventions.[28] The excessive compensation was a strong point of criticism following the tragedy. How much money is too much to pay for a clinical trial subject? When does it become an unfair inducement to attract the vulnerable to potential harm not worth the benefit?

In Canada, the case of Dr. Nancy Olivieri illustrates the influence of the pharmaceutical industry over decision makers at academic and health care institutions, ultimately hindering safe medical research and patient health to secure economic return. Olivieri reached international acclaim when she attempted to publish her research in the area of thalassemia, an

---

[27] Committee on assessing the system for protecting human research participants, Institute of Medicine, *Responsible Research: A Systems Approach to Protecting Research Participants* (Washington DC: National Academies Press, 2001), in Lemmens, T. Leopards in the Temple: restoring scientific integrity to the commercialized research scene, *International and Comparative Health Law & Ethics: A 25-Year Retrospective*, Winter 2004, pp. 641–657.

[28] Coghlan, A. Mystery over drug trial debacle deepens, http://www.newscientist.com/article.ns?id=dn9734), *New Scientist*, in http://en.wikipedia.org/wiki/TGN1412.

inherited disorder in which the red blood cells are defective, and was hindered by the corporate sponsor Apotex. She discovered the experimental drug, deferipone, which was meant to prevent iron overload in these patients, lost its effectiveness and caused liver damage. When she published her work, she was sued for breach of contract and ostracized by some of the hospital and university communities at the University of Toronto. It was discovered that Apotex was a major donor to the University.[29]

In contrast to these high profile scandals surrounding clinical trial tragedies in developed countries, bad outcomes and side effects in the developing world are silent except in fiction and drama such as in the novel (and later on film) by author John Le Carre, "The Constant Gardener," where a pharmaceutical company went to all lengths to get approval for a dangerous drug which killed and harmed vulnerable trial subjects in impoverished Africa.[30] In reality, inequities between the developing and developed world have caused debate about offering a proportion of a population possible life saving medications such as for AIDS, and offering nothing, the local standard of care, to others.

The controversy reached international recognition in 1994 when the ethics of short-course AZT treatment to stop perinatal transmission of HIV in Uganda came to light. The drug was to be compared to a placebo, the non-active treatment. Ethics guidelines such as the Helskinki Code, did not allow for placebo when an effective treatment is available. New drugs to be tested have to be compared to the most effective treatment presently available, as opposed to no treatment at all. Influential scientists and scholars debated the ethics of clinical trial standards in developing countries where the developed standard of care therapeutics is not available. At the time, Marcia Angell, the editor of the *New England Journal of Medicine* argued placebo controlled trials where a treatment is available is unethical. In contrast, Nobel Laureate Harold Varmus, while director of the US National Institutes of Health (NIH), and David Satcher of the Center for Disease Control (CDC) disagreed and argued that local cultural

---

[29] Lind, S.E. (1990). Finder's fees for research subjects, *New England Journal of Medicine* 323: 192–195; Ch. 73; pp. 377–378.
[30] LeCarre, J. (2001). *The Constant Gardener*, Hodder & Stouten.

variables and poor health infrastructures must be taken into consideration when determining a local standard of care for a trial, even when the trial is being performed for a developed country with effective treatment available for the condition of interest, in this case, HIV.[31]

The debate continues and is unresolved in the medical community, but the issue prompted a revision to the Helsinki Declaration in 2000. Although the revision reiterated a position against placebo controls when effective treatments are available, it added: "The benefits, risks, burdens, and effectiveness of a new method should be tested against those of the best current prophylactic, diagnostic, or therapeutic method exists" (World Medical Association 2000:3044).[32] The pharmaceutical industry has since worked with this definition using placebo controlled trials for maximum economic benefit to be gained in the developed world. The concerns for "just redistribution" in resource poor areas of the world, continues to be in limbo.

Recently, the varying standards of health within a country at local, district and provincial levels, has been raised. On 25 July 2004, the South African AIDS advocacy group, the Treatment Action Campaign, highlighted discrepancies and variability in the country's HIV antiretroviral drug rollout program which is desperately needed to combat HIV and AIDS in millions of affected individuals in their country. The issue was identified not for the inequity of available treatment for patients, but in the ethical conundrum for continuing clinical trials in these characteristically impoverished populations where placebos have been used.[33] Bioethicists and medical scholars are now debating as to how to define "standard of care" in a population where variability exists. Could the provision of antiretrovirals where they do not exist be seen as unfair inducement? Is a placebo unethical? Given the influence and power exerted by the pharmaceutical industry over clinical trials research and subjects finding loopholes through ethical guidelines and subjects' protection, it is not likely that placebo trials would be halted in the near future. It is to their

---

[31] *op cit*. Petryna, A., p. 187.
[32] *Ibid.* p. 188.
[33] Singh, J.A. (2004). Standards of care in the antiretroviral rollout world, *The Lancet*, 364: 920–922.

benefit to keep inequity present in this world. At present, no US legislation or transnational regulatory policy exists to control and monitor the globalization of clinical trials subjects.[34]

In addition to being without standard medical treatments available in developed countries, citizens in developing countries are further considered ideal for clinical trials participation due to their "treatment naïveté."[35] It is very difficult to find ideal research subjects fitting the long list of inclusion criteria to participate in a clinical trial in the US, Canada and Western Europe where it is common to have patients on multiple medications that can confound the treatment effects of the drug to be tested, or worse, suffer serious adverse events and harm from concurrent effects. Consequently, the results of clinical trials performed on populations differing than the ones where the drug will be sold and marketed, may not be comparable or accurate, and more importantly, dangerous. The consequences of adverse drug reactions since 2000 have been massive in terms of health, and deleterious economic impact on the pharmaceutical industry. Drug related adverse events have increased 500% between 2000 and 2005.[36] These bad reactions occurred after the drug was approved and on the market resulting in product liability for the pharmaceutical company and economic loss when the drug has been removed from the market. Given the loss of investment at such a late stage in product development and manufacture, pharmaceutical companies try to salvage the economic losses and find new indications for the failed and unsafe drug. This causes a vicious cycle of recruiting yet again more clinical trial subjects naive to the treatment and gullible enough to take a medication with known toxicity. The vulnerable in developing countries are approached again.

Such was the case for Trovan, a widely prescribed antibiotic in the US, until it was taken off the market in 1996, for serious liver toxicity.[37] In an effort to find a new indication for the drug, Pfizer created a trial for

---

[34] *op cit.* Petryna, A., p. 189.
[35] Ibid. p. 186.
[36] Petryna, A. (2005). Ethical variability: drug development and globalizing clinical trials, *American Ethnologist*, 32(2): 183–197.
[37] *op cit.* Petryna, A. p. 190.

pediatric bacterial meningitis. The trial was not approved by a US ethics committee and received very cursory review and approval by a local ethics committee in Kano, Nigeria where a meningitis outbreak was identified through the Internet and civil unrest under the Abachy military dictatorship contributed to the instability. Standard safe antibiotics were already being administered to children through Doctors Without Borders at a local hospital. The Pfizer team went to the hospital and selected 100 children in line as study subjects. Apparently the research nature of the treatment was not explained such that the parents could understand that their children were not receiving the expected treatment. They also did not understand that a new formulation of Trovan was being tested, never before tried in humans, or that some members of the control group received a lower dose of the standard antibiotic, inadequate for meningitis, but more likely to demonstrate treatment superiority in the Trovan group. The low dosing resulted in the deaths of 11 children, as argued by the lawyers representing the affected families who sued Pfizer in a US Court. With extensive financial backing, Pfizer put up a strong legal defence downplaying the enforceability of ethical codes and declarations versus the lacking rule of law in unstable vulnerable countries. The lawyers on behalf of the families outlined that many groups were culpable in this tragedy: Nigeria's military rulers and government officials, Ministry of Health officials, hospital administrators, FDA regulators who authorized an unapproved drug's export into Nigeria for "humanitarian" reasons, and Pfizer researchers selecting research subjects from a line of children waiting and hence consenting for standard care to treat meningitis.[38] It is very troubling to consider that such exploitation of vulnerable populations can be contorted into acceptability when applying the lens of developed world standards and judgment, and justifying their intervention as benevolent because the recipient has nothing, including dignity and respect for her human rights. In this case, if the Nigerian interests were not on the side of protection, but on making populations accessible for research, the exploitation by countries and industries guided by the rule of law, ethics and morality, is all the more reprehensible.

---

[38] Let alone the concern regarding conflict of interest on the part of Pfizer staff interacting directly with patients.

Strategies for Sustainable Health Care

The health of a nation and its citizens is highly dependent on numerous factors contributing to their physical, mental and social well-being: the political, economic, cultural, geographic, and intangible elements, all of which create the unique fabric of the society. In the new millennium, there is still great disparity in the health of the Earths' inhabitants. The effects of globalization are impacting to raise the standard of living in traditionally Third World communities, but at what pace? Could more be done to accelerate and raise the standard of living in these populations? Are the decisions by government, industry and individuals responsible and sustainable for tomorrow or short-sighted and immediate for today? Thus far, we have reviewed the examples of climate neglect, organ sales and trafficking, and the human subjects research business, which do not appear to fulfill the criteria for long term planning and sustainable vision in achieving health. Is there a model of a successful sustainable venture prioritizing the health of people and a nation?

The Brazilian Response to the AIDS/HIV Crises: A Model of Sustainable Decision-Making

In the early 1980s, Brazil was predicted to suffer an HIV/AIDS epidemic as presently being experienced in Africa and other countries where health care infrastructure was virtually non-existent. The predictions did not hold true however, given strategic decisions and investments made by the Brazilian Government and collaborations with people and organizations working together, despite their short term differences, for the long term good. It was estimated by the World Bank that Brazil would see 1.2 million cases of HIV infection by 2000. In reality, there were only 600,000, half of this projection.[39]

The first case of AIDS in Brazil was diagnosed in 1982. The country experienced a change in political power in 1985 moving towards democracy from military rule and in 1986, the National AIDS Control Program

---

[39] Ministry of Health of Brazil (2003) in http://en.wikipedia.org/wiki/HIV/AIDS_in_Brazil.

(NACP) came into existence through the efforts of the federal Ministry of Health. It was placed under the auspices of the National AIDS Control Committee, a group of interested scientists and civil society leaders, in 1987.[40]

Brazil approached the impending epidemic through a multi-pronged approach recognizing the multiple elements, such as social, financial, and cultural, which impact on health. Socially, it was imperative to recognize and work with the strong religious beliefs motivating behavior in the country. Brazil targeted the groups which accounted for a high percentage of HIV transmission and worked to educate them and prevent the spread. Unlike other countries that lagged behind in encouraging condom use, Brazil assured condoms were affordable and disseminated widely. Prostitute groups were embraced to distribute information materials and condoms. Despite the fact that Brazil has one of the largest populations of Roman Catholics in the world, a faith which frowns on premarital sex, prostitution and various sexual behaviors; there was little resistance to the condom campaign and the assistance from prostitutes to disseminate information. The Catholic Church did not demand their "abstinence only" programs and complaints regarding religion and morality were "mild."[41]

Furthermore, intravenous drug use was identified as a source of infection and needle exchange programs promptly implemented and supported. Between 1994 and 1998, 12 such programs were implemented and by 2000, 40, distributing approximately 1.5 million syringes in 2000. Nationwide blood bank screening began in 1988 and by 2000, when the incubation period for the virus was better understood and addressed through modern screening procedures, virtually no cases of HIV were spread through blood transfusions. Finally, Brazil implemented zidovudine treatment to prevent mother to child transmission in pregnancy and recommendations against breast feeding by mothers harbouring the virus. Given this measure, the rate of maternal fetal transmission of HIV is only 3%, comparable to developed countries.[40]

---

[40] Levi, G.C. and Vitoria, M.A.A. (2002). Fighting against AIDS: the Brazilian experience, *AIDS* 16: 2372–2383. in http://en.wikipedia.org/wiki/HIV/AIDS_in_Brazil.

[41] Reel, M. Where prostitutes also fight AIDS, *Washington Post*, 2 March 2006, p. A14, in http://en.wikipedia.org/wiki/HIV/AIDS_in_Brazil.

Arguably, the most significant strategy to combat HIV and AIDS in Brazil came through its free antiretroviral drug program, available to all afflicted Brazilian citizens. In December 1996, federal law 9313 came into effect assuring free universal access to anti-retroviral drugs including a specialized class of drugs called protease inhibitors. Each year the guidelines for antiretroviral therapy are reviewed and updated for the most appropriate contents of the "ARV cocktail." In 2003, all 125,000 Brazilian AIDS patients received the free treatment. It was traditionally argued that free ARV drugs would not impact on survival from AIDS if not disseminated in the context of minimal infrastructure and capacity. Despite the skepticism, the Brazilians receiving the drugs through their outpatient settings adhered to the prescribed regimen. Scientific research suggested that the antiretroviral treatments were the single independent factor contributing to their survival.[42]

The success for the program and the free ARV drugs could not succeed without the assistance of external funding bodies and organizations such as NGOs and the World Bank. In 1992, the NACP was restructured to include stronger linkages between the government and NGOs. AIDS Project 1 accrued US$90 million of domestic funding and received a US$160 million loan from the World Bank for a total investment of US$250 million between 1992 and 1998. AIDS Project 2 between 1998 and 2002 reached US$300 million of combined domestic and World Bank contributions.[43]

Brazil's drug costs for the free ARV program was less than half that of the developed world: US$4459 per patient versus US$10,000. In 2001, Brazil began manufacturing eight of the 12 drugs used in the ARV cocktail and by 2003, eight of the 15 drugs. By producing these generic alternatives locally, and obviating the need for patented imports, Brazil saved 32%. Between 1996 and 2000, Brazil's treatment costs were reduced by 72.5% by avoiding the patented imports.[44]

---

[42] Marins, J.R.P., Jamal, L.F.C., Sanny, Y.B., *et al*. (2003). Dramatic improvement in survival among adult Brazilian AIDS patients, *AIDS* 17: 1675–1682, in http://en.wikipedia.org/wiki/HIV/AIDS_in_Brazil.

[43] *op cit.* Leve, G.C. and Vitoria, M.A.A, p. 2374.

[44] Gilman, S. Brazil, AIDS, and intellectual property (http://www.americanedu/TED/brazil-aids.htm), *TED Case Studies*, January 2001, No. 649, in http://en.wikipedia.org/wiki/HIV/AIDS_in_Brazil.

Brazil enacted laws that protected the health of its people standing up to a powerful pharmaceutical industry in the midst of arguably weak international laws and regulations. Article 71 of the 1997 Brazilian patent law requires that foreign products be manufactured locally within three years of being granted a patent. This action can be taken without the consent or agreement of the foreign manufacturer through "compulsory licensing." Furthermore, Article 68 allows "parallel importing" from the lowest international generic bidder. These actions bring in competition, bring down prices and limit monopolies.[45]

The US and the powerful pharmaceutical lobby responded against the humanitarian practices of Brazil. The US threatened sanctions against Brazil and placed it on a "Special 301" watch list. They challenged Article 68 under the World Trade Organizations Agreement on Trade-Related Aspects of Intellectual Property Rights (TRIPs) for allegedly discriminating against imported products. But the agreements signed on 14 November 2001 at the WTO conference in Qatar reaffirmed that TRIPs "does not and should not prevent members from taking measures to protect public health" including "Medicines for all." The same year, the United Nations affirmed that access to AIDS drugs was a human right. The declaration was unanimous except for the US which abstained.[46]

Article 71 was invoked for the first time in August 2001 when a Brazilian Pharmaceutical company, Far Manguinho, was authorized to produce Nelfinavir, a drug patented by Pfizer but licensed to Roche for the Brazilian market. Following the Brazilian action, Merck and Roche agreed to reduce the prices of five drugs by 40% to 65%. The Brazilian Government stated: "Local manufacturing of many of the drugs used in

---

[45] Oxfam, G.B. (May 2001) *Drug Companies vs. Brazil: The Threat to Public Health* (http://www.oxfam.org.ok/cig-bin/parser.pl/0005/www.oxfam.org.uk/what_we_do/issues/health/drugcomp_brazil.htm) in http://en.wikipedia.org/wiki/HIV/AIDS_in_Brazil.

[46] WTO agreed in 2001 to TRIPS (Trade Related Aspects of Intellectual Property Rights). Establishes minimum patented protection for drugs which is 20 years from time of filing and marketing exclusivity; 140 nations signed who represent 90% of world trade, and provides a forum for dispute resolution. NAFTA is stronger than TRIPS in that it also provides pipeline protection.

the anti-AIDS cocktail is not a declaration of war against the drugs industry. It is simply a fight for life."[47]

Unfortunately, not all Latin American nations have fared as well in their attempts to provide affordable medicines for their AIDS patients. In 2005, the US, under the Bush Administration along with Costa Rica, El Salvador, Nicaragua, Honduras and the Dominican Republic ratified the controversial Dominican Republic-Central America Free Trade Agreement, or CAFTA-DR.[48] Proponents of CAFTA-DR espoused the benefits of the deal for American corporations to profit from new, developing markets while in return modernizing the living standards of the US's closest southern neighbors. One of the key components to the agreement was the implementation of the "data exclusivity" provision which allows brand name drug manufacturers the ability to conceal test data required for administration of the AVRs, for five years. Domestic generic manufacturers would have to conduct their own prohibitively expensive clinical trials, a practice indicated as unethical by Doctors Without Borders because human subjects would be put through experimental trials for which data were already available.[49] Thus, the perceived "modernizing" benefits of CAFTA-DR to less advantaged partners become arguable in light of the sacrifices made by AIDS sufferers within those nations who cannot afford the higher-priced, life saving non-generics.[50]

Sustainability in the Pharmaceutical Industry: Health for the Industry or the World

According to the 1997 Brundland Commission, "Sustainable development meets the needs of the present without compromising the ability of future generations to meet their own needs."[51]

---

[47] Wadia, R. (16 August 2001). Brazil's AIDS policy earns global lauds (http://archives.cnn.com/2001/WORLD/americas/08/14/brazil.AIDS/), *CNN*, in http://en.wikipedia.org/wiki/HIV/AIDS_in_Brazil.

[48] http://www.ustr.gov/assets/Trade_Agreements/Bilateral/CAFTA/Briefing_Book/asset_upload_file74_7284.pdf.

[49] http://www.doctorswithoutborders.org/publications/article.cfm?id=1361.

[50] Hearn, K. (2005). *Yale Global Online*, Independent Media Institute: http://yaleglobal.yale.edu/article.print?id=5764.

[51] http://www.worldinbalance.net/agreements/1987-brundtland.php.

Today, more than 150 million children are malnourished, more than 750 million people lack health services, more than 1250 million lack access to safe drinking water, and more than 850 million adults cannot read or write. Each year, infectious disease (ID) kills 14 million people of which most are in developing countries and most are in children under five.[52] The majority of diseases are preventable or treatable. Twelve different IDs account for 20% of the entire global disease and disability burden. IDs overall are responsible for 63% of deaths of children aged under five years. Poor countries carry 99% of the global burden of these 12 diseases.[53] Ninety percent of infectious diseases are in the developing countries but only 10% of global research and development spending is dedicated here.[54] The pharmaceutical industry invests billions annually into product development, research, and marketing, yet these statistics are staggering and troubling. Why such a stark contrast between abysmal health for some and the search for nirvana for others. Is this the world we want to leave for our children and descendents?

The goal of a business enterprise is " …to buy our products and use our services. We are here to serve you" and a sustainable business understands that it is there to serve "…your children, your children's children, and their children. When they are here, we will be here to serve them the same way that we serve the needs of the present without compromising the ability of future generations to meet their own needs."[55]

The triple bottom line describes corporate worth in terms of economic, social, and environmental value creation. Sustainability infers that all three "balance sheets" are "in the black." Industry, organizations, and governments must consider sustainability not only for fiscal corporate solvency, but in terms of human existence and the many factors influencing it. Social capital, natural capital, and financial capital are part of the new

---

[52] Oxfam, VSO, Save the Children. *Beyond Philanthropy: The Pharmaceutical Industry, Corporate Social Responsibility and the Developing World*, 2002, p. 8.

[53] *Ibid.* p. 25. Hepatitis B, HIV/AIDS, malaria, measles, onchoceriasis, polio, respiratory infections, TB, trypanosomiasis, trachoma, lymphatic filiariasis, leprosy.

[54] *Ibid.* p. 20.

[55] Kao, R., Kao, K. and Kao, R. (2003). *Entrepneurism: A Philosophy and Sensible Alternative for the Market Economy*, Imperial College Press.

dynamic equilibrium. Natural capital refers to resources, living systems, and ecosystem: financial capital; cash, investments and monetary instruments. And social capital is "the stock of active connections among people: the trust, mutual understanding and shared values and behaviors that bind the members of human networks and communities, and make cooperative action possible."[56] Given the open networks for communication in this globalized world today, organizations have never been better positioned to embrace the precepts for social capital.

In 1998, Oxfam published a review of the Pharmaceutical Industry (Pharma) in terms of sustainability as an industry and in their contributions for a sustainable world.[57] Health crises have many complex causes, including poverty, poor nutrition, persistent underinvestment in health systems, and political instability resulting in war and destruction. High prices of medicines are another cause. Pharma and other companies do not believe they are responsible for the world's poor, particularly their health care. This is the responsibility of the respective governments. Lacking the sustainability focus, they choose not to see the opportunity available to tap into this human capital resource as an investment for future earnings and loyalty.

The Oxfam report suggested that Pharma address five key areas in their core practices that would impact positively today and importantly tomorrow. First, appropriate pricing to make their products accessible to all populations, second, re-evaluation and easing of arguably excessive patent rules for intellectual property protections outlined in the TRIPS agreement, third, appropriate and ethical use of medicines, and fourth, targeting research and development expenditures towards world prevalent infectious diseases. According to Doctors without Borders, presently, 10% of global R&D expenditure is directed at diseases which account for 90% of the world's disease burden. In 2001, global R&D was estimated at US$70 billion. Arguably, the majority of research spending does not result in novel, innovative, "life saving" drugs, but in minor improvements to

---

[56] Cohen, D. and Prusak, L. (2000). In *Good Company: How Social Capital Makes Organizations Work*, Harvard Business School Press (ISBN: 978-0875-849133), 224 pp. McGraw Hill Press, p. 4.
[57] *op cit*. Oxfam. Reference 58.

existing drugs, "me to" drugs and "lifestyle" drugs. A redirection of research and development spending and practices would be a significant paradigm shift for the industry.

Lastly, the Oxfam report described the potential in Joint Public Private Initiatives (JPPIs), such as that outlined in the Brazilian AIDS initiatives. Such is a prototype for all organizations to follow in this increasingly networked world.

Companies, public health, philanthropic organizations, and financial bodies need to work together to target a specific disease or cause in developing countries or their local populations. JPPIs are networked organizations with common goals. They involve ongoing commitments to resolving targeted health problems as part of a company's long term business plans and do not exclude vulnerable segments of society. They state objectives for integration and strengthen national health systems reporting on their impact. Bringing together the WHO, World Bank, Pharma representatives, NGOs, governments, private foundations (such as Oxfam and the Bill and Melinda Gates' Foundation) and research institutes is a beginning to create a JPPI able to assist our vulnerable developing world brothers and sisters.

In the words of Chad Halliday regarding a vision of sustainable growth through science and technology: "I believe that if we use our creativity and scientific knowledge effectively, we can provide a strong return for our shareholders and grow our businesses — all while meeting the human needs of societies around the world and reducing the environmental footprint of our operations and products."[58]

We all have a role to play in addressing some of the deep inequities between rich and poor countries — inequalities which create and perpetuate poverty, disease, and deterioration of the world we have today for our descendants tomorrow. All organizations, industries and governments must consider how their processes and decisions will impact on humanitarian, environmental and global levels, not only today, but importantly, tomorrow. These are not new concepts and are recurring themes throughout

---

[58] Holliday, C., Shmidheiny, S. and Watts, P. (2002). *Walking the Talk: The Business Case for Sustainability*, Greenleaf Publishing Group.

civilization, most recently following the second world war, when "what emerged ... was a consensus that the world community had to come together and provide a framework for three big things if it was going to survive and prosper: peace and security, economic development, and human rights."[59] Perhaps these principles can finally be achieved and integrated into our actions for a world, if not better, then at least not worse, for our children.

---

[59] *op cit.* In Friedman, T.L. (2008). John Derbach teaches at Widener Law Harrisburg Penn and edited the book *Agenda for a Sustainable America*, p. 48.

6
MINIMIZATION OF RESOURCE DRAINS AND ENVIRONMENTAL DAMAGE

Peter Hing

Resource Drains and Environmental Damage cover a very wide area, and are complex and intricately interconnected issues. Resources cover energy and materials use in land, sea and air transportation, buildings, manufacturing and mining industries, commercial establishments, agriculture, food processing, defense, communications as well as lighting for the homes and public places. Resource drains also intrude in the area of migration of trained medical, healthcare, scientific, technical and economic personnel from poorer and developing countries to more developed economies, flight of capital from poor to rich countries. Resource drains can also include the mismanagement of organizations, industries, banks, stock markets and with countries resorting to wars, genocide to resolve border and international conflicts. The perpetuation of policies such as trade embargo, classification of countries as axis of evil powers, the breeding and harboring of terrorism, the greed for absolute military power at any cost, can also be classified under resource drains. Even the use of bottled water if carefully analyzed can also be considered huge resource drains. In the same note, the mismanagement of the economy, the water, mineral and human resources in many countries, the corruption in government, utility companies, stock markets, many banks and insurance companies can be classified as resource drains on a gigantic scale as witnessed in recent months.

In this chapter, the discussion is confined within two areas. One is on the development of sustainable lighting which can lead to enormous energy saving worldwide, and thus minimize emission of greenhouse gases, in particular, carbon dioxide in the atmosphere. The other is on the sustainable development of dispersed micro power generation which can incorporate the use of low carbon technologies, cost effective renewable energies. The move from giant utility companies providing power to the homes, commercial establishments and industries to on-site cost effective micro power generation has the potential of eliminating electrical power losses during distribution over long distances. Moreover, dispersed micropower generation technologies have been established and are currently being evaluated for long term durability. This will also be presented and discussed in this chapter. The adoption of dispersed micro power generation will slow the construction of coal fire stations, nuclear stations, ungainly, lossy and hazardous powerline distributions all over the countries. It will also lead to dramatic reduction in carbon dioxide, contribute to the stabilization of global warming, and a reduction in environmental damage worldwide.

PART I. DEVELOPMENT OF SUSTAINABLE LIGHTING FROM GASEOUS DISCHARGE

Introduction

In the first part of the chapter, I will discuss briefly lighting throughout the ages and then elaborate on the development of light sources from incandescent sources and gaseous discharge. I will then introduce the role of a wide range of functional materials needed for the construction of various types of lamps.

Scientists and lamp engineers are working very hard to improve the efficiency and the quality of the lighting, and are making valuable contributions to quality of life as well as contributing to the reduction in carbon dioxide emissions by improving the efficacy of all types of lamps and lighting design, as well as enhancing the quality of the light for general lighting applications.

Lighting companies have been in the forefront of developing low carbon emission devices, designing lighting systems that can make use of wasted heat instead of letting the excess heat generated being wasted. Whilst environmentalists are quick to point the finger at lighting companies for not doing enough, one needs to bear in mind the great technological challenges and ingenuity of scientists and engineers before Edison, and the perseverance of Edison in the US and Swan in the UK in the invention of the incandescent lamps, first with carbon filaments, then with tungsten filaments.

Whilst these incandescent lamps may not be efficient, emitting only 15 lumens per watt, and resulting in a lot of heat being generated, lighting engineers and architects have been working cooperatively to use the heat generated for heating and at the same time providing an extremely warm and pleasing light source in the home. The incandescent lamp has the highest color rendering index (CRI) of all the artificial lamps ever invented. If one day we could convert efficiently and cost effectively most of the infra-red radiation generated in the incandescent lamps and from other sources like the sun, it would be a great service to mankind. Research in this direction, however, is hampered partly by lack of funding. This is not helped also by the fact that to date very low energy conversion efficiency from infra-red to visible has been achieved using existing materials.

Clearly, lack of suitable phosphor materials to convert infra-red energy to visible is preventing its development. Such type of research should be encouraged and supported particularly as nanotechnology can today be fully deployed to assist the design and development of specialty materials with possibility of effecting the conversion of infra-red into visible more efficiently.

The development of light sources leading to the current energy saving compact fluorescent lamps (CFL) lamps is described on page 144. The CFL lamps are today the most extensively used general purpose lamps particularly in the developed and developing economies. These lamps give an average of 60 to 80 lumens per watt compared to around

15 lumens per watt for the incandescent lamps invented by Edison and Swan over a century ago.

In lamps and lighting, materials play an integral part in the development of advanced light sources. The contributions of materials to the development of sustainable lighting will be discussed. The introduction and widespread use of advanced and energy efficient compact fluorescent and other high efficiency discharge light sources worldwide have not only enhanced the quality of life in the homes, offices, public places, but also contributed to energy conservation and huge reduction in carbon emission.

Today, close to 20% of the electrical power generated in the developed economies is used for lighting public buildings, roads, factories and the homes. The power usage for lighting in less developed economies is even higher as close to 40% of the electrical power generated is used up in lighting.

The lighting engineers and scientists as well as solid state physicists have long been dreaming of the day when solid state lighting (SSL) can become possible and cost effective. The current development in SSL using light emitting diodes indicates that such types of lighting is very suited for displays, decorations, indicators and advertisements. These have been hugely successful as the light generated is very directional. However, it is still very expensive to have low cost, warm white light from SSL for lighting the homes, buildings and public places. Significant development and advances in the field of SSL have been made. This is discussed in more detail in part II of this chapter.

The development of SSL has often been referred to as the holy grail of lighting. Some recent advances in SSL are discussed in part II of this chapter. Solid state lamps could attain efficacy of 150 lumens or more per watt and (CRI) of 80 and over. This could revolutionize the way we lit our homes, buildings and public places in the not too distant future. Most lighting industries have now shifted a major part of their R&D activities to SSL in the race to develop cost effective, long life and high efficiency light emitting diodes from inorganic and organic semiconductors. Innovative exterior and interior applications of SSL will be highlighted, and its implications on energy conservation, reduction in carbon emission, and promotion of a sustainable economy are presented and discussed.

Lighting from the dawn of civilization to the 21st century

Evidence of primitive lights using torches and hollow stones with moss or grass, animal fats was found as far back as 70,000 BC. These artifacts were found in cave paintings in Altamira in Spain and Dordogne in France. Early Greek pottery lamps were unearthed dating back some 7000 BC. These lamps were made of rendered animal fat or oil as fuel. Throughout the 18th century whale oil lamps and candles were extensively used to provide lighting. In 1783, Argand, a Swiss chemist invented the hollow circular wick and glass chimney lamp. In 1784, the first use of coal gas as lighting fuel was introduced. In 1853, the first kerosene lamp was introduced in Germany. Edison improved the design of Thomas Woodward in 1870 to produce the first successful incandescent electric light bulb. Swan in the UK independently invented the filament lamp. Electric lighting was steadily replacing gas lighting. In the 20th century, electric lighting reigns almost supreme, although candles are still used today for blackouts.

The main purpose of lighting throughout the ages is to provide artificial lighting whenever natural darkness occurs. Later it was also used to create visual effects. In recent years the following important developments of lighting have been identified, namely, the science of lighting and seeing has been developed. This creates a need for the lighting engineers to work closely with architects to maximize the flow of light and participate in the active creation of beauty with the interplay of light, form and color. Later lighting and heating were utilized to provide a conducive environment to live and work in a sustainable manner.

Need for energy conservation and sustainability

In this section, the need for efficient lighting for energy conservation is presented and discussed. It is now estimated that close to 20% of the electrical power generated in developed countries is used for lighting; almost twice as much in less developed countries. Thus the large amount of electrical energy derived primarily from burning of fossil fuels emits a large amount of carbon dioxide into the atmosphere. The conversion of electrical power to light sources is still very inefficient. Theoretically every watt of electrical power should give 683 lumens at 550 nm under normal atmospheric conditions and room temperature. The most efficient light sources being the low pressure sodium lamp with efficacy over 200 lumens per watt but with extremely poor CRI. The most advanced high intensity discharge lamps like high pressure sodium lamps give around 140 lumens per watt for CRI less than 50; for higher CRI, the efficacy drops to around 100 lumens per watt. The metal halide lamps with white light source give also 100 lumens per watt with high CRI around 80 or so. The compact fluorescent lamps give at most 80 lumens per watt with CRI around 60 to 80. Theoretically, one can expect some 683 lumens per watt at 550 nm per watt for energy conversion in the visible spectrum. Unfortunately, the current efficacy of the discharge light sources is of the order of 80 to 140 lumens at best, partly because of large amount of energy being lost as heat and partly because our understanding of the plasma processes occurring leading to the emission of radiation are still not very well understood thus limiting the lumen output that could be realized. Generally as the CRI is improved, the efficacy drops.

For incandescent lamps invented by Edison and Swan over 100 years ago, the efficacy is of the order of 15 to 20 lumens per watt, but the CRI is the highest, and hence has the highest CRI. Incandescent lamps are very inefficient. Some 90% of the power used is turned into heat. In Europe, the manufacturing of the incandescent lamps is being phased out and being replaced by more compact and efficient fluorescent lamps. Intense research and development is also currently being conducted to commercialize SSL. The SSL originates from semiconductor junctions. This is discussed in part II of this chapter.

In part I, research and development that had led to the large scale manufacturing and use of these high intensity discharge light sources, including compact fluorescent lamps will be presented and discussed. The materials development for various types of discharge light sources will be highlighted. The high intensity discharge light sources such as in high pressure sodium and metal halide lamps operate at relatively high temperatures and pressures compared with fluorescent lamps. The materials requirements for these high intensity light sources are extremely stringent and demanding. The sustainable development of these materials will be discussed.

The first discharge lamp was shown at the Royal Society of London way back in 1860. The lamp induced a brilliant white light by the discharge of high voltage through carbon dioxide at low pressure. Around 1870s, Europe was well ahead in electrical arc light. Thomas Edison in the States went on to demonstrate his electric incandescent lamp made with carbon filament in 1879.

A wide range of materials are used in the lighting industries, including glasses and glass ceramics, ceramics, metallic materials, polymers, composites as well as various types of gases. In a previous article[1] materials development for discharge light sources was reviewed. In this chapter, sustainable materials development for both conventional and solid state lamps are presented and discussed.

For more efficient, cost effective and sustainable light sources in the future, considerable investment in SSL is now underway worldwide to meet the energy challenge, reduce carbon emission and mitigate the effect of global warming. The author will discuss the research and advances being made in the field of SSL. The role of science, engineering and technology (SET) in the development of sustainable lighting will be presented and discussed.

Moreover, the deployment of SET is emphasized in any sustainable economic development to meet the challenge of a rapidly rising world population expected to reach ten billion by 2050. The issue of climate change, carbon emission and carbon footprints, energy, water and food security, survival of human species, the preservation of all the wonderful biodiversity of planet earth, the eradication of poverty, illiteracy, and curable diseases in many parts of the world, terrorism, genocide, lack of understanding and tolerance of various cultures are some of the very grave issues facing mankind today.

How Radiation is Generated

An air gap kept at ambient between two spherical conductors gives a spark if the voltage between the two conductors is sufficiently high to induce the breakdown of the air. When some UV light is in the vicinity of

---

[1] Hing, P. (2008). Materials for discharge light sources, *Scientia Bruneiana*, 7/8: 81–101.

the two conductors, the voltages needed to generate the sparks are considerably reduced. When the air pressure inside a glass tube is reduced, lower voltage is needed to cause gaseous discharge. Residual air causes the gaseous discharge to be pinkish. The color of the discharge will be different for different gases.

Figure 1 summarizes the phenomena of gas discharge in air at various pressures. Some familiarity with the unit of pressure used in lamps fill is needed, namely, one bar is equivalent to 760 mm Hg or 10^5 Pa (Pascal). Thus 0.01 mm Hg, the pressure in Pascal is 1.316 Pa approximately. The gas pressure inside the lamp envelope is often quoted in Pascal. Low pressure discharge light source, pressure is of the order of 400 Pa to 2000 Pa. For high pressure sodium (HPS) lamp, the pressure ranges from 7000 to 10,000 Pa. In metal halide lamps, the pressure of the species is between 2500 Pa to 9000 Pa. During the operation of lamps, the pressure can attain several atmospheres in HPS lamps and up to tens of atmospheres in the case of metal halide (MH) lamps. The marked increase in pressure is caused by the high vapor pressure generated by the very volatile halide

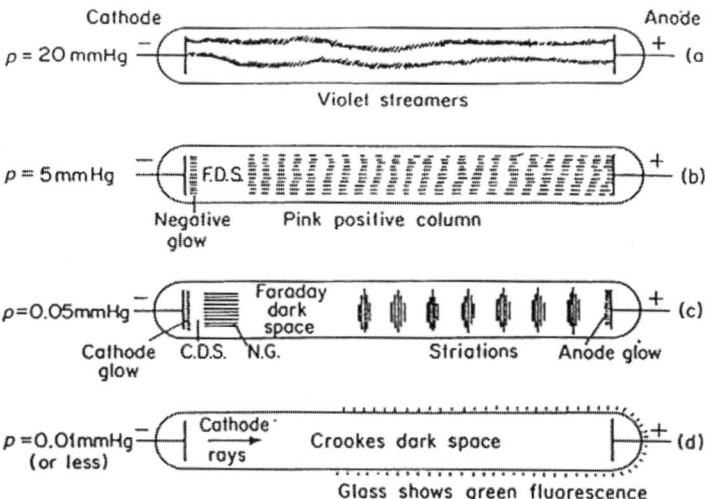

Fig. 1 Gaseous discharge as the pressure is reduced. FDS — Faraday Dark Space; CDS — Crookes Dark Space.

Source: Textbook on Physics by Duncan, J. and Starling, S.G., and Electricity and Magnetism by Starling, S.G.

species at elevated operating lamp temperatures. In these high intensity discharge light sources, the wall temperatures of the ceramic lamp envelope can reach 1300K and the center of arc is about 6000K! Thus the lamp materials have to withstand extremely hostile environments, making it extremely demanding on the materials.

The I-V characteristics of the gaseous discharge is shown in Fig. 2a. To maintain a self-sustaining discharge without a runaway current situation as indicated in the lower half of Fig. 2a, a resistance is needed in the circuit.

The mechanisms involved in the gaseous discharge, and the increasing current are briefly discussed with the aid of Figs. 2b and 2c. When the electric field is sufficiently large, breakdown of the gases occur and become conducting. The breakdown occurs as there is some ionization taking place by cosmic rays or natural radioactivity. The electrons are accelerated by the electric field, and acquires enough energy to ionize the atoms. At the same time there are recombination processes going where the electrons and ions recombine to form the neutral atom. When the rate of ionization exceeds the rate of recombination, the production of charged carriers increase more rapidly than the current. A consequence of this is

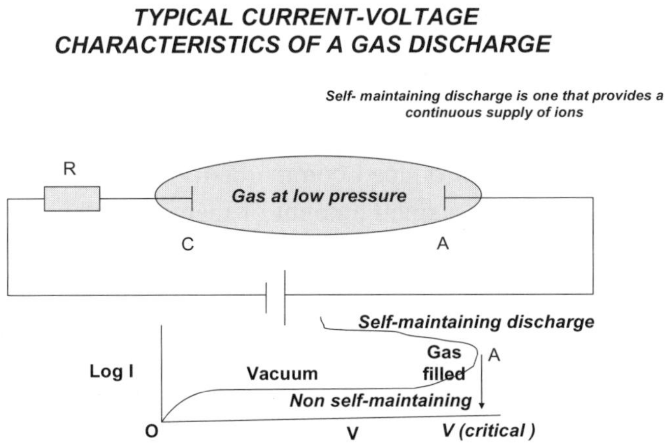

TYPICAL CURRENT-VOLTAGE CHARACTERISTICS OF A GAS DISCHARGE

Self- maintaining discharge is one that provides a continuous supply of ions

(a)

Fig. 2a Relationship between the current and the applied voltage.

Source: *Electricity and Magnetism* by Sears, F.W. (MIT Press).

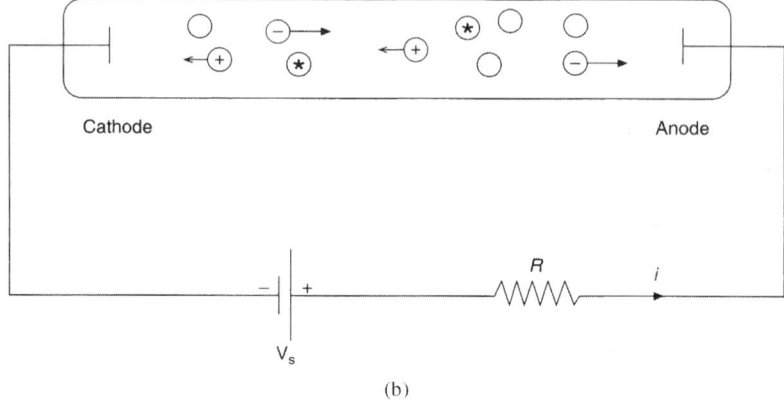

Fig. 2b Sows in ionization of the atom (empty circle) to produce a plasma. The applied electric field causes the electrons to move towards the anode, and the positive ions towards the cathode. The discharge current is due to the drift of the positive and negative particles caused by the electric field. The resistor R limits the magnitude of the current for the DC discharge.[2]

the electric field or voltage drop decreases as the current increases as shown in Fig. 2c.

The Development of Compact Fluorescent Lamps

Although discharge light sources were known as early as 1860, practical fluorescent lamps were introduced commercially only in the 1940s. All fluorescent lamps contain a small amount of mercury and some inert gas such as argon. The color of the light emitted depends on the type of gases used. For fluorescent lamp containing mercury and argon, UV radiation of 253.7 nm is generated. This is due to the de-excitation of the mercury atoms as depicted in Figs. 3 and 4, as much as 50% of the electrical power is converted into UV radiation. The efficacy is only about 6 lumens per watt without any phosphor. This is very low compared with the

---

[2] Wharmby, D.O. (1997). Radiation and light production, in Coaton, J.R. and Marsden, A.M. (eds.), Lamps and Lighting (4th Edn.), Arnold Publisher.

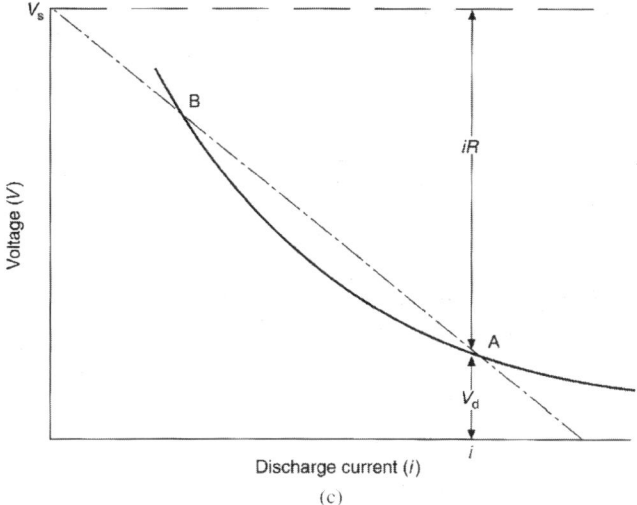

Fig. 2c Depicts the *I-V* characteristics of a discharge with the increasing current. Point A is where the discharge voltage is stable. This is where the supply voltage V_s is related to the discharge voltage V_d and the resistance losses iR by $V_s = V_{ds} + iR$ for the circuit shown in Fig. 2b.[2]

theoretical 683 lumens per watt for generation of monochromatic yellow-green light of 555 nm. One can expect some theoretical 250 lumens per watt for a broad spectrum of light simulating sunlight.

With a coating of narrow band phosphors inside the glass envelope, efficacy of the order of 90 lumens per watt and color rendering index (CRI) over 80 have been achieved.[1] The compact fluorescent lamps (CFLs) can now replace directly the incandescent lamps without changing the sockets. These CFLs have become very popular due to its lower power consumption leading to considerable saving in energy. These energy saving lamps are contributing to a dramatic reduction in carbon emission as less power is needed for lighting.

The development of useful, cost effective, and energy light sources requires interdisciplinary skills and expertise. Physicists, chemists, materials scientists, mechanical and electrical engineers are needed to develop useful light sources to meet societal needs.

The tasks of the lamp scientists and engineers are to devise means of converting the UV into the visible efficiently, develop low cost and

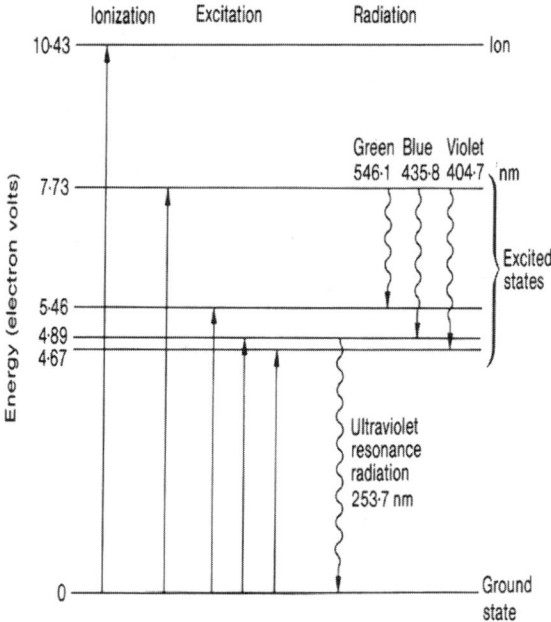

Fig. 3 Simplified energy level showing the excitation and de-excitation of mercury atoms giving ultraviolet resonance radiation of 253.7 nm (2537 A).[3]

reliable electronic starter, eliminate flicker, improve the lamp efficacy and lamp life. The author observes that most of the failures of the CFL are due to failures of the electronic starter built in with the CFL lamps.

The Development of Phosphors

A material that exhibits the phenomenon of phosphorescence is known as a phosphor. The material sustains continued glowing in the dark after exposure to light or to energized particles such as the electrons. The origin of the term phosphors stems from the glow of the phosphorus in the dark. The glow in phosphorus is, however, due to the oxidation of phosphorus rather than excitation with light.

---

[3] Ranby, P.W. (1983). Phosphors, in Cayless, M.A. and Marsden, A.M. (eds.), *Lamps and Lighting* (3rd Edn.), Edward Arnold.

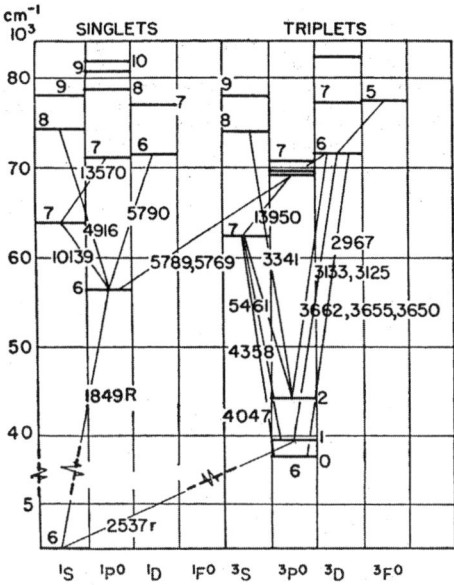

Fig. 4 A more detailed energy level diagram for mercury showing the origin of the 253 nm (2537 A) and 197 nm (1970 A) radiations.

Source: *American Institute of Physics Hand book*, 3rd Edn. (1972).

Inorganic and organic materials exhibit glow or emission of light. The term luminescence is now more appropriately used. Prefixes are used to differentiate types of phosphors. The glow arising from chemical reaction is termed chemi-luminescence, whilst that from heating a material is known as thermo-luminescence. Luminescence arising from electric field is known as electro-luminescence. The luminescence arising from interaction with light is known as photo-luminescence. However, the term phosphors has been kept for historical reasons.

In the lighting industries, the term phosphors are used for materials that exhibit luminescence when exposed to UV radiation. The term phosphors are kept for all materials that exhibit luminescence when subjected to not only UV radiation, but also radiation of shorter wavelength like X-rays, gamma rays, or to a stream of electrons. Some mechanisms of luminescence are shown in Fig. 5.

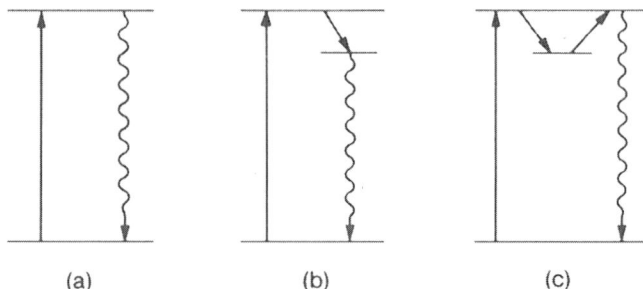

Fig. 5 Various mechanisms of luminescence.

Phosphors in cathode ray tubes (CRT)

To date, a wide range of materials have been used as phosphors in the cathode ray tubes. These include the zinc sulphide doped with various activators particularly from the rare earth elements. Some examples are ZnS doped with Ag, Cu, Al; Zn_2SiO_4 containing Mn and As activators; Y_2SiO_5 with Ce, Tb; ZnO with Ag; Gd_2O_3 with S and Tb; YAG with Ce, Tb; Indium Borates (InBo) with Th, Eu. These phosphors, with some modifications, have also been used for X-ray screens, neutron detectors, alpha particle scintillators, and photomultipliers for electrons.

In Fig. 5a, de-excitation to the ground state occurs, whilst in Fig. 5b de-excitation with relaxation in a meta stable state takes place; in Fig. 5c, de-excitation with trapping occurs.[2]

Phosphors for general lighting applications

Phosphors capable of converting UV into visible are known as Stoke phosphors. Figure 6a shows how these phosphors produce emission of radiation of higher wavelength. The phosphors for conversion of infra-red radiation (higher wavelength) into the visible (lower wavelength) are known as anti-Stoke phosphors. This is a much more difficult process, requiring very special phosphor materials. Currently the efficiency of anti-Stoke phosphors is well below 1%. Research in this area is needed to improve the efficiency of converting infra-red to visible. Breakthrough in this field has many applications, including the conversion of a large amount of infra-red from solar radiation into electrical power.

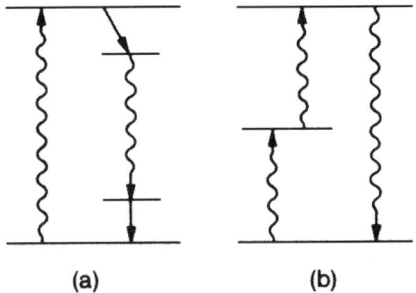

Fig. 6 (a) Stoke and (b) anti-Stoke phosphors.[3]

Phosphors used in dichromatic fluorescent lamps include barium and europium doped magnesium aluminate ($MgAl_{16}O_{27}$) as blue phosphors; (Ce, Tb) $MgAl_{11}O_{19}$ as green; Y_2O_3.Eu as red phosphors. These rare earth based phosphor materials are generally more expensive than phosphors based on the silicates, phosphates, tungstate, arsenates, vanadates, etc.

Conversion UV to Visible Using Phosphors

Ultraviolet radiation has short wavelengths, of the order of about 100 to 350 nm. The radiations are therefore more energetic than visible light with wavelength of the order of 450 to 600 nm. This is because the energy of a photon of light is given by $E = h\nu$ or hc/λ, where h is the Planck's constant, ν the frequency, c the velocity of light, and λ, the wavelength of the radiation. The energetic UV radiation is able to excite the activators (dopants) in the phosphor matrix to higher energy states. We can write the total efficiency η of the phosphor[3] as $\eta = \eta_{qe} \dfrac{\lambda_{ex}}{\lambda_{em}}$ where η_{qe} is the quantum efficiency, λ_{ex} is the wavelength of the radiation used to excite the phosphors, and λ_{em} the wavelength of the emitted radiation. Even if η_{qe} attains 100% (every quantum of radiation absorbed by the phosphors gives a quantum of visible radiation), the overall efficiency would still be less than 100% as λ_{ex} is less than λ_{em}.

To understand the mechanisms of the energy conversion, an understanding of the atomic energy levels associated with the activators in the host material is needed. We can associate the width of the spectral emission to the different crystal fields experienced by the activator ions in the host material. The environment of the activators and its oxidation states dictate the efficiency of the energy conversion. Phosphors are characterized by their emission color and the length of time the emission lasts.

The combination of red, blue and green emission produces white light. These tri-phosphors are exploited in fluorescent lamps which are basically white light with different correlated color temperature (CCT) ranging from 2500 K to 5000 K. Halo-phosphate phosphors are added as the first layer coating to improve the color of the white light generated by the triphosphors, and also reduce cost. Some early designs of energy saving compact fluorescent lamp developed at Thorn Lighting as early as the 1980s are shown in Fig. 7.

A typical tubular fluorescent lamp is shown on the top part of Fig. 8 (reproduced from the March 2008 issue of *Scientific American*).[4] Linear and circular types of fluorescent lamps found applications indoors in offices, condominiums, public and commercial buildings, kitchen areas

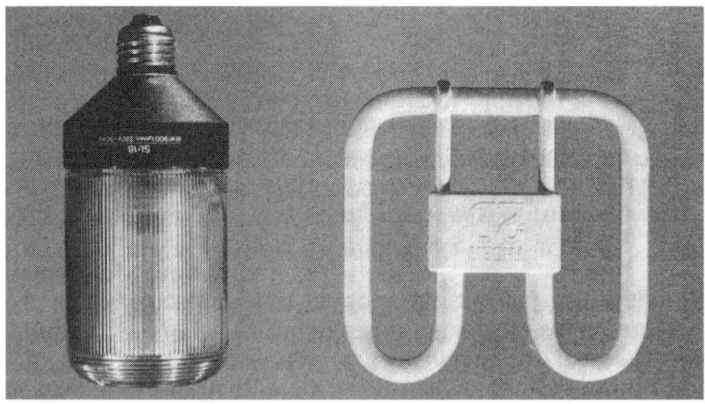

Fig. 7 Early designs of energy saving compact fluorescent lamps. These lamps are for direct replacement of the incandescent lamps.[3]

---

[4] Fischetti, M. (2008). The Switch On (an article on energy saving compact fluorescent lamps), reported in the March 2008 issue of *Scientific American*.

Development of Sustainable Lighting from Gaseous Discharge   151

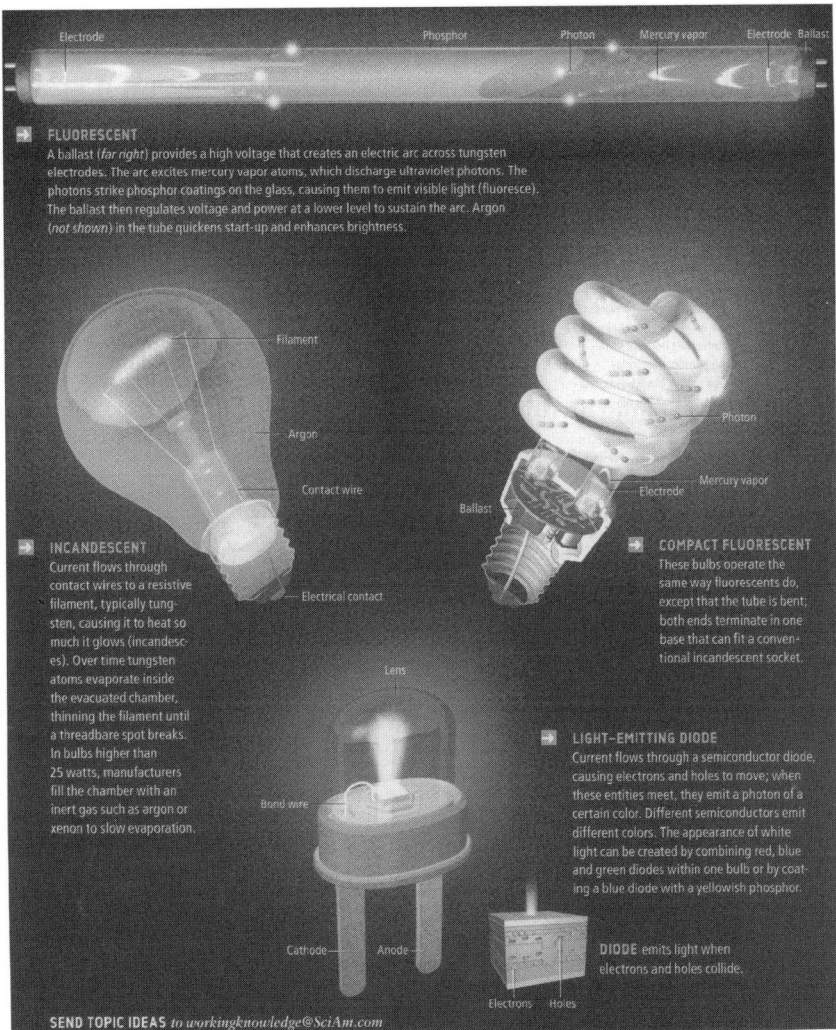

Fig. 8 Various types of lamps reported in an article in the March 2008 issue of *Scientific American* by Fischetti, M.[4]

and corridors. The various grades of white light ranging from warm to very cool white; the difference in the white color depends on the amount of red component of light generated from the conversion, and hence from the type and amount of phosphors used.

Compact Fluorescent Lamps (CFLs)

The latest development of tri-phosphors enable compact fluorescent lamps to give 80 lumens per watt. Although five to six times better than incandescent lamps, it is still low compared with the 250 lumens that can be obtained theoretically. The CFLs provide considerable energy saving. The incandescent lamps will no longer be manufactured in Europe by 2010; in the US, GE has stopped all research and development on incandescent lamps.

Energy conservation and energy efficiency are strategies to minimize the use of fossil fuels and to stabilize global warming with less carbon dioxide emission. However, the initial cost of replacing all the incandescent lamps with compact energy saving fluorescent lamps is high. The longer life of these lamps reduces the frequency of replacing these lamps, therefore contributing to marked energy and cost saving.

Today there are numerous designs of compact fluorescent lamps ranging from a few watts to 60 watt. Some typical shapes are shown in Fig. 9. The use of these compact energy saving lamps not only saves energy but in the long run also reduces the cost of lighting drastically. A 26 watt CFL is equivalent to a 100 watt incandescent lamp (Fig. 10).

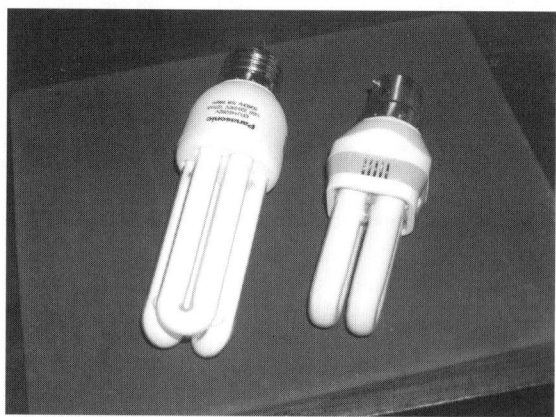

Fig. 9 Some designs of energy saving CFLs available on the market.

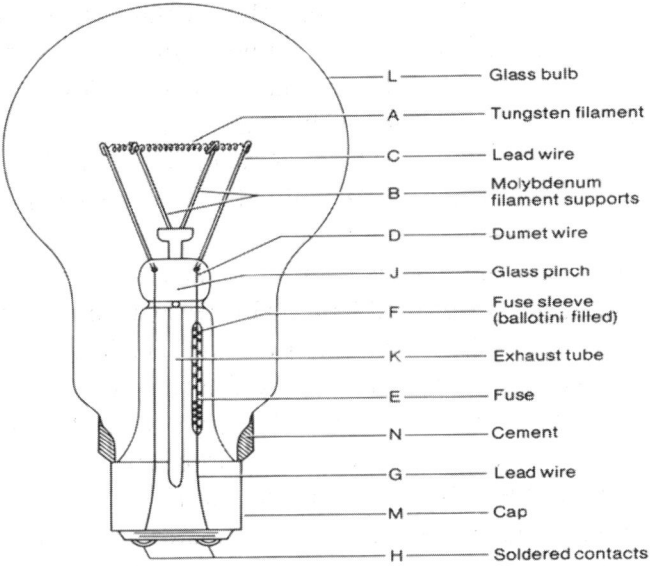

Fig. 10 The incandescent lamps invented by Edison and Swan.

Luminescence is an active area of research covering bio-, chemo-, thermo, electro-, and photo-luminescence. It is useful to discuss photo-luminescence using phosphors that lead to the development of efficient light sources. Electro-luminescence in the sense that electrical voltage is used to generate and maintain the discharge. Photo-luminescence where phosphor materials as coatings are used to convert UV (shorter wavelengths) radiation into visible (longer wavelengths).

Energy Conservation and Sustainable Development in Lighting

Developed and developing economies consume huge amounts of energy from fossil fuels. This is creating a concern on energy security as most of the fossil fuels are located in politically unstable countries. Gigatons of carbon dioxide and other greenhouse gases are emitted from the burning of fossil fuels, and its effect on global warming, biodiversity, and climate change are major problems of the 21st century. Development of sustainable lighting can conserve enormous amounts of energy, and mitigate global warming. Replacement of all incandescent lamps by energy saving compact fluorescent lamps worldwide represent an estimated 20 million tons of oil being used annually. The impact on the reduction of the carbon dioxide emitted to the atmosphere is very significant.

All fluorescent lamps contain a small amount of mercury. This requires careful disposal of used lamps. Greater awareness and publicity need to be given to this issue. Mercury is a toxic chemical. It is also being debated whether its continued use in the future is sustainable. Intense research to develop low cost reliable white light solid state lamps from semiconductors such as gallium nitride and from organic polymers light emitting diodes (OLED) is being conducted worldwide. Novel materials are being investigated to produce white light source without the use of the expensive phosphors. There is a race for the development of low cost solid state lighting, and the challenge is being taken very seriously by all major lamp manufacturers.

Advanced Ceramics and Composites for High Intensity Discharge Lamps

Lots of research and development were conducted to improve the sinterability, the in-line transmission, chemical resistance, thermal shock resistance, and thermo-mechanical properties. The relationship between processing, properties,[5–7] and performance in actual high intensity discharge

---

[5] Hing, P. (1990). Vacuum sintering of alumina to translucency, in Sale, P. (ed.), *Transaction of the British Ceramic Society*, paper was presented at the Conference on Novel Materials Processing, Manchester University.

[6] Hing, P. *et al.* (2007). The processing, properties and performance of alumina ceramics, paper presented at the *Sixth MP3 Processing for Properties and Performance Conference*, Beijing, 14–16 September 2007.

[7] Hing, P., Evans, D.T. and Marshall, R. (1979). United States Patent 4155758 on Lamps and Discharge Devices and Materials.

lamps, namely high pressure sodium (HPS) and in the experimental ceramic metal halide (CMH) lamps[8-11] were conducted.

A range of ceramic materials investigated for the ceramic discharge lamps include single crystal sapphire, polycrystalline alumina, magnesium aluminate spinal, $MgAl_2O_4$, yttrium aluminate (YAG), doped yttria (Y_2O_3), Mullite ($3Al_2O_3.2SiO_2$) aluminum oxynitride, (AlON) and Silicon Aluminum Oxynitride (SIALON). Figure 11 depicts the crystal structure of alumina ceramics, and the sintered translucent alumina starting from alumina powders is shown in Fig. 12.

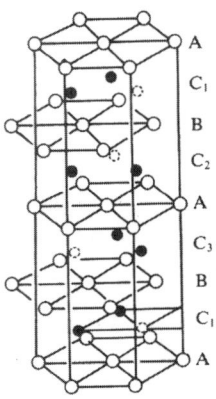

Fig. 11 Hexagonal crystal structure of alpha-alumina. Unfilled circle — O^{2-} ions, filled circles — Al^{3+} ions occupying two-thirds of the octahedral sites, broken unfilled circle — vacant octahedral site.[12]

---

[8] Evans, D.T. and Day, J. (1983). Lamp materials, in Cayless, M.A. and Marsden, A.M. (eds.), *Lamps and Lighting*, (3rd Edn.), Edward Arnold.

[9] Chiang, Y.-M., Birnie, D. and Kingery, W.D. (1997). *Physical Ceramics, Principles of Ceramic Science and Engineering*, by the MIT Series in Materials Science and Engineering, pp. 413–419.

[10] Brown, K.E., Chalmers, A.G. and Wharmby, D.O. (January 1982). Tin sodium halide lamps in ceramic envelopes, *Journal of IES*, pp. 106–114.

[11] Chalmers, A.G. and Brown, K., Thorn Lighting Ltd., 1982–1985. Private communication with author on deformation of alumina arc tube used in experimental ceramic metal halide lamps.

[12] Anderson, J.C., Leaver, R.D. and Alexander, J.M. (1991). *Materials Science*, (4th Edn.). Chapman and Hall.

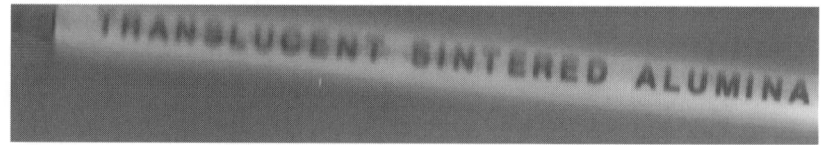

Fig. 12 Sintered translucent alumina arc tube for high intensity discharge lamps reported by the author.[13]

Sintered translucent polycrystalline alumina was found to be the most suitable arc tube material in terms of chemical resistance, refractoriness, thermal shock resistance, dimensional reproducibility, cost effectiveness, manufacturability, availability of starting materials, reliability and cost.

Note that the crystal structure of alpha alumina is shown in Fig. 11. Alpha alumina is also known as corundum and exists in various crystalline forms such as kappa, gamma alumina. Gamma has a cubic structure. The most stable form of alumina is the alpha alumina with a hexagonal crystal structure as shown in Fig. 11. The packing of the aluminum and oxygen atoms in the lattice represents a packing of about 0.84 or 84%.

Development of Alumina to Translucency

High purity alumina powders is obtained from alum (aluminum sulphate dodecahedra) precursors. This route is preferred as ultra high purity and reactive alpha alumina powders can be obtained. The starting materials should have surface areas of the order of preferably about 30 m^2/g, and submicron size powders. The purity should be at least 99.98% or higher.

For instance, it was found that alumina slurry containing soluble precursors of magnesia and yttria, as dopants have good spray drying characteristics due to the high solid content, typically above about 65% by weight of alumina in the alumina slurry. Moreover, low viscosity that can be formed and useful to pump the slurry into the atomizer.

The low viscosity and high solid content produces spray dried granules with excellent flowability and cold compaction behavior. In particular, the

---

[13] Hing, P. (2006). Materials for the development of high intensity discharge light sources, invited paper at *Fifth MP3 Materials Processing for Properties and Performance Conference*, Singapore, 11–15 December 2006.

incorporation of dopants in the form of soluble precursors had enabled both a small concentration of dopants, such as magnesia and yttria, typically in the region of 500 ppm to be uniformly dispersed in the alumina slurry.

These dopants, moreover, had enabled the sintering of the polycrystalline alumina to high density, minimal residual porosity and high translucency at temperatures as low as 1700°C. The best in-line transmission was achieved by the author when sintering was conducted at about 1900°C. A typical sintered translucent sintered alumina is shown in Fig. 12. The high in-line transmission is achieved at the expense of reducing the grain boundary areas and appreciable grain growth and abnormal grain growth (Fig. 13).

There is evidence of segregation of chemical species, and formation of second phases at the grain boundaries such as yttrium aluminate on the internal and external surfaces of the sintered polycrystalline alumina arc tubes. At very high temperatures, these second phases on the surface of the samples tend to disappear presumably due to volatilization.

Very high operating temperatures, around 1900°C, in a hydrogen atmosphere usually reduces the life of the molybdenum furnace, and increased the embrittlement of not only the refractory metal shields, but also the tubular molybdenum shields used as sample holder for supporting the alumina tube during the sintering process. Trials conducted

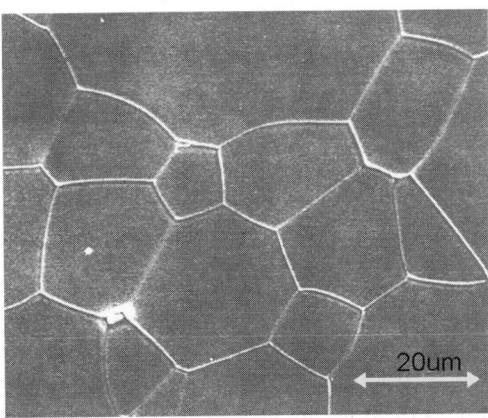

Fig. 13 Grain structure of sintered translucent alumina used as envelope for high pressure sodium and recently introduced ceramic metal halide lamps.

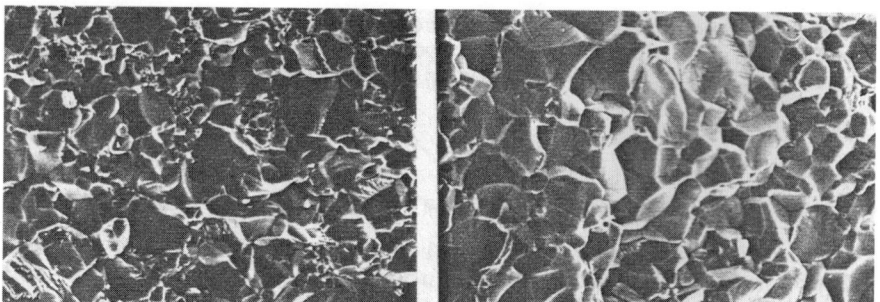

Fig. 14 Fracture surface of sintered translucent alumina sintered at 1850°C (LHS) and 1900°C (RHS). Magnification scale: 1 cm ≡ 20 μm.

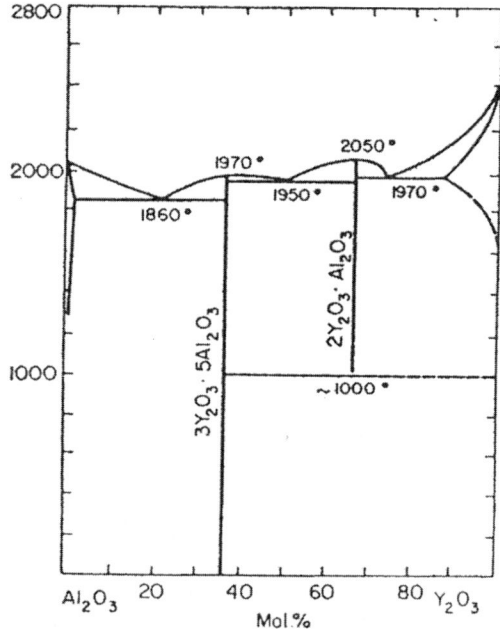

Fig. 15 The phase diagram of Al_2O_3–Y_2O_3 showing eutectic at 1860°C.

using experimental refractory cermets (ceramic-metal composites) as shields for the tubular components were also successfully conducted. These cermet tubes, moreover, proved to be lasting and did not suffer embrittlement compared with 100% molydenum metal shields (Figs. 14 and 15).

Wet and dry bag compaction were used for the fabrication of the arc tubes for ceramic lamp applications. In the wet bag processes, the polymer moulds or polymer colostomy were in contact with the pressure transmitting fluids during compaction. In the dry bag compaction, the polymer moulds did not make contact with the pressure transmitting fluids. This development coupled with the use of the free flowing spray dried ceramic granules have enabled the large volume manufacturing of the ceramic arc tubes to be carried out. Up to now, the most widely used material for the high intensity ceramic discharge light source is still alumina. The polycrystalline alumina has been sintered to very high translucency using pressureless sintering in a reducing atmosphere such as hydrogen.

Studies have also shown that cheaper gamma alumina powders of similar purity could also be used as starting materials for the fabrication of the sintered translucent alumina. However, the shrinkage is of the order of almost 50%. The large volume change requires retooling and changing the refractory metal shields for holding the sample. The advantages in saving from lower cost of starting materials and lower sintering temperature did not justify changes in the manufacturing process.

Experimental studies were also conducted on rapid sintering. Primary aims are to reduce the sintering time and increases the volume throughout. Although it was shown possible to sinter the green body to fully dense and translucent envelope within several minutes close to 1950°C and above, the distortion in the sintered components was dramatic.

However, the distortion was removed with longer sintering and holding time. The capital cost of changing the continuous high temperature hydrogen furnaces to a very low thermal mass furnace with considerable saving on hydrogen was not studied further.

Similarly vacuum sintering of the polycrystalline alumina to translucency was conducted successfully. It was shown that the payback would be about three years, which was considered too long in the industry, and thus combined with the high capital cost to replace existing continuous hydrogen furnaces was not pursued further. A large vacuum furnace using refractory tungsten mesh elements was constructed, and experiments were conducted successfully. The vacuum sintered components were also used in high pressure sodium lamps successfully.

We also investigated the sintering alumina in vacuum using carbon susceptor in an RF furnace. We were able to solve the blackening problems in both the refractory W mesh furnace and also in the carbon tube used as susceptor and sample holder. The experimental studies carried out at Balzers, Westlar, Germany, using large diameter vacuum furnaces showed that volume vacuum production of sintered translucent polycrystalline alumina was successful.

Cost analysis showed that the return on investment (ROI) was achievable within two years. Vacuum sintering was not pursued further due to huge capital investment in furnaces and the need to maintain and replace expensive refractory metal parts. The problems associated with darkening of the sintered translucent ceramics using carbon susceptors and sample holders were considered too risky as the thermodynamics of the processes need to be very carefully controlled. In particular the need to control or eliminate traces of moisture trapped inside the furnace parts such as carbon felt for insulation was vital. Similarly, the need to avoid reactions between the water vapor and the refractory metal such as molybdenum and tungsten in vacuum furnaces was necessary. This causes contamination in the sintered translucent alumina tubes. We have been able to control and fine tune the processing.

The development and continued refining of the ceramic processing and implementation of strict quality control in the manufacturing operation enabled elimination of various factors contributing to the residual porosity, cylindrical porosity, white specks, black specks, surface roughness, etc. This enabled volume production of these highly refractory, chemically resistant, with high in-line transmission, and a satisfactory high surface finish.

Another area where studies were conducted is ultra-rapid sintering of polycrystalline alumina to translucency in a low thermal mass furnace. In this study, it is shown that the sintering time can be dramatically reduced from several hours to less than ten minutes. The details of this study is being written up and will be presented at a materials processing conference, and submitted for publication as an innovative materials processing paper.

It was necessary to develop very high surface finish in the interior and external surfaces of the tubular polycrystalline alumina arc tube.

The development of effective materials processes contributed tremendously to the widespread use of the alumina ceramic envelopes, not only for the normal high pressure sodium (HPS) lamps but also in the improved color rendering index (CRI) HPS lamps which requires higher wall loading (Figs. 17 and 18).

The use of the polycrystalline alumina arc tube was extended to the development of compact high pressure, high intensity ceramic metal halide (CMH) lamps containing highly chemically reactive and volatile halide species.

The internal pressure of the lamp fill volatile species in the compact CMH lamps can reach tens of atmospheres as the thin-walled alumina tube was observed to bulge out over prolonged operation (private communication Chalmers, A.G. and Brown, K.) during the early stages of the development of these CMH lamps at Thorn Lighting Ltd (Leicester, UK).

Besides the development of the straight highly translucent polycrystalline alumina arc tubes, research were conducted on the development of highly translucent complex shape hollow ceramic tubular components with tapered ends using dry compaction techniques as well as wet forming units such as traditional slip casting and the more demanding blow moulding technique adopted from the glass and plastic industries.

Below are listed some important processes developed by the author, and critical problems solved during the development of compact HPS and CMH lamps.

(1) The role of a small amount of calcium oxide on the life and performance of the HPS lamps.
(2) The effect of surface finish of the green alumina arc tubes prior to sintering.
(3) The development of compact bulbous-shaped translucent arc tubes by blow moulding and slip casting.
(4) The development of dense sintered translucent polycrystalline alumina by rapid vacuum and reducing atmosphere sintering.
(5) The development of high surface finish translucent sintered polycrystalline alumina.
(6) The development of alumina arc tubes with external grooves for effecting quick start of the HPS and CMH lamps.

(7) The development of leak tight, strong, tough, electrically conducting alumina-metal (cermet) composites with matching thermal expansion with alumina.

Ceramic-Metal (Cermets) Composites for High Intensity Discharge Lamps

The high pressure sodium lamps using sintered translucent alumina as the envelope requires a niobium insert. The latter carries a tungsten electrode. Each end of the alumina tube is closed with the niobium insert. The reason niobium is used is because of the close thermal expansion between niobium and alumina. To obtain a hermetic seal, a silica free glass ceramic is used as the intermediate sealing material. This type of sealing material is covered in patents by lighting companies such as General Electric and GTE Sylvania in the US, Philips in the Netherlands, Orem in Germany, and Matshucita, Kyocera, Toshiba, Panasonic in Japan.

The use of the niobium metal insert with the intermediate glass ceramic seals provides a close match in thermal coefficient of expansion with the dense translucent polycrystalline alumina arc tube. The end closure can thus be thermally cycled over the life of the lamps without losing its hermeticity. The latter is vital for the containment of the gaseous vapor species inside the arc tubes. These could be alkali and mercury vapors together with some inert gases such as argon, krypton and xenon. The seals for the HPS lamps are generally highly reliable. Failure of the HPS lamps usually occurs by loss of emitter materials on the tungsten electrodes and due to the blackening inside the surfaces of the alumina arc tubes, particularly near the electrode regions. This leads to drastic reduction in lamp efficacy and lamp life.

It is of import to note that the use of niobium in contact with the highly reactive metal halide vapors such as sodium and tin iodide, bromide, chloride and fluoride leads to severe chemical attack of the electrodes and niobium. The silica envelope was also found to be attacked by the metal halide vapors. To overcome these problems, it was first reported by Philips in Eindhoven, that a new design of end closure material such

MICROSTRUCTURE OF ELECTRICALLY CONDUCTING AL$_2$O$_3$ CERMETS

Fig. 16 Microstructure of sintered alumina — tungsten cermets. Note the metallic tungsten surrounding the alumina granules. The ceramic-metal composites (known as cermet) was developed for the experimental ceramic metal halide lamps. 1 cm ≡ 100 μm.
Source: United States Patent: 4155758, Hing, P., Evans, D.T. and Marshall, R.[14]

as alumina-molybdenum cermet in place of the niobium-metal insert for the ceramic metal halide lamps.

Following this announcement by Philips in the 1980s, Thorn Lighting embarked on the development of ceramic–metal composites with different arrangement of the dispersed phases (Fig. 16). This development was led by the author, and resulted in several patents. The key to the development of the novel alumina–refractory metal composites (cermets) was the development of processes that enabled the refractory metallic particles in the micron range to coat the alumina granules and other types of ceramic granules formed either by pan granulation and other spherodization processes, including spray drying. Coatings can be effected by mixing the ceramic and metallic phases in a suitable manner

---

[14] Ceramic metal halide lamp having medium aspect ratio, United States Patent 6555962 (2003).

that minimizes the aggregation of the micron size metallic phases. The economical processes developed could be adopted for large scale processing of ceramic–metal composites. The development of the ceramic–metal composites enabled Thorn Lighting to have a substantial lead in the early development of very compact high intensity and efficiency CMH lamps (see Fig. 19).

Whilst cermets containing dispersed match phases are well known in the patent literature and journal publications, the development of

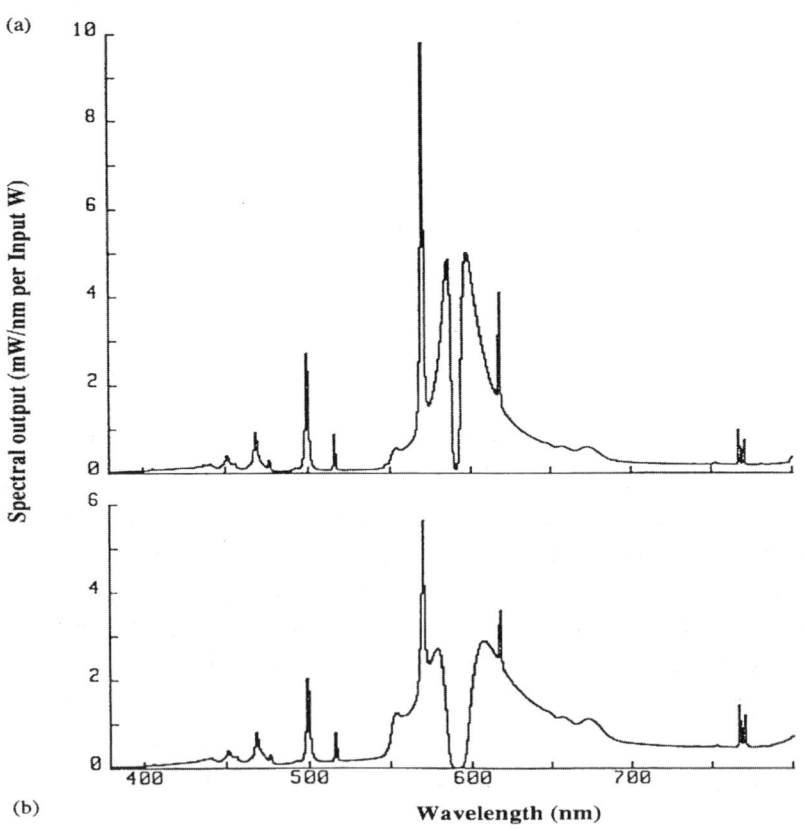

Fig. 17 Spectral distribution in HPS lamps at different pressures: **(a)** 250 watt at 104 Pa and **(b)** 250 watt at 4×104 Pa. Note improved color rendition at higher pressure of about 20 with golden yellow white light used on motorways, buildings, airports, etc. Note the predominant feature of HPS lamp is self-reversal of Na D lines (bottom spectrum).

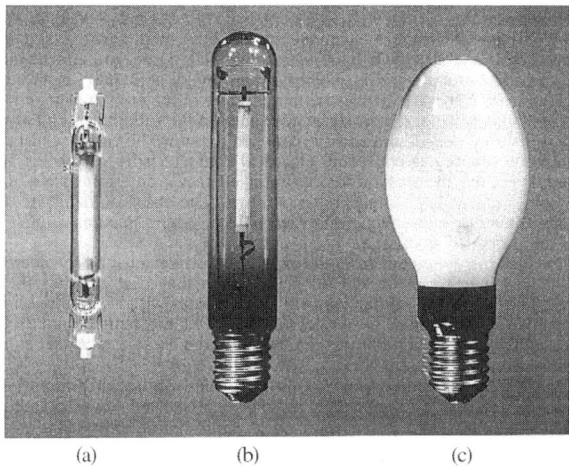

Fig. 18 High pressure sodium lamps (400 watt) using inner alumina arc tube. Note different types of outer glass envelope. **(a)** Fused quartz linear outer envelope, **(b)** larger linear borosilicate glass outer envelope, and **(c)** bulbous outer glass envelope with inner surface coated with phosphor.

Fig. 19 Experimental ceramic metal halide lamp.
Source: Chalmers, A.G., Wharmby, D. and Brown, K. *Thorn Lighting Technical Memorandum* (1989).

electrically conducting cermets with low volume fraction of metallic phases and with closely matching thermal expansion with the polycrystalline alumina arc tubes are novel. The cost effective technique of fabricating dense strong and tough composites with dispersed phases and a distribution of free flowing spray dried ceramic granules were pursued aggressively.

The author led the development of the ceramic-metal composite based on coating the ceramic granules with a layer of metallic phase. Two types of granules were investigated; those fabricated by spray drying of the high purity alumina slurry, and alumina granules prepared by mechanically rolling the mixture of the metal and ceramic phases. In this way, ceramic granules ranging from less than ten microns to several hundreds of microns can be produced. The processes were optimized and led to the development of very strong and tough cermet materials capable of carrying sintered–in tungsten electrodes. Such designs of enclosure with the cermet materials led to the granting of a US Patent.[7]

It was also found that the spray dried alumina granules developed relatively smooth surface finish and also had marked "dimpled" doughnut-like appearance. The spray dried granules were more difficult to coat with refractory metallic particles. Moreover, the metallic particles were found to lodge in the dimples in the spray dried alumina. This led to higher metal loading for electrical conduction. Some roughening of the surfaces were, however, found to be effective in filling the dimples with alumina debris first, and this is found to assist the metallization processes.

However, when the granules prepared by the simple granulation process we used at the time, it was found that the surfaces of the alumina granules were rough, but free of dimples. These types of ceramic granules were found to be easier to metallize as the particle spread more uniformly over the whole granules during the metallization process. The effectiveness of the metallization process was attributed partly to the mechanical entrapment of the micron size metallic particles on the rough surfaces. However, the physics of the adhesion processes were not investigated. This would be worth studying in more detail. In particular the nature of the charge and charge distribution on the various sizes of the granules, and the effect of residual moisture, humidity effect, additives, etc. would be worth investigating in more detail to elucidate the mechanisms of sticktion of the metallic particles on the various types of ceramic granules.

Moreover, further enhancement in the thermo-mechanical properties of the ceramic-metal composites were obtained by dispersing discrete metallic phases in the alumina granules. This resulted in stronger and tougher dense sintered cermets. The improvement in the mechanical strengths was attributed to the inhibition of grain growth due to the dispersed metallic particles. The spatial distribution of the metallic phases on the sinterability and thermo-mechanical properties of the ceramic metal composites were reported in several *Proceedings of the Science of Ceramics* by Hing, P.[15,16]

Development of Glass Ceramic Sealing Materials for the Ceramic Halide Lamps

The construction of the seals for the HPS lamps consists of a niobium tube as an insert into the alumina arc tube. The niobium carries a coiled tungsten electrode coated with emitter materials to reduce the work function. Niobium is chosen as an insert because of the fairly close match in thermal expansion with the alumina. Hermetic seal is obtained using a silica free glass ceramics. The composition is proprietary as each lamp company has their own compositions. Basically it contains magnesia, alumina, barium oxide and boric oxide with some other alkaline earth-like strontium oxide. The sealing glasses for the HPS lamps were found to be inadequate for sealing of the ceramic metal halide lamps as the metal halides attack these glasses during the lamp operation.

Thus there was a need to develop sealing materials capable of withstanding the highly reactive metal halide species inside the alumina arc tubes. There is a growing trend to use ceramic arc tube instead of the fused silica as envelope as ceramics are more refractory, and also capable of withstanding higher internal pressures of the gases during the lamp operation.

Conventional ceramic powder processing route, sol gel processing and melt formed routes have been used to prepare experimental materials for evaluation as potential sealing materials. One simple test was to first

---

[15] Hing, P. (1984). Spatial distribution of tungsten on the physical properties of Al_2O_3-W cermets, *Science of Ceramics*, 12: 87–94.

[16] Hing, P. (1980). The strength and fracture properties of dense sintered Al_2O_3 cermet materials, *Science of Ceramics*, 11: 521–528.

cold press the chemically prepared glass compositions and premelt on the sintered translucent alumina discs in air to study the melting characteristics and its wettability on the alumina substrate. The glass compositions should preferably melt below 1500°C and exhibit good wettability. The molten glass should spread easily with low contact with the substrate. Nucleation and crystallization heat treatments of the premelted glasses were also carried in a muffle furnace in air. Sealing compositions resulting in crack free substrates and glass ceramics after nucleation and crystallization heat treatments are selected for further studies.

Development of Compact White Light High Pressure Sodium Lamps

Figure 20 depicts typical energy level of sodium atom. As the pressure of the lamp fill in the high pressure sodium lamp is increased, the spectrum is broadened as shown in Fig. 17(b).

Development of Seals for the Ceramic Metal Halide (CMH) Lamps

Figures 19, 21 and 22 show experimental metal halide lamps constructed with alumina ceramic envelope. The seal consists of a cermet end plug joined to an alumina ceramic arc tube. A glass ceramic sealing compound is used to join the cermet end to the translucent alumina tube. The cermet carries an electrode that is sintered inside the cermet enclosure at both ends.

The CMH lamps shown in Fig. 19 and 21 are double ended lamps meaning that there is an electrode at each end of the tube. The seals must be fully hermetic, implying that gases inside the sealed arc tube necessary for the operation of the lamp must not leak out, nor should any gas in the outer envelope of the lamp leak in externally through the interfaces of the glass ceramic seals.

Hermeticity tests were usually conducted on sealed arc tube containing argon and metal halides pellets. The seals were thermally cycled at

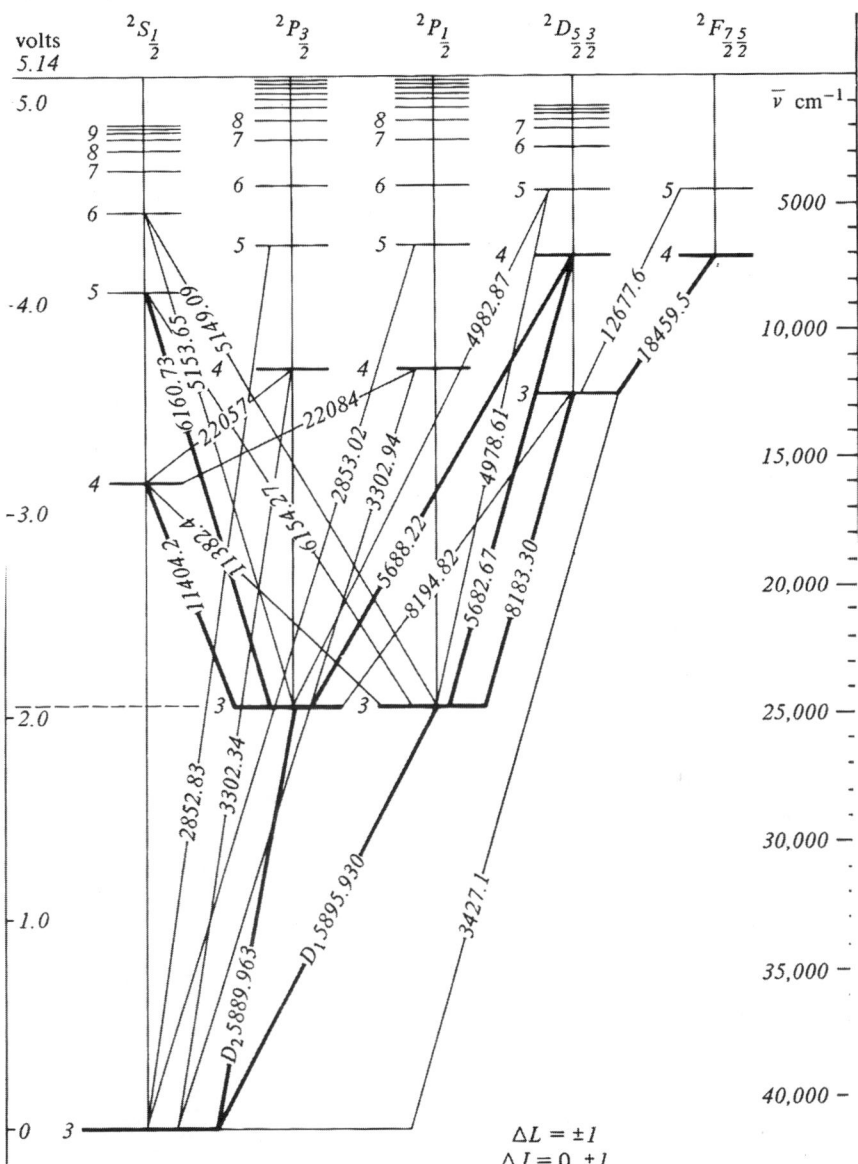

Fig. 20 Energy level diagram in eV (LHS) and wavenumber (RHS) for sodium.
Source: Introduction to Atomic Physics by Semat, H.

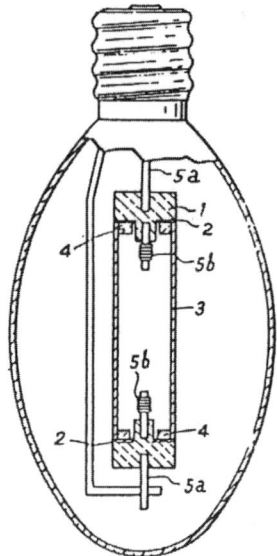

Fig. 21 Ceramic metal halide lamps developed at Thorn Lighting Ltd., UK, using proprietary ceramic–metal (cermet) composite end closure and glass sealing compositions.

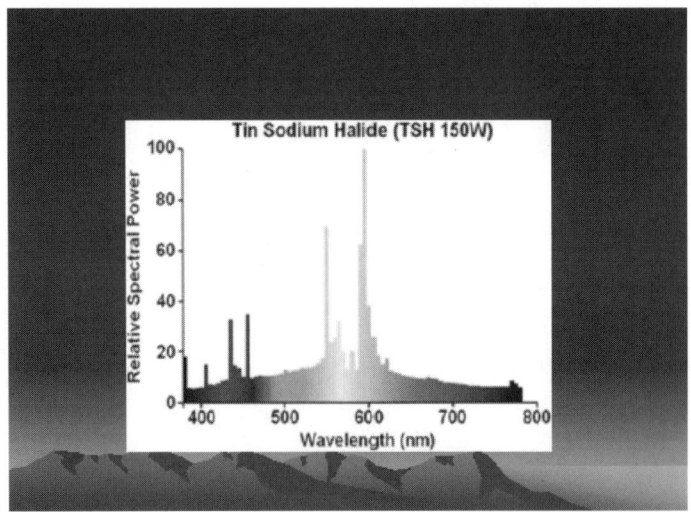

Fig. 22 Spectrum of white light source in experimental CMH lamp.

various temperatures. One technique of assessing quickly whether the seals were leaky was to observe the color of the cold discharge produced using a Tesla coil applied at one end of the sealed ceramic envelope.

A leaky seal produced a distinct violet/purple discharge, while a hermetic seal gives a distinct bluish discharge. A bluish discharge must be maintained for months under various cycling conditions. A bluish discharge indicates a leak tight seal. The sealed arc tube can be thermally cycled to simulate service performance of the lamp. Maintenance of the bluish discharge over prolonged thermal cycling indicates that the seals are fully hermetic.

The chemical resistance was also tested in experimental metal halide lamps under actual service conditions. The techniques of containing the metal halides at relatively high sealing temperatures without loss of metal halides required special sealing techniques. The technology will be discussed separately.

Materials Systems Investigated to Produce Refractory and Metal Halide Resistant Glass Seals

Most of the experimental investigations were conducted in silica containing glasses. The systems which were most investigated are:-

$MgO.Al_2O_3.SiO_2$
$SrO.ZrO_2.SiO_2$
$Y_2O_3.Al_2O_3.SiO_2$
$SrO.MgO.SiO_2$

To make the seals, frit rings were fabricated by uniaxial compaction using specially designed stainless steel dies. In all the four systems investigated we have identified various compositions that have potential for the construction of experimental ceramic halide lamps. These will be discussed. The development of the glass ceramic sealing had involved extensive research. It is more appropriate to discuss this aspect of the materials development in more detail in a separate article.

Conclusions

In the first part of the review, it is shown that the development and use of functional ceramics and ceramic composites as well as glass ceramic seals were necessary in the construction of high intensity discharge light sources such as compact high pressure sodium and ceramic metal halide lamps. Whilst these high intensity ceramic discharge lamps are now available commercially, the early development required extensive materials development and design.

This material development has enabled the commercialization of these compact high efficacy and high color rendering high intensity discharge light sources. These lamps can be operated cost effectively, safely and reliably. Even today, research and development on discharge light sources are still needed as the efficiency can still be further improved. This is because most of these light sources are far from achieving its theoretical 683 lumens per watt for monochromatic radiation, and about 250 lumens per watt for the white light distribution. The most efficient high pressure sodium lamps is of the order of 140 lumens per watt, and the ceramic metal halide white light source of the order of 100 to 120 lumens per watt.

The author believes that there is possibility of developing high intensity discharge light sources with 200 lumens per watt if R&D is focused on identifying all the mechanisms of energy losses in the plasma, across the walls of the sintered ceramic envelope, understanding the physics and chemistry of the discharge, the development of more refractory high temperature and chemically resistant sealing materials and transparent envelope materials with nano or sub-nano surface finish.

PART II. DEVELOPMENT OF SUSTAINABLE SOLID STATE LIGHTING

In the second part of the discussion on sustainable lighting, the development of solid state lighting will be reviewed.

Introduction

In part II of the chapter on Minimization of Resource Drains and Environmental Damage, the development of sustainable solid state lighting is reviewed. In particular, recent advances in this field will be presented. As a reminder, solid state lighting (SSL) refers to light sources completely different from conventional lighting which requires heating a filament in an inert atmosphere; with the filament being enclosed in a glass envelope containing inert gases or converting the gaseous discharge into useful light sources. Conventional lighting also includes light sources obtained from various types of gaseous discharge as in fluorescent lamps, high pressure sodium, high pressure mercury, low pressure sodium and metal halide vapor lamps as discussed in part I of this chapter.

Historically, silicon carbide (SiC) was the first material noted to emit "cold" light. It was first observed around 1907 and reported by Round.[1] Here the term cold refers to the emission without the need to heat the filament as in the case of incandescent lamp using tungsten filaments or from gas discharges. In these lamps, black body radiation is involved. It was only in the 1940s that the mechanism of cold light emission was recognized as coming from a *p-n* junction.[2] Work conducted in the early 1950s reported light emission from various metal-semiconductor contacts in GaP,[3] GaAs, GaSb, InP,[4] Ge and Si.[5]

---

[1] Round, H.J. (1907). A note on carborundum, *Electrical World*, 49: 309.
[2] Lehovec, K., Accardo, C.A. and Jamjochian, J.E. (1951). Injected light emission of silicon carbide crystals, *Physical Review*, 83: 603–607.
[3] Wolff, G.A., Hebert, R.A. and Broder, J.D. (1955). Electroluminescence of GaP, *Physical Review*, 100: 1144–1145.
[4] Braunstein, R. (1955). Radiative transition in semiconductors, *Physical Review*, 99: 1892–1893.
[5] Haynes, J.R. and Briggs, H.B. (1952). Radiation produced in germanium and silicon by electron–hole recombination, *Proceedings of American Physical Society Meeting*, Columbus, Ohio. Also in *Phys. Rev.* 86: 647 (1952).

Working as a Consulting Scientist at GE, Nick Holonyak Jr. invented the first visible red Light Emitting Diode (LED) in 1962. Holonyak worked on the red LED using gallium phosphide (GaP) and obtained milli lumen per watt. Today the red LED delivers over 100 lumens per watt — a remarkable achievement.[6] There has been serious research and development of the LEDs for SSL at Thorn Lighting in the 1970s and 1980.[7,8]

There was considerable research and development on all colors of LED[9] prior to the invention of the blue LED. It may be of interest to note that blue emission was also reported in Boron Nitride (BN)[10] and great hope was placed on obtaining useful blue emission from silicon carbide. Around 1990, a group of Japanese researchers[10–12] published some early work on the luminescence in GaN. It was then that Shuji Nakamura in his own words mentioned that he shifted his interest into GaN as most people are working on other materials such as ZnSe and SiC. The author and his team also found blue emission in a PZT, a lead zirconate titanate ceramic with perovskite structure.[13]

Up to 1994, most of the colors of light can be obtained from LEDs using different types of wide band gap materials from III-V semiconductors,

---

[6] Holonyak, N. and Bevacqua, S.F. (1962). Coherent (visible) light emission from $GaAs_{1-x}P_x$ junction, *Applied Physics Letters*, 1: 82–83.

[7] Williams, E.W. and Hall, R. (1978). Luminescence and light emitting diodes, in Pampling B.R. (ed.), *International Series on Science of Solid State*, Vol. 13. Pergammon.

[8] Cayless, M.A. and Marsden, A.M. (eds.) (1983). *Lamps and Lighting*, 3rd edn.

[9] Sakai, S., Chang, S.S., Ramaswamy, R.V., Kim, J.-H., Radhakrishnan, G., Liu, J.K. and Katz, J. (1988). $Al_{0.3}Ga_{0.7}As/Al_{0.5}Ga_{0.95}$ as light emitting diodes on GaAs-coated Si substrates grown by liquid phase epitaxy, *Applied Physics Letters*, 53: 1201–1203.

[10] Mishima, O., Era, K., Tanaka, J. and Yamaoka, S. (1988). Ultraviolet light-emitting diode of a cubic boron nitride pn junction made at high pressure, *Applied Physics Letters*, 53: 962–964.

[11] Akasaki, I., Amano, H., Kito, M. and Hiramatsu, R. (1991). Photoluminescence of Mg-doped p-type GaN and electroluminescence of GaN p-n junction LED, *Journal of Luminescence*, 48/49: 666.

[12] Amano, H., Asahi, T., Kito, M. and Akasaki, I. (1991). Stimulated emission in MOVPE-grown GaN film, *Journal of Luminescence*, 48/49: 889–892.

[13] Sun, C.Q., Jin, D., Zhou, J., Li, S., Tay, B.K., Lau, S.P., Sun, X.W., Huang, H.T. and Hing, P. (2001). Intense and stable blue-light emission of $Pb(Zr_xTi_{1-x})O_3$, *Applied Physics Letters*, 79: 1082.

except blue light. Most of the research was on ZnSe to obtain blue emission as it has the right band gap. However, in 1994, LED that emitted blue radiation was found in GaN at Nichia, Japan. Dr. Shuji Nakamura was credited with the invention of the blue LED.[14-16] This has since transformed the fortune of a small unknown chemical company that is also leading the development of the blue diode lasers extensively used in DVDs.

Dr. Shuji Nakamura has since moved to the University of California, Santa Barbara Berkeley, where he has been appointed to Professor. He won a substantial lawsuit of several million dollars from Nichia. Professor Shuji Nakamura was awarded the 2006 Millenium Prize in Technology for his invention of the revolutionary blue LED, white emitting diode and blue laser diode using GaN.

The race to commercialize SSL is now on with the announcement of Philips no longer supporting research and development on compact fluorescent lamps (CFL). Most of the major lighting companies are now conducting intensive R&D to develop cost effective SSL.

It would not be surprising to see LED exceeding 150 lumens, and possibly approaching 200 lumens per watt if Haitz's law which states that that every decade the price of LED lights falls a factor of ten while performance grows by a factor of two. This is the equivalent to Moore's law in microelectronics which states that silicon chip performance doubles in performance every 18 months, but the price is reduced every year.

These long-lasting, low-heat light sources (LED) illuminate everything from alarm clocks to the NASDAQ billboard in New York's Times Square. These light-emitting diodes produce more lumens per watt than both incandescent and halogen lighting sources, thus making them more

---

[14] Nakamura, S., Mukai, T. and Sengh, M. (1994). Candela-class high brightness InGaN-AlGaN double heterostructure blue light-emitting diodes, *Applied Physics Letters*, 64(13): 1687–1689.

[15] Nakamura, S., *et al.* (1995). High-brightness InGaN blue, green and yellow light-emitting diodes with quantum well structures, *Japanese Journal of Applied Physics*, 34(7A): L797–L799.

[16] Nakamura, S., *et al.* (1995). Superbright green InGaN single-quantum-well-structure light-emitting diodes, *Japanese Journal of Applied Physics*, 34(10B): L1332–L1335.

environmentally friendly and cost effective. The LED's life span is about ten times longer than an incandescent bulb making it ideal for use in automotive dashboards and taillights, traffic signals and consumer electronics.

SSL refers primarily to the light coming from semiconductor junctions. There is no gaseous discharge involved. Since the discovery of the red light emitting diode with a fraction of lumen per watt, to over 100 lumens per watt today, one can say that the progress in the field of SSL is phenomenal.

Professor Colin Humphreys stated at the British Association's Festival of Science in Sheffield, UK, "I think that gallium nitride is the most important new material since silicon." A mission funded by DTI, UK, reported that Nichia has already developed white LEDs that gives 113 lumens per watt as shown in Fig. 1.[17] The white LEDs with

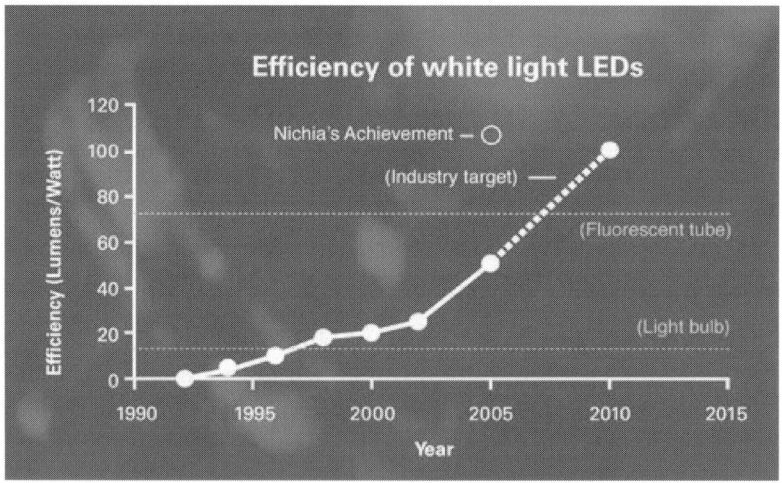

Fig. 1 Efficiency of white LED reported by Nichia, Japan in 2006.[18]

---

[17] Nakamura, S., et al. (1996). InGaN-based multi-quantum-well-structure laser diodes, *Japanese Journal of Applied Physics* (Part 2), 35(1B): L74–L76.
[18] See Nichia website: http://www.nichia.com.

efficiency greater than 100 lumens per watt is better than the fluorescent lamps, and is approaching the efficiency of high pressure sodium lamps at 140 lumens per watt and as high if not higher than the white light source from the high intensity ceramic metal halide lamps. However, one major disadvantage is that the light from LED is directional, and therefore not suited for general illumination but can be used for other applications.

By doping GaN with indium the color can be changed from pinkish to red. White light can be obtained by converting the blue with a coating of phosphor as in the fluorescent lamp. Blue laser using GaN has also been developed and used for reading and storing huge amounts of data. A single CD can now store all the songs from the Beatles or Madonna.

The US Department of Energy now has a program that accelerates advances in SSL. SSL is considered to be a pivotal emerging technology that will fundamentally alter the way we light our homes, public and commercial buildings, and sidewalks in the future. The L Prize Competition worth up to US$20 million by the Department of Energy challenges the lighting industries in America to develop high performance and energy saving SSL sources — a 21st century lamp.[19]

The SSLs used a fifth of the power of a conventional lamp, and can thus reduce carbon emission. Some 20% of the electrical power generated is used by developed countries for lighting; and over 40% in less developed parts of the world. The cost of SSLs is still very high and needs to come down by an order of magnitude or more. We expect that in the next five to ten years, SSL will be commonplace just like compact fluorescent lamps today.

Nichia and other companies have developed blue LEDs and blue lasers based on GaN.[18,20] Semiconductor lasers have many applications

---

[19] See DOE, USA website: http://www.energy.gov.
[20] Narukawa, Y., *et al.* (1997). Role of self-formed InGaN quantum dots for exciton localization in the purple laser-diode emitting at 420 nm, *Applied Physics Letters*, 70(8): 981–983.

ranging from reading and writing on compact discs for storing and retrieving of information to optical communication.

Organic Light Emitting Diodes (OLEDs)

Another development which has potential as SSL is the discovery of organic light emitting diodes (OLEDs).[21–25] The field is developing very fast. We can expect low cost large flexible panel being used as general area illumination. The illumination is much lower than that of the SSL from semiconductor LEDs such as GaN, GaInN, GaInMgN, GaP, etc. At present it is unlikely to match the performance of semiconductor based SSL.

OLED is also known as light emitting polymer (LEP) or another more elaborate name is organic electroluminescence (OEL). OLED is any light emitting diode, the electroluminescent layer contains a polymer that allows suitable organic compounds to be deposited. These are deposited in rows and columns on a flat carrier by a printing process. The matrix of pixels can emit light of different colors on application of an electric field. OLEDs have many applications ranging from television screens to computer displays, portable cell phones, personal assistant (PDA), advertising, etc. It is more beneficial than liquid crystal (LCD) displays which require back illumination. Degradation of OLED materials has, however, limited its use. There is active research to minimize degradation of the OLED. As the field is developing very fast, a review on the OLED and its applications at this stage will soon be outdated.

---

[21] Bernanose, A., Comte, M. and Vouaux, P. (1953). *J. Chim. Phys.*, 50: 64.

[22] Burroughes, J.H., Bradley, D.D.C., Brown, A.R., Marks, R.N., Mackay, K., Friend, R.H., Burn, P.L. and Holmes, A.B. (1990). Light-emitting diodes based on conjugated polymers, *Nature*, 347: 539–541.

[23] Heeger, A.J. (1993). In Salaneck, W.R., Lundstrom, I. and Ranby, B. (eds.), *Conjugated Polymers and Related Materials*. Oxford, pp. 27–62.

[24] Gustafsson, G., Cao, Y., Treacy, G.M., Klavetter, F., Colaneri, N. and Heeger, A.J. (1992). Flexible light-emitting diodes made from soluble conducting polymers, *Nature*, 357: 477–479.

[25] Friend, R.H., Gymer, R.W., Holmes, A.B., Burroughes, J.H., Marks, R.N., Taliani, C., Bradley, D.D.C., Dos Santos, D.A., Brédas, J.L., Lögdlund, M. and Salaneck, W.R. (1999). Electroluminescence in conjugated polymers, *Nature*, 397: 121–128.

Footnotes 10 to 33 provide a comprehensive coverage of the subject. On 23 November 2008, Samsung reported the discovery of true blue light emission from organic light emitting material.[31] The days of low cost large panel solid state white light source is getting closer.

Basic Principle of Solid State Lamps Obtained from Light Emitting Diodes

In this section, the basic principle behind the light emitting diode (LED) based on semiconductors is discussed briefly. Semiconductors fall between metal and insulators in terms of their electrical conductivity. Intrinsic or pure semiconductor is not a good electrical conductor, and its resistivity decreases as temperature increases. The reason for this is that the heat supplied breaks the covalent bonds in semiconductors like silicon or compound semiconductors like gallium arsenide (GaAs) and indium antimonide (InSb) and releases electrons for electrical conduction. This is an expensive process to obtain valence electrons for conduction because of the energy supplied which must be of the order of the band gap of the semiconductor which can range from a fraction of electron volt (eV) to several electron volt (say 0.1 to 3 eV).

A smarter way to obtain a huge supply of free electrons is to replace some of the atoms of the elemental semiconductor like silicon or compound semiconductors like those obtained from the alloys obtained from

---

[26] Kiebooms, R., Menon, R. and Lee, K. (2001). In Nalwa, H.S. (ed.), *Handbook of Advanced Electronic and Photonic Materials and Devices*, Vol. 8. Academic Press, pp. 1–86.

[27] Hebner, T.R., Wu, C.C., Marcy, D., Lu, M.H. and Sturm, J.C. (1998). Ink-jet printing of doped polymers for organic light emitting devices, *Applied Physics Letters*, 72: 519.

[28] Wood, D. (1994). *Optoelectronics Semiconductor Devices*. Prentice Hall.

[29] Wilson, J. and Hawkes, J.F.B. (1989). *Optoelectronics: An Introduction* (2nd Edn.). Prentice Hall.

[30] Yariv, A. (1991). *Optoelectronics* (4th Edn.). Harcourt Brace Janovich College Publishers.

[31] Retrieved on 24 October 2008 from: http://en.wikipedia.org/wiki/image/E27 with 38LED.JPG.

[32] Wearnes, L.A.A. (1990). *Electronic Materials*. MacMillan.

[33] Retrieved on 4 December 2008 from: http://www.ledinside.com/Joliet+Technology+offered+LED+street+Lighting+with+energy+savings+of+up+to+80%25_20080715.

elements from group III and V of the periodic table. By incorporating say a donor atom from group V elements like phosphorus in the silicon semiconductor, effectively, one extra electron is released and free to take part in the electrical conduction. This is because four of the electrons from the phosphorus atom are used up to form the complete four covalent bonds in the covalent semiconductors like silicon or germanium. Semiconductors with excess electrons are known as *n* type. One can easily imagine the number of atoms in a meter cube of semiconductor. Now if every 10^8 silicon atoms are replaced by one phosphorus atom, we will have 10^{20} phosphorus atoms; if each phosphorus atom gives an extra valence electron as it is easily ionized, then there will be some 10^{20} electrons per meter cube. Thus the number of electrons available for electrical conduction is very large.

In the same way if we replace a silicon atom with an atom from group III in the periodic table like boron, there will be insufficient electron to complete the sharing of the electrons to form the four covalent bonds with the Si neighbors, or other covalent type semiconductors. In this case, only three complete covalent bonds are formed. One of the incomplete covalent bond is acting as a vacant site, or absence of an electron. The vacant site is known as a hole and carries a positive charge, whereas the electron carries a negative charge. Semiconductors with holes as carriers are known as *p* type semiconductors.

When the *n* and *p* type semiconductors are joined to form a junction, the junction is known as a *p-n* junction as shown in Fig. 2. The *p-n* junction is made by a special lithography and thin film deposition process. LED is obtained when an electric field is applied between the *p* and *n* junction. For efficient light emission, the semiconductor must be a direct semiconductor rather than an indirect semiconductor. Silicon and germanium are indirect semiconductors, whereas most of the III-V compound semiconductors are direct semiconductors. Direct semiconductors allow the light to be emitted more easily from the *p-n* junction.

The mechanisms of the light emission are more involved. First we must apply the voltage across the *p-n* junction so that it is in the forward biased mode, meaning the *p* type part of the semiconductor is kept at a higher potential (+) and the *n* type part of the semiconductor is at a lower potential (−). When the forward bias is applied, the junction will emit light

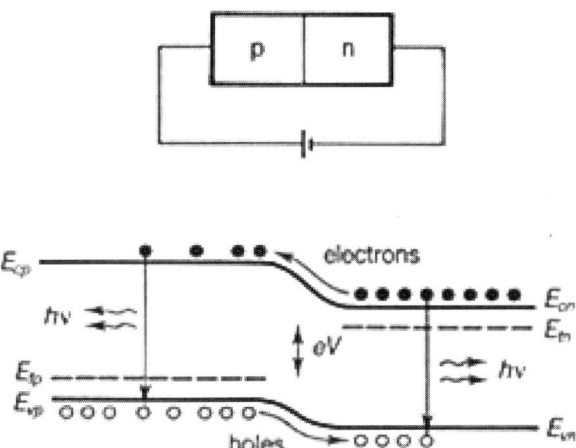

Fig. 2 A p-n junction for a semiconductor in the forward biased configuration. The emission of the radiation is shown on the left and right side of the energy diagram when an electron from the conduction band drops into the hole in the valence band. The arrows indicate emission of radiation. This is also known as the injection electroluminescence of the p-n junction under forward biased.[28]

of various colors depending on the band gap of the semiconductor. Each type of semiconductor has a certain band gap or forbidden energy band expressed in electron volt (eV). The band gap is separated by the valence and a conduction band. The origin of the band gap is very complicated, and need to apply quantum mechanics to see how the electrons in the solids interact with the periodic potential associated with the periodic arrangement of the atoms.[28]

The energy of the valence electrons are arranged as energy levels; because there are so many energy levels with energy between the energy levels of the order of 10^{-12} eV. In view of this large number of energy level so closely spaced, it is best to describe the energy of the electrons as being arranged into energy bands. Thus all the valence electrons in the solids reside in the valence band at zero degree Kelvin (0 K), and none in the conduction band. The electrons obey the Fermi-Dirac statistics. Above 0 K some of the electrons will be excited to the conduction band and leave holes in the valence band. In the same way, the application of a forward bias will cause the electrons from the n type semiconductor to move to the

p type semiconductor which is kept at a higher potential. The holes with the positive charge will move across the p-n junction to the n side of the semiconductor which is kept at a lower (negative) potential. This will give rise to a net junction current vital for the operation of microelectronics devices.

At the p-n junction, recombination process takes place when inter band transitions occur, i.e. when electrons from the conduction band drops into the holes in the valence band. The probability of inter band transitions is high for direct semiconductors, i.e. for semiconductors in which the bottom of the conduction band falls directly on top of the valence band.

It is of interest to mention that free electrons are removed from the valence band to the conduction band, creating vacant sites or holes in the valence band above 0 K. At equilibrium, the rate of electron-hole creation is the same as the rate of recombination of electron. The process is illustrated schematically in Figs. 2 to 4, and the semiconductor LED based on this principle is shown in Fig. 5.[27–30]

When free electrons combine with the holes, the process is known as recombination. Recombination releases energy in the form of radiation, $h\nu$, where h is the Planck's constant and ν the frequency of the radiation emitted.

In microelectronic devices with transistors where speed of the charge carriers are important for electrical conduction, we do not want

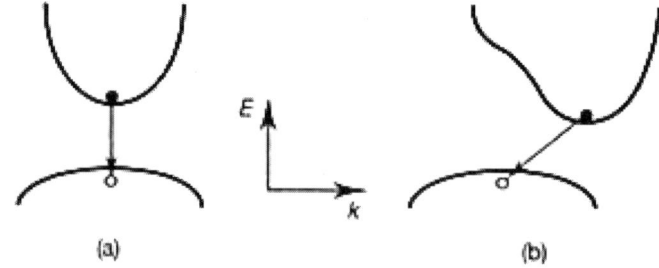

Fig. 3 The energy diagram as a function of the wave vector k or the E-k diagram. (**a**) A direct band gap semiconductor where the bottom of the conduction band (upper curve) falls directly on top of the valence band, i.e. at the same k value. (**b**) An indirect band gap semiconductor, where the bottom of the conduction band (upper curve) does not fall directly on top of the valence band. Note a direct band gap semiconductor leads to a more efficient LED.[28]

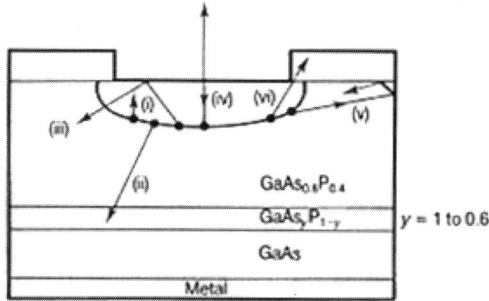

Fig. 4 Surface light emitting LED using GaAs doped with phosphorus. Note the internal reflection, emission and absorption of the light emitted from the *p-n* junction.[28–30]

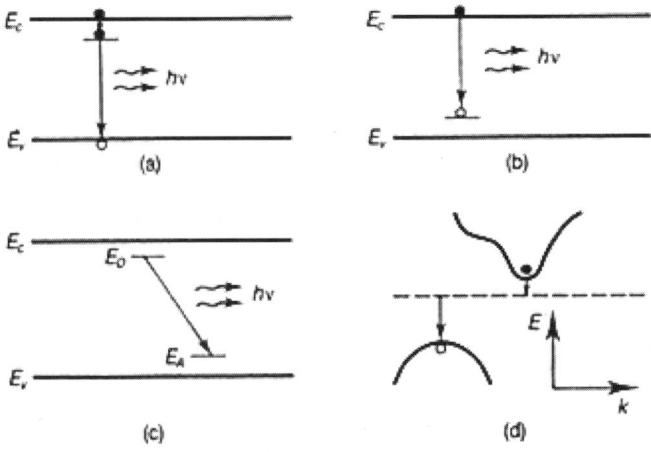

Fig. 5 Various ways in which the electrons can recombine with holes. (**a**) From donor center to holes in valence band. (**b**) electrons from conduction band into vacant sites (holes) in the acceptor energy levels, (**c**) electrons from donor energy level recombining with holes in the acceptors, (**d**) an indirect semiconductor behaving like a direct conductor when the semiconductor is doped with the same valence dopant as the semiconductor.[28–30]

recombination if we are considering only microelectronic devices. It is necessary to minimize recombination. LEDs, however, depend on recombination processes to release radiation.

For LEDs, however, we are more interested in the radiation emitted. Also in LEDs, recombination processes that lead to photon generation are not desirable as the efficiency will drop. The wavelength, λ, of the radiation is given by $E = h\nu = hc/\lambda$ since $c = \nu\lambda$, where c is the velocity of light, h the Planck's constant, and ν the frequency. Thus the wavelength associated with the emission of the radiation from a semiconductor with $E = E_g$ the band gap gives $\lambda = hc/E_g$.

In Fig. 5, various ways in which the electrons can combine with the holes are discussed. In Fig. 5a, the electrons from the donor centers drop into the holes in the valence band emitting radiation with energy $h\nu$. In Fig. 5b, the electrons drop into the holes in the acceptor energy levels, emitting radiation with energy $h\nu$.

The other way involves the electrons from donor levels recombining with holes in the acceptor levels as illustrated in Fig. 5c. Another mechanism in which electrons from the conduction band in an indirect semiconductor combines with the holes in the valence band is to make the semiconductor behave as if it is a direct semiconductor by doping the indirect semiconductor with a dopant of the same valence as the indirect semiconductor. This is illustrated in Fig. 5d. Example GaP doped with nitrogen; both phosphorus and nitrogen have the same valence, and the semiconductor behaves like a direct semiconductor and emits in the green.

For example, when GaP is doped with nitrogen, with same valence as the phosphorus atom in GaP. This is why such centers are known as "isoelectric" centers. The nitrogen atoms form a shallow energy below the conduction band. It does not contribute to electrical conduction, but plays a vital role in the indirect radiative recombination.

Materials Used for LEDs

It is instructive at this stage to introduce the selection of materials for LEDs. If certain wavelength λ of the emitted radiation is required, use is made of the relation $E = h\nu = hc/\lambda$, where h is the Planck's constant, c the velocity of light, λ the wavelength, and ν the frequency. The wavelength corresponding to a material with a certain band gap $E = E_g$ given by hc/E_g is shown in Table 1. For emission of the visible radiation ranging at 700 nm or so, the material needs to have a band gap E_g of about 1.7 eV.

For CdSe, with E_g of 1.74 ev, λ is 714 nm; for lower λ the band gap of the materials is higher. For λ of 555 nm, the band gap of the GaP

Table 1 Materials with different band gap emit radiation with different wavelengths[32]

Material	Gap Energy (eV)	Group in Periodic Table	λ_g (nm)
C	5.4[i]	IV	230
Si	1.11	IV	1,110
Ge	0.66[i]	IV	1,880
β-SiC	2.3[i]	IV-IV	540
α-SiC	2.86[i]	IV-IV	434
AlP	2.45[i]	III-V	497
AlAs	2.17[i]	III-V	573
AlSb	1.60[i]	III-V	776
GaP	2.24[i]	III-V	555
GaAs	1.42	III-V	875
GaSb	0.70	III-V	1,775
InP	1.35	III-V	978
InAs	0.36	III-V	3,450
InSb	0.17	III-V	7,310
CdS	2.42	II-VI	513
CdSe	1.74	II-VI	714
CdTe	1.44	II-VI	863

[i] Indirect gap.

Notes: λ_g is the wavelength of a photon of energy, E_g. If $\lambda_g > \sim 700$ nm, the material is opaque.

is 2.24 eV. The materials for emission of radiation in the visible need to have a wide band gap. As the wavelength of the radiation moves in the infra-red region, the materials selected must have a lower band gap. Thus engineering of the band gap is required to enable precise radiation to be emitted in the *p-n* junction of the semiconductor.

LEDs have two distinct roles, in optoelectronics, one for communication and one in displays. We need to add another role since the combination of the colors from LEDs can generate white light source. With the discovery of blue emission from the gallium nitride semiconductor, the possibility of generating low cost white light from solid state without incandescence and/or gaseous discharge is a reality. It can be seen that materials from III-V and II-VI are suitable materials for emission in the visible ranging from 400 to 800 nm. However, III-V compounds are eminently suited, and majority of LEDs and semiconductor lasers are fabricated using the III-V compounds, as these semiconductors can be doped to produce n and p types more readily than II-VI semiconductors.

From Table 1, it is not surprising that the majority of the LEDs for displays are made from III-V compounds, in particular from $GaAs_{1-y}P_y$ and $Ga_{1-x}Al_x As$, as these cover band gaps are ranging from 1.42 to 2.24 eV (880 to 558 nm).

Figure 6 shows how the band gap changes with the composition for substitution of phosphorus (P) for arsenic (As) in GaAs. The efficiency of LED with indirect semiconductor is low, and this can be remedied with substitution of nitrogen for phosphorus in indirect semiconductors. The reason for the large increase in the efficiency is due to the formation of energy of about 10 mev below the conduction band.

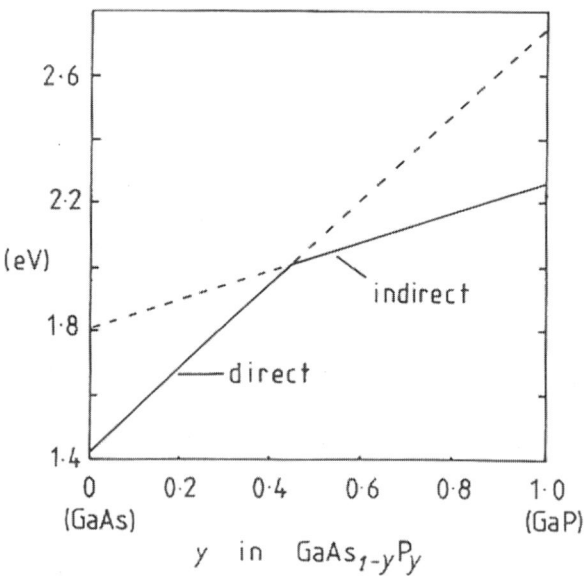

Fig. 6 Band gap (eV) for substitution of As for P. For $y < 0.44$, the semiconductors are direct; for $y > 0.44$, the semiconductors are indirect type.[32]

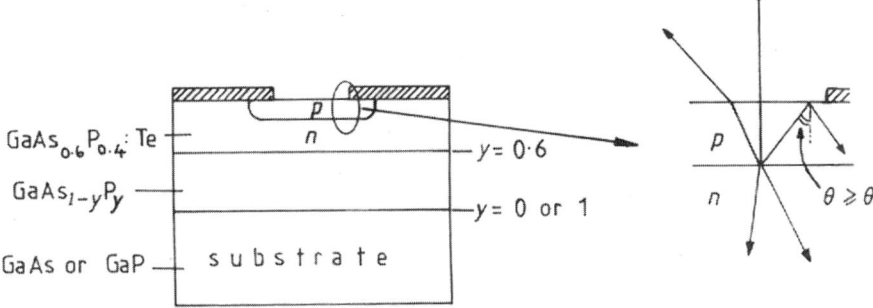

Fig. 7 Structure of a LED chip. The figure on the RHS shows that when $\theta \geq \theta_c$, internal reflection occurs.[32]

The construction of a LED is shown in Fig. 7. It is made up of a *p-n* junction formed by diffusion of zinc, a *p* type dopant. If the material is $GaAs_{1-y}.P_y$, the substrate can be either GaAs ($y = 0$) or GaP ($y = 1$) onto which a graded layer of $GaAs_{1-y}.P_y$ is grown by chemical vapor deposition (CVD). The process is carried out using GaCl from Ga/HCl to transport the gallium, and phosphine (PH_3) and arsine (AsH_3) to transport phosphorus and arsenic.

The graded layer starts at $y = 0$ for GaAs and $y = 1$ for GaP substrate, and ends at $y = 0.6$ for $GaAs_{0.4} P_{0.6}$. An *n* type layer of about one-micron of $GaAs_{0.6} P_{0.4}$ is grown on top of $GaAs_{0.4} P_{0.6}$. The *n* type is formed by using selenium or tellurium from group VI elements to provide extra electrons. The upper contact to the *p* layer is made so that the aperture allows maximum light emitted to emerge from the top surface. It is important to design the *p-n* junction as close to the surface as possible for optimal efficiency.

If the substrate is GaAs, it is opaque as the band gap is small and the wavelength associated with GaAs is large, then the photons emitted downward from the *p-n* junction is absorbed. And the photons reflected back from the top interfaces are absorbed.

If the substrate is made of GaP, then the photons emitted at the *p-n* junctions are reflected back to the surface, and thus more light emerges from the aperture. This reflection is because the band gap of GaP is large, the wavelength associated with GaP is small. Materials with large band

Internal Efficiency of LEDs

The efficiency η of LEDs can be defined as the ratio of the optical power output over the electrical power overall efficiency output. This is approximately equal to the ratio of the number of photons emitted to the number of recombinations taking place. The efficiency η is made up of the internal or quantum efficiency η_i, and external efficiency η_e giving an overall efficiency of $\eta = \eta_i \eta_e$.

The quantum efficiency depends on whether direct or indirect transitions take place, and whether there are intermediate energy levels formed in the band gap as a result of doping, for example, with nitrogen atoms. Even if direct transition is achieved, it will not necessarily produce an optical photon.

The internal efficiency can be quantified in various ways, but the definition is always the same. It can also be defined as the ratio of the number of photons created at the junction to the number of electron–hole pairs generated in that region. The internal efficiency, η_i, can therefore be related to the ratio of the relative recombination rates for radiative transition to the relative rates of non-radiative transition:

$$\eta_i = \frac{\Delta r_{nr}}{\Delta r_r + \Delta r_{nr}}$$

where Δr_r, Δr_{nr} are the relative recombination rates for the radiative transitions and non-radiative transitions, respectively. Note Δr_r, Δr_{nr} is the difference between the operating recombination rates and the thermal equilibrium value.

The internal efficiency can also be written as follows:

$$\eta_i = \frac{\tau_{nr}}{\tau_r + \tau_{nr}},$$

where τ_{nr} and τ_r are the lifetime of the non-radiative and radiative transitions, respectively.

It can be shown that the lifetimes τ_r for semiconductor in which $p_o \gg n_o$ where p_o and n_o are the equilibrium concentration of holes and electrons respectively, is given by the relation τ_r (electrons) = $1/BN_a$, where B is a constant whose magnitude depends on the semiconductor and N_a the concentration of acceptor atoms. The above relation is for the lifetime of minority carrier (electron in this case) in a p type semiconductor.

We can also obtain a similar relation for the lifetime of the minority carriers (holes) in an n type semiconductor as τ_r (holes) = $1/BN_d$. The recombination constant B has significance as shown in Table 2 for various semiconductors. Example, for n type GaAs, the recombination constant B is of the order of 7.2×10^{-10}, and for n type silicon this is of the order 10^{-15}. Thus for the same concentration of dopants say N_d of the order of 10^{18} per cm^3, the lifetime of the minority carrier in an n^+-p junction in an n-GaAs is of the order of $1/(7.2^{-10} \times 10^{18})$ or 278×10^{-12} second. Similar calculation for n-Si gives lifetime of minority carriers as 111×10^{-6} second.

Assuming that the lifetime of the non-radiative τ_{nr} electron hole recombination is 2 ns, and τ_r is of the order of 278 pico (278×10^{-12}) second, η_i is then 0.88 or 88% for a doping density of 10^{18}cm^{-3} on n^+ side of a n^+-p junction of GaAs. Similar calculation for Si shows that the

Table 2 The values of constant B for various semiconductors this is needed to determine the lifetime of the semiconductor[28]

Semiconductor	Recombination Constant B (cm^3 s^{-1}) At or Near Room Temperature
Si	1.79×10^{-15}
Ge	5.25×10^{-14}
GaP	5.37×10^{-14}
GaAs	7.21×10^{-10}
GaSb	2.39×10^{-10}
InP	1.26×10^{-9}
InAs	8.50×10^{-11}
InSb	4.58×10^{-11}

efficiency is of the order of 10^{-5} or 10^{-3}% or 0.003%. Small values of the lifetimes is beneficial for LED as in the case of n-GaAs. Large lifetimes in intrinsic or doped Si is of no use for LED.

The external efficiency is dictated by the ease of the light getting out of the device. The problem is due to the refractive index difference between the semiconductor and air. It is well known that the fraction of light transmitted between two media is given by $T = 1 - R$, where R is the reflectivity at the boundary between the two media. T can be further written as

$$T = 1 - \left[\frac{n_1 \cos v_1 - n_2 \cos v_2}{n_1 \cos v_1 + n_2 \cos v_2} \right]^2,$$

where n_1 and n_2 are the refractive index for media 1 and 2, v_1 and v_2 the angle of incidence and the angle of refraction normal to the two media. According to Snell's law, $n_1 \sin v_1 = n_2 \sin v_2$. The high refractive index of say GaAs as 3.4 would reduce the T to 0.7 or 70% of initial value. Worst is the internal reflection as the incident angle exceeds the critical angle. The device engineer needs to design the LED to reduce the mismatch of the refractive indices. Thus a dome shaped design using a transparent epoxy polymer with an intermediate refractive index of 1.8 reduces the reflection losses appreciably. Figure 8 shows refraction with a curved matching layer of polymer epoxy. This explains why practically all LEDs have tiny dome shaped appearance.

Figure 9 depicts a large geodesic sphere with Waterford crystals consisting of over 32,000 LEDs used to light up Times Square in New York on the eve of 2009.

The new crystal ball can produce millions of vibrant colors and billions of patterns and will be able to withstand the hostile weather environment in New York. The ball will be covered with 2668 triangular Waterford crystals and lit by 32,236 Philips LEDs. The geodesic sphere is 12 feet in diameter and weighs 12,000 pounds. It is designed to withstand all types of weather.

Figure 10 shows an advertisement for V-LEDs, which are now available from Sylvania to replace automobile lamps. By simply quoting the

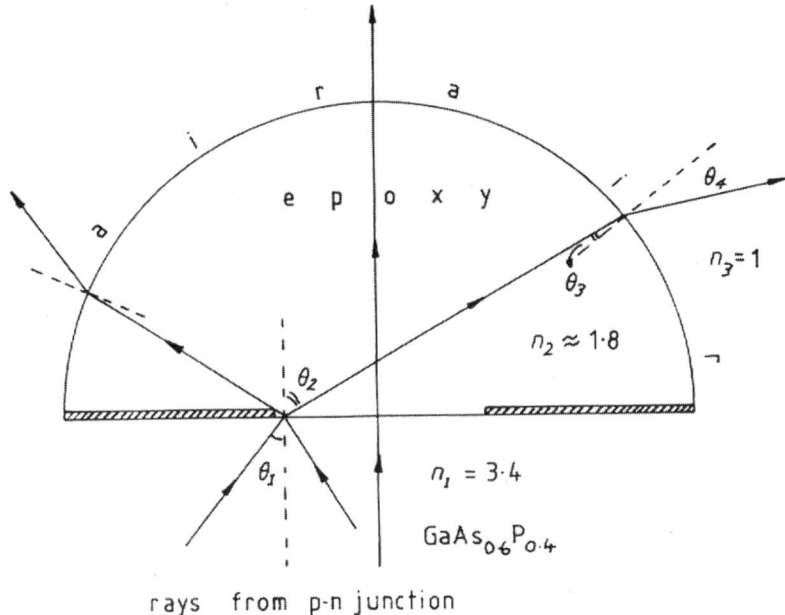

Fig. 8 Refraction with a curved matching layer of epoxy. The design enables LEDs to be produced with minimal internal reflection and optimum light output.[32]

type and number of the light bulbs in one's vehicles, replacement LEDs lamps, known as V-LEDs (vehicle LEDs) can be purchased and fitted easily. The lighting company and e-Bay are offering advice on-line on how to select and replace vehicle bulbs with V-LEDs.

What we are witnessing currently is the LED taking a substantial share of the conventional lighting business. GE Lighting has also announced that the company is no longer pursuing any R&D on incandescent lamps and concentrating on the development of LEDs for general lighting applications. Cree Inc. is already offering all kinds of up and down lighting for the homes, and has extended their LEDs lighting business to exterior lighting as well. Some of the applications of LEDs, at shown in Figs. 11 and 12, are interesting and innovative.

Some companies are now producing LED lamps with color correlated temperatures between 2600 K to 5000 K, with efficacy of LEDs of up to

Fig. 9 New York Times Square LEDs were lit up with over 32,000 LEDs in a giant ball on the eve of 2009. This is to announce the arrival of solid state lighting in a big way. (Retrieved on 3 December 2008 from www.treehugger.com/files/2005/12/times square.[34]

Fig. 10 V-LEDs or vehicle LEDs lamps from Sylvania, USA http://www.sylvania.com.[35]

124 lumens per watt at 700 mA and for CCT of 3000 K of up to 65 lumens per watt at 350 mA.

Joliet Technology, a leader in renewable energy, is offering solar LEDs for street lighting as shown in Fig. 11. This is innovative as it is

---

[34] http://www.treehugger.com/files/2005/12/times.
[35] http://www.sylvania.com.

Development of Sustainable Solid State Lighting   193

Fig. 11   LEDs for street lighting.[33]

Fig. 12 Tianjin University — a member of the LED University. Retrieved from http://www.leduniversity.org.[36]

challenging the dominance of low and high pressure sodium lamps discussed in part I of this chapter.

The solar LEDs for street lighting claims the following advantages over conventional lamps: no external power supply, long life of over ten years, flicker free, lower cost, clean technology with no toxic substance like mercury, immediate lighting without preheating, one battery only, substantial reduction in CO_2, integral daylight sensors, failure of one LED will not lead to failure of the whole lamp, long life PV module (over 20 years), and giving exceptional return on investment. The solar LEDs are also being evaluated in remote communities using power from solar energy stored in batteries. Such type of lighting is sustainable as it does not use grid power and relies on renewable sources.

According to Joliet Technology, a 400 watt high pressure sodium lamp and an equivalent JOL168 watt high power LED lamp based on

---

[36] http://leduniversity.org.

12 hours usage per 24-hour period shows a saving of 12.25 kWh as the 400 watt HPS lamp energy consumption on a daily basis is 14.83 kWh and that of JOL168 watt is only 2.58 kWh.[33]

There is currently expanding government and industry parties under the name of LED City. The interested parties are working to evaluate, deploy and promote LED lighting technology across the whole of the municipal infrastructures with the aims of saving energy, protecting the environment, reducing maintenance cost and providing better quality of light for improved visibility and safety. In the US, some 22% of the electrical power generated is used in lighting. With increasing cost of fossil fuels, carbon emission, global warming, and sustainability of the environment with increasing human activities, there is an urgent need to introduce a revolution in lighting. LEDs are revolutionary solid state lighting now challenging the conventional lighting as discussed in part I.

According to the US Department of Energy, switching to LEDs in the next 20 years can reduce electricity demands by over 60%, eliminate over 250 million tons of CO_2, avoid building of over 130 power plants, and a potential saving of close to US$300 billion. Those involved with municipal infrastructures development, management and town planning will benefit from joining the LED City as participants.

In the same way as LED City, there is now LED University parties promoting LED lighting. Figures 12 to 14 show some of the major universities across the world leading the LED University promotion.

Fig. 13 University of North Carolina — a member of the LED University. Retrieved from http://www.leduniversity.org.[36]

Fig. 14 University of California Santa Barbara (UCSB) — a member of the LED University. Retrieved from http://www.leduniversity.org.[36]

Likewise there are parties promoting LEDs at the workplace as shown in Fig. 15 and service station in Fig. 16.

Various Colors of LED and White LEDs

As mentioned earlier, by doping gallium nitride (GaN) with indium, the color in the LED can be changed from pinkish to red. White light source for solid state lighting can be obtained by converting the blue from GaN with a coating of phosphor such as yttrium aluminate doped with cerium ions (YAG.Ce) or blue light through a yellow color window or substrate such as zinc selenide (ZnSe).

Three approaches are being used to obtain white light sources for solid state lighting using LEDs, namely wavelength conversion, color mixing, use of quantum dot, and homoeptaxial ZnSe.

- Wavelength conversion involves the use of blue light from a LED to excite a phosphor coating which then re-emits yellow light.

Fig. 15 Environmental friendly restaurant with LED lighting. Retrieved from http://www.ledworkplace.org.[37]

Fig. 16 LED lighting at a gas filling station. Retrieved from http://www.ledworkplace.org.[37]

---

[37] http://ledworkplace.org.

This balanced mixing of yellow and blue lights results in the appearance of white light. The color rendition or color rendering index (CRI) is poor.
- Mixing of different colors to produce white light source. In this case, the UV light, say from GaN, is used to excite different phosphors. The colors red, green and blue are mixed resulting in a white light with the rich and broad wavelength spectrum.
- Blue LED and quantum dot. This is a process where a thin layer of nanocrystal particles containing 30 to 40 pairs of atoms, primarily cadmium and selenium are coated on top of the LED. The blue light excites the quantum dots which results in a white light with a wavelength spectrum similar to UV LEDs.
- Homoepitaxial ZnSe is a new technology developed by Sumomito Electric. In this case, the LED is grown on a zinc selenide (ZnSe) substrate. This simultaneously produces blue light from the active region and yellow emission from the substrate. The resulting white light has a wavelength spectrum on par with UV LEDs. No phosphors are used. The efficiency is higher than white light from LED.

For solid state lighting (SSL), several LEDs are placed close together in a lamp to enhance the illumination as shown in Fig. 17.[31] This is because

Fig. 17 A solid state lamp containing several LEDs with Edison Screw developed to replace incandescent and fluorescent lamps. This spot lamp type E27 JDR has 38 light emitting diodes. This solid state lamp is rated at 1.4 watt and operate on 230 Volt.[31]

an individual LED produces only a small amount of light. In the case where white LEDs are utilized in SSL, this is a relatively simple task, as all LEDs are of the same color. The LEDs can be arranged in any manner.

The color mixing method is more difficult to generate equivalent brightness when compared to using white LEDs. Degradation of different LEDs at various times in a color-mixed lamp can lead to an uneven color output. Because of the inherent benefits and greater number of applications for white LEDs for SSL, most designs today focus on utilizing these white LEDs.

Discussion

The current use of compact fluorescent lamps is an interim solution to the energy saving lighting. The lumen efficiency per watt in energy saving fluorescent lamp is still low compared with the theoretical value of 683 lumens per watt at 550 nm or 250–300 lumens over a broad range of wavelengths to simulate the sun's spectrum. The use of even a small amount of mercury, a toxic substance, is a problem with fluorescent lamps, and its use is associated with a toxic waste disposal problem. The used CFL and other types of fluorescent lamps need to be carefully managed to recover the mercury instead of finding its way in landfills. In most countries, the disposal of toxic waste from consumer products find its way in landfills or in the oceans due to a non-existent system of managing and/or recycling toxic waste.

Major lighting companies have now switched most of their research and development in incandescent and fluorescent lighting to solid state lighting. In the 1970s and 1980s most of the lighting companies practically shelved their R&D efforts on solid state lighting. Since the announcement of the blue LED using gallium nitride (GaN) first reported by Nichia, the situation has changed dramatically. This invention of the blue LEDs by Shuji Nakamura has since turned the fortune of a small unknown chemical company in Japan into a major chemical company with their range of patents on blue and white LEDs and blue lasers. The invention also signals the arrival of solid state lighting — the holy grail of lighting.

The principle behind solid state lighting is now fairly well understood. Lighting companies are currently intensifying their R&D to capitalize on this holy grail of lighting, namely developing a really cost effective and efficient solid state lighting that can replace incandescent and other types of light sources. The L Prize of over US$20 million from the US Department of Energy (DOE) will be presented to the American Company that can come up with novel, cost effective and efficient solid state lighting which can replace compact fluorescent lamps.

The DOE is also supporting research on the development of the growth of bulk dislocation free gallium nitride substrates, thin films, phosphors, thermal management of the devices, and manufacturing processes. In Europe, under several framework programs, substantial research and development grants on renewable energy and clean technologies, and other low carbon technologies are being implemented in order to meet the commitment of having 20% of the energy generated by renewable sources by 2020 and reducing the carbon dioxide emission under the Kyoto Protocol. The development of solid state lighting ranks very high in the EU Framework Program on clean technologies and renewable energy.

There is now a Haitz's law which states that the price of LED falls by a factor of ten every decade but the performance doubles every 18 months. This is the equivalent of Moore's law in microelectronics which states that the performance of the silicon chip doubles every 18 months, with a reduction in manufacturing cost which benefits the consumer.

The latest study conducted by Professor E.F. Schubert and Assistant Research Professor Jong Kyu Kim from Rennslaer Polytechnic Institute (RPI) showed that if all the world's light bulbs are replaced by LEDs, the power saving is in Tera watt hour, the amount of saving is close to two trillion dollars, and the reduction in carbon dioxide is of the order of 10.68 Gigatons.[38]

Conclusion

In part II of this chapter, the historical development on the search for blue light leading to the invention of the blue LEDs based on gallium nitride (a III-V compound semiconductor in 1994) is outlined. The work of small

---

[38] 38RPI News and Events — Researchers lay out vision for lighting released on 18 December 2008.

groups of researchers in the universities on gallium nitride have paved the way to the development of the blue LEDs. This has since accelerated the pace of development in solid state lighting. It is expected that cost effective and efficient white LEDs will be used extensively in many lighting applications. However, since the light source from LEDs are directional, it may not be the most suitable for general lighting. Recently, Cree Inc. has announced the development of warm white light source from LEDs for general lighting applications, with correlated temperature from 2700 K to 3300 K as well as offering over 50 lumens per watt. Such types of advances would completely revolutionize the way we light our homes and workplaces in a truly sustainable manner in the not too distant future.

The principles behind the semiconductor LEDs are also discussed. This is primarily to highlight the role of science and technology behind the quest for sustainable economic development, the insight and contributions of scientists, engineers and technologists to enable sustainable lighting.

Continued investments in research and development in the science and engineering of materials, in designing manufacturing processes that combine the best of Moore's and Haitz's law will lead to low cost and affordable solid state lighting. These revolutionary lighting will bring enormous benefits to all mankind in terms of energy and cost saving, reduction in carbon dioxide, contribution to the stabilization of global warming and reduction in environmental damage. We can expect substantial reduction in mercury being used following the large scale transition to solid state lighting in the years ahead. This would also minimize environmental damage.

The lighting industries worldwide are also fully aware of the urgent need to provide truly cost effective sustainable and smart lighting. Universities are also setting up Smart Solid State Lighting Centers to undertake collaborative research to speed up the introduction of low cost solid state lamps and smart lighting systems for general lighting.

PART III. SUSTAINABLE DISPERSED COMBINED MICRO POWER AND HEAT GENERATION

In part III of this chapter on Minimization of Resource Drains and Environmental Damage, studies on sustainable dispersed micro power and heat generation are presented. In particular, combined micro power and heat generation from solid oxide fuel cells (SOFCs) will be discussed in more detail as this is presently in the advanced stages of development. Prototype systems are being assessed for durability, reliability, performance for domestic application to provide electrical power and heat at high efficiency. The potential of combining micro power generation with cost effective renewable energy sources are also areas of intensive research and development. The development of low cost and affordable systems for micro power and heat generation is an area of considerable research and development worldwide.

In this part III, the studies being conducted on combined dispersed micro power and heat generation are reviewed. The more promising technologies that are being advanced for dispersed power generation are briefly discussed. This is followed with a discussion on fuel cell technologies. In particular, the recent developments in SOFCs are discussed. More emphasis being given to SOFC as it has very good potential of contributing substantially to the sustainable development of cost effective dispersed micro power and heat generation for the homes, rural areas, remote locations such as off shores, commercial buildings, and other small enterprises without the need for inter grid connection. Currently, inter grid connection has still many unresolved technical and legal issues.

Fuel cell converts chemical energy directly into electrical power, with water as the end product. Among various types of fuel cells that have been developed, the proton electrolyte membrane (PEM) fuel cells and the SOFCs are likely to contribute to the development of a truly sustainable economy. PEM fuel cells are being developed for vehicles and the SOFCs for providing combined electrical power and heat in the home. SOFCs have considerable potential for dispersed micro power and heat generation thus making the development of a compact, low cost and reliable micro combined heat and power (MCHP) power supply that is environmental friendly. Moreover, the heat generated can be used for domestic and industrial water heating, thus providing combined heat and power (CHP). If the cost of installing SOFC can be reduced below US$400 per kW, then the economics become very promising and can compete seriously with grid power.

In this discussion, the focus is on dispersed micro power generation for the homes, small enterprises and remote locations. In particular, power generation in the kilowatt range without grid interconnection. Dispersed combined heat and power generation in the megawatt range are also being extensively evaluated for industries, schools, hospitals, and commercial buildings.

Introduction

This section on sustainable dispersed combined micro power and heat generation focuses on the development of fuel cell technology and discusses its implications on energy security, and its use for transport, industries, business and domestic use. In particular, the development of intermediate and low temperature solid oxide fuel cells (SOFCs) for dispersed micro power and heat generation for the homes will be reviewed.

Sir William Grove, a Welshman, jurist and physicist, demonstrated in 1839 at the Royal Institution, London, the production of electricity and water by combining oxygen and hydrogen. Grove used two inverted test tubes, each carrying a platinum electrode. The inverted tubes were placed in a bath of dilute sulfuric acid which acts as the electrolyte.

With an electric current, electrolysis of water gave hydrogen and oxygen, which were collected in the inverted test tubes. The electric current was switched off, the hydrogen was in contact with the platinum anode, and the oxygen in contact with the platinum cathode reacted with the hydrogen passing through the electrolyte to form water and generate a direct current. This type of battery was named by Grove as the gas battery.[1] It was also the first fuel cell conceived, where the fuels were outside the electrodes, and the electrolyte was sulfuric acid.

---

[1] Grove, W.R. (December 1842). On a gaseous voltaic battery, *Philosophical Magazine*, 21: 417–421.

In the 1930s, F.T. Bacon, FRS, a chemist in Southern England, looked systematically into the findings of Sir William Grove, FRS, namely, the direct conversion of chemical energy into electrical energy. Bacon worked on alkaline fuel cells with porous metal electrodes and alkaline based electrolytes. His work was continued after the war, and in the 1960s, the fuel cell based on Bacon's successful design[2] was first used as auxiliary power supply for the Apollo and Gemini spacecraft. The development was conducted under NASA Space Fuel Cells.

The concept of dispersed micro power generation has received less publicity compared with the campaign for energy efficient lamps such as the compact fluorescent lamps, and more recently solid state lighting. However, there is currently intense research and development for a low cost, reliable and efficient dispersed power and heat generation system for the home, business and industries. SOFCs benefit from the flexibility of fuels that can be used. This ranges from hydrogen to natural gas and thus well suited to take advantage of the dispersed power generation as the gas distribution network is well developed. Other advantages of SOFCs are high tolerance of sulfur in the fuel stream, no need for external reformer, no flooding of the electrolyte or electrodes, robust and reliable constructions. Use of the heat developed for domestic and industrial applications give efficiency of 80% or more. There is no NOx and SOx and reduced CO_2 output. Moreover, gas line already exists particularly in urban areas and can be directly connected to the SOFCs system. In remote communities where cylinders containing gases and liquids like LPG (liquid propane gas) can be delivered, the potential of using SOFCs as dispersed power generation is also very promising, particularly for schools, hospitals and community centers.

The research on the development of solid oxide electrolytes for intermediate temperature SOFCs conducted at the Nanyang Technological University, Singapore, in collaboration with Professor John Kilner in the Materials Department, Imperial College, London, will be reviewed. The research activities on the development of low cost compact, high efficiency, and low temperature SOFCs in the Physics

---

[2] Bacon, F.T. (21 May 1960). Fuel C: will they become soon a major source of electrical energy?, *Nature*, 186: 589–592.

Department, Faculty of Science, University of Brunei Darussalam will also be highlighted.

Rationale for combined dispersed power and heat generation

Just like the liberalization of the communication industry, the liberalization of the energy market has opened up possibilities of combined dispersed power and heat generation in homes, industries and remote areas without the need for the grid. Moreover, environmental concerns, energy security and supply mean that the concept of distributed or dispersed generation combined with heat generation has considerable potential for supporting a truly sustainable combined power generation and heating cost effectively and efficiently.

The power losses during distribution of power are also eliminated. Heat generated in stand alone systems can be used for domestic and/or industrial heating. Most of the dispersed power generation reported are primarily for business premises, industries, schools and hospitals, with power generation in 100 kW to 1 MW.[3,4] This review is more concerned with stand alone, low cost sustainable micro power generation in the homes, small enterprises, and remote locations ranging from less than a kW to a few tens of kW primarily without the need for grid interconnection. Grid interconnection raises numerous issues with utility companies, and many of these issues have yet to be resolved.[5]

Technologies being developed to support micro dispersed power generation

There are several technologies that can support dispersed power generation. The following technologies are being developed:

- advanced internal combustion engine with CHP,
- micro turbines,
- stirling engines,

---

[3] Kordesch, K. and Simader, G. (1991). *Fuel Cell and Its Applications*. VCH.
[4] Energy Center of Wisconsin (ECW) Report Number 193-2 on Review of the Art Fuel Cell Technologies for Distributed Generation.
[5] Thellen, L.L.P. Distributed power generation in the US — practical issues affecting project development, Construction Weblink.

- flywheels,
- renewables like photovoltaics, solar heating, wind, geothermal, and
- fuel cells.

Each of these technologies have their advantages and also disadvantages. However, fuel cells, in particular SOFCs, have considerable potential for sustainable micro dispersed power generation. This is due to the fact that the SOFC produces electricity at twice the efficiency of traditional generators. The SOFCs is not only robust and durable, it uses a wide range of fuels, including natural gas, propane, biofuels, LPG or hydrogen. It does not require an external reformer or a boost compressor. The power generation is clean with very low carbon emission. SOFC can be combined with solar and wind for hybrid power generation.

Similar SOFC technologies are also being developed for distributed power generation in the megawatt range with interconnection with the grid. In this case, the legal and technical issues need to be resolved between the utilities, suppliers of dispersed micro power, and the end users.

Application of solid oxide fuel cell for dispersed micro power generation

A comparison of various micro power generation systems in Table 1[6] shows that SOFC holds the greatest promise in terms of efficiency and other advantages.

Micro power from SOFCs can be used in:

- homes,
- farms,
- military bases,
- pig and poultry farms,
- dairy,
- saw mills,
- green houses, and
- cottage industries.

---

[6] Retrieved on 11 December 2008 from http://powergeneration.siemens.com/products-solution.services/products-packages/fuel-cells/benefits-features.

Table 1 Comparison of tubular solid oxide fuel cells with other fuel cells and other distributed options[6]

Comparison of Fuel Cells and Other Distributed Generation Options

The table compares tubular SOFC systems with other fuel cell systems and other distributed generation options of comparable size.

	PEM	PAFC	MCFC	SOFC	Micro-GT	Diesel Engine	Stirling Engine
Electrical efficiency using natural gas (net AC/LHV), %	35	40	45–50	45–50*	30	35	30
Performance degradation, %/1000 hrs	>1	0.44	0.60	<0.10	0.20	0.20	na
Emissions using natural gas: NOx, g/MWh	<20	<10	<10	<10	300	700	200
SOx, g/MWh	<0.1	<0.1	<0.1	<0.1	1	1	1
Noise, dBA @ 10 m	<60	60	65	65	65	80–90	60
Water consumption, gal/MWh	0	90	88	0	0	0	0
Total fuel efficiency using natural gas (net AC/LHV), %	35	65	70	80–85	~75	~78	~77

Data obtained from various published sources.
* Target for pressurized SOFC hybrids is 70%.

Dispersed micro power without grid interconnection

At present there are still a lot of legal and technical issues which need to be resolved between the utilities companies concerning interconnection with the grid. Interconnection between grid (utility companies), distributed power suppliers and end users have considerable differences that have yet to be resolved.

Similar technical and legal problems are likely to be encountered if excess power generated by micro power generation systems are to be exported to the grid. The practical issues affecting the development on distributed power generation was presented by Thellen Consultants and Lawyers at the International Bar Conference in 2004 in San Francisco.[5]

In the case of the dispersed micro power generation without the need for grid interconnection to accept excess power generated, particularly in the case of the homes and small enterprises ranging from a few kilowatt to hundreds of kilowatt, there will not be any legal and technical issues with utility companies.

Utility companies are unlikely to stop the trend towards dispersed power generation particularly as the cost comes down, and the end users become more aware of the reliability and environmental friendly way of generating electrical power and heat in the homes and own premises.

The concept of dispersed power generation whether on a micro scale as mentioned above or in the megawatt range associated with distributed generation for industries and commercial enterprises will become popular only by creating greater awareness of its potential benefits such as energy security, energy reliability, low carbon emission and hence it potential of stabilizing global warming. So there is an urgent need to engage the public at an early stage.

At present the best way forward is to engage the public in debate and create greater awareness of the importance of dispersed power generation in the media. To avoid the technical and legal issues of grid interconnection, the grid power can simply be used as top up. It is, moreover, not necessary to return excess power generated to the grid as this can be stored in batteries and used later. With the promise of electric cars soon to be launched on the market, there will be a need to use any excess power generated to charge the car batteries overnight at home or at work.

Moreover, universities and research organizations should continue with the development of ultra low cost dispersed power systems from fuel cells and other technologies. This will enable a highly competitive, cost effective and sustainable dispersed micro power generation to be established.

Already companies such as Acumentrics, Ceres Power, Fuel Cell Inc., Kyocera, Siemens, General Electric, Westinghouse and several others are poised to capture a large share of the sustainable multibillion dollar micropower generation business.

Review of Fuel Cell Technologies

Principle of fuel cell

Fuel cell basically converts chemical energy directly into electrical energy. It consists basically of an anode, a cathode and a solid oxide electrolyte. The thermodynamic efficiency defined as the ratio of the free energy change ΔG over change of enthalpy ΔH, i.e. $\Delta G/\Delta H$ can be as high as 95% at 200°C, decreases to about 75% at 1400°C and about 60% at 1500°C. The Carnot cycle efficiency is $(T_1-T_2)/T_1$, where the source temperature T_1 is much greater than sink T_2. In case of Carnot efficiency, the higher the operating temperature T_1 and lower the sink temperature T_2, the greater the efficiency (see Figs. 1 to 3).

Materials development

Materials development leading to the development of high temperature solid oxide fuel cells operating around 1000°C is reviewed. This is followed by a more detailed discussion on the materials development that led

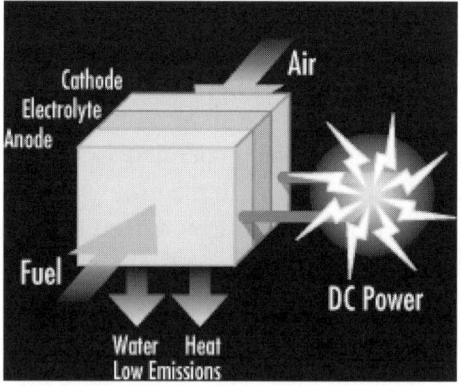

Fig. 1 Schematic of a fuel cell.
Source: Ceres Power Website — General Brochure.[7]

---

[7] Retrieved from http://www.csa.com/discoveryguides/fuecel/overview.php.

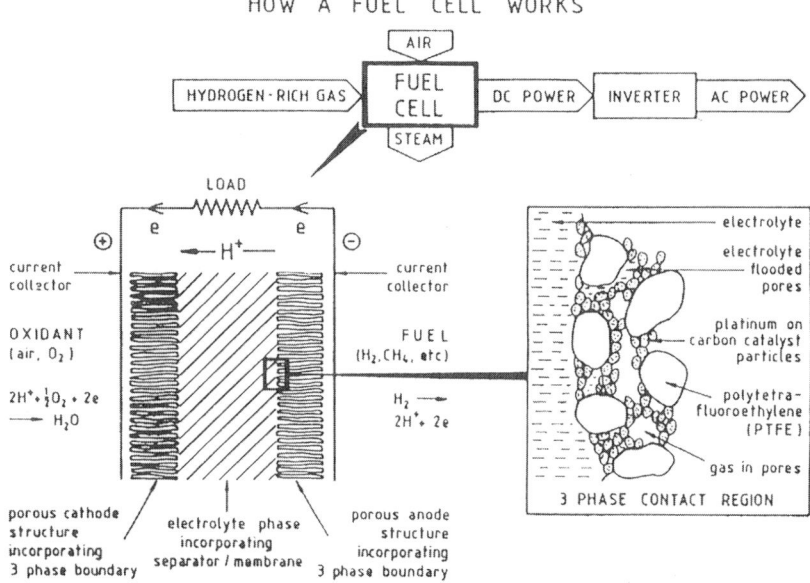

Fig. 2 Schematic showing how a fuel cell works and processes occurring at the anode and cathode of a H_2/O_2 fuel cell. Note enlarged view of the three-phase boundary (electrolyte, electrode and reacting gas).[8]

to the recent prototypes intermediate temperature solid oxide fuel cells (ITSOFCs). Several prototypes are being evaluated by the National Research Council, NRC, Canada, General Electric (USA), and a consortium led by SECA in the US. In particular, materials for solid oxide electrolytes, electrodes, interconnect and sealing materials will be presented and discussed in greater detail. This will be followed by materials development conducted by the authors. In particular, the processing, properties and microstructures of ceramics derived from cerium oxide and cerium oxide-gadolinium oxide with potential for use as intermediate solid oxide electrolytes are presented and discussed. In particular, the importance of minor additions on the sinterability, thermo-mechanical and

---

[8] Steele, B. (1991). *Electronic Ceramics, Electrical Ceramics for Fuel Cells and High Energy Batteries*.

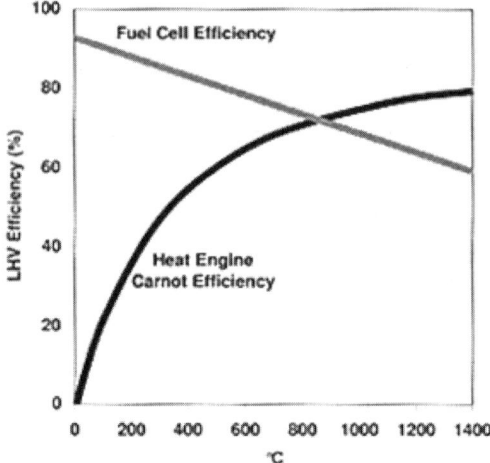

Fig. 3 The thermodynamic efficiency of a fuel cell versus the Carnot cycle efficiency at different temperatures. Note that the Carnot cycle efficiency increases as the temperature between source and sink increases. This is opposite to the thermodynamic efficiency in fuel cell which shows a decrease in efficiency with temperature.[9]

electrical conductivity of cerium oxide and cerium oxide-gadolinium oxide will be highlighted.

Thermodynamic Efficiency and EMF of Fuel Cells

The thermodynamic efficiency of an electrochemical converter such as in a fuel cell is given by the relation $\eta = \Delta G/\Delta H$ where ΔG is the Gibbs free energy and ΔH is the enthalpy of the reaction. The relation is derived from the Gibbs free energy relation $G = H - TS$, H enthalpy, S the entropy, and T the temperature in K. Thus, $\Delta G/\Delta H = 1 - T\Delta S/\Delta H$. In case of reactions where ΔS is 0, then $\Delta G/\Delta H = 1$. In most cases encountered in fuel cells, the chemical reactions is such that the term $T\Delta S/\Delta H$ is positive, thus giving thermodynamic efficiency less than one.

---

[9] Olaf, G.A., Goeppert, A. and Prakash, G.K.S. (2006). *Beyond Oil and Gas, the Methanol Economy*. Wiley.

Kiukkola and Wagner[10] obtained a relation between the electrochemical potential E for an ionic conductor sandwiched between two electrodes given by

$$E = \frac{1}{ZF} \int_{\mu_2}^{\mu_1} t_1$$

where Z is the absolute value of the valency of the mobile ions in the electrolyte, F is the Faraday constant, μ_1 and μ_2 are the chemical potentials of the electrodes, t_1 is the transference number; and t_1 is the ratio of the electrical conductivity of the ion and the total electrical conductivity of the ion and the electronic conductivity. Moreover, there is a relation between the free energy change in a cell reaction and the cell potential which are given in standard inorganic chemistry textbooks.[11,12] It can be shown that the change in the free energy ΔG is given by $\Delta G = -nFE$, where E is the electromotive force of the cell, n is the number of electrons transferred, and F is the Faraday constant. The emf E is given by $E_P = E_{P_o} - (\Delta nRT/nF) \ln P/P_o$, where E_P and E_{P_o} are the cell potentials at total pressures and P_o at standard pressure. E_P can be written as $E_P = E_{P_o} - 1/nF \int_{P_o}^{P} \Delta V dp$, where ΔV is the volume change of the reaction. For reactions involving liquids and solids, the volume change is small, the effect of pressure is small. For reactions involving gases as in the case of the fuel cells, the volume change is large, and pressure effect must be taken into account. For a pressure change of one to ten atmospheres in a H_2–O_2 fuel cell, the cell potential changes by 45 mV. The open circuit voltage based on Nernst's equation for the H_2–O_2 fuel cell can be written as[13]

$$E_P = E_{P_o} + \frac{RT}{2F} \ln \frac{P_{H_2} P_{O_2}}{P_{H_2O}}.$$

---

[10] Kiukkola, K. and Wagner, C. (1957). *J. Electrochem*, 104: 308; also in 104: 379.
[11] Glastone, S. and Lewis, D. (1968). *Elements of Inorganic Chemistry*. MacMillan.
[12] Abrash, H.I. and Hardcastle, K.I. (1961). *Chemistry*. Glencoe Publishing Co., Inc.
[13] Yahiro, H., Eguchi, Y., Eguchi, K. and Arai, H. (1988). *J. App. Electrochem*. 18: 527–531.

The operating voltage of a fuel cell E can be written as

$$E = Eo - [IR_i + \eta_c + \eta_a]$$

where I is the current, R_i the internal resistance of the electrolyte and other cell components, and η_c and η_a are the polarization losses at the cathode and anode. Polarization losses are due to slow electrochemical reactions rates, and also due to slow diffusion of fuel at the interfaces of the anode and oxidant at the electrolytes. However, precise mechanisms involved are not well understood and will be addressed in the research being proposed at the University of Brunei Energy Program (see Figs. 4 and 5).

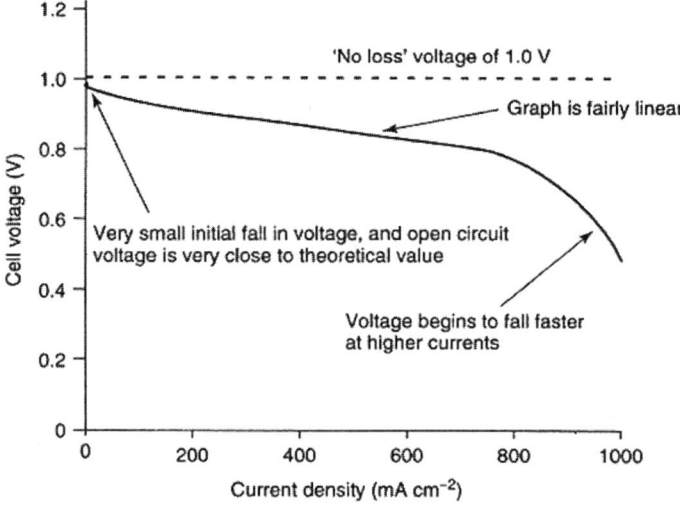

Fig. 4 Irreversible losses occurring in a fuel. Retrieved from http://www.mc-wap.cetena.it/public/athens/1_MC-WAP_CAF-Oct2007.pdf.[14]

---

[14] Retrieved from http://www.mc-wap.cetena.it/public/athens/1_MC-WAP_CAF-Oct2007.pdf.

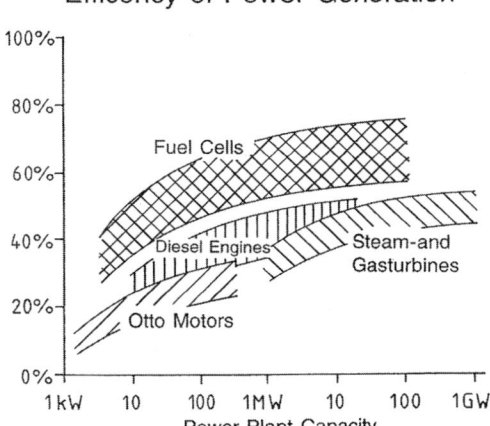

Fig. 5 Efficiency of various types of power generating systems versus fuel cell.[3]

Types of Fuel Cells

There are several broad types of fuel cells. One type uses liquid electrolytes and the other solid based electrolytes. Among the liquid electrolyte fuel cells are alkaline fuel cell (AFC), phosphoric acid fuel cell (PAFC) and molten carbonate fuel cell (MCFC). Those using solid electrolytes are polymer electrolyte membrane fuel cell (PEMFC), solid oxide fuel cell (SOFC) and direct methanol fuel cell (DMFC). Each type of fuel cell has its advantages and disadvantages. A review of the whole range of fuel cell systems would need a fair amount of discussion to do justice to the milestones achieved in fuel cell technology to date.[3,7,11,13,15–19]

A large number of fuel cell projects, however, have also been abandoned or shelved due to high cost of installation and power generated,

---

[15] Retrieved from NFCRC Activities — Research Studies — Research Archives — Siemens Westinghouse 25 kW Tubular Solid Oxide Fuel Cell.htm.
[16] Retrieved from Ceres Power website (2008) — General Brochure.
[17] Retrieved from NRC, Canada website on Solid Oxide Fuel Cell SOFC600C.
[18] Retrieved from GE Eco Technology website.
[19] Minh, N.Q. (1993). Ceramic fuel cells, *Journal of the American Ceramic Society*, 76: 563–588.

insufficient reliability and poor prospects of commercialization in the short term. Presently there are intense interests in commercializing PEMFC for transport, SOFCs for modular power generation for domestic and other applications, and DMFCs for portable power pack for laptop and hand held devices.

The direct conversion of chemical into electrical energy has since attracted intense studies. This is particularly the case in the last two decades following the realization of depleting fossil fuel, issues of energy security, the increasing cost of recovering fossil fuel, the increasing price of oil, increasing carbon emissions to the atmosphere and its impact on global warming and climate change. Over the years, various types of fuel cells, besides SOFCs using different electrolytes and electrodes have been developed. These include:

- proton membrane (PEM) fuel cell,
- alkaline fuel cell (AFC),
- molten carbonate fuel cell (MCFC),
- phosphoric acid fuel cell (PAFC),
- methanol fuel cell (MFC), and
- ethanol fuel cell (EthFC)

For more information on these different types of fuel cells, references[3,7,9,11,13,15–22] are highly recommended.

However, it is instructive to discuss briefly some advances made in the various types of fuel cells. This will give a more balanced account of the range of fuel cells available, the advantages and disadvantages of each type of fuel cells.

PEM fuel cells are being considered as more suitable for transportation. SOFC is more suited for dispersed micro power generation in the 2–10 kW range for domestic applications. For large commercial buildings, hospitals, schools, 100 kW to several MW rated SOFC fuel cells are being evaluated.

---

[20] Zhang, T., Hing, P., Huang, H. and Kilner, J. (2001). Effect of F_2O_3 doping on the shrinkage of Ceria, *Journal of Materials Processing Technology*, 113: 463–468.

[21] Zhang, T. (2003). Ph.D. Thesis, School of Materials Science and Engineering, Advanced Materials Research Centre, Nanyang Technological University, Singapore.

[22] Zhang, T., Hing, P., Huang H. and Kilner, J. (2002). *Mater. Sci. Lett.*, 21: 1167–1169.

PEM fuel cells

PEM was considered for the space shuttle, but the performance was inferior to AFC which has efficiency approaching 70%, and could provide clean water for drinking as well as electrical power. However, with improvement in the polymer electrolyte, PEM fuel cell has become very fashionable again. Today, the PEM fuel cell is being developed commercially for vehicle applications. A typical PEM fuel cell is shown in Fig. 6.

The basic principle is the hydrogen entering the anode is split into protons and the electrons by a platinum based catalyst. The protons moved through the solid polymer membrane to the cathode. At the cathode, the oxygen combines with the electrons and the protons forming water with the aid of platinum catalyst. The reactions occurring at the anode, cathode and the overall redox reactions occurring in the PEM fuel cell are shown in the insert of Fig. 6.

Car manufacturers like Honda, Toyota, Renault, Volkswagen, Daimler–Chrysler are currently conducting extensive tests on a fleet of

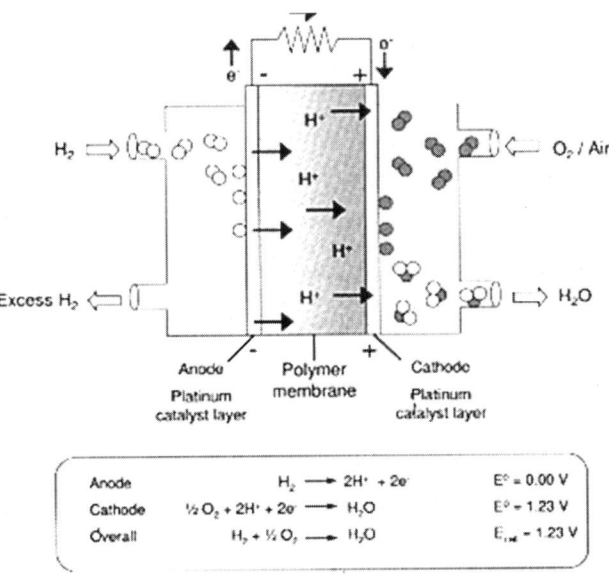

Fig. 6 Typical PEM fuel cell.[9]

cars in normal everyday running conditions to evaluate the long term performance of all FCV vehicles.

The major problems at the moment with fuel cell cars is the lack of space needed to store hydrogen, high cost, need for technical breakthroughs in solid hydrogen storage, improvement in safety, and the infrastructure to supply hydrogen for the fuel cell vehicles.

Advances are being made in improving the performance of PEM solid polymer membrane such as Nafion from Dupont de Nemours first introduced in the 1960s. The early solid polymer electrolyte for the US Gemini Space Program included hydrocarbon–type polymers such as cross-linked polystyrene-divinylbenzene sulfonic acids and sulfhonated phenol formaldehyde. The major problem was the instability caused by the C–H bond cleavage at the alpha-sites where the functional groups are attached. However, when these polymers were substituted with the fluorine, for example by polyfluorostyrene sulfhonic acid, the life of the membrane increased by a factor of five.

The Nafion family of solid electrolyte polymer has since been much improved and used up to now. Moreover, extensive research and development on solid polymer electrolyte materials are being conducted by Asahi, Dow, Ballard and other companies for PEM fuel cells. Currently, research is being carried out to develop solid polymer electrolytes that can be operated at higher temperature, preferably exceeding 200°C to mininize the water management problem. For example, the steam formed can be used for heating and hydrogen generation instead of flooding the electrodes.

Alkaline fuel cell

The alkaline fuel cell was first introduced by F. Bacon and subsequently used in the Gemini and Apollo Space Program as mentioned in the Introduction. In the AFC, instead of the protons moving through the electrolytes, the hydroxide OH^- ions move from the cathode to the anode. Pure hydrogen is used as the fuel injected on the anode side. The reaction occurring at the electrodes is summarized in the insert of Fig. 7. A dynamic AFC with circulating liquid electrolyte is shown in Fig. 8.[3] The fuel cell with circulating electrolytes has advantages over the static AFC as the circulating electrolytes can act as an effective barrier to reactant gas leakage. Moreover, it can remove accumulated impurities and carbonates.

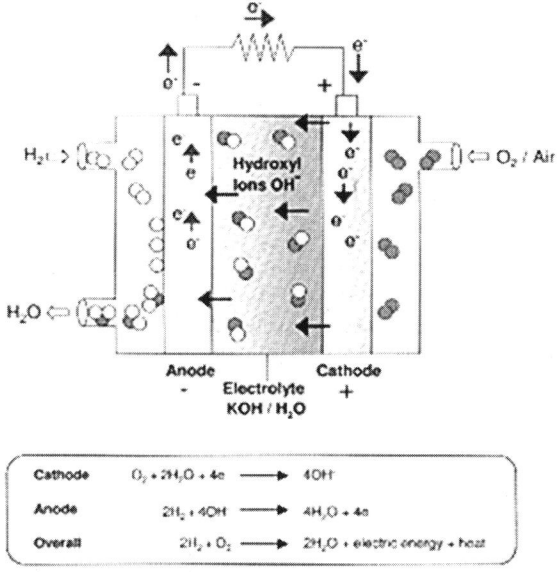

Fig. 7 A static alkaline fuel cell using potassium hydroxide as electrolytes.[9]

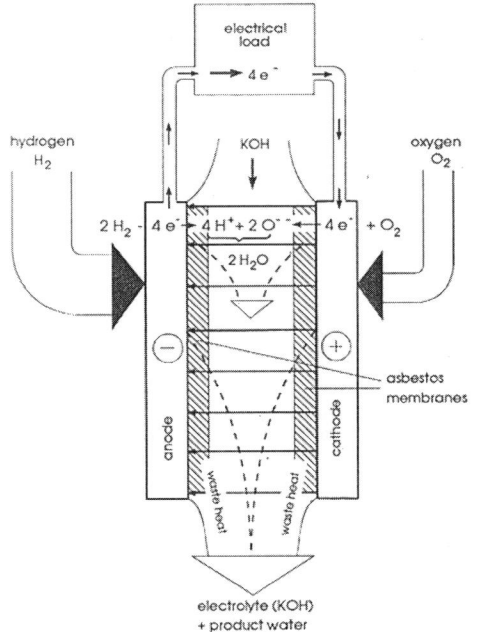

Fig. 8 A dynamic alkaline fuel cell with circulating potassium hydroxide electrolytes.[3]

The main advantage of circulating electrolytes is that it can be used as a cooling liquid and as a method of removing the water formed. The disadvantages of circulating liquid electrolyte is that it develops parasitic currents through the ionically conducting liquid electrolyte junctions of the series connected cells and parallel electrolyte flow. This parasitic current must be minimized.

The scientific community today is focusing more on PEMFC, MCFC and SOFC. The AFC for military and space applications are not constrained by cost, whereas for consumer and industrial applications cost is a major issue. There is now some development using low cost porous carbon electrodes.

Molten carbonate fuel cell (MCFC)

The molten carbonate fuel cell makes use of lithium potassium carbonates as the electrolyte. This is heated up to about 650°C. A typical setup for the MCFC is shown in Fig. 9. At the anode, the hydrogen reacts with the CO_3^- ions giving water, carbon dioxide and electrons. The reaction is shown in the insert of Fig. 9. The oxidant is oxygen or air. It can be seen in Fig. 9

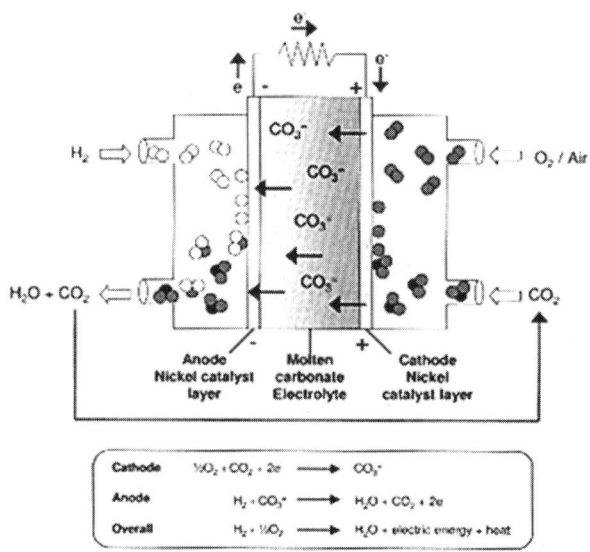

Fig. 9 A typical setup of a molten carbonate MCFC kept at 650°C.[9]

that the carbon dioxide is recycled and returned to the cathode, making it a low carbon emission energy conversion device.

The fuel is mainly hydrogen. However, because of the high temperature operation, any hydrocarbon such as natural gas can be internally converted to hydrogen. Moreover, methanol and ethanol can also be converted to hydrogen internally. Without reformer, efficiency of MCFC can reach up to 50%. The higher operating temperature enables porous nickel to be used as catalysts instead of expensive platinium/gold electrodes.

However, molten carbonates are highly corrosive, and long term reliability is still being evaluated. Fuel Cell Energy Inc. in collaboration with the US Department of Energy (DOE) are currently evaluating a hybrid system consisting of MCFC and a gas turbine power plant for power generation. The aim is to develop efficient energy generation hybrid system with efficiency as high as 75%.

Phosphoric acid fuel cell (PAFC)

This is another example of liquid electrolyte used in the fuel cell. Because of its bulky nature, it is used for stationary power generation. The electrolyte is kept at about 200°C and pure hydrogen is used as fuel pumped at the anode. A typical setup for the PAFC is shown in Fig. 10.

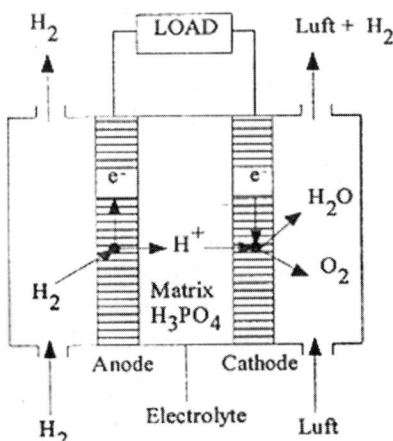

Fig. 10 Setup for a typical PAFC using phosphoric acid as liquid electrolyte.[3]

The hydrogen splits into protons H⁺ and electrons, which travel to the cathode. The protons move from the anode to the cathode where they react with the oxygen ions to form water. Excess oxygen, with water and hydrogen generated are removed.

PAFC, together with MCFC, SOFC and PEM, is presently one of the most studied fuel cells. PAFC is available from United Technologies Corp. The electrodes are made up of carbon coated with dispersed platinum catalyst. Hydrogen is obtained by reforming methane, with efficiency of 37% to 40%. With combined generation of power and heat, efficiency as high as 88% is achievable. The cost of generating 1 kW from PAFC is around US$4500 compared with a few hundred dollars per kilowatt from the grid. Despite the high cost, PAFC has a niche market, for example banks, hospitals, airports, military bases, etc. where very stable, clean, reliable energy sources are required.

Direct methanol fuel cell (DMFC)

The DMFC is now being developed as a micro fuel cell capable of replacing rechargeable battery. Soon we may be able to purchase DMFCs capable of supporting the laptop for over ten hours of continuous use. Several major companies have invested heavily in the development of a portable power pack to replace existing rechargeable batteries used in laptop computers. A typical DMFC is depicted in Fig. 11. The major problem is methanol flooding of the PEM membrane and poisoning of the catalysts. There is a need for research and development for polymer membranes capable of operating around 200°C to 300°C.

Solid oxide fuel cell (SOFC)

The first high temperature solid oxide fuel cell (HTSOFC) using yttria stabilized zirconia ($Y_2O_3.ZrO_2$) as the solid electrolyte operating around 1000°C was first developed by Westinghouse in 1962.[23] Several designs of tubular SOFCs have been tested, and one design has been operating for

---

[23] Chandra, S. (1981). *Superionic Solids*. Varanasi (UP) India.

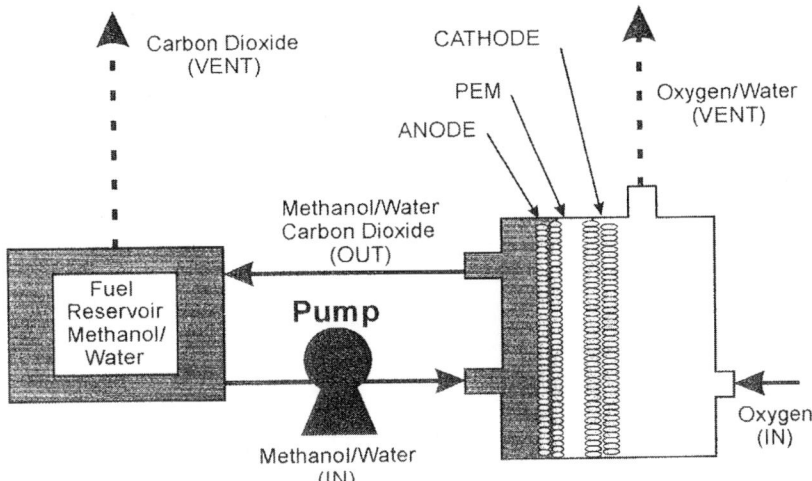

Fig. 11 A typical setup for a direct methanol fuel cell (DMFC).[3]

eight years in the Netherlands. Stationary SOFCs based on the yttria stabilized zirconia is now a reality.

With energy security issues in the forefront, the SOFC technology for power generation in the 100 to 250 MW range can be expected. Already Canada is evaluating a 200 MW SOFC supplied by Westinghouse.

The main features such as oxidant, fuel and operating temperatures of five types of fuel cells are summarized in Fig. 12. Note that for SOFCs, the solid oxide membrane must be very good oxygen ion conductors. The efficiency of fuel cells for power generation is higher than any other type of power plants as summarized in Fig. 13.[8]

Design of Solid Oxide Fuel Cells

Although there are four or five main designs of the SOFC, the planar and tubular designs are the two most commonly mentioned as shown in Figs. 14 and 15. The design of the SOFC is also strongly influenced by the performance of a single cell at the operating temperature. For instance under load, typical performance of a planar design is 0.7 V at current density of 150 mA/cm^2 (0.15 A /cm^2). Therefore for a 1000 W (1 kW) SOFC,

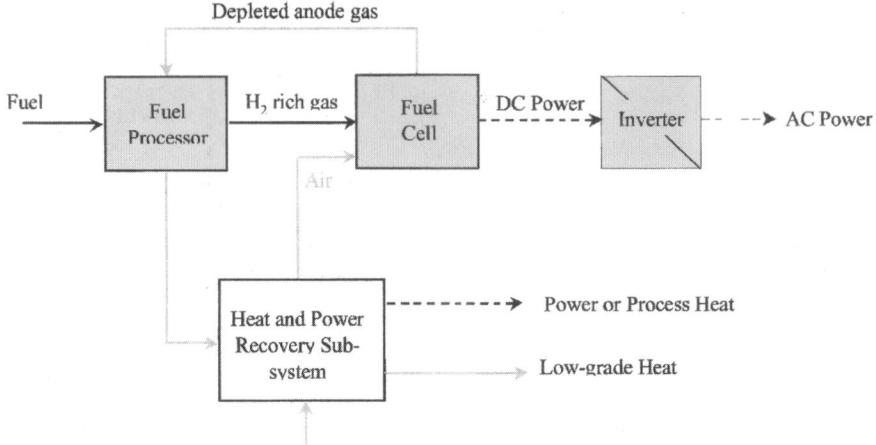

Fig. 12 A generic fuel cell system from Biomen and Mugewa (1993).[4,24]

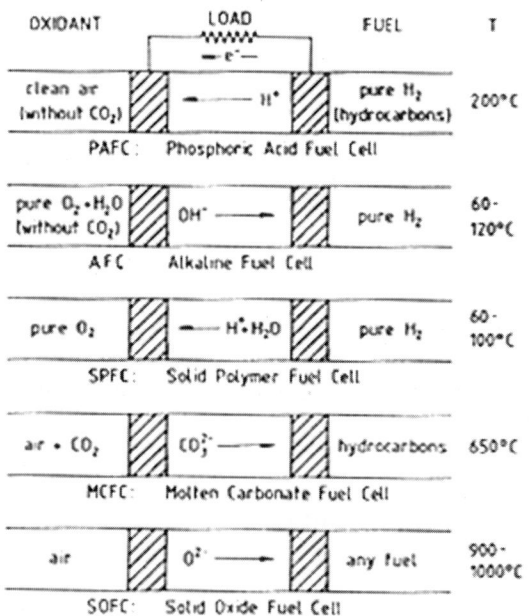

Fig. 13 The main features of five major types of fuel cells being developed.[8]

---

[24] Wereszazak, A., Laracuirzio, E. and Bansal, N.P. (eds.) (2006). *Advances in Solid Oxide Fuel Cells, Ceramic Engineering and Science Proceedings, Cocoa Beach*, Vol 27, No. 4. Wiley Interscience.

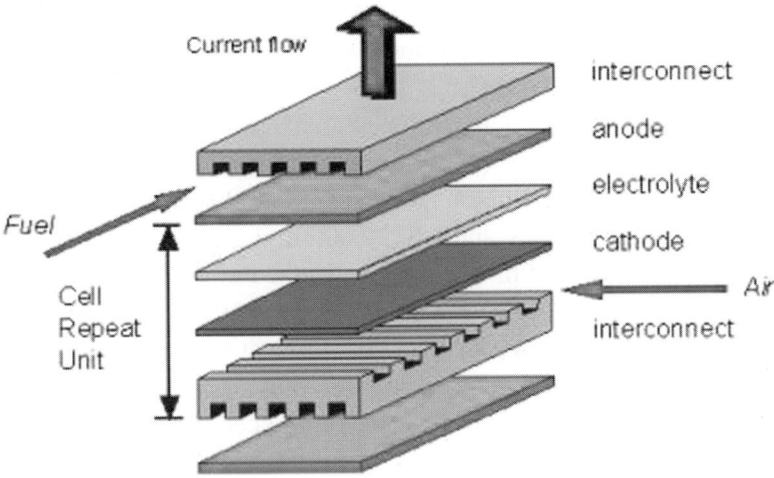

Fig. 14 Design of planar solid oxide fuel cells. Note the range of functional ceramics used (cermets, solid oxide electrolytes, ceramic cathode, interconnects, sealing materials for hermeticity) to prevent gases from leaking out the solid oxide fuel cells.[7]

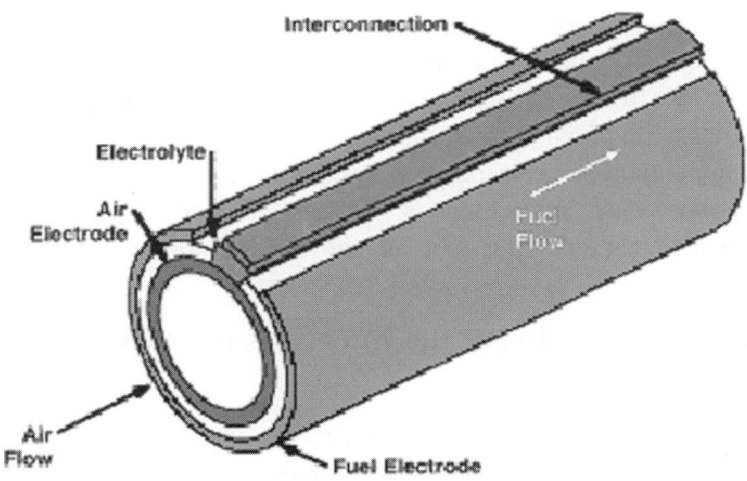

Fig. 15 Westinghouse tubular design. Note that the planar and tubular designs of solid oxide fuel cells (two of the most popular designs of solid oxide fuel cells). (Retrieved from NFCRC Activities — Research Studies — Research Archives — Siemens Westinghouse 25 kW Tubular Solid Oxide Fuel Cell.htm.)[15]

we will need a cell of one meter square. A more practical way is to have a cell of 10×10 cm or 100 cm^2, thus 100 cells will give us 10,000 cm^2 or 1 m^2 will give us 1 kW SOFC.

A typical home in the UK will need an average of about 6 kW power supply, whereas in the US a 10 kW unit will be required. If the cost of the power unit including installation is around US$2000 per kilowatt, one will need US$12,000 in the UK and US$20,000 in the US.

Current cost of 1 kW hr of power consumed in the US is 30 cents; in some places like California around 32 cents. If the average household consumes 5 kW $\times$ 365 days $\times$ 6, the cost of electricity per month will be 10,950.00 kWh $\times$ $0.30/kW = $3285 per year or $275 per month, and likely to continue to increase if the price of oil keeps rising. At the time of completing this manuscript the price of oil has decreased from a high of US$147 per barrel to below US$50 per barrel due to the economic downturn and financial credit crunch. As the economy picks up, more likely the price of oil will go up again as demand exceeds supply. Of greater concern is the continued dependence on fossil fuels, carbon emission, global warming, extreme consequences of climate change particularly on less developed economies, and threats to biodiversity.

It would take about six years to get to the return on investment, which is acceptable if one considers contribution to the environment. If the SOFC has a life of ten years or more, it will be beneficial to install such a stand alone micropower generating system in the home. The capital outlay for an average family home is still high, and currently there is as yet no guarantee that the SOFC will last ten years or more.

Reactions Occurring at the Interfaces of the Anode, Cathode and Electrolyte

The SOFC can operate in various modes. For instance it can operate as a chemical reactor producing oxygen or hydrogen and other feedstocks.

It is of interest to note that the reactor produces oxygen at electrode 2 from air (oxygen and nitrogen) from electrode 1 as shown in Table 2.[8] Thus the ceramic electrolyte membrane acts as an oxygen separator. In the last reaction, the reactor produces hydrogen (H_2) in electrode 1 from ethane

Table 2 Reactions occurring at electrodes in a ceramic electrochemical reactor

Electrode 1	Electrolyte	Electrode 2
$1/2O + 2e \rightarrow O^{2-}$	O^{2-}	$O^{2-} + H_2 \rightarrow H_2O + 2e$
$O^2 \rightarrow 1/2O_2 + 2e$	O^{2-}	$H_2O + 2e \rightarrow H_2 + O^{2-}$
$1/2O_2 + 2e \rightarrow O^{2-}$	O^{2-}	$O^{2-} + 1/4CH_4 \rightarrow 1/4CO_2 + H_2O + 2e$
$1/2O_2 + 2e \rightarrow O^{2-}$	O^{2-}	$O^{2-} + 2CH_4 \rightarrow C_2H_6 + 1/2H_2O + 2e$
$1/2O_2(N_2) + 2e \rightarrow O^{2-}$	O^{2-}	$O^{2-} \rightarrow 1/2O_2 + 2e$
$H^+ + e \rightarrow 1/2H_2$	H^+	$1/2C_2H_6 + 1/2C_2H_4 + H^+ + e$

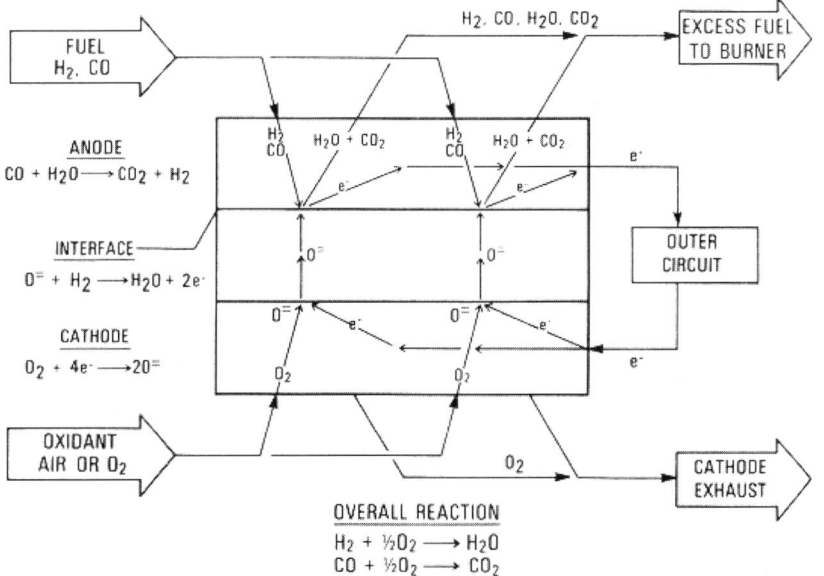

Fig. 16 Chemical reactions occurring at the anode and cathode in the solid oxide fuel cell.[19] Similar diagram is also discussed in another type of fuel cell such as the phosphoric acid fuel cell (PAFC).[14]

(C_2H_6) in electrode 2. In this case, the reactor is acting as an internal reformer (no need for a separate reformer) producing hydrogen in electrode 1 and ethylene as feedstock from ethane.[8] Chemical reactions occurring at the interfaces is depicted in Fig. 16.

Current Development of Intermediate Temperature Solid Oxide Fuel Cells (ITSOFCs)

Intensive development in a decade or so has enabled prototype intermediate temperature solid oxide fuel cells (ITSOFCs) operating around 600°C to be developed as illustrated in some of the prototypes (Figs. 17–19). Organizations like the National Research Council (NRC) of Canada, Ceres Power in the UK, General Electric (GE) in the US, Kyocera in Japan, Acumentrics in the US/Canada, Ceramic Fuel Ltd. in Australia, ECN, and Fuel Cell Inc., have produced prototype ITSOFCs which are being evaluated for long term durability, performance and reliability.

Current Status of Research in Solid Oxide Fuel Cells Worldwide

The Department of Energy (DOE) in the US has recently initiated a ten year R&D program involving several leading universities and with

Fig. 17 Latest development of intermediate temperature solid oxide fuel cell with $Gd_2O_3.CeO_2$ electrolyte by Ceres Power. The unit is being developed for long term performance and durability as dispersed power supply for home.
Source: Ceres Power Website.[16]

Fig. 18 Latest development in intermediate temperature solid oxide fuel cell 600°C by NRC, Canada, under Framework 6 with EU. The unit is being evaluated for long term durability and performance until 2010.

Source: NRC website.[17]

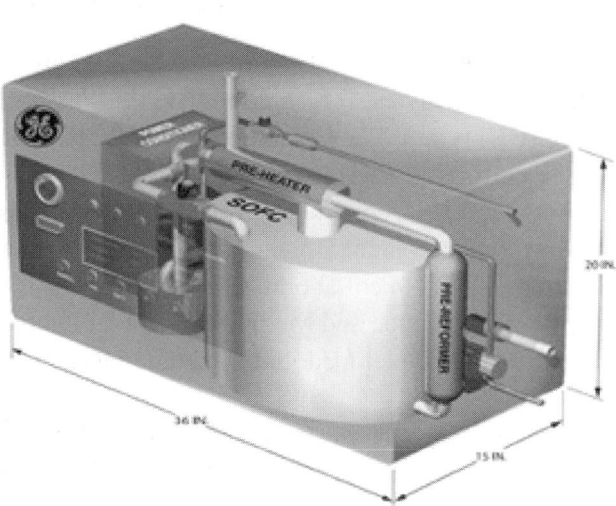

Fig. 19 GE latest 6 kW solid oxide fuel cell being evaluated at the DOE (USA) for long durability.

Source: GE Eco Technology and DOE websites.[18]

Solid State Energy Conversion Alliance (SECA), a consortium of several leading companies in the field of SOFCs. SECA is to conduct research and development to enable low cost, high efficiency and durable SOFCs to be produced. A manufacturing cost of US$400 per kilowatt or lower is among the main objectives of current research initiative on SOFCs. This cost must be competitive with grid power.

In Japan, Kyocera is developing advanced low cost SOFC for stand alone applications and targeting domestic applications. A similar research trend is taking place in Europe. There is an increasing trend to link SOFCs with development of clean coal technology. SOFCs using liquid based fuels such as methanol, ethanol, diesels, LPG, etc. are being developed.

There is also increasing emphasis to model processes occurring at the electrodes and the solid electrolyte interfaces and to understand the relationship between the microstructures and the interfacial polarization resistances. Worldwide there is also an increasing trend to reduce the operating temperatures from 1000° to 600°C and below.

Research Carried Out by the Author and His Group

In the following sections, the research carried out on the development of low cost ceramic electrolytes for intermediate SOFC are described. Imperial College, UK, is well known in the field of SOFCs. The research on solid oxide electrolytes for intermediate SOFCs, in the Materials Science and Engineering Department, Advanced Materials Research Centre at Nanyang Technological University Temperature Fuel Cell, was initiated by P. Hing in 2000 in collaboration with Professor J. Kilner from the Imperial College of Science and Medicine. Some of the results on sinterability, microstructures developed and ionic conductivity are depicted in Figs. 20–24.

The result in Fig. 24 on grain boundary conductivity represents an extensive amount of investigations and analysis on ceramic materials processing, and materials characterization using impedance spectroscopy.[18] The microstructures developed in the Ceria doped samples are shown in Figs. 22 and 24.

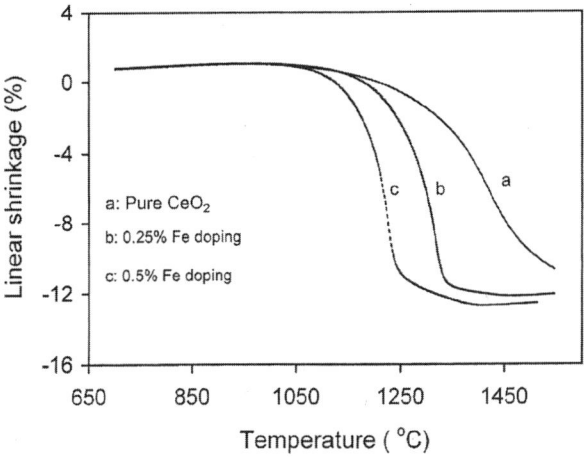

Fig. 20 Effect of F_2O_3 doping on the shrinkage of Ceria.[20]

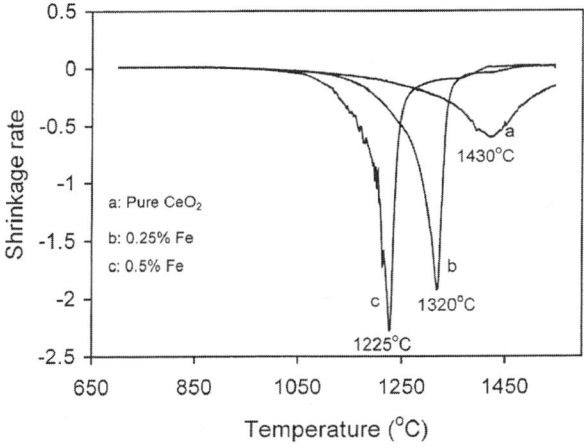

Fig. 21 Sintering rate of iron doped ceria at different temperatures.[20]

Discussion

The high temperature solid oxide fuel cell is a proven technology capable of generating power up to megawatt either as a stand alone power plant, or combine with turbine power generation to further increase the efficiency of the power generation in the combined heat and power (CHP)

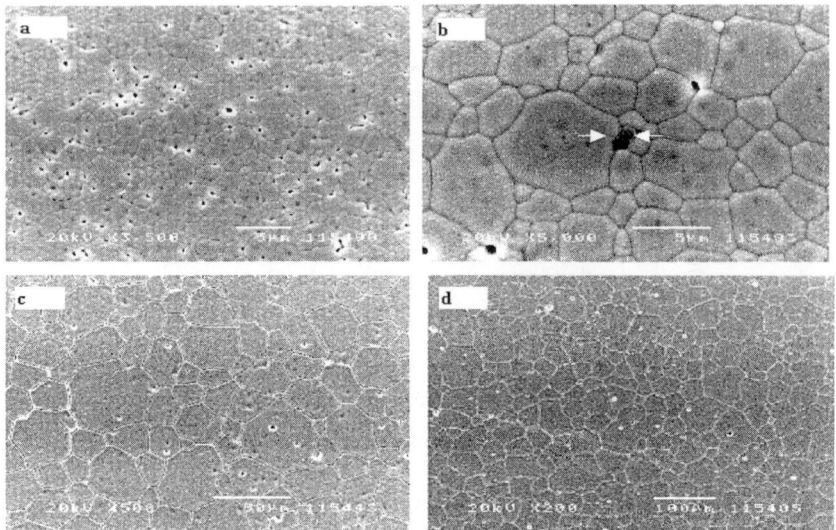

Fig. 22 Microstructures of Ceria doped with 0.5% Fe in the form of ferric oxide and sintered for one hour in air at (**a**) 1200°C, (**b**) 1300°C, (**c**) 1500°C, and (**d**) 1600°C.[21]

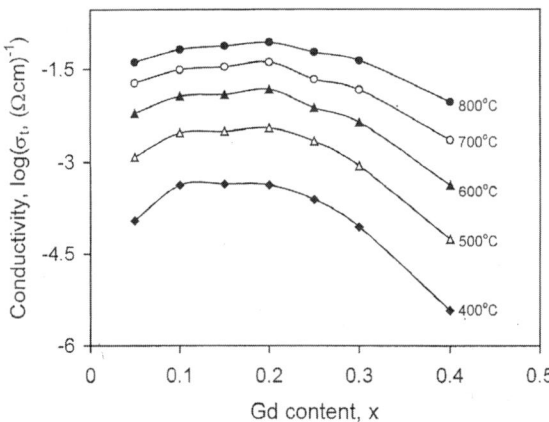

Fig. 23 Dependence of grain boundary conductivity σ_{gb} for $Ce_xGd_xO_{2-\delta}$ on Gd content at different temperatures.[22]

process. As the high temperature solid fuel cell operates in the region of 900°C to 1000°C, a range of fuels can be used without the need to reform the gases to hydrogen. The fuel flexibility is a major advantage of the high temperature SOFCs.

Sustainable Dispersed Combined Micro Power and Heat Generation 231

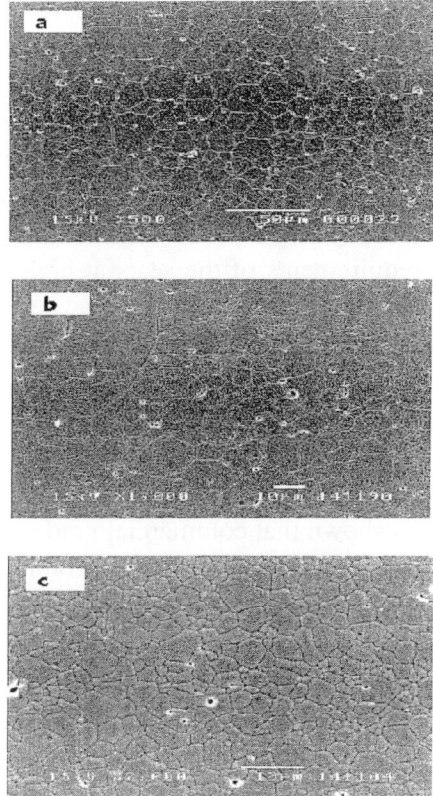

Fig. 24 Effect of Gd content on microstructures of $Ce_{1-x}Gd_xO_{2-\delta}$ sintered at 1600°C for five hours in air.[21]

For application in the home, the power requirements for a stand alone unit is around the 6 to 10 kW range. Using high temperature SOFCs may not be viable, because of the high installation and maintenance cost. The justifications for developing SOFCs operating at temperatures lower than 600°C is that the thermodynamic efficiency increases at lower temperatures. This is in sharp contrast with the energy system based on the Carnot cycle where its efficiency is $1-T_2/T_1$, with T_1 as the operating temperature (source) and T_2 the sink temperature. Moreover, it is well known that material components and devices operating at elevated temperatures degrade much more rapidly and thus reduces the life of the components, and increase maintenance cost.

This is because the speed of chemical reaction increases exponentially with temperatures. Low operating temperatures, moreover, prevent the sintering of the porous electrodes, thus altering the performance of the fuel cells. High temperature oxidation materials are needed as interconnects for high temperature SOFCs. The need to use expensive nickel based alloys in the aerospace industries increases substantially the cost of the SOFCs. Special sealing materials are also needed in the stack design of the SOFCs. The requirements of the seals at high operating temperatures become more stringent.

The development of intermediate temperature solid oxide fuel cells (ITSOFCs) operating around 600°C or lower has better potential for commercialization because of lower installation and maintenance cost and greater durability. To date, the US, Canada, EU, Japan, China, Korea, Taiwan are testing several prototype ITSOFCs.

In this review, it is shown that commercial grade cerium oxide can be sintered close to theoretical density using transition metals. The sintering of some ceramic compositions in the cerium oxide–gadolinium oxide close to the theoretical density will also be presented and discussed. The dense materials also have high ionic conductivity around 500°C–600°C indicating potential of using the GCO ceramics as solid electrolytes for ITSOFCs. Several companies like Ceres Power (UK), NRC (Canada) and GE (USA) have incorporated these oxygen ion conductors as solid oxide electrolytes for their prototype ITSOFC 600°C.[7,15,16] The cost per kilowatt is of the order of US$3000–4000, and thus falls outside the requirements of the DOE.

For dispersed power unit capable of meeting the domestic requirements in an average house in Europe and the US, a stand alone unit of 5–10 kW would be ideal. Substantial saving can be achieved using ITSOFC to generate power and heat in the home if the cost of installation per kilowatt can be reduced to about US$400 per kilowatt or lower and the unit can last for ten years, and the maintenance cost minimized.

Note the cost of using 1 kW hr of electricity in the US is now 30 cents and in the UK around 9 pence per kilowatt. The SOFC power generating unit and accessories must last a minimum of five years, preferably ten years. Thus, the stand alone power unit still requires extensive evaluation for performance, reliability and durability. There are justifications to continue intensive research in solid oxide fuel cells mainly to:

1. drastically reduce the cost of constructing both the high and intermediate temperature solid oxide fuel cells for the homes, individual buildings, commercial establishments, hospitals, schools, etc.;
2. reducing the operating temperatures further preferably below 600°C without affecting the efficiency;
3. improving the reliability and durability;
4. reducing the maintenance cost;
5. improving the ease of replacing worn parts;
6. reducing drastically the cost of manufacturing materials components for solid oxide fuel cells; and
7. developing novel and more cost effective materials for electrodes, electrolytes separators, etc.

Key to achieving the above objectives is mounting a comprehensive program on the science and engineering of the critical materials used for the construction of the next generation of solid oxide fuel cells. The need for a more focused investment in research and development also applies to other types of fuel cells for portable devices and transport. The literature on solid oxide fuel cells is extensive.[3,4,19–22,25–30] This will further assist

---

[25] Biomen, L. and Mugerwa, M.N. (eds.) (1993). *Fuel Cell Systems*. New York: Plenum Press.

[26] Singhal, S.C. and Kendall, K. (2004). *High Temperature Solid Oxide Fuel Cells: Fundamentals, Design, and Applications*. Elsevier.

[27] Bove, R. and Ubertini, S. (June 2008). *Modeling of Solid Oxide Fuel Cells: Methods, Procedures and Techniques. Fuel Cells and Hydrogen Energy*. Springer.

[28] *Progress in Solid Oxide Fuel Cells*, American Ceramic Society (ACERS), July 2006.

[29] O'Hayre, R., Collella, W., Cha, S.W. and Prinz, F.B. (2009). *Fuel Cell Fundamentals* 2nd Edn. Wiley Interscience.

[30] Hing, P., Zhang, T. and Kilner, J. (2008). Development of intermediate temperature solid oxide fuel cells in CD format, in the Proceedings of the First International Conference organized by the Institute of Engineering and Technology in Brunei Darussalam, 26–28 May 2008 on *Sustainable Energy Management in an Era of Information Technology and Communication Technology*.

researchers in the field to develop novel materials, processes and systems leading to low cost, compact, long life, high efficiency, high reliability, and sustainable micro power generation to meet increasing societal needs not only in remote areas, but also in the urban environment.

It is also of interest to end this discussion with a mention of the 2.7 million pounds collaboration between Ceres Power and British Gas which is trading as Centrica PLC for the development of micro combined heat and power generation system using intermediate temperature solid oxide fuel cells[31] and the release of a November 2008 report on dispersed power generation from Argonne Research Laboratory by A. Elgwainy and M.Q. Wong.[32] The authors concluded that fuel cell technologies exhibited lower greenhouse gases than US electricity grid and other combustion technologies — solid oxide fuel cells and molten carbonate fuel cells.

Summary

In this review, differences between high and intermediate temperature solid oxide fuel cells are highlighted. The intermediate temperature solid oxide fuel cells are considered more appropriate for stand alone power generation in the home. The high temperature solid oxide fuel cells with large amount of heat generated are more useful for large scale distributed power generation in commercial premises, hospitals and schools. It is already used for advanced combined heat and power (CHP) generation in large scale power plants.

The dense ceramics obtained from the ceria-gadolinia system have high ionic conduction useful for the development of intermediate temperature solid oxide systems. To enable low cost solid oxide fuel cells to be developed and introduced on a large scale as stand alone applications in the home and commercial premises, some focused areas of research and development have been identified.

---

[31] Press release by Ceres Power (20 March 2006).
[32] Report by Argonne Research Laboratory: *Fuel Cell Cycle Comparison of Distributed Power Generation Technologies* (ANL/ESD/08-4).

There is high hope that this time round, maybe within five years, solid oxide fuel cell technology will be adopted on a large scale commercially for domestic and other dispersed power applications. From the number of companies that have invested heavily in developing and evaluating the long term performance of the low power solid oxide fuel cells mentioned earlier, there will be intense competition for market share for supplying combined dispersed micro power and heat generation systems.

The competition will be highly beneficial not only to consumers, business and commerce but also to the environment as solid oxide fuel cell is basically a very low carbon emission energy conversion device. The survey conducted to date shows that the application of solid oxide fuel cells as a combined dispersed micro power and heat generation for stand alone applications will play a very vital role in supporting a green and sustainable economy worldwide. It will contribute to the engine of growth for a green economy, and create enormous opportunities for gainful employment and sustainable wealth creation, reduction in greenhouse gases, and environmental damage.

7
BUILDING A SUSTAINABLE FUTURE FOR OURSELVES AND OUR COMMON HOME

Mirian Vilela

"Earth, our home is alive with a unique community of life."[1] Our sense of home normally brings us a deep feeling of care, care for our space, for our well-being and care for where we sleep and for those with whom we share this space. The thing is, we normally do not relate to Earth, or to the community of life, with that same feeling of closeness and level of care, because our vision of home is usually limited to the walls and roof where we live and does not include the bigger whole which our house is part of. To a certain extent we unfortunately relate to Earth with some level of detachment, without clearly seeing that we are dependent on it and interdependent with its living systems.

This is probably why our Earth's ecological systems and the larger community of life are being harmed and, instead, economic interests have been driving the direction of national and international policies and plans. Often decisions are made according to the interests of those holding economic power, with a considerable lack of care for the whole and little understanding of our interconnectedness with Earth and its systems.

Everyday we make a number of decisions, big and small, personal or for our organization, work or community. Each of these daily life decisions has consequences. Some are small, and others are significantly

---

[1] Earth Charter (2000).

bigger; some will have short term effects, and others will have long lasting consequences. To be inactive and not act on issues where we could make a difference is also a decision.

We often do not realize the scope of the consequences of our decisions, such as their impact in people's lives, on the economy, on the environment and Earth's ecological systems and also on the future generation's quality of life. On this last point, Earth Charter sub-principle 4 (a) reminds us "that the freedom of action of each generation is qualified by the needs of future generations."[2] This refers to a profound sense of intergenerational responsibility and sensitivity, regarding the needs of future generations, that should inform, guide and limit the ways in which we exercise our freedom. Once we understand this, we then have the responsibility to act in view of this understanding; considering, of course, that "with increased freedom, knowledge and power comes increased responsibility to promote the common good."[3] We must, therefore, accept responsibility for the consequences of our actions and decisions.

But will we dare to make decisions that are guided by what is good for the whole rather than just our own interests? Will we take the stand to seek different voices and different knowledge to help inform our decisions and also ensure that we consider the short as well as the long term consequences of our decisions and actions? Will we make these decisions that benefits the whole even if the results are not what we "originally envisioned" or end up being something that will not directly benefit "me, my house, my company or my country" in the short run? This is where ethical dilemmas sometimes emerge. As the Earth Charter states: "life often involves tensions between important values. This can mean difficult choices. However we must find ways to harmonize diversity with unity, the exercise of freedom with the common good, short-term objectives with long-term goals."[4]

In this paper I suggest the following three key avenues for rising above the current world social, economic and ecological crisis caused by short-sightedness, greed and selfishness and how to start building a more

---

[2] Earth Charter (2000). Principle 4 (a).
[3] Earth Charter (2000). Principle 2 (b).
[4] Earth Charter (2000). The Way Forward.

just and sustainable Earth Community. I believe in order to address the current world challenges and crisis it is necessary to:

a) incorporate ethical reflections into our daily lives and decisions,
b) have an integrated approach to decision making and planning, and
c) rethink our governance systems and strengthen participatory processes of decision making.

In this reflection I will be using the Earth Charter[5] as my main reference, as in it the fundamental principles and vision of sustainability are well-articulated. In this Charter we can find a call for accepting shared responsibility, taking action and a new vision of hope and interdependence. We can also find a specific warning that "Humanity stands at a critical moment in Earth's history, a time when humanity must choose its future." Given this current situation, the Charter also calls on us "to join together to bring forth a sustainable global society founded on respect for nature, universal human rights, economic justice and a culture of peace."[6]

Incorporating Ethical Reflections in Our Daily Lives and Decisions

The processes of problem solving, planning and decision-making require that we have a clear vision of the whole and an attitude of caring along with a profound sense of responsibility. This means caring for ourselves, for our community, the larger community of life and the Earth. This entails an ethical reflection that helps us realize what is right or wrong not just for ourselves, but also for society as a whole. It helps us think of the choices we have to make, our actions, each step we take and the impact of our decisions in the social sphere.

What could be an unethical choice or decision? Some examples include not taking responsibility for the consequences of our decisions

---

[5] The Earth Charter is a declaration of fundamental principles for building a just, sustainable, and peaceful global society. It was launched in the year 2000. It is the result of a worldwide participatory consultation process that took place during most of the decade of the 1990s.

[6] Earth Charter (2000). Preamble.

and actions, not respecting or ignoring the planetary ecological boundaries or limits, or doing something for our own benefit knowing well that this will significantly harm others.

In the increasingly interdependent world that we live in, global ethics based on care and respect that bring together a set of widely shared values and principles which can guide our decisions are becoming more and more necessary. This has to do with strengthening the values of compassion, shared responsibility for the betterment of society, social equity and economic justice instead of the greed and purely economic interests that seem to dominate our relations in the world and societies.

Given that we share a common home, Earth, we need to have a common platform, a common understanding among humans of how we are to live. This common platform should outline a global ethic with a set of widely shared values and beliefs that we have in common, on what is the right way to share life on Earth. For this, we need to have a certain consensus regarding how we should live on this same ground, this same home — Earth. If we don't have it, how can we possibly coexist peacefully in the long run? Reaching a common understanding happens with members of a house or an organization; a common understanding is set forth for us to be able to share a common roof regarding how we are going to live together and share this space despite the diversity in styles, tastes, priorities and interests. In the midst of our cultural diversity, interests and priorities, we can find a number of commonalities as humans. For instance, before identifying with or feeling that I am a citizen of a country, a member of an organization or a company, I need to see that I am a citizen of Earth. In other words, a human being has the responsibility to care for the human family and the larger community of life on Earth. My sense of attachment to Earth and the larger community of life should supersede my attachment to my country, my company and my culture. Of course this is a very controversial and sensitive subject, because we are taught from a very young age to be loyal first and above to certain structures that society has created including our national border. For this, it helps to think that much of my well-being depends on Earth's ecological well-being as a whole. These are not detached from one another.

Even if I look at this topic with an anthropocentric view, I should see that not taking care of the environment will be bad for me in the long run, it will be bad for my business as it will not have the same environmental conditions and natural resources that I need for my business to function. A healthy environment and good Earth conditions are the first ingredients that any business would need in the long run. We can and should also try not to be limited to an anthropocentric approach but to embrace a strong eco-centric view that balances the way in which we relate to others, the larger community of life and Earth. If I have an eco-centric view, I would see and feel that Earth deserves respect anyway.

In this regard, the Earth Charter reminds us that we need to "recognize that all beings are interdependent and every form of life has value regardless of its worth to human beings."[7] This means we need to "respect Earth and life in all its diversity[8] in spite of its utility to me and independently of where is my focus or interest. What happens when I am not respecting Earth? I am ignoring it, I am dumping waste on it, I am digging more resources than I should from it, and I am not allowing it to go through its self-regenerating processes.

The question is, how can this global ethic be ingrained in our modus operandi; or how can we promote this kind of sensitivity and vision if many values and ethics have been taken away from our formal education system? For instance, in most of the business schools or in the training of future engineers or politicians, the study of ethics and the common good is not part of the curriculum. There is a need to rethink and re-orient the current education system (formal and informal) that has been promoting and focusing on the individual's own success or the success of one's own community to the detriment of another and with too much focus on material wealth.

Excessive materialism is clearly not bringing self-fulfillment to people, but rather an existential emptiness which they vainly seek to fill with consumerism. In many societies, certainly through the news and marketing campaigns, the best or the only way to measure success is portrayed as the amount or kind of things someone possesses rather than looking at the person and how much they are able to contribute to the

---

[7] Earth Charter (2000). Principle 1 (a).
[8] Earth Charter (2000). Principle 1.

betterment of others in society. If we look at it from another perspective, we normally look at a company's, organization's or country's financial growth, or its GDP, to evaluate how well they are doing, but it does not show their contribution to Earth and society as a whole. This is a very narrow and limited way to measure success.

Peter Singer, in his book *How Are We to Live?*, stresses that "in a society in which the narrow pursuit of material self-interest is the norm, the shift to an ethical stance is more radical than many people realize;" for instance, "the preservation of old-growth forest should override our desire to use disposable paper towels. An ethical approach to life does not forbid having fun or enjoying food and wine, but it changes our sense of priorities."[9]

In addition, a wrong relationship with nature, with a simple and narrow utilitarian view focusing mainly on what nature can give us, leads us to a disenchanted view of the world. The Earth Charter emphasizes that "we must realize that when basic needs have been met, human development is primarily about being more, not having more."[10] How can we focus our attention on being more compassionate, respectful and caring human beings or organizations if the social pressure is fully focused on our material achievements? This requires determination and a profound change in perceiving the ways we function and how things work.

The reality is that we have a myopic way of thinking, in which quality of life is based on the kind of house we live in, the kind of car we drive, the financial profit of our company, the economic growth rate of a country, etc. We need to transition to the idea that the value and quality of our lives are not determined solely by our individual financial and material possessions, but also by our contributions to the larger community, to the common good. This obviously will lead us to shift away from the sole focus on individual or self-growth and progress to focus more on social betterment and Earth's systems.

Business groups, non-governmental organizations, universities and governments are key players in the improvement of our society. Their

---

[9] Singer, P. (1993). *How Are We to Live? Ethics in an Age of Self-Interest.* Oxford University Press, p. 277.
[10] Earth Charter (2000). Preamble.

purpose ought to be mainly to benefit the whole (or rather to serve the common good) and not just to seek their own material wealth. The same goes for individuals. However, there is the mistaken perception that contributing to the common good goes against one's self-interest. In some cases it could be true, if we are looking at it from a short-sighted perspective, but in the long run, what is good for the whole will have positive impacts on "me, my family or my company." This vision will help us all find a sense of purpose and meaning in life. We should envision the sense of fulfillment an individual or organization would gain from helping our society and our common home — Earth.

It is essential that we challenge the notion that self-interest should supersede collective interest. We should turn it around and envision a society that will place the common good as the top priority, and realize that achieving the common good and having a right relationship with Earth and others will be in our own best interest in the long run.

Can we infuse society with a deep sense of belonging and responsibility, so that whatever we do as business people, lawyers, academics, or as citizens, should help improve society and other people's lives? Our skills, knowledge and capacities should mainly be used to serve a greater whole and contribute to the realization of the common good. In the long run this will be good for us or our company.

As Peter Singer reminds us

> *"we will find that to live an ethical life is not self-sacrifice, but self-fulfillment... If we can detach ourselves from our own immediate preoccupations and look at the world as a whole and our place in it, there is something absurd about the idea that people should have trouble finding something to live for."*[11]

For that to happen, we need to dare to make things different, but, will we be open enough to see the other side and listen to others' perspectives? As the Earth Charter states: "fundamental changes are needed in our

---

[11] Singer, P. (1993). *How Are We to Live? Ethics in an Age of Self-Interest.* Oxford University Press, Preface for the first edition, p. 1.

values, institutions, and ways of living."[12] "This requires a change of mind and heart. It requires a new sense of global interdependence and universal responsibility."[13] Fortunately, there are a number of movements that can help us to break our inertia and conformity to the status quo.

The Earth Charter is a framework that offers us a vision of what this kind of an ethic of care and responsibility looks like. Principle 2 states that we need to "care for the community of life with understanding, compassion, and love."[14] This is certainly not what we are taught to do in our schools and universities, but it is what needs to be central to our societies.

Despite the fact that the world news is quite focused on the current financial crisis, which indeed is of great concern, there is a much deeper and latent crisis that does not receive much news coverage. This is the health of the Earth and its systems, as well as a crisis of the values of humanity.

We can and should live an ethical life that is constantly reflected by our decisions and actions. What the world is facing in terms of social disparity, misery, lack of access to basic needs and disregard for the well-being of the larger community of life, is largely an ethical problem. We can and should turn that around.

Integrated Approach to Decision Making and Planning

Sustainability has a lot to do with limits, long-term vision and the inter-relationship of things. It concerns our understanding of the limits and the capacity of Earth's ecological systems to give humanity its services of water, air, natural resources, absorption of waste, etc. Sustainability also deals with long-term approaches. For instance, if we look at a situation with a short-term perspective we might make a completely different decision than if we look at the same situation with a long-term vision, due to the differing levels of sensitivity and consideration with regard to the cascade of consequences that come after a decision. In addition,

---

[12] Earth Charter (2000). Preamble 4th paragraph.
[13] Earth Charter (2000). The Way Forward.
[14] Earth Charter (2000). Principle 2.

sustainability also focuses on the relationship of things which requires a systemic vision of a given situation (we can also call it a holistic or integrated approach).

To illustrate that, let us imagine when a specific part of our body is aching, say the stomach; we can make a quick decision to take medicine that will immediately address the stomachache. That might be good in the short run and we will quickly be relieved, but we soon may realize that that same medicine generated other problems, worse than the previous one, in our heart, blood pressure or kidneys, or even that it caused our death. This shows the importance of being sensitive and aware of the side effects of a quick-fix decision and acting accordingly. Given this, we need to look at the whole system of our body before a decision is made to take a certain medicine. This is the same with our social, economic and environmental systems particularly because they are so closely interconnected.

Time and again everything is seen in a disconnected or fragmented way; for example, the priority of national and international policies or the business world, is normally given to economic growth and development. Understanding the notion of sustainability, however, brings to our attention the close relationship between economic development and the natural and social systems. The reason for persisting in this "business as usual" way of thinking is that our academic disciplines, as well as the way institutions are organized, show a strong division and separation of areas and disciplines. There is a lot of knowledge and expertise out there concentrated in realms or focus areas that unfortunately are often disconnected from one another or do not seek collaboration in problem solving neither has the interest to generate joint solutions. This is as if knowledge is mostly available in pieces. Often people believe that their area of expertise is the most important and produces most of the answers without spending time to look around in other areas of expertise to seek different perceptions.

Therefore, the large majority of international and local efforts are undertaken in a fragmented and narrow way. This means that they are mostly focused on addressing a specific topic without considering the possibility of multiple causes or the effects and future ramifications of any intervention. Such compartmentalization of institutions, governments and academia is not effective, and, therefore, requires a fundamental change in the way we learn, think, plan and organize ourselves.

We must realize that what affects society affects business; a depleted environment will also affect the success of a business. Business goals cannot succeed in societies that fail because of social problems, such as poor education or conflicts, nor can they succeed in an environment that is so polluted and degraded that it cannot provide wood, water, oil, bauxite or other valuable raw materials and natural resources. What could be the attitude of a business person or a company that can see these relationships and think long-term? We know that businesses are increasingly vulnerable to consumer preferences that are becoming more demanding and selective regarding the environmental and social practices used to produce the products they buy. Businesses are also further challenged by a changing political climate where there are increasingly more government regulations setting parameters for sustainable development. This is good, and it is helping to empower conscientious consumers to create new rules of the game.

Dialogues in the 1991 movie *Mindwalk* (produced by Bernt A. Capra and based on the book *Turning Point* by Frijof Capra) focuses on the importance of a "fundamental shift of perception from the world as a machine to the world as a living system." The movie's emphasis on the interdependent and interconnected relationships in the world is an important lesson. Therefore, in order to fully understand how to effectively implement sustainable practices it is necessary to be able to see the whole system, to think systemically.

With the above, it is clear, in order that to better understand the complexity of our current challenges; we need to look at the whole situation through multidisciplinary lenses. Once we fully understand the complexity of our challenges, there needs to be a concerted effort in shifting from a fragmented approach of thinking, planning and learning to an integrated approach to problem solving and planning. This process should also involve the reorientation of our educational systems to make future generations aware of the relationships and interdependence of the different parts of systems. The transition should be informed by an ethical framework that will ensure the common good.

The Earth Charter offers an integrated perspective and a reference tool that recognizes that economic development, environmental protection, human rights and peace are closely interrelated, and therefore it reminds us that in order to address one of these dimensions, one requires a vision of the whole.

It is increasingly recognized that we have crossed the limits of our natural resources with the current patterns of consumption and production. There are numerous reports and studies calling our attention to this, affirming that the current "patterns of production and consumption are causing environmental devastation, the depletion of resources, and a massive extinction of species."[15] The issue is that many people still do not see how these problems are related to them, to their daily lives or their business. This is not just a question of being an environmentalist or caring about ecology, it is also a question of caring for ourselves in the long run, if we want to look at it through a very anthropocentric lens. It is obsolete to think that being a business person focused on increasing profits precludes us from being a social activist and/or environmentalist. These disparate interests actually have similar goals when we think about ensuring long-term survivability. We should overcome our differing perceptions and find points of convergence as we address our common challenges.

The economy that we live in produces most everything derived from the natural resources available (renewable and non-renewable) through processes that generate a lot of waste. This affects Earth's health, and its capacity to continue providing humanity with the basic natural resources and its ability to assimilate the waste that we dump back on it (humanity is certainly dumping much more than what it can absorb). This cannot continue for much longer, we need to ingrain the notion of limits and care into our current systems.

We are living in a wasteful society. Do we ever stop to think if we really need what we are buying? Or do we ever think of what these products are made of? What were the natural resources used to produce the products that we use? Who were the people involved in the manufacturing process of this or that product that we need? Who was empowered or disempowered by the process of production of those things that we buy? Just think about the economic, social and environmental aspects and the

---

[15] Earth Charter (2000). Preamble.

impact of the food we eat or the products we use in our daily lives, such as the chair you are sitting on or the shoes you are wearing today.

Responsible consumers today will be looking beyond impulses and immediate gratification because they will give significant value to products that reflect ethical values and cohere with the well-being of societies and the environment. We have to be ready to take the responsibility of the long-term effects of our choices. Not only the consequences for our lives and our own health, but for the whole, including the Earth's health. Therefore, "we must adopt patterns of production, consumption, and reproduction that safeguard Earth's regenerative capacities, human rights, and community well-being."[16]

Industries need to simultaneously think of the way things are produced and designed from the beginning and look for alternative ways of production, particularly if they want to continue in the business. The authors of the book *Cradle to Cradle: Remaking the Way We Make Things* tell us that it is not enough just to recycle and reduce the energy used in the process of production. In other words, it is not enough to be eco-efficient, as this makes us just "less bad." There is an urgent need to re-invent the way things are made in order to be eco-effective, which means designing processes that are right from the beginning. According to them, product design is currently focused upon disposable and discardable products, but this needs to shift toward design that would allow products to be returned to the product cycle once used. They said that "Eco-effective design demands a coherent set of principles based on nature's laws and the opportunity for constant diversity of expression."[17]

This means that for a company to become sustainable or coherent with the values of sustainability and committed to contributing to the common good it is not enough to only establish a department that will take care of environmental and social corporate responsibility or have another department dedicated to sustainability. In order to be effective, this requires a systemic change, a new vision and commitment that are in

---

[16] Earth Charter (2000). Principle 7.
[17] McDonough, W. and Braungart, M. (2002). *Cradle to Cradle: Remaking the Way We Make Things*. North Point Press.

every corner, division and section of the company, following a new vision of how things are to be done and therefore it should be part of everything that goes on in the company. It should be in the whole system, not just one organ. In other words, it should be part of its "blood system."

If we have the knowledge and the technology to provide for all and to reduce our impact on the environment why don't we do it? We need to infuse sensitivity, awareness and a deep sense of responsibility in all of us, but particularly in those who carry the decision making power that will affect many. Principle 2 (a) of the Earth Charter makes us think that we need to "accept that with the right to own, manage, and use natural resources comes the duty to prevent environmental harm and to protect the rights of people." This is a responsibility that we need to carry, but it needs to be infused into our formal and informal education settings.

Frijof Capra says that "the goal of the global economy is to maximize the wealth and power of its elites; the goal of eco-design is to maximize the sustainability of the web of life." He continues by adding that "the great challenge of the 21st century will be to change the value system underlying the global economy, so as to make it compatible with the demands of human dignity and ecological sustainability."[18] Again, this requires a new vision of what our common good really is and an integrated ethical framework to be used as a map, a compass or as a reference tool for our decisions.

Participatory Governance as a Way to Ensure an Integrated Approach to Decisions

"How we decide and who gets to decide often determines what we will decide... Governance is about decisions and how we make them. It is about the exercise of authority."[19]

The belief that the answers to our societies' problems can only come from our governments, as the best and unique representatives of people,

---

[18] Capra, F. (2002). *The Hidden Connections: Integrating the Biological, Cognitive, and Social Dimensions of Life Into a Science of Sustainability*. Doubleday, p. 262.
[19] World Resources Institute, (2003). *World Resources 2002–2004: Decisions for the Earth: Balance, Voice and Power*. Introduction and p. 6.

is a limited approach to international, national and local governance. This is particularly true if we consider the multiple interests and levels of capacity, power and knowledge existing in our communities and countries. Not to mention the relatively limited capacity of our governments to address our social and environmental problems.

According to the 2002–2004 World Resources Institute report, the end of the cold war, the emergence of civil society, the proliferation of new information and communication technology, the shrinking role of nation-states and the clear dominance of the private sector through the wave of privatization are critical geopolitical changes that took place in the past 20 years. Within that context, new global governance is necessary to address the interrelated challenges of our global society; this must involve inclusive participatory processes in the development and implementation of policies.[20]

Given this, there is still much need to improve the processes by which policies and strategies in different realms at the global, national and local levels are developed and implemented. One of the reasons is because policies are developed, but are not connected to the situations they are meant to address. This is evident particularly in relation to those who will actually end up implementing the policies or those who will be affected by them. This generates difficulties in the process of implementation. Improving such processes requires the willingness of all to appreciate a variety of perspectives and to utilize local knowledge, concerns and experiences in contributing to and influencing the process of decision making as well as the implementation of sustainability. There are high possibilities that this, if it effectively happens, will enrich the outcomes of the decision making process, given the cross-fertilization of knowledge, information and perspectives from different levels and fields of action. Increased participation in governance will also help to ensure that international and national policies are actually localized and put into practice, particularly as it builds a sense of ownership and makes it easier to forge partnerships.

---

[20] World Resources Institute, (2003). *World Resources 2002–2004: Decisions for the Earth: Balance, Voice and Power*, p. 24.

Principle 13 of the Earth Charter re-affirms this notion of inclusive participation in decision making and sub-principle 13 (b) states: "Support local, regional and global civil society, and promote the meaningful participation of all interested individuals and organizations in decision making." Clearly, much of the realization of this idea depends on the context and the kind of decision that is being made. For instance, meaningful participation can be crystallized by (a) just offering a space for different voices to express their concerns or perspectives, or (b) by offering a safe space to collect advice that will clearly influence decisions being made, or (c) by fully opening the process for participatory and collective decisions, which is a different story in itself.

If we imagine what happens when interested groups are not involved in a planning process or policy design we could easily visualize the added value of a participatory process in decision making. In these situations, the process lacks their input, their engagement, their support and particularly the opportunity to generate collaboration and partnerships. Actually, many times, just because of the way decisions are made, the implementation process will face not just lack of collaboration but also opposition, due to a sense of exclusion generated beforehand.

Such processes can be improved by generating spaces for dialogue among various sector representatives and interest groups, where knowledge and interests can be shared in a safe environment and where the focus of all should be the search for a shared vision of the common good and genuine collaboration. These are to be spaces that would bring together government representatives, interest groups of civil society, academia and business leaders, among others, to foster better decisions that meet the needs of people and ecosystems with equity and balance. This is a different exercise from the role a number of civil society groups participating in the so-called "anti-movements" (that create a lot of resistance). It is an opportunity to explore alternative ways to collectively overcome challenges and differences, by focusing on the needs and priorities of the collective while, at the same time, building consensus and alliances.

Given this, our global society needs to look for innovative ways to enrich the processes of decision making in places such as the United Nations as well as at the national and local levels. Consequently I will explore some examples of the role of non-state actors which include "persons, institutions and organizations that have the goal of advancing or expressing a common purpose through ideas, actions, and demands on governments"[21] in contributing to the transition towards sustainability and the related process of setting up policies.

I will look at a couple of examples that illustrate new ways of incorporating different voices in the sustainability debate that are attempting to improve participatory approaches in decision making. With that in mind, I will first look at the progress of non-state actors' participation in intergovernmental policy making processes, particularly between the 1992 Rio Earth Summit and the 2002 Johannesburg Summit on Sustainable Development.

Historic overview

The formal "participation" of Non-Governmental Organizations (NGOs) in the UN system dates back to the origins of the UN itself, as Article 71 of its Charter states "The Economic and Social Council (ECOSOC) may make suitable arrangements for consultation with non-governmental organizations which are concerned with matters within its competence."[22]

Over the years, particularly since early 1990, due to the exponential increase of civil society interest in UN decisions, some changes were introduced to clarify procedures such as accreditation, but the general framework of NGO status continues to be similar. Currently national and international NGOs can submit requests for accreditation for consultative status which are:

- general consultative status — reserved for large, international NGOs that work on most of the issues on ECOSOC's agenda;
- special consultative status — for NGOs that have competence in only a few of ECOSOC's areas; or

---

[21] Gemmill, B. and Bamidele-Izu, A. (2002). The role of NGOs and civil society in global environment governance, in Esty, D. and Ivanova, M. (eds.), *Global Environmental Governance: Options and Opportunities*. Yale School of Forest and Environmental Studies.
[22] United Nations Charter Article 71.

- ECOSOC roster — other NGOs that do not have or qualify for consultative status.

The basic difference is that NGOs in consultative status have a political relationship with ECOSOC, and, therefore, have certain rights that allow some direct participation in the intergovernmental process. These rights are related to participating in public or some UN plenary meetings, space to submit written statements and to make oral presentations at some point in the debate. NGO accreditation to conferences allows considerable participation and space for lobbying in informal sessions and, with this, influencing the decision making process of the intergovernmental deliberations.

Along these lines, it is interesting to note the detail that the color of the accreditation badge for participants in key UN conferences is the same for all non-state actors, including, business groups, local governments, indigenous peoples, NGOs, farmers and the academic and scientific communities. This means that formally all these groups (that are certainly not homogeneous and do not carry the same perspectives, nor priorities, neither have the same level of influence) are in the same category of "major groups" from the UN Secretariat perspective and have similar "rights." Formally they are also similarly limited to the space given to non-state actors.

It is widely recognized that the process leading up to the 1992 United Nations Conference on Environment and Development (UNCED), known as the Earth Summit, generated unprecedented public interest, thus environmental and social organizations increased their capacity to better understand and influence the international policy making process. Since then, involvement of non-state actors in global governance has continuously increased and almost became the norm. As a matter of a fact, the 1992 Earth Summit re-affirmed that the commitment and genuine involvement of non-state actors are critical to reaching sustainable development goals. Article 10 of the 1992 Rio Declaration states "Environmental issues are best handled with the participation of all concerned citizens at the relevant level." Furthermore, the UN Commission on Sustainable Development was created to help follow up and advance the implementation of the 1992 Summit agreements and has, as part of its mandate, to work through an inclusive process of international deliberations and decision making. Let us see how this has been evolving.

Participation from Rio-92 to Johannesburg Summit in 2002

In the process leading up to the 92 Rio Earth Summit, for the first time NGOs that did not have ECOSOC consultative status were allowed to request for accreditation to attend such a conference as observers, this was an expression of commitment by the Summit organizers, to open the space for participation. This generated the need to review how the UN would relate to non-state actors. At the Earth Summit and during its preparatory process the clear notion of "major groups" in the "UN terms" did not exist as it was created as an outcome of the Summit. However, thousands of representatives of civil society participated in the Summit, mostly NGOs, youth and women. It was also the first time that the UN gave so much space for the representation of the business sector. So much so that some groups were suspicious and uneasy with that.

The Conference Secretariat would evaluate the applications and recommended lists of non-state organizations for accreditation to the Summit Preparatory Committee. Along this process, key NGOs in consultative status with the ECOSOC could be given an opportunity to briefly address plenary meetings of the Preparatory Committee and meetings of Working Groups. During the Summit itself, some of them were able to make oral statements upon invitation by the Chair. NGOs were also able to distribute written statements, which they did in addition to advocating and lobbying governments in corridors and informal sessions.

In parallel to the intergovernmental Summit event, the 92 Global Forum was organized, to allow unlimited civil society organizations to participate in the process. Prior to this, there was little NGO coordination to work on common positions on different issues. The NGO Global Forum held numerous meetings, seminars and exhibits on environment and development issues for the public. During this Global Forum a series of alternative treaties were prepared not only to influence the governmental agenda, but also as a way to express civil society commitment and aspirations. The themes of the treaties vary from environmental concerns to youth, women or indigenous people's rights. This alternative process was put together with certain anticipation that the intergovernmental negotiating process was unlikely to deliver outcomes reflecting what was expected and demanded by many.

The Summit program of implementation, known as Agenda 21, an agreed plan of action for implementing sustainability in the 21st century, identified (in its session III, from chapters 24 to 32) nine sectors as 'major groups', as key players in decision-making, that should be involved in the inter-governmental sessions being NGOs, local authorities, business and industry, farmers, trade unions, scientists and technological communities, Women, Indigenous Peoples and Youth. These groups represent sectors of society considered to be playing crucial role in the development and implementation of policies for sustainable development.[23] They were invited to participate in the follow up process of the 92 Summit.

Multi-stakeholder dialogues

Later on during the UN General Assembly Special Session (for the five years evaluation since the Earth Summit), held in 1997, the CSD was instructed to reinforce its high level policy debate with more extensive interaction with non-state representatives: the "major groups." Since then an interesting and innovative mechanism was created: a two-day multi-stakeholder dialogue has been integrated as an official segment in the CSD intergovernmental annual sessions.

With the attempt to implement the principle of inclusion in international deliberations, these two days of "dialogues" have offered space to representatives from all nine major groups, to present their concerns and recommendations during official intergovernmental sessions. The first such session took place during the CSD-6 held in '98, and was facilitated by the elected chair of the year. Since then the outcomes of the

---

[23] Consensus Building Institute (2001). *Multi-Stakeholder Dialogues: Learning from the UNCSD Experience*. Working paper, p. 11.

multi-stakeholder dialogues are part of the CSD Chair's summary and have been incorporated in the official records of the meetings. Generally, the Chairman's summary largely reflects the key points raised by major groups, but with little coherence and structure of the information. This summary does not mean that the recommendations will be reflected in the final decisions of the session.

Despite the fact that these dialogues have not been amply dynamic, it has been relatively positive and part of a learning process for states and non-state representatives, particularly because none of these actors were used to interact in formal sessions. It could be said that it is even more difficult for governmental representatives to listen to what non-state members have to say throughout these sessions with the same level of interest as if it was a purely intergovernmental session. The expectations about this innovative process differ; for the UN Secretariat the dialogues are mainly to provide an opportunity for government and major groups to exchange ideas about issues of concern. For the major groups this exercise is mainly used to influence negotiations and have their recommendations incorporated in the outcomes of negotiated decisions.

Over the years, this experience has shown the overlap of issues raised, recommendations and support between major groups. On other occasions there have been extensive clashes, particularly between NGOs or farmers and the business groups. In 2001, the Consensus Building Institute made a study on this experience highlighting some elements that have not positively contributed to this multi-stakeholder dialogue. These are: the lack of focus of these multi-stakeholder dialogues, too short a time for real dialogue, the style of facilitation by the chair lacks dynamism, the short time allocated for each major group intervention and the formal way in which representatives make their intervention reading from a text that had been drafted by many rather than indeed having a dialogue with informal interventions.[24]

Overall, the format of the multi-stakeholder sessions has not allowed significant real dialogue or exchange by going beyond pure presentations. Although it has been positive as a mechanism to exchange information, there is still doubt about how effective and useful it has been.

---

[24] Consensus Building Institute (2001). *Multi-Stakeholder Dialogues: Learning from the UNCSD Experience*. Working paper, p. 7.

During the Johannesburg Summit in 2002 the Chair of the negotiations did not have the role of facilitating the multi-stakeholder dialogue as at other times, instead Jan Pronk, the UN Secretary General Special Envoy to the Summit took this role and brought significant dynamism to the experience. Through a series of questions he engaged "major groups'" representatives and the audience to move away from the typical reading statement practice of these dialogues. This shows that over time the dialogue structure can get better and even the UN can sometimes shift away from the accustomed stiff way of exchanging positions and intervening. This type of structure and new vision entail building consensus in a way that had not taken place before, that is why the role of the chair or facilitator is so crucial in leading an effective and real dialogue as well as in bringing coherence.

The UN Secretariat stressed that this Summit was not supposed to be focused on political debate, but rather on actions and results. Indeed, targets, timetables and a number of commitments were agreed upon at Johannesburg. But the event itself mobilized groups from every region in the world and from all sectors. According to the organizers, the Summit "also marked a major departure from previous UN conferences in many ways, in structure and in outcome that could have a major effect on the way the international community approaches problem solving in the future."[25] These differences have to do mostly with the increased level of participation and commitment of non-state organizations and also the development of partnerships among non-state actors and governments.

In any case, the "new" participation within the UN-CSD has been significant as a space to influence governments and to voice concerns from different perspectives. Even if "major groups" are still limited and only allowed to intervene in a few formal and open meetings. For instance, very often contentious issues are taken to closed-door meetings where only government representatives can participate. Generally these are not plenary meetings but are sessions held by groups that hold shared interests. Some examples are European Union government representatives meeting to discuss about certain topics of the agenda, African countries or

---

[25] United Nations. *The Johannesburg Summit Test: What Will Change?*, featured story at the summit website: http://www.johannesburgsummit.org/html/whats_new/feature_story41.html.

the Group of 77 and China meeting behind closed doors to talk about sensitive matters. These group meetings may opt to allow the presence of "major groups," but often they do not. Therefore, in these cases only "major group" representatives who are part of their official national government delegation and wearing a government badge of accreditation will be allowed to enter in the room of the so called "closed door meetings." Moreover, even though they may be able to follow the discussion, they will not be allowed to intervene unless it is through the goodwill of their government representative.

In addition, the "rights" of general consultative status NGOs to participate in the debate of formal meetings is really far from a reality, as it is in fact only used when prior permission has been given. Even considering these deficiencies, I believe the CSD offers an interesting space to improve this unique experience of participatory governance that should be replicated in other UN fora and local communities. There seems to be a wide range of variation with regards to member states response and openness to this innovative way of undertaking UN meetings and negotiations. Above all this experience offers good precedents for slowly shifting the mind set of bureaucrats that start acknowledging the added value of civil society participation in the process of decision making. Particularly because government delegations often change every four to five years, but non-state actors and representatives normally stay throughout the years and carry the experience and history that helps ensure long term implementation and flow of knowledge.

Although the process of including the multi-stakeholder voices in the international policy making negotiations has been relatively slow and far from perfect, there are reasons to believe that in the future there will be new ways of developing policies and making decisions. Some governments are now including "major group's" representatives as part of their official delegations to international conferences. There has been some effort to get each of these "major groups" organized, also to clarify issues of representation and get the various parties used to the idea.

This new participatory approach requires time, openness, good facilitation and significant political will in order to be effective and help the necessary transition from the traditional power structures.

A crucial moment to show improvement and creative ways in engaging different groups in addressing our collective world challenges will be at the upcoming World Summit in 2012. This Summit has been set up by the United Nations as an occasion to "undertake an overall review and appraisal of the progress achieved in, and to identify further measures for enhancing, the implementation of Agenda 21 and the outcomes of the World Summit on Sustainable Development."[26]

We could look at the participatory process of decision making as examples that could be adapted to stimulate openness and interest of a specific company in engaging with the community where it is situated.

National processes

Looking at another dimension, it is also important to ensure that such processes or similar mechanisms are available at the national level. Chapter 37 of Agenda 21 reminds us that "The ability of a country to follow sustainable development paths is determined to a large extent by the capacity of its people and its institutions as well as by its ecological and geographical conditions."[27] It further stresses the need to "promote an ongoing participatory process to define country needs and priorities in promoting Agenda 21 and to give importance to technical and professional human resource development and development of institutional capacities and capabilities on the agenda of countries…"[28]

Given that a number of countries created National Councils for Sustainable Developments (NCSD) or similar entities, to help bring the 1992 agreements and subsequent ones to the national levels. The NCSDs are interesting multi-stakeholder mechanisms of policy making, that generally bring together different groups of the society in a country to help develop an integrated development plan. In many ways, the NCSDs also help the national government to prepare for the global meetings of sustainable development, such as the Johannesburg Summit; their members are also selected to participate in the official government delegation to the UN negotiations.

---

[26] United National General Assembly Resolution A/C.2/63/L.27 of 4 November 2008.
[27] United Nations (1992). Agenda 21. Chapter 37, paragraph 37.1.
[28] United Nations (1992). Agenda 21. Chapter 37, paragraph 37.3 (a).

In some cases such as in Mexico, the NCSD is attached to the Secretary of Environment and as such acts only as advisory body to members of the cabinet through the Environment Minister. They have a quite interesting process of elected representatives in all states of the country that bring the voices and perspectives from the non-governmental, academic, grassroots or business sectors.

In other cases, such as in Niger or Honduras, the NCSD has more than an advisory mandate; it is located in the office of the Prime-Minister, specifically to facilitate the interaction among all cabinet ministers, together with the academic and business sectors. The exercise is an attempt to integrate public and private interests in a space that brings various concerns and recommendations for an integrated national plan for development. These may be seen as models of new participatory governance for sustainable development policies.

In the following section I would like to broadly illustrate some examples of efforts to engage different groups (stakeholders) in the decision making process at the community level that ultimately seek the betterment of society and the conditions of life on Earth. At the local levels there are a number of ways such endeavors are being undertaken.

Processes of developing Local Agenda 21

For years the government of Brazil, through its Ministry of Environment, has undertaken a concerted effort to promote the development of Local Agenda 21 throughout the country. Local Agenda 21 processes are expected to generate a plan of action for the local community or city. The outcome is important, but the process of getting different groups of a community together to collectively identify the community challenges and priorities, analyze the community situation, as well as to develop a common vision of the communities future is as important if not more as it also helps to generate collaborations in the process of making this vision a reality. To offer guidance and further stimulate such undertakings, the Ministry of Environment has developed guidelines, which are in a manual for local communities on how to undertake a process of developing its own Local Agenda 21. In addition, the national government has also been facilitating a national network of

Local Agenda 21s to stimulate continuity in this effort and exchange experiences.

There are similar efforts been undertaken in other parts of the world related to the setting up of Local Agenda 21s. The UN-Habitat and the Local Government Initiatives (ICLEI) have both developed useful and interesting guides for local communities to carry out participatory processes in developing their Local Agenda 21s as action plans to implement sustainability at the community level (see www.unhabitat and www.iclei.org). These processes of developing Agenda 21s in the form of local action plans for sustainability can be initiated by the local authority or by any group within the community: the schools, the private sector, NGOs or others. Are these participatory processes perfect? No, but they are a good beginning to engage the community in a process that requires the engagement, help and commitment of all if it is to be successful and become a reality.

Co-management of protected areas

Co-management of protected areas is another example of situations in which the most appropriate arrangement, to accommodate all parties involved, is to have co-management which involves the local community and the government. This comes as an alternative to the classic or conventional way of undertaking such decision through a centralized national policy. For instance the central government decides to declare a protected area in a given place and fully manages it, without considering the local communities that live there or without seriously considering what such a decision could entail for their livelihoods. These are typical cases where a decision is taken with partial knowledge of the context and with limited viewpoints showing only one side of the situation; focusing only on the issue and need of conservation, for example, without a systemic approach taking into considerations the social impact of such decision. There are numerous cases in all regions of the world that went through this process by first undertaking a centralized or top down approach then, after facing opposition, having to reconsider the decision and open the process for discussion. Each story has its own characteristics and also a number of similarities. In Cahuita National Park in Costa

Rica, for example, a decision was made by the government to charge high fees to enter the national park. The local community demanded the possibility to be fully engaged in the process of managing what they felt was their protected area, as it is located in their community, and to benefit from the funds and ensure good implementation.

Another example is the case of The Sokhulu people of the Mapelaine Reserve on South Africa's northeast coast, a traditional community located near Durban in South Africa. The Sokhulu people had their livelihood and security jeopardized for some years due to a short-sighted decision taken at the central government. In this case when the Mapelaine Nature Reserve was declared a protected area, the natives or traditional people living there for hundreds of years were suddenly prevented from harvesting mussels for their basic needs. This generated conflict with the park guards and authorities until the different parties could together determine the sustainable level of harvesting mussels and agree on a co-management plan for that protected area.[29]

Situations like these come from regions where the local community can freely live and enjoy the benefits of their surroundings, as well as base their livelihoods on the benefits of the natural resources (in a relatively sustainable way), to where the native cultures are suddenly precluded from making use of their land in traditional ways, which generates a problem, to a situation in which the government, the local community and many times the academics, join forces, share knowledge, overcome differences and agree on a type of co-management of a protected area.

These cases show us that if we can see how useful it is to engage in the decision-making process those who will be affected by the consequences of a decision, we could avoid numerous misunderstandings, problems in implementing policies and lack of support in the implementation phase.

Participatory budgeting

A number of local governments have experimented the participatory budgeting approach, and they have entered into a process of decentralizing, to

---

[29] World Resources Institute (2003). *World Resources 2002–2004: Decisions for the Earth: Balance, Voice and Power*, p. 174.

a certain extent, the decision making process of what to do with the public budget.

Porto Alegre, a pioneering city in the southern part of Brazil, is an international reference point with regard to giving civil society the opportunity to echo their voices and collectively decide how a certain percentage of the public funds should be used. In this case, the local authority takes a courageous decision to share the decision making power of how to allocate a portion of the public funds. So they invite the local society to help define the priorities that need to be addressed and how to allocate the municipal public funds.

We can consider participatory budget as a model of leadership openness as it really requires the willingness from the leadership to share power and as an instrument to build participatory democracy.

It is possible that a number of other cities after seeing the good results of such an undertaking would be willing to adopt similar paths and adapt it to their own contexts. There are no single recipes of how to undertake participatory processes of decision making, much of it will depend on the context, on the level of problems to be addressed, the complexity of the situation, the capacity of governments and other actors in society to address them, and the goodwill and commitment of leadership.

The whole concept of sustainability involves systemic thinking for bringing together the environmental, social, political and economic dimensions of policy making. Participation of different groups of civil society in the processes of policy design, planning and strategic development at the global, national and local levels is essential to enrich the process. This brings diverse knowledge and perspectives, generates a sense of ownership and long term commitment to implementation, as well as giving legitimacy to the processes. In addition to mobilizing public opinion on specific issues, "major groups" can help vocalize the interests of persons not well-represented in the traditional policy making arenas.

In conclusion, there are a number of existing different models and mechanisms of participatory governance. Participatory processes require time, flexibility, patience, understanding the perspective of different stakeholders, good and open leadership, committed citizens and the goodwill of all. The positive side of it is that it generates an important sense of ownership and a better understanding of the overall situation. It also helps generate partnerships that bring with it additional human and financial resources and increase the implementation capacity of a decision. Much of it will also depend on the context, such as the capacity of national or local governments and non-governmental institutions to manage, regulate, control, generate information or actually improve the overall situation.

In this paper the evolving process of civil society, private sector and academia participation in policy and decision making was briefly illustrated to stimulate our thinking with regards to future possibilities. This should help us shape ideas of possible future scenarios for environment and sustainability governance. It is certain that new models are emerging following changes that our society and organized systems are undergoing. These changes will hopefully strengthen a profound sense of shared responsibility and commitment of all to building a more just and sustainable world. The challenges of reinventing current institutions and rethinking our power structures can be envisioned and realized. This will eventually lead us to the necessary structural changes in our governance systems.

If we see the interdependence of local and world challenges and understand linkages between key problems we could address them with an integrated approach. We would then easily realize that caring for Earth and its large community of life also means caring for ourselves and that we need to collaborate across borders. This will help humanity overcome the short-sightedness and selfishness that seems to dominate the way we make decisions. Then a new ethic of care and responsibility with one another and our common home, Earth, would naturally become part of ourselves, our lifestyles and decisions without the limitation of artificial borders created by our outdated systems.

III. ENTREPRENEURSHIP EDUCATION

8
SUSTAINABILITY AND ENTREPRENEURSHIP EDUCATION AT THE UNIVERSITY LEVEL

Lloyd W. Fernald

Introduction

Sustainability has been defined and presented to the reader several times throughout this volume. Nevertheless, for those who may select this chapter alone, solely as a matter of special interest, it is important to discuss sustainability and its relationship to business before providing the reader with the role of entrepreneurship education in achieving global sustainability.

Sustainability means "meeting the needs of the present without compromising the ability of future generations to meet their own needs." (EPA, 2008) "We have a responsibility to sustain — if not enhance — our natural environment and the nation's economy for future generations." (Johnson, 2008) Wikipedia, the free encyclopedia, defines sustainability as "...a characteristic of a process or state that can be maintained at a certain level indefinitely. Historically, complex human societies have died, sometimes as a result of their growth-associated impacts on ecological support systems. The implication is that today's industrial society will also collapse as a result of continued growth in both scale and complexity." (Wiki, 2008a).

Sustainability is directly associated with two of the major issues of the 21st century. The first is the successful management of human resources. The second is the growing pressure from governments and the general public for organizations to adopt environmentally responsible operations.

With respect to the former, human resources challenges are faced with increased turnover, decreased loyalty, rising stress levels, corporate-community relations and social responsibility. Thus, sustainability provides leaders of organizations, both large and small, with a framework for understanding and adopting the practices that contribute to a renewable, sustainable workforce and environment. Those that can achieve both human and ecological sustainability will be the leaders of the new sustainable economy. Other leaders face possible extinction (Dunphy *et al.*, 2000).

A third issue regarding sustainability is globalization. Interactions between the complexities of globalization and the evolving sustainability agenda may very well define the marketplace of the 21st century. Implications for the corporate responsibility and sustainability development agendas will differ based on different regions of the world and different timeframes (ROG, 2008).

When sustainability is viewed from a systems approach, it lessens the emphasis on profits only and the consequent suffering and damaging disruption of human social and economic systems. It assists in developing policy options for a transition to a sustainable way of life that does not cause significant environmental or social degradation or destruction. It does not significantly compromise the lives of future generations while utilizing the resources of the world wisely to ensure a relatively indefinite future for human society and other forms of life (Clayton *et al.*, 1996).

Indicators of sustainability are different from traditional indicators. Traditional indicators such as stockholder profits, production materials, and jobs, measure changes in one part of the community as if it was entirely independent of other parts. Communities are a web of interactions among the environment, the economy, and society. Sustainability indicators reflect the reality that there is interconnectedness among these three communities. Natural resources provide the materials for production on which stockholder profits result. Jobs affect the poverty rate and the poverty rate is related to the crime rate. Air and water quality affect health. Poor air and water quality also impact on profits if they incur the extra expense of being cleaned up during the manufacturing process. In addition, health problems caused by poor air quality or exposure to toxic materials have an adverse effect on worker productivity and contribute to the rising costs of healthcare. Thus, sustainability requires an integrated view of the world and multidimensional indicators that show the links among a community's economy, environment, and society (Hart, 2006).

Entrepreneurship/Small and Medium Sized Enterprises (SMEs) will play an important role in sustainability efforts, as well as in the case of economic development of the world's economies. But the role of economic development involves more than increases in per capita output and income. It involves initiating and changing the structure of business and society. Entrepreneurs are innovators. Innovation is often the key, not only in developing new products and/or services, but also in stimulating investment interest in the new ventures created (Hisrich et al., 2005). These new ventures must give thoughtful consideration to how human and ecological resources will be used or abused in providing society with new products and services.

The growth rate for entrepreneurship/self-employment in the United States since the early 1980s has been greater than the general work force. This same trend has been seen in other economies as well. Entrepreneurship has experienced dynamic growth, especially among young people. Many of them have been extremely successful in the computer/computer-related industries (Megginson et al., 2005).

Entrepreneurs are resourceful and creative. They develop new markets, creating customers and/or buyers. They discover new sources of materials because of their innovative nature. Entrepreneurs are also the organizers and coordinators of the major factors of production, such as land, labor, and capital. They introduce new technologies, new industries and new products, and especially important, they create jobs (Wiki, 2008b).

The understanding of entrepreneurship is generally based on the work of economist Joseph Schumpeter, one of the most influential economists of the 20th century. He wrote, in his book entitled *Capitalism, Socialism and Democracy* that an entrepreneur is a person who is willing and able to convert a new idea or invention into a successful innovation. He further stated that entrepreneurship forces "creative destruction" across markets and industries, simultaneously creating new products and new ways of doing business. Schumpeter saw the innovative entry of entrepreneurs into the market as the force that sustained long term economic growth, even as it destroyed the value of established companies (Wiki, 2008c).

Clearly, the role of entrepreneurship in worldwide sustainability is crucial. How that role is played could depend considerably on entrepreneurship education, first in making aspiring entrepreneurs knowledgeable of the sustainability issue and, second, making them aware of how they can harness sustainability for profit. This is a mammoth challenge when viewed in light of current global business practices related to sustainability.

Current Global Business Sustainability Practices

By definition, "A business is sustainable if it has adapted to practices for the use of renewable resources and holds itself accountable for the environmental and human rights impacts of its activities." (Wiki, 2007) Sustainability perspectives for resources and business are essential. The present growth trends in world population, industrialization (China and India for examples), food production, and resource depletion, continue unchanged. The worldwide limits to growth will be reached sometime within the next 100 years. A potential result could be a sudden and uncontrollable decline in both population and industrial capacity (Loucks, 1999).

A study by the Economist Intelligent Unit (EIU) surveyed 1200 senior business executives across Europe, North America, Asia-Pacific, Latin America, the Middle East and Africa. The survey revealed that many executives do not perceive sustainability as an integral part of strategic planning success. Almost one-half of the respondents believed that sustainability programs would improve brand value, but only 20 percent of the respondents believed that sustainability programs could improve profitability. Almost one-third of them admitted that their company's sustainability efforts are focused on communication, not actual change (Bigger Thinking, 2008).

It is increasingly evident that the current patterns of consumption and production, however, are not sustainable. The enormous growth in worldwide economies and population during the last four decades threaten the health and well-being of all life as we know it today. Examples of these threats include depletion of the ozone, change in climate (global warming), depletion and fouling of natural resources, and a considerable loss of biodiversity and habitat (SCN, 2004). For these reasons, corporations are under increasing pressure from their stakeholders to embrace social and environmental responsibility. But Wall Street demands quarterly financial results, a strict return on investment, and a short payback period. Regrettably, there has been limited evidence expressed in business language showing the benefits to these three critical factors through sustainability practices. This is clearly changing, albeit slowly. Willard (2002), an author, scholar, and environmental activist, has provided business leaders with a pragmatic discussion of the benefits of sustainability development strategies. He presented seven sustainability strategies in a practical guide that would lead to significant business opportunities. These included reducing hiring and retention costs, improving productivity, decreasing expenses, and increasing revenues and shareholder value.

One study, published in 2002, drew on 70 case histories of companies around the world. It showed how the three pillars of sustainable development, economic growth, ecological balance, and social progress, work to improve the bottom line even as they create a better world. This was seen as a first in which major business leaders argued that sustainability was not only compatible with, but crucial to, business success (Holliday *et al.*, 2002).

Another study argued that organizational and cultural change is the missing key ingredient in the operationalization of sustainable development. The study provided a theoretical framework and a change-management guide for business managers to use in leading their organizations to embrace sustainability (Doppelt, 2003). Another initiative is the Vancouver Sun Sustainable Living Expo, a celebration of leading companies who care about their customers, their communities, and the environment. Their EPIC Sustainability Initiative is a framework of management practices that guide their decisions according to sound principles of environmental, social, and economic sustainability. The objectives of the initiative are (1) reducing the consumption of resources and associated generation of wastes and pollution; (2) ensuring that the environmental aspects related to their products and services are minimized; and (3) actively engaging all involved through promotions and communications as they prepare for the 8–10 May 2009 expo (EPIC, 2008).

Schaltegger and Wagner (2006) have compiled insights on a large number of aspects of the link between sustainability performance, business competitiveness, and economic success in an attempt to provide a comprehensive view of how these variables are related. Also provided are (1) case histories of companies that have been successful in integrating social, environmental, and economic issues, (2) analyses of the causal and empirical relationship between environmental and/or social performance, business performance, and firm-level competitiveness, (3) assessment of factors influencing operational sustainability strategies and their economic impact, and (4) comparisons of interactions between sustainability performance and firm competitiveness across industry sectors and countries.

Small business leaders are beginning to respond with innovative new solutions. Small businesses such as A.O.K. Auto Body and Vic's Market are progressing beyond regulatory compliance in favor of more positive roles in finding solutions to sustainability issues. Perhaps the single most influential factor motivating such actions is that waste reduction, energy efficiency, and prevention of pollution make economic sense, thus improving the bottom line of the business (SCN, 2004). There also are companies from emerging markets that are finding considerable success in the global business community, but only a few are known for their environmental and social management. These companies are gaining a competitive advantage by developing business strategies to become environmentally and socially responsible. It suggests that companies from emerging markets, even more than in developed countries, can lead the way in sustainable innovations, which makes them strong market differentiators (Giraud et al., 2008).

Clearly, the case for businesses, large and small, to make sustainability an important part of their strategic planning and to implement such planning has grown considerably over the past five or six years. Corporations and SMEs are realizing there are profits to be made by sustainable practices. It now is the role of universities to provide future business leaders, and especially our future entrepreneurs, with the philosophies or theories, programs, practices and procedures needed to guide them in their successful pursuit of profits, while at the same time achieving sustainability of economic, ecological, and social or human resources.

Entrepreneurship Education

Entrepreneurship is a key driver of the economy. Wealth and a majority of jobs are created by SMEs started by entrepreneurially minded individuals, many of whom later create large businesses. Individuals exposed to entrepreneurship frequently express that they have more opportunity to exercise creativity, higher self-esteem, and a greater sense of control over their lives. For these reasons, many business men and women, politicians, economists and educators support fostering a robust entrepreneurial culture in order to maximize individual and collective economic and social success (Entrepreneur Education, 2008). This includes a demand for entrepreneurship education.

Entrepreneurship education has experienced remarkable growth over the past 50 years, increasing from a single course offering to a diverse range of educational opportunities available at more than 1500 colleges and universities around the world (Charney and Libecap, 2000). The 1985 prediction that the number of course offerings should increase at an expanding rate (Vesper, 1985) held true. In 1985, 253 American colleges or universities offered courses in small business management or entrepreneurship. In 1993, 441 entrepreneurship courses were available (Gartner and Vesper, 1994). Foote (1999) reported that student enrollment in entrepreneurship courses at five top American business schools increased 92 percent from 1996 to 1999 (from a total of 3078 to 5913 courses), and the number of entrepreneurship courses offered increased 74 percent.

The 1990–2005 period witnessed the growth of small business management and entrepreneurship courses offered at both the two- and four-year college and university levels in the US (Solomon and Fernald, 1991). A 2001 estimate suggested that entrepreneurship and small business education were being offered in as many as 1200 post-secondary institutions in the US alone (Solomon, 2001). Although numbers differ based on sampling techniques of the researchers, however, other specific examples of the growth of entrepreneur education include: (1) 16 American universities/colleges were offering courses in 1970 versus 400 in 1995 (Vesper and Gartner, 1997); (2) 400 American courses were being offered

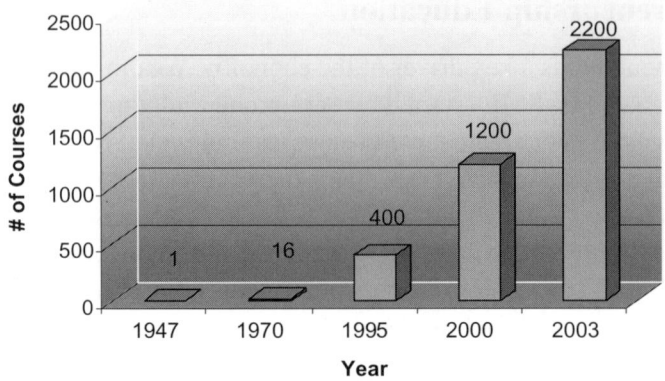

Fig. 1 Growth of entrepreneurship courses at unversities in the US.

in 1995 versus 1200 in the year 2000 (Solomon et al., 2002); (3) an increase from the first university class in 1947 to 2200 courses at over 1600 schools in the US in 2003 (Kirby, 2003); and (4) at least 1800 American universities were offering at least one course by the year 2005 (Cone, 2005) (Fig. 1).

The offering of small business management and entrepreneurship courses at both the two- and four-year college and university levels have grown in the US in both number and diversity of content. This expansion of educational offerings has been fuelled in part by dissatisfaction, voiced by students and accreditation bodies, with the traditional Fortune 500 focus of business education (Solomon and Fernald, 1991). If entrepreneurship education is to produce real entrepreneurs capable of generating real enterprise growth and wealth, the challenge to educators will be to craft courses, programs and major fields of study that meet the rigors of academia while keeping a reality-based focus and entrepreneurial climate in the learning environment (Solomon et al., 2002).

In 1995 there were no textbooks available to describe how to operate a business in an ecologically sustainable way. A handful of companies, however, were becoming ecological pioneers, at the same time becoming very successful in their businesses. They realized that students and business executives were still being taught the virtues of growth and ever higher profits, strategies for global expansion and how to use an ever-expanding worldwide web. But there were few, if any, schools teaching that profit and growth curves are not limitless and that global expansion of businesses was creating environmental and social disintegration. They also realized it was time for business schools to develop workshops or even a full curriculum for business leaders to not only account for profit and loss, but how to account for natural resources, ecological and human (Capra and Pauli, 1995).

The Kauffman Foundation in the US works to catalyze an entrepreneurial society in which job creation, innovation, and the economy flourish. They work with leading educators, researchers, and other partners to further the understanding "of the powerful economic impact of entrepreneurship, to train the nation's next generation of entrepreneurial leaders, to develop and disseminate proven programs that enhance entrepreneurial skills and abilities, and to improve the environment in which entrepreneurs start and grow businesses." (Kauffman Foundation, 2008) They recently were cited by *USA Today* as stating that entrepreneurship education must address opportunity recognition, marshalling of resources, and initiating and operating an entrepreneurial venture in the face of risk (USA Today, 2008). Although these are obviously broad and generally accepted goals, it is noted that the sustainability issue apparently has not yet gained sufficient priority to be included within this definition of entrepreneurship education.

Loucks (1999) authored what may be considered an early reference for students and professionals involved in business and other fields to help them understand how business and science, as professional communities, are adapting to new information about risks to the environment. He emphasized two key concepts, the concept of needs, that is, the essential needs of the world's poor, and the idea of limitation imposed by the state of technology and social organization in the environment's ability to meet present and future needs. There is an obligation to do what is environmentally and socially right, as well as what is economically expedient. He wrote that actions may be deemed right when they tend to preserve the integrity, stability, and beauty of the biotic community; wrong when they tend otherwise.

There are many challenges facing educators in the field of sustainability. An evolving field, still in its infancy as a management discipline, there is a need to overcome the underlying assumption that many environmental and social issues represent non-value-added effort. A wide mix of approaches is indicated, many of them are experimental and new to management learning. It has been suggested that they all share an experiential element and attempt to bring the theory across in a way that makes it relevant to the practitioner. Thus, educators need to link the learning to the students' perception of the "real" world. In addition, there is a need to provide holistic and interdisciplinary learning. The concept of sustainability does not easily lend itself to a narrow approach because it crosses over to all business functional areas, as well as to the ecology, engineering, and biology fields (Galea, 2004). This is reflected in the Owen Graduate School of Management's entrepreneurship program, which is the epicenter of leading-edge, cross-disciplinary work among their graduate schools. Projects involve students and faculty from their law school, medical center physicians, and engineering and science graduate students (Vanderbilt, 2009).

Universities have always existed to nurture healthy economies through education. The University of British Columbia (UBC) is among hundreds of educational institutions pledged to make sustainability the foundation for campus operations, research and teaching. In 1997 UBC became the first university to adopt a sustainable development policy. One year later it became Canada's first university to open a campus Sustainability Office and they now offer over 300 sustainability-related courses (Sustainability Office, 2008). In fact, this review found that Canadian universities appear to be leading the way in incorporating sustainability into their curriculum. For another example, the Schulich School of Business at York University was recently ranked #3 in the world and #1 in Canada in a global ranking of the top 100 MBA programs that are incorporating social and environmental business issues into the main curriculum (Schulich, 2008).

Babson College cited five key areas in entrepreneurship education. They are: (1) new venture creation, (2) entrepreneurial finance, (3) technology, (4) public policy, and (5) social entrepreneurship. Social entrepreneurship was defined as the process of identifying opportunities, organizing resources and providing leadership to solve people and planet problems while generating societal and economic value. People issues include healthcare, education, poverty, homelessness and security. Planet issues include the environment, energy, water, waste and clean technology. They believe that by leveraging their expertise in entrepreneurship, social entrepreneurship courses and programs will educate entrepreneurs to develop and grow businesses for a better world (Babson College, 2008).

The Stanford Graduate School of Business has scheduled a program, entitled "Business Strategies for Environmental Sustainability," based on the belief that true innovators set the bar. They re-define the terms of competition and determine the future. The program was designed to provide (1) a framework for understanding how to strike a balance between business and environmental objectives while maintaining stakeholders confidence, (2) strategies to gain competitive advantage through environmentally sustainable practices, (3) a deeper awareness of best practices across industries, and (4) the leadership skills needed to enable action as an internal change agent (Stanford, 2008).

The Kenan-Flagler Business School at the University of North Carolina offered a sustainable enterprise-related concentration for their MBA program during the 2007–2008 academic year. In addition to the courses, students could receive credit towards the Sustainable Enterprise concentration for independent study projects. Course titles included: (1) Strategic Corporate Social Responsibility, (2) Entrepreneurship and Minority Economic Development, (3) Global Supply Chain Management, (4) Product Stewardship and Sustainability, (5) Climate Change: Turning the Heat Up on Business, (6) Sustainable Enterprise, (7) Systems Thinking for Sustainability, and (8) Social Entrepreneurship (UNC, 2008). In 2007, the Kelley School of Business' MBA program at Indiana University was awarded the National Model MBA in Entrepreneurship Program for developing an exemplary program in entrepreneurship that reflected innovation, quality, effectiveness, comprehensiveness, sustainability, transferability, depth of support and impact on a national or global level (Kuratko, 2007). It should be noted, however, that no course titles included the word "sustainability."

Many other universities are now offering sustainability-related entrepreneurship courses to their MBA/entrepreneurship programs. Table 1 provides a summary listing of selected programs (see Note 1 below).

Table 1 Sustainability programs and courses at selected universities and colleges

Bainbridge Graduate Institute	Offers an MBA in Sustainable Business.	http://www.bgiedu.org/
Boston College	Recently joined the Association for the Advancement of Sustainability in High Education (AASHE) and the US Green Building Council (USGBC). Plan to incorporate sustainability theme in many BC courses.	http://www.bc.edu/offices/sustainability/sustainability.html
Center for Environmental Policy and Management, University of Louisville	Seeks to improve the economic efficiency and environmental efficacy outcomes of governmental and business environmental management practices.	http://cepm.louisville.edu/
Fairleigh Dickinson University	Conference covered business opportunities in renewable energy, clean water technology, biofuels, alternative transportation, green building and construction technologies, waste management, industrial transformation, sustainable and urban agriculture, carbon sequestration, green investing, and sustainability education. Additional topics may be added, based on registration interest.	http://inside.fdu.edu/prpt/greeexpo.html

(*Continued*)

Table 1 (Continued)

Frederick A. and Barbara M. Erb Institute, University of Michigan	Corporate Management Program equips students with skills and knowledge necessary to create environmentally and economically sustainable organizations.	http://www.erb.umich.edu/
Green Design Institute, Carnegie Mellon University	Undergraduate and graduate students at CMU are offered elective courses that provide a deeper understanding of scientific, engineering, economic, social and policy issues relating to the environment.	http://www.ce.cmu.edu/GreenDesign/education/index.html
Haas School of Business, University of California, Berkeley	Interdisciplinary program that integrates Business Ethics, Global Corporate Social Responsibility, Social Enterprise and Environmental Management.	http://www.haas.berkeley.edu/
Harvard Business Publishing	Harvard Business Online's Leading Green blog covers leadership, innovation, strategy, execution, marketing and so on all from a green perspective.	http://blogs.harvardbusiness.org/leadinggreen/
Haub Program in Business and Sustainability, Schulich School of Business, York University	Provides graduate courses in Management Practices and Strategies for Sustainability; education and tools needed to champion sustainable development.	http://mba.schulich.yorku.ca/SSB-Extra/BSUSnew.nsf/docs/History

(Continued)

Table 1 (*Continued*)

Institute for Technology, Entrepreneurship and Commercialization, Boston University	Dedicated to the new entrepreneur who is pursuing technologies, products, and services that meet pressing global needs in healthcare, life sciences, alternative energy, and many other sectors.	http://www.bu.edu/phpbin/news-cms/news/?dept=6444&id=44120
Jonkoping International Business School (JIBS)	Measure success by enabling JIBS and partners to generate new revenues and profits in an environmentally sustainable way.	http://www.ihh.hj.se/doc/1667.
Kelley School of Business, Indiana University	Program includes innovation, quality, effectiveness, comprehensiveness, sustainability, transferability, depth of support & impact on a national or global level.	http://www.indiana.edu/~grdschl/graduate-programs-and-degrees.php.
Leeds School of Business, University of Colorado	Specializes in helping students create companies that are eco-friendly and socially progressive.	http://leeds.colorado.edu/about/interior.aspx?id=542,585,2128

(*Continued*)

Table 1 (Continued)

Loyola Marymount University, Los Angeles, CA	MBAB 650 • Environmental Strategy: Sensitizes students to the broad range of environmental issues affecting business and society today; examines how society's increasing concern for the natural environment is having a major impact on business firms, as well as how business is affecting the natural environment.	http://www.lmu.edu/AssetFactory.aspx?did=10889
New York University	Catherin B. Reynolds Foundation Program in Social Entrepreneurship. Provides sustainability practices classes that relate to specific courses.	http://www.nyu.edu/reynolds/social/index.flash.html
San Francisco State University	MBA with Sustainable Business emphasis will provide students with an in-depth appreciation of the environmental and social dimensions of conducting business in a global market. Also, BUS 858 (Sustainability and Business Opportunity).	http://www.sfsu.edu/~bulletin/current/programs/busgrad.htm#subumba

(Continued)

Table 1 *(Continued)*

San Jose State University	BUS 297D: Sustainability — Understanding the management of sustainability is vital as we face rising costs for energy, water and other scarce resources as well as problems associated with greenhouse gas emissions (GHG).	http://search.sjsu.edu/query.html?q=entrepreneurship+sustainability&goSearch=GO
Simmons College School of Management	Has agreed to adhere to the United Nations' Principles for Responsible Management Education, which provides a framework for academic institutions to incorporate universal values into curricula and research.	http://management.simmons.edu/som/news/3172.shtml
Sloan School of Business, MIT	Sustainability Lab course started in Spring 2007 includes systems view and active learning.	mitsloan.mit.edu/sustainability/tools/StermanPresentation070912.ppt.
University of Calgary	Strategies for Sustainable Development: The strategic context for making business decisions with respect to sustainable development issues.	http://www.ucalgary.ca/pubs/calendar/2008/what/courses/BSEN.htm
University of Florida	Honors Introduction to Social Entrepreneurship — IDH3931, 2252.	http://www.clas.ufl.edu/users/kjoos/spring06/idh3931/readings.html

(Continued)

Table 1 *(Continued)*

University of Massachusetts	ECON 308 Political Economy of the Environment: Application of the theories of political economy to environmental problems and issues. Topics include regulatory and market approaches to pollution and natural resource depletion; cost-benefit analysis and its economic and political foundations; and case studies of specific environmental problems such as acid rain, deforestation, and global warming.	http://www.umass.edu/umext/jgerber/bdic300.htm
University of Pennsylvania	GAFL-520-001 Non-Profits and Social Entrepreneurship: Self Sufficient Agents of Change.	http://209.85.215.104/univ/upenn?q=cache:eiyg8uKJ4rsJ:www.fels.upenn.edu/Syllabi/GAFL520.pdf+entrepreneurship+sustainability&hl=en&ct=clnk&cd=1&gl=us&ie=UTF-8

(Continued)

Table 1 (Continued)

University of Vermont	CDAE 237 — *Economics of Sustainability.* Economic analysis that integrates natural resource and community planning for sustainable development at local, national and international levels. Examples include land use, sustainable agriculture and green business.	http://www.uvm.edu/academics/catalogue2008-09/?Page=courses/coursecatalogue.php&SM=coursemenu.html&category=CDAE
University of Washington	*Global Social Entrepreneurship Competition,* focus on social entrepreneurship requires that teams find creative and commercially sustainable ways to improve the quality of life in developing countries.	http://foster.washington.edu/new/full_stories/gsec.html
W. P. Carey School of Business, Arizona State University	Bachelor of Arts in Business with a Sustainability Concentration.	http://wpcarey.asu.edu/up/future-students/at-a-glance/degree-programs.cfm#BS

Conclusions

Sustainability is no longer an issue of to do or not to do. With the acceleration of globalization, new markets are being opened. There is a rapid evolution of technology and global connectivity, a growing prominence of developing countries, and a large increase in both the number and reach of multinational businesses. This globalized world has interconnected financial markets with positive and negative consequences. It has unprecedented urbanization reflecting strong underlying trends associated with the way people earn a living, with growing divides and potentially explosive disparities between the rich and the poor. It also has challenges to diversity, in its biological, ecological, human and social forms, as well as concerns about the climate and environment (ROG, 2008).

Although sustainability has been a concern of many in recent decades, it appears that the next sustainability wave is the buy-in of business. The idea of sustainability has been embraced enthusiastically by some businesses and rejected by others. It appears that corporate commitment to sustainability strategies will depend on their understanding that it is not only the right thing to do, but can yield increased profits over time. It also will increasingly occur as a result of a combination of threatening market forces that range from climate change to the rising demands of stakeholders. These two drivers are triggering the need for change and providing a vision of business success if the transition to sustainable operations, products, and services is properly managed (Willard, 2005).

Entrepreneurship is a lifelong learning process. It starts as early as elementary school and progresses through all levels of education, including adult and executive education programs. In addition to being a lifelong learning process, it should also be multidisciplinary.

Entrepreneurs are engaged in areas other than business such as the fields of engineering, environmentalists, health and medicine, and biology. Universities are increasingly recognizing this by offering entrepreneurship courses to other than business students (Entrepreneurship Education, 2008).

Education is a key factor in rallying businesses, large and small, to integrate sustainability into their strategic planning. The United Nations declared a Decade of Education for Sustainable Development starting in

January 2005 (Wiki, 2008a). Book authors began writing about the role of business in sustainability as early as 1995 (Capra and Pauli, 1995).

Consistent with the move toward social entrepreneurship and giving increased emphasis on sustainability in entrepreneurship education, Kao made a strong case for substituting stewardship-based economics for the current ownership-based economics. He clearly stated how the classic doctrine of

> **Note 1:** The web pages for hundreds of universities worldwide were reviewed using the key words of entrepreneurship and sustainability. Only those with courses or programs meeting this requirement were included. In many cases, the word "sustainability" referred to sustainability of operations, etc., however, and was not applicable to this study.

ownership, individual rights of private property ownership, and the market economy, all succeeds in wealth accumulation for the rich at the expense of the poor, the environment, and our children's children. On the other hand, stewardship-based economics is about life and living. Each individual has the right to live and share the earth's resources. Decisions are made to allocate resources sensibly for both self-interest and the interest of fellow human beings for long term sustainability for the future of humanity. He provides a model, Social Equity, Inc., which would correct our current methods of wealth distribution, thereby relieving poverty and helping the environment (Kao, 2007). It appears to be a far more ethical approach for businesses of the future and, for that reason, can easily be used as a textbook for university entrepreneurship courses.

Entrepreneurship has been declared the most significant driver in the future development of societal welfare. Businesses, organizations and individuals should be motivated for, and develop competence in, perceiving new opportunities through reflective action and hence participating in the creation of change and growth in society. This capacity and inclination for change and innovation is conceived as an important human trait, which has come to be known as "enterprising behavior" in international research

(Blenker *et al.*, 2006). Universities have started workshops for business executives, followed by courses for MBA students, during this decade. Entrepreneurship courses and programs which include sustainability have come into prominence only during the past several years, and then only among a minority of universities. While not complete, this review of sustainability in entrepreneurship education at the university level includes a selection of universities that understand and have accepted the challenges being faced in the world's future. They not only believe in the importance of the full contribution of human beings and the environment, these universities and colleges understand they will have an important influence on their students, the young men and women who will be the leaders of sustainability in the business world of tomorrow.

References

Babson College (2008). *Social Entrepreneurship at Babson*, The Arthur M. Blank Center for Entrepreneurship. Retrieved 23 May 2008 from Babson College website: http://www3.babson.edu/ESHIP/programs/socialeship.cfm.

Bigger Thinking (2008). *Harnessing Sustainability for Profit*. Retrieved 21 February 2008 from BiggerThinking website: http://www.biggerthinking.com/en/sustainability/actionor aspiration.aspx.

Blenker, P., Dreisler, P. and Kjeldsen, J. (2006). *Entrepreneurship Education at University Level: Contextual Challenges*, Working Papers 151, School of Economics and Business Administration, Tallinn University of Technology.

Capra, F. and Pauli, G. (eds.) (1995). *Steering Business Toward Sustainability*. Tokyo: United Nations University Press.

Charney, A. and Libecap, G. (2000). *Impact of entrepreneurship education*, in *Insights: A Kauffman Research Series*. Kauffman Center for Entrepreneurial Leadership.

Clayton, T., Clayton, A.M.H. and Radcliffe, N.J. (1996). *Sustainability: A Systems Approach*. Washington, DC: Island Press.

Cone, C. (2005). *Are Entrepreneurs Born or Made? (Can We Learn/Teach Entrepreneurship?*. Retrieved 14 June 2008 from stvp.stanford.edu/documents/about/presentations/OSV_Byers_2007.pdf.

Doppelt, B. (2003). *Leading Change Toward Sustainability: A Change-Management Guide for Business*. Sheffield, United Kingdom: Greenleaf Publishing.

Dunphy, D., Benveniste, J., Griffiths, A. and Sutton, P. (2000). *Sustainability: The Corporate Challenge of the 21st Century.* Australia: Allen & Unwin.

Entrepreneurship Education (2008). *Importance of Entrepreneurship Education.* Retrieved 27 February 2008 from the Consortium for Entrepreneurship Education website: http://www.entre-ed.org/.

EPA (2008). *Supporting Sustainability.* Retrieved 27 February 2008 from Environmental Protection Agency website: http://www.epa.gove/sustainability/24 p.1.

EPIC (2008). *Ethical, Progressive, Intelligent, Consumer, the Vancouver Sun Sustainable Living Expo*, The Globe Foundation of Canada, Vancouver, British Columbia.

Foote, D. (1999). Show Us The Money! *Newsweek*, 19 April, pp. 43–44.

Galea, C. (2004). *Teaching Business Sustainability.* Sheffield, United Kingdom: Greenleaf Publishing.

Gartner, W.B. and Vesper, K.H. (1994). Executive forum: experiments in entrepreneurship education: Successes and Failures, *Journal of Business Venturing*, 9: 179–187.

Giraud, L., Mak, M.A. and Thorpe, J. (2008). *News Release: Emerging Market Companies Win by Using Innovative Strategies for Sustainable Business*, International Finance Corporation, The World Bank, Washington DC, 16 January.

Hart, M. (2006). *Indicators of Sustainability.* Retrieved 24 April 2008 from Sustainable Measures website: http://www.sustainablemeasures.com/Indicators/index.html (copyright@1998–2006).

Hisrich, R.D., Peters, M.P. and Shepherd, D.A. (2005). *Entrepreneurship* (6th Edn.). Boston: McGraw-Hill Irwin.

Holliday, C.O., Schmidheiny, S. and Watts, P. (2002). *Walking the Talk: the Business Case for Sustainable Development.* San Francisco: Berrett-Koehler Publishers.

Johnson, S. (2008). *Supporting Sustainability.* Retrieved 27 February 2008 from US Environmental Protection Agency website: http://www.epa.gove/sustainability/24 p. 1.

Kao, R.W.Y. (2007). *Stewardship-Based Economics.* Singapore: World Scientific Publishing Company.

Kauffman Foundation (2008). *About the Foundation.* Retrieved 14 March 2008 from Kauffman Foundation website: http://www.kauffman.org/foundation.cfm, page 1.

Kirby, D.A. (2003). Entrepreneurship education: can business schools meet the challenge?, paper presented at the *Internationalizing Entrepreneurship Education and Training Conference*, November.

Kuratko, D.F. (2007). *Kelley School of Business Entrepreneurship Program*. Retrieved 22 April 2008 from the Indiana University website: http://newsinfo.iu.edu/news/page/normal/4692.html.

Loucks, O.L. (1999). *Sustainability Perspectives for Resources and Business*. Boca Raton, FL: CRC Press.

Megginson, L.C., Megginson, W.C. and Byrd, M.J. (2005). *Small Business Management: An Entrepreneur's Guidebook*. Boston: Irwin.

ROG (2008). *Raising Our Game: Can We Sustain Globalization?*, Retrieved 3 May 2008 from SustainAbility Compass website: http://www.sustainability.com/raising-our-game.

Schaltegger, S. and Wagner, M. (2006). *Managing the Business Case for Sustainability: The Integration of Social, Environmental and Economic Performances*. Sheffield, United Kingdom: Greenleaf Publishing.

Schulich (2008). *Business and Sustainability*. Retrieved 23 May 2008 from Schulich School of Business, York University website: http://mba.schulich.yorku.ca/SSB-Extra/BSUSnew.nsf/docs/History.

SCN (2004). *Sustainable Business*. Retrieved 6 May 2008 from Smart Communities Network website: http://www.smartcommunities.ncat.org/business/buintro.shtml.

Solomon, G.T. (2001). *Interview*. The George Washington University School of Business and Public Management, 22 October.

Solomon, G.T., Duffy, S. and Tarabishy, A. (2002). The state of entrepreneurship education in the United States: a nationwide survey and analysis, *International Journal of Entrepreneurship Education*, 1(1): 65–86.

Solomon, G.T. and Fernald, L.W., Jr. (1991). Trends in small business management and entrepreneurship education in the United States, *Entrepreneurship Theory and Practice*, 15(3): 25–40.

Stanford (2008). *Business Strategies for Environmental Sustainability*. Retrieved 30 May 2008 from Stanford Graduate School of Business, Executive Education website: http://www.gsb.stanford.edu/exed/bses/index.html.

Sustainability Office (2008). *Get Sustainable*. Retrieved 17 May 2008 from the University of British Columbia website: http://www.sustain.ubc.ca/.

UNC (2008). *MBA Sustainable Enterprise Concentration*. Retrieved 8 April 2008, from Kenan-Flagler Business School, University of North Carolina website: http://www.kenan-flagler.unc.edu/KI/cse/newmbasec.cfm.

USA Today (2008). *Entrepreneurship Education for Children and Youth*. Retrieved 27 February 2008 from USA Today website: http://www.Usatoday.com/educate/Kauffmanpresentation.htm.

Vanderbilt (2009). *The Owen Entrepreneurship Center*. Retrieved 26 August 2009 from http://mba.vanderbilt.edu/vanderbilt/About/faculty-research/research-centers-of-excellence/own-entrepreneurship-center.

Vesper, K.H. (1985). *Entrepreneurship Education*. Wellesley, MA: Babson College Press.

Vesper, K.H. and Gartner, W.B. (1997). Measuring progress in entrepreneurship education, *Journal of Business Venturing*, 12(5): 403–421.

Wiki. (2007). *Sustainable Business*. Retrieved 16 July 2008 from Wikipedia website: http://en.wikipedia.org/wiki/Sustainable_business.

Wiki. (2008a). *Sustainability*. Retrieved 9 May 2008 from Wikipedia website: http://www.en.wikipedia.org/wiki/Sustainability.

Wiki. (2008b). *Entrepreneurship*. Retrieved 27 April 2008 from Wikipedia website: http://en.wikipedia.org/wiki/Entrepreneurship.

Wiki. (2008c). *Creative Destruction*. Retrieved 27 April 2008 from Wikipedia website: http://en.wikipedia.org/wiki/Creative_destruction.

Willard, B. (2002). *The Sustainability Advantage (Seven Business Case Benefits of a Triple Bottom Line)*. Gabriola Island, BC, Canada: New Society Publishers.

Willard, B. (2005). *The Next Sustainability Wave: Building Boardroom Buy-In (Conscientious Commerce)*. Gabriola Island, BC, Canada: New Society Publishers.

9
FROM ENTREPRENEURSHIP TO STEWARDSHIP-BASED ECONOMICS*

Raymond W. Y. Kao, Rowland R. Kao and Kenneth R. Kao

> *This paper is prepared on the basis of the authors' previous work in this area along with a selection of noted contributions made by other writers since 1703. Its purpose is to provide readers a brief account of the evolution of the important knowledge discipline — Entrepreneurship: How it impacts our life, living, environment and resources as well their diversity(?) in the past 100 years.*
>
> *Raymond W.Y. Kao*
> *Rowland R. Kao*
> *Kenneth R. Kao*

Entrepreneurship

Introduction — the matter of definition

It was at an Entrepreneurship Conference, held in Shanghai 1995, a joint effort between China's Fu-Dan University, and Nanyang Technological University of Singapore. After the senior author delivered the opening address with a reference that Entrepreneurship should be noted as creative

---

* To be published in *Entrepreneurship Encyclopedia*, edited by Leo Paul Dana.

and innovative human activity for self-interest and the common good, a young person commented: "In your address, you said that people in the drug trafficking business are not entrepreneurs, but I think you are wrong. Drug trafficking is a business, and traffickers are just as much entrepreneurs as any other venture founders. They created the business, make money for themselves, and provide jobs for others. Why don't you consider them as entrepreneurs?" The senior author responded: "Well, I don't know about China, but in Singapore, a drug trafficker, if caught and found guilty as charged can be sentenced to death by hanging."

This short conversation indicates more or less what a definition means, and how important it is. A definition can be misused to justify actions for those who wish to make it to serve their own means.

A definition was made to serve man as a guide, in a learning environment, helping to communicate knowledge amongst those concerned. All of us would agree, including our legal system, that laws are created on the basis of justice to enforce human behavior and/or business conduct within the framework of the law. But the law is not justice itself. To enforce and interpret justice in the law is the task of the judge — a person, or a group of persons (jury). Similarly, a definition is supposed to be based on a sound purpose, intended to be used in practice. To uphold what a definition is intended to do for us, however, is still a human problem.

The jungle of definitions

(A) The Entrepreneur

It would be difficult to verify that the dinosaurs went extinct because they were not entrepreneurs who could innovate to adapt to a changing environment. In the less "innovative and creative society," prehistoric human beings lived without "Entrepreneurship" as hunter-gatherers. They certainly had no automobiles, LCDs or plasma TVs, MSN video communication, million dollar mansions, and personal jets just for the sake of one's own pleasure. Although all these things may not be everyone's preference, nevertheless, it is the creative and innovative activities that give all those luxuries to those who desire them. However, not all those in the privileged classes are innovative and creative. They can cheat, lie, manipulate the system, and for some, even kill others to get what they want. In today's world of well-to-do countries, the desire for more is not just a matter of words, but action, and perhaps this is how entrepreneurship was spurred.

(1) *Self-employed with uncertain return*

As a knowledge-based discipline, the word, *Entrepreneurship* has at least 300 years of history, but it was not until Cantillon (1710), followed by a number of writers (see summary below), who the needed criteria to form a definition, was it developed, and up this day they are still widely quoted. In Cantillon's words, an entrepreneur is someone who is "self-employed with uncertain returns" characterized by the following:

(a) An entrepreneur is a person
(b) The person is self-employed and assumed in the self-created business venture
(c) The venture is in the exchange system.
(d) He/she depends on the venture for his/her livelihood.
(e) Uncertainty signifies risk taking attributes.

These elements suggest that in a simple way, although an entrepreneur is a person, this person is at the center of entrepreneurship knowledge.

The above, by-and-large, fits well with the supply functions of economic analysis, including

(a) Factor of distribution — income or profit.
(b) Factor of exchange — income can only be generated from an exchange system under the market economy.
(c) Factors of production — the process of innovation and creation.

(2) *The challenges that come along with definition*

As it is a closely related economic discipline the ownership-based (self-employed) definition leaves two areas of concern as to the further search for the property of an entrepreneur (see Table 1) — what are his attributes?

(a) Dual status of self-employed "business entity"

Based on Cantillon's definition, the enterprise under a self-employed individual has dual status: the enterprise is both an economic entity and social entity. As an economic entity, the "self-employed has the proprietary decision-making right to make decisions in allocating the "uncertain returns" for him/herself. As a social entity, he/she is accountable as a

Table 1 A summary of entrepreneur definitions

Richard Cantillon	1710	A self-employed person with uncertain return.
Abbe Nicollas	1767	A leader of men, a manager of resources, an innovator of ideas, including new scientific ideas, and a risk taker.
Jean-Baptiste Say	1801/1810	A coordinator of production with management talent.
Joseph Schumpeter	1910	A creative innovator.
Frank Knight	1921	A manager responsible for direction and control, who bears uncertainty.
Edith Penrose	1959	A person with managerial capabilities separate from entrepreneurial capabilities, and able to identify opportunities and develop small enterprises.
J.E. Stepanek	1960	A moderate risk taker.
D.C. McCelland	1961	A person with a high need for achievement.
Robert E. Budner	1962	A person who has a high tolerance for ambiguity.
Orvis F. Collins	1964	A person with a high need for autonomy.
W.D. Litzinger	1965	Low need for support and conformity, leadership, decisiveness, determination, perseverance and integrity.
J.B. Rotter	1976	Internal locus of control.
Israel Kirzner	1979	An arbitrageur.
J.A. Timmons	1985	"A" type behavior pattern.

steward for resources to see that all resource-providers will receive a fair share of return for their contribution (including to restore what was taken from nature and a fair share of the fruits of labor).

If the requirement to sustain a definition of entrepreneur is risk taking, along with other attributes (see summary), all of them can be the attributes of some, although not one possesses all those attributes (including the self-employed "entrepreneur"), but they could have those attributes the same as the self-employed. Then, there are complicated matters involving the factor of earned uncertain income distribution (*profit*). *Must all goes to the proprietary decision maker (owner) or viewed as residual for redistribution to all those who had made the contribution?*

(b) Issues concerning "Income" or "Profit" distribution

   (i) Wages to workers to be paid first before "Income" — Since the entrepreneur is self-employed, he/she would be the decision maker to allocate resources (including human resources) according to his/her desire including, in particular, "earned uncertain return" or "profit." However, the risk factor does not involve just whether there shall be any income or profit, as those who worked in his/her enterprise would have to be paid first before income or profit can be earned in order for them to continue working in the enterprise.

   (ii) A point of dispute — In accordance with Cantillon's definition, it is the matter of making proprietary decisions (traditionally ownership decision) that counts. However, the definition leads to two issues. *First*, the definition seems to suggest that a self-employed person is the only entrepreneur. *Second*, the distribution of uncertain income or profit is entirely at the discretion of the self-employed entrepreneur.

   (iii) Seeding for socialism — If those who work under the self-employed entrepreneur are dissatisfied with his/her decision to award him/her the entire uncertain return or profit, there could be the possibility for those who work in the enterprise to challenge that decision. In a broader scale, this is how socialism/communism takes the route to challenge the entrepreneur's decision.

(B) Entrepreneur Attributes

Over the years, there have been a large number of contributions with respect to the subject of the entrepreneur and entrepreneurship. The emphasis placed on the "entrepreneur" as a person has not satisfied concerned individuals for many reasons. Aside from the issue of the social entity, there are questions about the entrepreneur and his/her firm. In a firm, there can be others who have similar attributes as those of the owner/entrepreneur. As a form of reporting, every level has a decision maker that has the need to make proprietary or stewardship decisions. They, like the owner/entrepreneur, need to possess and have the ability to exercise characteristics such as confidence, creativity and innovative ability to assure a firm's success. There are, in fact many known attributes of successful entrepreneurs. Hornaday and Gibb's works are used here to highlight the essentials (see Table 2 below):

Table 2 A comparison of identified entrepreneur attributes between the works or Hornaday and Gibb

Hornaday	Gibb
Self-confidence	Creativity
Perseverance, determination	Initiative
Energy, diligence	High achievement
Resourcefulness	Risk taking (moderate)
Ability to take risks	Leadership
Need to achieve	Autonomy and independence
Creativity	Analytical ability
Initiative	Hard work
Flexibility	Good communication skill
Independence	
Foresight	
Dynamic leadership	
Ability to get along with people	
Criticism	
Profit orientation	
Perceptiveness	
Optimism	

In fact, over a period of approximately 150 years, academics have done a great deal in an attempt to define who an entrepreneur is and what is entrepreneurship. Carl Manger (1871) defined Entrepreneurship as: involving obtaining information, calculation, an act of will and supervision. Although in recent years, the search for the meaning of entrepreneurship extends beyond its limited scope of "small business commercial undertakings for the pursuit of profit making." Kathleen R. Allen gave the following description:

> *Entrepreneurship is a mindset or a way of thinking that is opportunity focused, innovative, and growth oriented. Although entrepreneurship is most commonly thought of in conjunction with starting a business, the entrepreneurial mindset can be found within a large corporation, in socially responsible non-profit organizations, and anywhere individuals and teams are desiring to differentiate themselves from the crowd and apply their passion and drive to executing business opportunities.*
> (In *Launching New Ventures*, 4th Edn. Boston, New York: Houghton Mifflin, p. 4.)

It is certainly a notable effort to extend "entrepreneurship' from the narrow confined means of just small business, to include all business undertakings, large or small. It should also be recognized, however, that entrepreneurs (creative and innovative individuals) exist in other organizations, such as not for profit organizations, governments etc.

(C) Enterprise Culture

As it is so commonly referred to, entrepreneurship signifies the development of human assets, of an individual, and/or for a group as a culture. The entrepreneur culture needs to be recognized in any organization, where it is needed to sustain development and growth. It can be said that for a healthy enterprise culture, any organization is built on the academic discipline for research and learning. A. A. Gibb provided some useful guides for enterprise culture development based on strong entrepreneur attributes within every individual in the organization.

There are surprisingly many writers and researchers who have offered their thoughts on, or who have worked on definitions of "entrepreneur," as well as on entrepreneurial attributes. There is, however, only a limited amount of work on an actual definition of "Entrepreneurship." The earliest perhaps known to the authors is the work of Carl Manger (1871); defining Entrepreneurship as involving obtaining information, calculation, an act of will and supervision. Some four decades later, Schumpeter advanced his definition: "Entrepreneurship is in its essence the finding and promoting of new combination of productive factors" (see Table 3).

From Fig. 1, it is clear that the entire discipline of entrepreneurship is based on the human need to create and innovate. The reason is simple enough to appreciate; the limited resources available on Earth constrains the needs of humans, whose endless desires have resulted in continuous expansion and exploitation.

It is clear that the entire discipline of entrepreneurship is based on the human need to create and innovate. The reason is simple enough to appreciate; resources available on Earth above and under are limited while

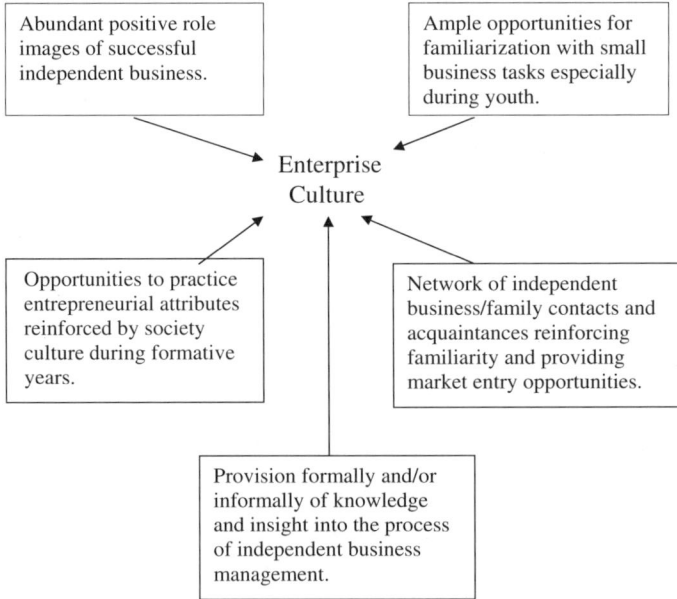

Fig. 1 Enterprise culture

Source: Gibb, A. A. (1987). Enterprise culture — its meaning and implications for education and training, *Journal of European Industrial Training*, 11(2): 2–38.

Table 3 Summary of entrepreneurship definitions

Contributor	Period	Contribution
Carl Manger	1871	Entrepreneurship involves obtaining information, calculation, an act of will and supervision
Joseph Schumpeter	1910	Entrepreneurship is in its essence the finding and promoting of new combinations of productive factors
Harvey Leibenstein	1970	Entrepreneurship is the reduction of organizational inefficiency and the reversal of organizational entropy
Israel Kirzner	1975	The identification of market arbitrage opportunities
W. Ed. McMillan and Wayne A. Long	1990	Entrepreneurship is the building of growth organization
Howard H. Stevenson	1992	Entrepreneurship is the pursuit of opportunity beyond the resources currently under your control

human's needs and wants have resulted in an upwardly continuous expansion. Consequently, entrepreneurship, creation and innovation efforts under a market system are the pillar to make everything possible to satisfy human needs. The desire to create and innovate is for many individuals, however, is an activity independent of market objectives. The efforts of these individuals are, in a fundamental sense, to contribute to the common good, to make life better for future generations. Unfortunately the spectre of human greed makes good things disputable, much like: "The tale of the rat that got into a pot of soup."

Note: *The tale of a rat that got into a pot of soup*

The Chinese have had many tales, stories, a number of them reflect situations either good or bad. One such tale implies that there are plenty of good things in life, but one bad seed can turn the good thing into a harmful senseless waste. Entrepreneurship is a wonderful human endeavor, with definitions that dwell on profit making. It happens that "Profit" is also a word, that reflects the human craving for money with no regard for the common good. To the senior author, this is much the same as a pot of deliciously wonderful nutritious soup, within which is found a rat which undoubtedly spoils the soup.

The kernel of an entrepreneur is the characteristic of an individual who simply has the desire to create and innovate regardless of the desire to accumulate wealth. The greedy accumulation of wealth does not necessarily require entrepreneurial activity. Should the corporate raider who liquidates the assets of companies, and dips into employees' pension funds to accumulate personal sums of money be considered an "Entrepreneur"? Is the central figure in the movie the "Godfather" the portrayal of an entrepreneur? Or do they just happen to be rats dropped in pots of soup?

The unfortunate reality

The definition of entrepreneurship must include the specific criterion of "for the common good." Without this qualification, drug traffickers could easily justify their harmful trade by stating that they are "job providers." How does this compare to a rat in the soup analogy?

Note: *Common good attached to the definition of Entrepreneurship is rooted in two sources*:

(1) *From the* second Vatican Council: *Factors that contribute to the common good and the overall conditions of life in society that allow the different groups and their members to be active in their own perfection more fully and more easily (p. 75).*
(2) *From* Wikipedia: *The Common Good is a term that can refer to several different concepts. In the popular meaning, it describes a specific "good" that is shared and beneficial for all (or most) members of a given* community*. This is also how the common good is broadly defined in* philosophy*,* ethics*, and* political science*.*

Human beings, as we are told by an old scholar, Moen-Tzu, can be born good or bad, those with good nature will do good for others, the bad will take advantage of others. Accordingly, most of us can be influenced (by example from others), learned, or taught to be either good or bad. For those who were either born bad, and those characterized as bad through the influence of others can be taught and/or learn to be good.

A meaningful definition will serve as a guide for action, but a guide is only a guide, and the actions are still in the hands of people. For example, job creation is one of many benefits to society resulting from the creation of a new venture. It is hardly a benefit to society; however, to allow drug traffickers whose activity is aimed at making profit at the cost of human misery, to claim they are providing jobs. The idea of "constructive destruction" has been used by manufacturers of products that maximize the short term with a built-in obsolescene strategy that causes resources drain, creation of undue waste and contamination of the environment. These are just a few negative repercussions that result when people have abused a sound definition for their own benefit, with no concern for the common good.

Defining Entrepreneurship, Past, Present and Future

The definition of entrepreneurship is a human-made statement that can be applied to guide actions for useful and sustainable value-adding processes. It is therefore a definition that should be complete for the individual's interest and the interest of humanity. As such, the authors offer the following based on what we have been taught by Schumpeter:

(1) The making of different combinations.
(2) Everyone has been an entrepreneur some time, not everyone can be entrepreneur all the time.

Entrepreneurship is and has been an all encompassing term covering all human creative and innovative endeavors, not just in profit-making commercial undertakings and not-for-profit making organizations but as well as, any individual who has the urge to do something new and something different, first as motivation for self-interest, then as always part of a group as whatever he/she does must be of benefit to others as well. Therefore, the definition of entrepreneurship needs to be welded from three components. These are:

(1) Wealth-creating and value-adding process.
(2) Actions involved in wealth creating and adding value to the process through venture formation and/or undertaking of entrepreneurial endeavors.
(3) Wealth for the individual and value for society.

The definition emphasizes the importance of creating wealth and adding value. As well, it includes all such activities, and as such departs from Cantillon's self-employed individual (1993). In the inaugural issue of the *Journal of Enterprising Culture*, the editorial board decided to place the definition on the inside front cover with a refinement to include who is an entrepreneur in a two-part definition as follows:

What is Entrepreneurship?

Entrepreneurship is "The process of doing something new and something different for the purpose of creating wealth for the individual and adding value to society.

Who is an Entrepreneur?

An Entrepreneur is a person who undertakes a wealth creating and value adding process, through incubating ideas, assembling resources and making things happen.

These definitions have led to a further refinement in the authors' later work to replace "adding value to society" with "the common good," this same definition leading to the development into the doctrine of Entrepreneurism.

Evolution of Entrepreneurial Thought

Entrepreneurism is thought of as being any human activity and thought that evolves over time (see Table 4). The early period began with Cantillon's

Table 4 Evolution of entrepreneurial thought*

Prior 1960s	Innovation and creation are fashionable words, yet were referring to mostly small owner managed business.
The 1960s	The thought and practice was on "big is better." Small may be beautiful, but bigger is better. The term "independent business" seemed to have sprung out of the National Federation of Independent Business in the US, and the Canadian Federation of Independent Business in Canada. Academics seemed to give a great deal of attention, the definition jungle became filled with ideas. Although, the word "entrepreneurship" is still difficult for people to pronounce clearly.
The 1970s	The growing concern for international competition and technological advancement, and the terms of intrapreneurship, interpreneurship, and technoneurship splurged out in the market place making a very colorful display. It is also in this period that a large number of universities took the initiative to offer "Entrepreneurship chairs" and offered PhD degrees in this discipline in the US.
The 1980s	Small is better seemed to catch everyone's attention: lean and mean, administrative (paperwork) challenges, small firms and takeovers filled the most part of the decade.
The 1990s	Money matters, creative financing, something seemed to be new at the period.
The early 21st century	Environment, poverty and resources drain become the urging issue. Social responsibility and concern for the common good drawn greater attention and action. Entrepreneurism draws needed attention, stewardship accountability applies to all entrepreneurial undertakings.

* Based on the senior author's working experience while serving as a member of the Minister's Consultative Committee for ten years, and as president of International Council for Small Business.

self-employed person with uncertain income, and then moved on to Carl Manger and Schumpeter's broader terms of creation and innovative activities and action-finding and promoting new combinations. This was followed by Timmons and OECD narrowing to actions involving searching and sizing business opportunities. At the same time, a few others seemed focused on pushing entrepreneurship development including business development, enterprise development and growth. Unfortunately, despite countless efforts, both in academic pursuits and practice in the private sector, the challenge of the "Common Good" has not been noted, although some academic efforts directed to social responsibility should be noted. The summary in Table 4 marks the noted changes in entrepreneurship throughout the past one-half of a century.

Entrepreneurism

(1) An ideology and philosophy

Entrepreneurism is an ideology proposed as a sensible alternative to capitalism on the one hand, and socialism on the other. The essence of it is based on the "common good." It is not just about making money, nor is it merely about starting up a venture or owning a small business — it is a way of life, applicable to all human economic activities. Living on a planet with finite resources, humanity is sustainable only if there is constant pursuit of innovation and creativity, not just for personal gain but also for the common good. It is also a philosophy, as it is based on: "To create and innovate is not a matter of choice, but necessity."

(2) The matter of self-interest and common good

Contrary to traditional belief, "Entrepreneurism" is not just about making money, nor is it merely about starting up a venture or owning a small business — it is a way of life, applicable to all human economic activities. Living on a planet with finite resources, humanity is sustainable only if there is constant pursuit of innovation and creativity, not just for personal gain but also for the common good. As a practical measure that to reassess the meaning of "Profit," it is more appropriate to advocate the use of residual to reduce harmful social injustice, avoiding unnecessary human conflict, still within the market system, to formulate an affordable means that will ease off human conflict. A definition of "Entrepreneurism" is therefore created on the basis of the fact that our understanding that "All humans are driven by two fundamental desires: the desire to own and the desire to create. Ownership is not just the titular holding of property-physical, intellectual or otherwise — but the right to make decisions, or put another way, the right to free choice. "The desire to create and desire to take that which is there, and to alter its form to suit our purpose, bringing into being something that did not exist before." However, it must be fully recognized, that there is a world of difference between ownership and stewardship.

> *Entrepreneurism is all about making human proprietary decisions. Exercising ownership right on the one hand, and assuring stewardship responsibilities on the other.*

This statement is the same as those who consider that capitalism is built on Schumpeter's notion of constructive destruction, Entrepreneurism is built on the weakness of two extremes. Capitalism on the one hand claims private property ownership without due consideration for the common good. Consequently, the accumulation of capital, further aggregation beyond personal consumption and luxury capacity can possibly accommodate, exploitation labor value and over demand on renewable and exhaustion of non-renewable resources at the same time. Unfortunately to rely on a market system to make adjustment itself may have to wait until there is a sub-system to make the "invisible hand" to see human misery and desperate pleas from "environmental damage" and "resources drain."

(3) Its practical application

Entrepreneurism is an ideology in which an individual is a creative and innovative agent with the desire for ownership and the right to make proprietary decisions, with the common good to guide action. As a body of knowledge, it presupposes the involvement of three independent yet interrelated entities: the state, business entity and individuals.

(a) The state: entrepreneurial government

Under Entrepreneurism, the state is the infrastructure consisting of individuals committed to serving people for the common good that will facilitate them in realizing their economic freedom, their right to acquire ownership to harvest their labor, and their right and obligations to protect the environment.

(b) The individual: entrepreneurial person

An individual is at the center, and as a stakeholder in any undertaking is responsible to him/herself. The individual views entrepreneurship and working as an entrepreneur as a way of life.

(c) The business entity: entrepreneurial entity and entity entrepreneurial managers.

Entrepreneurship on the other hand is a process of doing something new (creative) and doing something different (innovative) for the purpose of creating wealth for the individual and adding value to society. Through entrepreneurship, the doctrine of Entrepreneurism reigns over all economic endeavors. The entrepreneurial approach is applicable to business management in general, including the creation of new ventures, managing one's own business, business with family members, government and public institutions, charitable and not-for-profit organizations as well as professionals and professional organizations. It goes without saying that the entrepreneurial approach to corporate management is an integral part of entrepreneurial contemplation.

In addition to the instinctive entrepreneurial contemplation in individuals, governments, organizational businesses and otherwise, Entrepreneurism also puts forward the examination of accounting practice in matters of profit determination and cost recognition leading to the consideration of adopting "residual" for measurement and as a basis for redistribution. Human effort, in particular, the redistribution of the fruits of labor, relieves the pressure on global poverty and environmental damage and replacement of depleted resources where possible.

Stewardship-Based Economics

It is all because of ownership

Ownership-based economics has led to the rapid development and apparent universal success of the market economy. It is a system built on the deception of unlimited resource availability, ill-defined profit, and is misled by the idea that an "invisible hand" alone can be an equitable system of distribution. It has resulted in a high living standard for a few select individuals, but at the expense of mankind and nature, ultimately culminating in the development of human conflict. It must be borne in mind however, that the ownership-based system induces human desire to acquire more.The undisciplined craving for more in the advantaged few, fuelled through the market system, creates poverty, damages environmental and human health, and drains limited resources which are supposedly there, indeed for us, but for the future as well. As long as our economy functions based on ownership, we will hardly see the end of poverty, and among other things, environmental damage and resources drain. Although we can not under the circumstance abolish the market system, we must realize that the "ownership" idea may be legal, but it has deceptively led us into a vicious circle of addiction out of which we may be unable to emerge.

While Entrepreneurism serves as a guide based on our creative and innovative natures, the real issue of "ownership" challenge, is that it fundamentally is little more than a struggle for "owning." Indeed, the origin of human conflict throughout history is rooted in greed and forceful acquisition of ownership. In recent years, economic expansion has seen its share of unfairly acquiring ownership over resources by the fabrication of information to commit criminal activities ranging from cheating innocent investors in the market system to inflicting civil war on a foreign country.

Ownership-based economy

Consideration for human poverty

Classic economics, which is rooted in Adam Smith's *Wealth of Nations* lies at the foundation of the Western countries. Although Smith's idea of wealth in the market system, is "To create wealth for me and for you as well," the unfortunate reality in today's market economy is quite different from what Smith had in mind: "For me, to be rich is splendid; to create wealth for you is not my business." This, is what the market economy is: all justice in based on the matter of competition, based on the decision made by invisible hands." To some people this ownership-based system is "the only system" for our ever expanding economy therefore, we would have to accept that poverty is common, natural, and inevitable, if:

(1) greed is the sole motivation to be rich,
(2) the rich and powerful prefer to make the rich richer, and
(3) the political policy favors the rich.

It is money that matters, it will make one rich or poor: the bank system

The rich-dominated monetary and banking system tends for the rich to create barriers against the poor getting better. Manipulation of lending interest rates combined with promoting "a better life through ownership" through mass marketing, squeezes the middle-class or low income people further into debt. Like an inflating balloon, it pushes the mid-class to low income individuals into poverty (in Western countries meaning those living with any form of income below the poverty line). Interest policy is in fact, nothing more than a weapon to further the indebtedness of the middle-class and people in poverty to the privileged few.

There is no single sub-system within the market system to help ease the pressure on poverty. Religion, government policy and charitable organizations are all helpful, and significant efforts ease the pain. Bear in mind, both rich and poor are relative, the only absolute is greed — an irrational desire for more. The fundamental problem is that while greed dictates that the "sky is the limit," we have no idea what that limit is.

Resources drain and environmental health

The depletion of non-renewable resources and erosion of environmental health available to present generations will mean there will be less for our descendants. Unless the creative and innovative efforts can restore what was once there for the future, we will have to expect that "Humans landing on Mars" will be our only hope for the future. But how, will this help to relieve the pressure on poverty, resources drain and environmental disaster?

Stewardship-based economics

Stewardship-based economics recognizes the importance of the market system. It is irreplaceable, but we cannot take advantage of the system merely to satisfy an individual's wants and greed at the expense of others' labor, limited resources and freely provided living environment without giving due consideration that "we may be part of Earth, but we don't own it." What we all need is to exercise our right to make proprietary decisions, but we must also assume stewardship responsibility. While proprietary decision-making might give us a two-fold approach to easing the pressure on both the human race and the opportunity to allocate resources for self-interest it is necessary to accept the responsibility to ensure all decisions made are also for the common good.

Stewardship economics provides concise definitions of "entrepreneurism," "entrepreneurship," "entrepreneur" and "entrepreneurial" for education and application within the framework of the market economy. It acts as a signpost pointing the way toward balancing the short-term need for survival with the long-term need for sustainable growth; and serves as a philosophical beacon that will guide individuals, particularly, business leaders, toward actions in the interest of humanity.

As stewardship-based economics was developed from early works on Entrepreneurship and Entrepreneurism, it places a great deal of emphasis on acting now to be responsible stewards for making resources allocation decisions, as well as the need for education to consider a few key areas:

- We have only one Earth, and everything on it is meant for everyone. Some are strong, others may be weak, but everyone is entitled to his share of what the Earth has to offer.
- The number of countries with their diversity of people, culture and background makes it difficult to generalize. Nonetheless, it is clear that no individual can live alone, and no one should take resources ruthlessly just for his personal use. The sharing of resources should be a way of life. Nonetheless, it is clear that no individual can live alone, and no one should take resources ruthlessly just for his personal use. The sharing of resources should be a way of life.

- Resources are finite. The challenge lies not in deciding who should or should not have them but rather in finding more sustainable and renewable resources through creation and innovation.
- As stewards, everyone has the right to make proprietary decisions while in control of the resources. Stewardship responsibility must, however, be exercised during decision-making, and there must be accountability for the consequences of actions taken based on any decision.

From Entrepreneurship to Stewardship-Based Economics

```
┌─────────────────────────────────────────┐
│ Entrepreneurship: Doing                 │
│ something new and something             │
│ different for self-interest and         │
│ common good                             │
└─────────────────────────────────────────┘
                    ⇩
┌─────────────────────────────────────────┐
│ Entrepreneurism is all about making     │
│ human proprietary decisions.            │
│ Exercising ownership rights on the one  │
│ hand, and assuring stewardship          │
│ responsibilities on the other.          │
└─────────────────────────────────────────┘
                    ⇩
┌─────────────────────────────────────────┐
│ Stewardship-based economics developed from early works │
│ on Entrepreneurship and Entrepreneurism, it places a great │
│ deal of emphasis on acting now to be responsible steward for │
│ making resources allocation decision, there is the need for │
│ education and to educate others to act and think likewise. A │
│ broad knowledge-based discipline to overcome difficulties │
│ experienced by human beings through our past, of poverty, │
│ human conflict, environmental damages, resources drain. │
└─────────────────────────────────────────┘
```

IV. ENTREPRENEURSHIP AND SMALL VENTURE DEVELOPMENT FOR SUSTAINABILITY

10
SMALL IS STILL BEAUTIFUL AND SUSTAINABLE

Wee-Liang Tan

Schumacher — Advocate of the Small and Creative

When Raymond approached me to write a chapter for this collection of essays on sustainable entrepreneurship, I initially paid attention to the virtue of smallness but quickly realized the need to address *Small Is Beautiful* — Ed Schumacher's (1973) book by that title. At that point in time in post-World War II history when Schumacher wrote, mankind is faced with a number of key challenges all of which Schumacher highlighted in his book *Small is Beautiful*. We are faced with global warming and the looming environmental disaster. The poverty levels have not decreased since the time he wrote about the poor. The projections of population growth he anticipated have been exceeded. The economic doctrines he criticized have contributed to the global credit crisis. When Schumacher (1973) wrote his book *Small is Beautiful*, he argued against mainstream thinking in economics. He questioned the current thinking of his day that still persists in many respects today. He questioned the thinking that big is better. The problem of production had not been solved, he said.

Schumacher was a far-sighted prophet. However, as with all prophets, they are often not heeded till after their time and, more often than not, only when it is too late and their pronouncements imminent. In this sense, *Small is Beautiful* is still beautiful because Schumacher's ideas are still current. His examples may need to be updated. Many know of his book but no one will ever know how many have applied his ideas. More likely than not, many may know of the title and what if signifies rather than be familiar with his ideas. This author bought a secondhand copy in 1997 from a Harvard Square bookstore. It sat on the bookshelf for some time before it was read. This request from Raymond to contribute a chapter led to a revisit of this classic.

It would be remiss of this author to attempt to summarize what Schumacher has propounded in broad brush strokes. Instead it is proposed in this chapter to examine some of his thoughts and the relevance they have for the future for, if one were to read *Small is Beautiful*, one cannot help but agree that much of what he said is still relevant today and in that regard, still beautiful and sustainable.

Schumacher's foresight and vision is appreciable when one considers what one knows today. He was the advocate for an economics of permanence that requires mankind to be cognizant and account for the impact on the environment, which he called natural assets, and the limits to the earth's supply of fossil fuels. One of his key arguments is that there would be issues with the purely capitalist way in which economics is conceived with no regard for fossil fuels, Nature and the poor. It is not proposed to take up his arguments afresh. Instead this essay will look at his ideas from the perspective of entrepreneurship. First, it briefly points out aspects of his ideas that are still pertinent today and hence beautiful. Second, it takes up the argument that the beauty of his ideas see completion through entrepreneurship for entrepreneurship embodies his ideas of economic freedom, the innovativeness that lies in the individuals and communities even if they come from the Third World, and the beauty in smallness. Third, it further argues that the work for us as educators is not finished as many entrepreneurship training programs although addressing the needs of individuals and respecting human endeavor, function on the principles of economics and ignore the environment.

Still Relevant Today

Many of Schumacher's ideas are still relevant today. He argued against the notion that all that matters is whether things are economic or non-economic. The reduction of evaluation of human activity to material measures of value, in his opinion, robbed society of much that is of value and meaningful. Stemming from this emphasis on the economic is the well-entrenched idea that all that matters is profit. It implies that many activities of a non-economic nature would not be considered. The evaluation of an activity as non-economic relegated the proponent of the deemed non-economic activity to disdain or relative inattention from society. Yet there are many so-called non-economic activities that deliver value and could be subjected to objective evaluation. In his own way, he questioned the validity of resolving all matters on the basis of profit without considering all costs. He indirectly questioned the notion of profit. Others have since done the same (see for example Kao's own work in 1995, 1997 and 2007). Labeling activities as non-economic or not profitable skews human choices between activities, rendering activities addressing social needs or the environment to be ranked lower on the agenda since they do not address the bottom line. Further, it also skews career choices and public financing allocations.

Schumacher's ideas preceded the ideas of sustainability. Before sustainability became a buzz-word, Schumacher questioned with prescience, the assumptions made in his day that the earth would be able to continue to provide for the world's population. It is only recently that the governments and corporations grudgingly took cognizance of the issues of the environment and global warming. He used the term "economics of permanence" instead. With this label he pointed out the need for a change in economic thinking. The problem of production had not been solved because the solution offered by economists ignores the cost of human production on nature. Nature, he argued, is not a readily renewable asset. Most of nature's assets that are utilized in production are not renewable. It is capital that if not replenished, would lead to scarcity that would return to haunt the human race. He questioned the thinking of his day that fossil fuels would be sufficient as an energy source and that it could be augmented through nuclear power.

The failure to impute costs to business activities just because there is no direct immediate cost is what he was alarmed about. Since then, there have been numerous methods developed to determine the costs of ignoring the environment. When faced with the argument that there is no way to objectively quantify the costs, economists have employed techniques such as NIMBY (Not In My Backyard). Two former colleagues at the Nanyang Technological University have published a book on this technique

(Quah and Tan, 2002). While advances have been made, the prevalent view is to act upon the environmental issues as a necessary evil. Global warming or not, corporations are only beginning to grapple with its impact on business and only because it contributes to their reputational capital to be perceived as being environmentally conscious. More often than not, it is more of a necessary evil. The *locus classicus* is the recent appeal for a US government bailout by the US automakers. The automakers were lambasted by the Congress and the press for traveling in private owned jets to seek a bailout without proposals to work on energy saving cars then decided it was expedient to include this item in their subsequent appearance to ask for aid (Chemnick, 2008; Robinson, 2008).

However, his key argument that economics as a system should incorporate values of society has not gained ground. He had deliberately used Buddhism to illustrate his argument that there should be economics that reflects the specific values of the society to which is it being applied. He suggested that there be Buddhist economics. Until the recent global economic downturn, the economic thinking that has prevailed from Schumacher's book had gained ascendency since the fall of the Iron Curtain. With socialism losing ground through the failure of economies that adopted its extreme form, communism, there has been little attempt if at all to consider economics with some element of a human face. Even China with its avowed socialist agenda has employed capitalist mechanisms such as the market system. It would be interesting to see how China embodies the national values as it continues to progress.

Smallness and Entrepreneurship

Schumacher's choice of a book title and his stand on the role of creativity and innovation by individuals and communities aligns him with entrepreneurship. These ideas inspired the development of entrepreneurship as a field. With his belief in the need for the system of production to recognize and permit the role of individuals, small groups and communities in creativity and innovation, he is an advocate for entrepreneurship although he did not directly refer to it. He was not in favor of confining production only to large corporations. Smaller firms or communities could at worst only damage a small portion of the environment. However, he had faith in the benefits of their human endeavor.

Of particular interest is his argument that there should be room for the individuals and small firms of this world and their creativity. Schumacher was a believer in smallness. In this argument lies the support for entrepreneurship and economic freedom. He did not despise small beginnings as the saying goes, "Despise not the day of small beginnings." The adage "oak trees from little acorns grow" holds true for innovations and entrepreneurial endeavors. While many are fascinated by size, might and strength of enterprises, this lopsided view of things ignores the truth that the giants all had beginnings. Beginnings are always small relative to other firms, groups, industries, and nations. It also ignores that innovations and inventions started mostly by small teams.

There is admiration for the large conglomerates. Yet the events in the last quarter of 2008 have revealed how the great can fall in a short period of time from little undetected fissures. It is in times like these that the small, nimble and quick are able to maneuver. They also happen to be the ones to create the jobs the large remove (Birch, 1981).

The field of entrepreneurship identifies with Schumacher as entrepreneurship concerns itself with newness, innovation and creativity. It also concerns itself with ventures that add value to society and create wealth. Entrepreneurship is entrepreneurship only when the new ideas and firms that entrepreneurs champion have legitimacy in society and they only have legitimacy if society gains from their existence. As a field, it has grown over the years gaining respectability. Initially there were those who considered entrepreneurship merely as small business or the discipline that concerns itself with craftsmen and artisans. It has expanded in scope from those early days.

The field has developed much since Schumacher's book. Numerous events were taking place at the same time while not in concert. The *Journal of Business Venturing* was established. There are now many academic journals whose focus is entrepreneurship. Raymond Kao, editor of this volume, has been responsible for starting one, the *Journal of Small Business and Entrepreneurship* and encouraging another, *Journal of Enterprising Culture*. There are many trade books as well as texts on entrepreneurship and related areas. The International Council for Small Business evolved from its American roots, entrepreneurship education programs began to proliferate first in the US, then Europe and even to the rest of the world. Education programs have been established and many conferences are organized to promote entrepreneurship research and education. The contributors to this volume have in one way or another been responsible for furthering the cause of entrepreneurship. The field has come far from the early days when the first Babson conference was organized in 1981.

It has captured the attention of policy makers worldwide through the Global Entrepreneurship Monitor. Policy makers are now interested in spurring the Total Entrepreneurial Activity (TEA) defined as the increase in early stage start-up activities.

Small moves in larger organizations

Schumacher was wise in highlighting the potential of the small. Corporations have adopted the idea that they should initiate new projects and organizational units to be entrepreneurial. They are considering ways in which to harness the efforts of the individual workers and small teams. Corporate entrepreneurship is not confined to the few on top or the some in middle management. It has increasingly become clear that all have to be involved from the top to the rank and file of an organization. Entrepreneurship of various forms and in different shapes needs to be present in any company. The efforts can no longer be confined to the few whether as a special or R&D unit.

In a sense the advent of the knowledge economy has substantiated the smallness argument. The implication of the knowledge economy is that knowledge is tacit and often resides in the workers. Knowledge management and corporate entrepreneurship have a commonality in seeking to harness the knowledge generated within corporations to codify it and translate it for use and for innovations.

Entrepreneurship still beautiful

With these developments, one might be tempted to think that the pioneering work of entrepreneurship has been achieved. That entrepreneurship has arrived — it is already part and parcel of "the establishment;" since few governments would ignore entrepreneurship development. One might be tempted to think that as entrepreneurship has developed as a field and in its contributions, that "small is beautiful" has become *passé*, part of the established thinking.

Not so, the interest in entrepreneurship is fairly recent compared to the traditional disciplines in universities. It has only gained entry over the last 25 years. To track the progress made, one could refer to the proceedings of the IntEnt conference (http://www.intent-conference.de) that has as its goal the study of the internationalization of entrepreneurship education. It has not been an easy passage. There has been grudging acceptance of the field by the preceding disciplines in management.

Further, there are areas that need research and examination. While smallness possesses beauty, one cannot disregard the liability of smallness. The aspects that remain for investigation lie in the means of overcoming the liabilities associated with small size in domestic and international activities. Cooperation is a key to overcoming the liability of smallness. Smallness in size has implications for the firm in the resource view of the world, where size implies that there are resources. Cooperation permits the pooling of resources and the sharing of risks enabling the small firms to leverage on the strengths and resources of others.

Clusters are formed when entrepreneurs and SMEs "congregate" at one location (geographical or otherwise), share and pool resources. Many economies have introduced policies and committed resources for the creation of clusters with the view of fostering new high growth entrepreneurial ventures. Integral to these clusters is cooperation between entrepreneurial firms. Cooperation between entrepreneurs and firms is one area for which research is needed to identify the means for initiating and effecting cooperation while retaining the spirit of enterprise. Networks of entrepreneurial firms could also be another means to overcome smallness. How do these networks form? What are the ideal forms of governance?

In the realm of international entrepreneurship, there is much to be explored as many assume that the principles for large firms engaged to international business would apply. This approach harks to the early days when interest in entrepreneurship as field of study began as "small business" or "small business management." Some cynical scholars then opined that all that applied to small business could be distilled from all that applied to big business — that entrepreneurship only covered what applied to small business at the early stage of firm growth or scaled down. Yet there are different considerations where entrepreneurial firms are concerned that do not directly translate from the big business international business principles. For one thing, entrepreneurial firms do not have the resources large firms are endowed with. Entrepreneurial firms are also opportunistic as opposed to being rational in their selection of locations to begin new overseas operations.

Social entrepreneurship has recently become an area of development as communities, individuals and successful entrepreneurs seek ways to address social problems through new and innovative ways distinct from simple giving (philanthropy). This is a new field of entrepreneurship education and research that has sparked opportunities for research and development of programs at universities.

While the avenues for research have received very brief mention, there are implications for entrepreneurship education. Research is needed and important but the impact to be made for change comes through education and here is where Schumacher's impassioned cry for smallness can truly make even more headway.

Implications for Entrepreneurship Education — The Gaps that Remain

While it is easy to see how the field of entrepreneurship owes much to Schumacher's advocacy for creative and innovative production at the level of the small, there is much in entrepreneurship education that has not addressed Schumacher's concerns. Entrepreneurship education does much to further Schumacher's cause — that production and contribution to economic activity is not confined to the large; that is should involve the small. Entrepreneurship education speaks of free enterprise. It educates the individuals, the firms and even the corporations to embark on creative opportunities and to innovate. In so doing, entrepreneurship education provides the small with the know-how and tool kits to embark on their ventures. How does entrepreneurship education come up short in meeting Schumacher's other concerns, one might ask?

Schumacher had suggested that there is a role for entrepreneurship and for economics that took hold of the issues in life that cannot be computed in terms of profit. He took a brave step to stand against the tide. He argued for the need to be concerned about the issues of business as usual. For entrepreneurship education to take cognizance of this and to implement it, education programs must, augment the business agenda to embrace sustainability and the non-economic.

Introduce sustainability. Entrepreneurship education has not abandoned the key idea in economics that Schumacher remonstrated against — looking only at profit; operating as if nature did not matter; assuming all is well so long as the entrepreneur or the firm made its tidy bundle of profit. Sustainability has yet to be a central business tenet. It is only at most the equivalent of what the information systems people call an "add-in" or "plug-in" — something added in just to patch what is needed. This "plug-in" is now called corporate social responsibility. The idea is not new. It has been around for more than 40 years. Even as recent as December 2008, the prevalent way to get companies to consider social responsibility is to address the profit imperative (Roberts, 2008). Yet it is clear that unless sustainability becomes integral to the quest for businesses, the harm to be done to the environment will continue unabated. Only a few entrepreneurship courses and programs include it as an item of the curriculum. This writer's brief scan of sustainability in entrepreneurship programs revealed that there are number of concentrations (also known as minors or immersions) in sustainable enterprises. Examples include the MSc minor in Sustainable Business at the Copenhagen Business School, the Sustainable Enterprise Concentration at Kenan-Flagler and the Sustainable Enterprise Immersion at the Johnson School at Cornell University. The cursory scan did not reveal as many courses compared to courses being developed by colleges in the area of social entrepreneurship.

While the notion of sustainability has only crept into entrepreneurship literature in recent times, beginning in the early 21st century. Raymond has been greatly concerned for it since the beginning of the 1990s, first in his article and then through his book in 1995. He did not use the word sustainability. His call was for a larger purpose over and above the environment although it encompassed it. He mandated that any action claiming to be entrepreneurial has to add value to society. Schumacher had preceded him when he called into the question the economics of greed and size. More recently, others like Peter Senge, Bryan Smith, Nina Kruschwitz, Joe Laur and Sara Schley (2008) have joined the voices calling for a revolution — the necessary revolution for corporations, individuals and groups.

Review the mission of enterprises. The non-economic has not been incorporated in the missions of enterprises. Entrepreneurship programs, has in the same fashion as other business management programs, sought the same basis for business legitimacy — profit. It has assumed profitability or feasibility (the alternative term) as the touchstone. Yet research and anecdotal evidence declares that entrepreneurs start enterprises for other compelling reasons. It would be easy to decry profit and this writer does not wish the reader to think that this is all that is being done. Instead, this is a call for a consideration of the mission of entrepreneurial activities. The mission would be shaped by personal beliefs, national values, culture and societal concerns. Entrepreneurship educators need to consider compelling a re-consideration of other values to be included in mission statements when assisting the entrepreneurs in crafting their business plans. Profit and profit alone should not be the sole purpose of the enterprise. Perhaps all that is required is the inclusion of a discussion of the purpose of business. It might require a new prescriptive definition of entrepreneurship that integrates wealth and contribution to society as Raymond has provided since 1992 (Kao, 1991). There is power in ideas and this is a fact that Schumacher drew upon as he spoke about in his chapter on education. A definition that encompasses contribution to society, that is wide enough to envisage sustainability may appear to be just an idea. However, the definition impacts behavior. Just consider the examples such as "true and fair" in accounting regulations, customer satisfaction in marketing, or the "reasonable man" in law. Simply requiring the strategic actors whether entrepreneurs, or managers in corporations to consider before engaging in their entrepreneurial actions, the contribution of such actions to society would do much in shaping the decisions taken.

The goals of a startup can address goals in addition to profit which rank equal to the profit motive. It is possible not to refer to profit at all but some other measure that the founders desire. The mission could specify the means by which the firm operates. If the firm declares that it would only use fair trade ingredients and that it would employ a certain percentage of the disadvantaged, these principles would direct the behavior of the managers and employees. The enterprise could also stipulate how the wealth that is generated from its economic activities will be shared. There is the well-known example that Ben & Jerry's whose social mission is interrelated with its economic mission. The social responsible behavior that saw the growth of the firm from its inception still continues today even though Ben & Jerry's has become part of Unilever since 2000. It continues to shine as a socially responsible company striving for values-led innovation. American consumers rated Ben & Jerry's the most socially responsible company in the United States in 2006, in the fourth national survey of corporate citizenship conducted by Golin Ferris (Freese, 2006).

Going beyond production to distribution. Schumacher lamented the attention focused on the large in production. To address the needs of the poor, they should be equipped with what he called "the middle technology" as opposed to the "super-technology" available to and used by larger firms. Equipping the poor with the techniques of production only provides the means for economic freedom and enables them to harness the enterprise system. The number in the population who engage in entrepreneurship is not high. Self-employment as a means of alleviating poverty only goes that far, as entrepreneurship calls for resources that are in themselves limited. The question still remains for the larger firms and even the entrepreneurs, who start their businesses, how to share the wealth with the masses. Entrepreneurship has thus far addressed the smallness in production in seeking to empower individuals to engage in creative and innovative economic activity that produces goods and services to meet society's needs with the view of creating wealth for the entrepreneurs.

Yet the distribution challenge poses two questions for entrepreneurship. First, do entrepreneurship educators, including this writer, only seek to develop entrepreneurs to produce, innovate and create to satisfy current consumption needs in society or to meet market needs? Second, does entrepreneurship in addition to creating wealth address distribution of the wealth? The first question is discussed under the heading wealth creation because entrepreneurship should through wealth creation re-dress inequalities; these inequalities give rise to needs. Discussion of the second question proceeds under the heading of wealth distribution. The mission of the enterprise discussed earlier should involve a consideration of both questions. Entrepreneurs and leaders of entrepreneurial firms should consider how they could create wealth in ways that impact the distribution of wealth and how, they could distribute wealth, if their wealth creation does not involve distribution.

Wealth creation. Granted that entrepreneurs and new ventures exist to meet consumption needs, however, when they address consumption needs, there is an obligation to address greater societal needs. Addressing market needs only requires ingenuity to "make money." The vistas for entrepreneurship should extend beyond the target market segments. When dreaming of the new venture, the needs of society should not only feature in the initial PEST (Political, Economic, Societal and Technological Trends) assessment. Do entrepreneurs produce variants of goods for the poor? Entrepreneurship educators need to draw the attention of students and participants in their programs to these vistas.

Entrepreneurs in the computer industry addressed their product offerings only to the people who could afford to pay. They only lowered their prices when there is competition. Yet for the poor, it took time, philanthropic money and a dream of creating a US$100 computer for the masses in the case of the MIT's XO PC for India's poor. The dream has yet to become reality although the race has begun between the MIT's XO PC and the Novatium's NetTV one (Overdorf, 2008). The MIT PC aims to address the basic computing needs of the poor in India while Novatium's founder and chairman, Jain, wants to develop a device that allows access to computing for the middle class in India. These two companies exemplify the entrepreneurial efforts to address the bottom of the pyramid in different ways. C.K. Prahalad (2005) in his book, *The Fortune at the Bottom of the Pyramid* highlighted the opportunities that exist amongst the sector ignored by most businesses — the poor.

In the past, entrepreneurs working on renewable energy and clean, potable water also seek to create wealth in ways that impact the general population. An example of one such firm is Hyflux, Asia's leading water and environmental company specializing in membrane-based seawater desalination, drinking water treatment, wastewater reclamation, water recycling, and raw water purification. Hyflux has built several water treatment facilities worldwide producing over 300 million cubic metres of potable and industrial water per year. It began as an engineering firm. Its founder, Olivia Lum, chanced upon Israeli membrane technology for which she then obtained a licence. It first traded as a membrane distributor before innovating and transforming itself into a manufacturer of proprietary membranes as well as a builder of water reclamation and reclamation facilities. It is a global player having established water reclamation systems for China and India.

Vestas is another example. Vestas, a Danish multinational company that has built its capabilities in wind power as an alternative energy when other companies were content to rely on fossil fuel. They began their venture into wind turbines in 1979. It originated in 1945 when the founder on leaving his father's blacksmith business established VEstjysk STaalteknik A/S (abbreviated Vestas) to manufacture household appliances (www.vestas.com). In the 1970s, it was in crane production. With the advent of the second oil crisis in 1978, began exploring alternative energy by experimenting with whisks. On its website it is recorded that the first experiment, the Darrieus wind turbine, ended up looking like a whisk standing upright (Vestas, 2007). Today it is a global producer of high technological wind turbine systems for alternative energy with over 15,000 people employed.

Entrepreneurship could also create wealth in the non-profit sector. Community-based entrepreneurship, social entrepreneurship and social innovations seek to create wealth and address social needs. These forms of entrepreneurship to the extent that their activities extend create wealth and share it. Social entrepreneurship courses and projects that harness the energy of the participants in addressing social causes with entrepreneurship should be encouraged. Since the development of social entrepreneurship programs is recent, there is an opportunity to document the developments and track the successes in individuals, programs and organizations. While the efforts of the students, individuals, community foundations or corporations are, as Schumacher would have loved, small efforts in creativity. When aggregated over time they would not necessarily in terms deemed "economic," would have benefited some disadvantaged, non-profit organizations and tested new models of addressing social problems. There is a rising number of social entrepreneurship programs around the world. A search of websites by this author identified 21 universities with social entrepreneurship education taking the following forms:

- executive programs (e.g. at Stanford, Harvard, Duke, Columbia),
- undergraduate courses (e.g. at University of Alberta),
- concentrations at the undergraduate and MBA levels, and
- MBA programs (e.g. at Duke, Tata Institute for Social Sciences).

It has also sprouted competitions such as the SIFE World Cup organized by Students in Free Enterprise (www.sife.org), the Global Social Entrepreneurship Competition organized by the University of Washington, and at the high school level, the SAGE World Cup organized by Students for the Advancement of Global Entrepreneurship (www.sageglobal.org). These competitions together with the education programs will help spur interest in creating wealth in novel ways to help the non-traditional target markets. The role of educators, this writer included, is to ensure that the competitions do not become competitions for their own sake but learning opportunities that shape future choices.

Wealth distribution. Entrepreneurs and the firms contributed to society in the past by way of donations and philanthropic acts. It is one of the ways entrepreneurs contribute to wealth re-distribution (see e.g. Acs and Dana, 2001). Successful entrepreneurs in different cultures have donated, albeit through different mechanisms and for different motivations. The reach of these activities is limited to the agendas of each of the philanthropists. Foundations such as the Gates Foundation means selected projects, programs and reach. Philanthropy should continue to be encouraged. More entrepreneurs should be involved. It should be included as part of the entrepreneurship curriculum as one way in which entrepreneurs have contributed to society in addition to the jobs, the technologies, innovations and wealth they create. Philanthropy is not part of the staple of most entrepreneurship programs.

The advent of entrepreneurship into the non-profit sector to address social problems is a welcome development. Social entrepreneurship creates wealth when there are new social innovations, programs, institutions or services that are directed at social problems. Social entrepreneurship through the enterprises established can also distribute wealth to the disadvantaged. It is the disadvantaged and the poor, who do not always benefit from the products and services resulting from entrepreneurship. With social entrepreneurship, there is the possibility of providing employment through work integration social enterprises such as the Greyston Bakery in America (www.greystonbakery.com) or Bizlink in Singapore (www. www.bizlink.org.sg), social innovations such as micro-credit or innovative use of cooperatives, and the development of new programs, etc. The Greyston Bakery runs a profitable bakery hiring from within the community in the Bronx where it was first established. There is some indirect distribution of the wealth through the employment of disadvantaged such as ex-prisoners and single parents. The bakery's generated profit is used to provide affordable childcare for community, affordable housing for the homeless and low income families, and affordable healthcare for persons with HIV. Bizlink, a charity in Singapore established to assist the disabled with employment, has established its social enterprise unit to seek to generate revenue from its projects while involving the disabled who are not ready to work in open employment. The revenue from its project contributed 45% of its total funding in 2007 and 35% in 2008.

It is all well and good to praise this development as it is certainly an advance over the previous means of contribution to society by way of philanthropy. However, more ways need to be encouraged through entrepreneurship education. The challenge has to be issued to our students, whether nascent or experienced entrepreneurs to consider ways in which wealth can be distributed or shared. Some entrepreneurs do so through the sourcing of the ingredients that they use for their products or services. One other way could be to distribute one's products or services through other small firms, the disadvantaged or the needy. Depending on the business environment, it might be feasible for goods from entrepreneurial firms to be distributed through community cooperatives or agents or representatives who might operate like the Avon ladies. Some social enterprises are already using the poor in distributing the products and services and in turn benefiting other disadvantaged. The United Nations established the convene the Commission on the Private Sector and Development in 2004 to answer two questions: how can the potential of the private sector and entrepreneurship be unleashed in developing countries; and how can the existing private sector be engaged in meeting that challenge? The commission's report led to the Growing Inclusive Markets Initiative under the auspices of the UNDP. The first report in its series *Creating Value for All* (UNDP, 2008) highlights case examples of how businesses across the globe have attempted to include the poor and the strategies that have been adopted. Far be it for this writer to dream up all the avenues. The UNDP report provides illustrations. The task remains for entrepreneurship educators to challenge the participants and students, to highlight the distribution problem as a factor in their considerations when starting businesses or new projects within organizations. It is incumbent on educators to advance the challenge otherwise the problem of distribution will not be addressed and the UN report remains a report that may go unnoticed and not acted upon.

Revisit the theory of the firm — it is not perfect. It may be necessary for the basic assumption in the theory of the firm to be reviewed. If the assumption remains profitable, the theory of the firm will continue to drive the other disciplines in business education. The pervasive assumption that an enterprise only glitters if there is profit, is seen in all the disciplines in management. Human resource management and now called human capital management is focused on managing human capital to derive the optimum outcome from the staff. Strategy, according to Igor Ansoff (1965), regarded by many as the father of corporate strategy, is for the purpose of improving the corporation's ROI. There needs to be a change to the root cause of the present inaction, which is propagated by the self-proclaimed father of all social science, economics, that efficiency is all that matters. Schumacher was critical of the measure of efficiency in the form of cost and benefit analysis because it did not include benefits for which there was no direct visible value and failed to include the cost to the environment.

Tools and methods available. Implementing the ideas in entrepreneurship education will involve curriculum change to incorporate new ideas and concepts in the course content. The concepts can effect changes in the mindsets of the participants. Even merely articulating a definition of entrepreneurship, that features wealth for self and contribution to society to undergraduates in Singapore, led to cognitive changes in conceptualization of entrepreneurship within varying time frames of one class to three months (Tan, 2002). It could take the form of case discussions of sustainable entrepreneurship. Projects are another way of engaging the participants with the desired ideas. Interviews with champions in eco-entrepreneurship and innovators in renewable energy and the like, are other means of furthering the agenda. The methodologies are, in this writer's opinion, the obstacle. Educators need to first, take on board the necessary revolution in their courses and programs. Individuals, groups and corporations need to be innovative, creative and entrepreneurial with sustainability and non-economic goals in mind, but academics and educators have the potential to shape the agendas of those they train and influence.

Conclusion

Can it be done? Will it be possible to conceive of people and firms acting in a sustainable fashion in pursuit of entrepreneurial goals? Will the beauty of small beginnings, small firms and creativity be appreciated and nurtured so as to flourish to benefit more people? There are examples of individuals and firms that need not be repeated here. Yet on a larger scale, one could take a leaf from nations that are small and constrained in resources. Switzerland is a land-locked nation comprising of cantons that has innovated in various ways to become known for its financial institutions, its craftsmen in watches, and food (and this includes more than just Swiss chocolates). Israel has little in resources and is constrained by scarcity in land, water, and natural resources or oil, yet it has managed in some respects to restore life to deserts and non-arable land through drip irrigation of which it is a world leader, developed an aircraft industry building upon the refurbishment of old planes from developed countries in the case of Israel Aircraft Industries (Perman, 2004). Singapore has like Israel sought to translate ideas from developed countries and improve them. It is also lacking in land but has become a leader in land reclamation from the sea and is developing expertise in desalination and reverse osmosis.

What will it take for this to happen? In this essay, the focus has been on the tribe that the writer belongs to — academics. In addition to the research and education mentioned above, there is a need for policymakers not to despise the day of small beginnings. They should allow for small beginnings in new start-ups, innovations, experimentation and ideas. Those with influence, power and ability should encourage the development of small beginnings whether in the form of improvements, new ventures, innovations and inventions. These beginnings should also start with the small people — educating the young and youth. It is here that the quest begins for new beginnings, ideas, dreams that see fulfillment in adulthood and through their lives. In truth, the spark, that accounts for the ideas that see commercialization or world changing technology, may be small, often beginning as a hunch, a gnawing irritation that becomes a solution, or a question seeking an answer. These should be nurtured and provided with leeway for development. However, if the emphasis is only placed on large firms, large projects, large institutions, and big ideas, then there may be opportunities lost in ignoring small beginnings. One of the virtues of smallness that Schumacher noted is the likely damage. He noted that being small, the damage done is limited to the small firm, community, group or individual. One must hasten to add, that the virtue of smallness is that the individuals, firms or organizations involved are more likely than not to remember their roots and to recall their communities or others that are in the category of small. Being small, it is also hoped that they do not become greedy and allow greed to supplant their good intentions. Even so, being small, the damage done through greed would be limited.

Schumacher appealed to the Bible at various points in his book. While the humanists reading this might doubt the validity of arguments stemming from intelligent design, the Holy Scriptures have also advocated the virtue of small beginnings and smallness. Of greater significance, there is the core idea of stewardship, that the human race is accountable as stewards of the resources in this world left for its use. Stewardship has also been a banner cry from Raymond Kao (2007) in his book, *Stewardship-Based Economics*. This idea, if inculcated in the human psyche, would shape behavior. Then the steps, being embarked upon by all, however small, would collectively make an impact.

References

Acs, Z. and Dana, L.P. (2001). Contrasting two models of wealth redistribution, *Small Business Economics*, 1: 63–74.

Birch, D. (1981). Who creates jobs?, *Public Interest*, 65: 3–14.

Chemnick, J. (2008). US automakers pledge efficiency amid bailout pressure, *Platts News*, http://www.platts.com/Oil/News/6037327.xml, accessed on 27 December 2008.

Freese, W. (2006). Ben & Jerry's chief euphoria officer report 2006, http://www.benjerry.com/our_company/about_us/social_mission/social_and its/2006_sear/sear06_1.0.cfm, accessed on 27 December 2008.

Kao, R.W.Y. (1991). Defining entrepreneurship: past, present and ?, *Creativity and Innovation Management*, 2(1): 69–70.

Kao, R.W.Y. (1995). *Entrepreneurship: A Wealth-Creation and Value Adding Process*. Singapore: Prentice-Hall.

Kao, R.W.Y. (1997). An *Entrepreneurial Approach to Corporate Management*. Singapore: Prentice-Hall.

Kao, R.W.Y. (2007). *Stewardship-Based Economics*. Singapore: World Scientific Publishers.

Overdorf, J. (2008). The $100 Un-PC Rajesh Jain thinks the next billion computer users hold the key to the industry's next big innovation. *Newsweek Online Exclusive*, http://www.newsweek.com/id/42955/, accessed on 27 December 2008.

Perman, S. (2004). *Spies, Inc.: Business Innovation from Israel's Masters of Espionage*. London: Financial Times.

Prahalad, C.K. (2005). *The Fortune at the Bottom of the Pyramid: Eradicating Poverty Through Profits*. Upper Saddle River, NJ: Wharton School Publishing.

Quah, T.E.E. and Tan, K.C. (2002). *Siting Environmentally Unwanted Facilities: Risks, Trade-Offs and Choices*. UK: Aldershot, Edward Elgar Publishers.

Roberts, C. (2008). Environmental challenges and profit opportunities, *Social Innovations Conversations Network* pod cast of address at the Stanford Center for Social Innovation, http://odeo.com/episodes/23756505-Carter-Roberts-Environmental-Challenges-Profit-Opportunities, accessed on 27 December 2008.

Robinson, D. (2008). US automakers pledge restructuring in new bid for loans, *VOA News.com*, 2 December 2008, http://www.voanews.com/english/2008-12-02-voa36.cfm?renderforprint=1&textonly=1&&TEXTMODE=1&CFID=82094904&CFTOKEN=32091595, accessed on 27 December 2008.

Schumacher, E.F. (1973). *Small is Beautiful*. New York: Harper & Row.

Senge, P., Smith, B., Kruschwitz, N., Laur, J. and Schley, S. (2008). *The Necessary Revolution: How Individuals and Organizations are Working Together to Create a Sustainable World*. New York: Doubleday Books.

Smith, A. (1776). *The Wealth of Nations*. Oxford: Clarendon Press.

Tan, W.-L. (2002). The inculcation of entrepreneurship as a mindset, in Tan, W.-L. (ed.), *The Dynamics of Entrepreneurship: Growth and Strategy.* Singapore: Prentice-Hall, pp. 262–287.

United Nations Development Program (2008). *Creating Value for All: Strategies for Doing Business with the Poor.* New York: United Nations. The pdf version of the report and the cases can be accessed at http://www.growinginclusivemarkets.org.

Vestas (2007). Corporate history, http://www.vestas.com, accessed on 28 December 2008.

11
INNOVATION AND ENTERPRISE SUSTAINABILITY

Gary Oster

> *"The dogmas of the quiet past are inadequate to the stormy present. The occasion is piled high with difficulty, and we must rise with the occasion. As our case is new, so we must think anew and act anew."*
>
> — Abraham Lincoln

Introduction

Every successful society is built upon the foundation of a healthy free enterprise system (Schramm, 2006). While the most visible goal of each corporation is to generate profit for its owners, enterprises are more importantly an efficient mechanism to allocate scarce resources to create wealth and add value for individuals and the common good (Kao, 1997; Kao *et al.*, 2002). Successful companies, regardless of their size or industry, are the engine of societal prosperity. The hope, opportunity, and hard work in responsible entrepreneurism is a major force in eliminating poverty and crime and building a healthy society (Hall, 2001). Crucial to the success of those companies is the capability and motivation to change and innovate. In essence, the only long-term source of profit and reliable security for any company is its ability to innovate better and longer than competitors (Schwartz, 2004, Davila *et al.*, 2006). Innovation must be radical and extensive to help companies differentiate themselves from competitors, harness discontinuities, discover and correct faults with current products or services, understand the unarticulated needs of customers, take advantage of latent opportunities that others miss, and extend the utilization of existing successful products, services, or ideas (Hamel, 2002). Superior innovation provides valuable opportunities to grow faster and better than their competitors and ultimately to positively influence the direction of their industry" (Davila et al., 2006). Innovation is also important to overcome the inevitability of strategic entropy (Hamel, 2002), meaning that the specific strategies that successfully brought a corporation to a point in time have already been copied by other firms, are declining in impact because of environmental changes, or have been obviated by technological innovation wrought by other companies within the same or adjacent industries. Ignoring the inevitability of change and the necessity of innovation may ultimately imperil the viability of the organization (Gryskiewicz, 1999). Never in world history has innovation been so important than in the present hyper-competitive global economic environment. Corporate leaders are increasingly hearing the innovation mandate from their board of directors, shareholders, and media. Their personal compensation and tenure are often directly tied to the development of a consistently innovative organization. There is growing global acknowledgement of innovation as the centerpiece of corporate strategies and initiatives (Kelley, 2001).

The main objective of this chapter is to investigate the importance of innovation to enterprise sustainability and to consider the key elements that contribute to innovation success in organizations. The chapter is structured as follows: The first two sections briefly review the literature of corporate innovation, especially as it relates to the important antecedent activity of idea generation. The next two sections consider the sources of and impediments to innovative ideas in the enterprise. The next section reviews five key areas of focus for innovative organizations. Finally, the chapter ends with concluding comments.

Innovation Based on Fresh Ideas

Because we live in an increasingly nonlinear world, only nonlinear ideas have the power to change customer expectations, alter industry economics and redefine the basis for competitive advantage (Hamel, 2002). The primary method to acquire some innovative and useful ideas is to generate *many* ideas (Salk, 1972), and only challenges and surprises can move a company forward (Davila *et al.*, 2006). In most instances, companies cannot create the future by imagining entirely novel solutions to customer needs and dramatically cost-effective ways of meeting those needs unless they abandon their historical trajectory and the shackles of policy, tradition, and orthodoxy. To routinely generate valuable innovative ideas requires intentionality. To build an organization where innovation is a way of life often requires employees to discard, and often reverse, their deeply ingrained beliefs about how to consider ideas, make decisions, and manage their implementation. Individuals and companies focused on efficiencies and near-term profits often consider these changes to be counterintuitive, troubling, or even downright wrong (Sutton, 2002).

The Source of Innovative Ideas

If enterprises are to efficiently allocate scarce resources to create wealth for individuals and society, they must function much like a constructive intellectual arena, where new ideas are constantly pitted against each other and the best ideas win out (Sutton, 2002). There must be routine, significant variation in what people think about, do, and produce. Regrettably, companies myopically focused on efficiency and quick profits consider such variations to be unwelcome errors and mutations in a system. Heterogeneity in decision-making and problem-solving styles is an important avenue to innovative ideas. Innovative organizations regularly change the "rules of engagement" with ideas (Kawasaki, 1999), isolate and define problems in new and unusual ways, and look harder for plausible solutions (Schwartz, 2004).

The successful generation of new, *different* ideas is based largely upon the diversity of motivations, experience, and thought among corporate employees (Sutton, 2002). Such diversity is intentional (Amabile, 1998) and must extend far beyond race and gender (Andrew and Sirkin, 2006). The mixing of different skills and abilities, attitudes and behaviors generates enthusiasm, refreshing new ideas, and remarkable new opportunities (Andrew and Sirkin, 2006). Because people are creative and innovative by nature, it is employees who ultimately make the different combinations behind all technological and scientific discoveries (Kao *et al.*, 2002). Broad skill sets and attitudes are important, positive factors in the development of innovative ideas in organizations (Bennis and Biederman, 1997; Andrew and Sirkin, 2006; Skarzynski and Gibson, 2008). Understanding, accepting, and actively promoting diversity of people and thought helps connect the great variety of gifts that people bring to the work and service of the organization (DePree, 1989). Innovative ideas may be sparked when alignment occurs with the right person in the right place with the right skill set, motivation, and approach (Andrew and Sirkin, 2006). Creativity in teams may be likewise substantially enhanced by deliberately seeking divergent pairs of employees (Hirschberg, 1998), and selecting members with a broad range of backgrounds and skills (Gryskiewicz, 1999).

Because employees are the locus of innovative ideas in a corporation, the organization's hiring practices are very important. True diversity in an organization requires employees who differ in age, race, country of origin, gender, education, etc. Despite being from substantially different ethnic backgrounds, three young men from the same area of Dallas probably have more in common than they have different. Diversity needs to be *deeper*. In addition to characteristics that may be obvious to the observer, an innovative workforce is also composed of people with diverse experiences and attitudes. When leaders undertake the task of improving the performance of their innovation activities, their efforts frequently involve the identification and closing of specific capabilities gaps through corporate human resource programs (Andrew and Sirkin, 2006). Recruiting the most talented and appropriately diverse employees is the first task of any leader with a goal of improving innovation outcomes (Bennis and Biederman, 1997).

Employees who propagate valuable innovation ideas often possess an unusual personality or routinely disagree with company policies or methodologies. Almost by definition, innovative employees eschew conventional wisdom and are thinking differently about the business. They may be mavericks who are congenitally unhappy with the direction of the business, or talented outliers in technology or sales departments with insights into customers and technologies that give them ideas for new businesses (Day and Schoemaker, 2006). Innovative employees are almost never insiders or corporate types on the fast track, and may lack traditionally accepted credentials or exist on the margins of their professions (Bennis and Biederman, 1997). Successfully innovative companies welcome those who routinely dissent, often have the zeal of recent converts, and harbor personal idiosyncrasies (Bennis and Biederman, 1997). They generally solve problems by being unconventional, determined, or even obtuse, far different from the majority of people who are normally "thinking in train tracks" (Dyson, 2003).

Constraints to Workplace Innovation

Hindering new ideas because they seem out of step with the historical trajectory of the firm or devising barriers to protect against the disruptions from outside forces puts the organization at immediate risk of becoming outdated and left behind in the marketplace (Gryskiewicz, 1999). Dissent and opposition to corporate innovation efforts may be muted and may only be evidenced by projects that are not done on time, are done poorly, or by those who do not share their knowledge or sit in silence in staff meetings (Horibe, 2001). Empirical research has shown that the internal infrastructure, motivation, and methodologies of innovation are oftentimes distorted during downsizing (Oster and Gandolfi, 2008). When employees suspect that additional waves of downsizing may soon occur, knowledge becomes a new form of currency and is hoarded by individual employees and departments. Information sharing and organizational learning slow to a crawl. In some instances, corporations aid and abet innovation resistance by rewarding employees for their allegiance to the historical past of the company (Pfeffer and Sutton, 2000) and sanctioning any change from the earlier corporate trajectory (Sutton, 2002). On a very human level, people generally dislike receiving new ideas especially if that knowledge is conveyed by people seemingly different from them (Von Krogh *et al.*, 2000). The qualities that make for great innovation — passion, drive, out-of-the-box thinking — are viewed as arrogance, unreasonableness, and uncompromising behavior by many peer employees and organizations (Horibe, 2001).

The ability of an individual or organization to recognize and formulate innovative concepts is limited by their rational boundaries (Manu, 2007).

If employees all resemble one another, those limits would be perilously short, therefore variation in ideas and experience is crucial. Unfortunately, corporate hiring policies more often do not support the hiring of people who increase variation. Current hiring procedures both buttress and homogenize the existing character and orientation of a company, adding numbers but failing to enlarge the range of a company's capabilities and the breadth of its vision (Hirshberg, 1998). Company leaders often wrongly believe a uniform workforce promotes harmony and unity in the workplace and leads to efficiency. Through human resource policies, hiring and training procedures, and managerial preference, many corporations are *intentionally* populated with employees who are alike, limiting important new ideas and actions. The fountain of *new* ideas originates in the broad diversity of the organization's thought leaders. If innovation is *essential* to the viability of corporations, and innovative ideas are dependent upon a diverse workforce, why is there currently so much "sameness" among company employees? The propensity to favor a uniform workforce shapes hiring and promotion policies, resulting in "homosocial reproduction" (Kanter, 1977). Kanter showed that corporate executives often rely on outward characteristics to determine who is the "right sort of person" to fit into the organization. Although detrimental to innovation in a company, it is not unusual for corporations to purposely hire the vast majority of workers from a specific geographic area, school, religious institution, club, or sport. Homosocial reproduction limits the range of a company's innovation capabilities and may ultimately derail the future success of the organization (Sutton, 2002).

No matter how tightly woven the protection from outside competitors, organizations often fail to consider an enemy from within, usually referred to as an *innovation antibody*, *organizational antibody*, or *devil's advocate*. Regardless of the soundness of a company's products and organization, one well-place innovation antibody can quietly reinterpret corporate strategies to co-workers and ultimately wreak havoc on the corporation's future. First, it is essential to emphasize that, just because a person who has an unusual personality or disagrees with company policies or methodologies, is not necessarily an "innovation antibody." To encourage the innovation that determines corporate viability, companies absolutely *need* those employees. Typically, the more radical the innovation and the more it challenges the status quo, the more and stronger are the antibodies. Also, the greater the past successes of the company, the greater are the organizational antibodies (Davila *et al.*, 2006). Innovation antibodies are considered by many to be the most dangerous idea-wreckers, as they always assume the most negative possible perspective, one that sees only the downside, the problems, the disasters-in-waiting, and that drown every new initiative in negativity (Kelley, 2001; Oster, 2008c). Innovation antibodies are determined to slow or eliminate innovation and change in the organization. The success of innovation antibodies intimidates other employees (Dundon, 2002). A historical review of innovation demonstrates that personal rejection has often been the reward for innovative people (Berkun, 2007), and that those who were successful at innovation ignored, dismissed, or overcame the organizational antibodies that inevitably came out to attack and defeat innovations (Davila *et al.*, 2006). It is an important role of corporate leadership to help corporate antibodies successfully integrate into the productive fabric of the company, or to be abruptly excised from it.

What are useful methods for thwarting innovation antibodies? First, early innovation efforts should begin with small, rapid, inexpensive experiments that most often keep innovative ideas "off radar" to organizational power brokers (Hamel, 2002). Secondly, corporate leadership must intentionally deconstruct the barriers in work habits and ecologies (Manu, 2007), and develop leadership styles that focus on first identifying and then incorporating polarized viewpoints (Hirshberg, 1998). Finally, to neutralize innovation antibodies, the organization must develop learning systems and activities that allow the firm to differentiate good change from bad change. Otherwise, innovation antibodies become unselective, attacking and disrupting *all* change (Davila *et al.*, 2006).

Encouraging Successful Corporate Innovation

There is no "secret sauce" that guarantees successful corporate innovation. Companies in many countries who feature remarkably varied organizational schemes, innovation policies and procedures, and with widely diverse personnel characteristics, regularly succeed at innovation. There are, however, specific attributes present in *all* organizations that successfully innovate. Five important strategies that help ignite and focus corporate innovation are explored hereafter.

Develop appropriate innovation metrics

The foundation of useful innovation metrics is honesty, realism, and transparency (DePree, 1989). Although most business people consider themselves to be realists, it is more common to find wishful thinking, denial, and other forms of reality avoidance deeply embedded in most corporate cultures (Bossidy and Charan, 2004). Corporate leaders sometimes recognize the world as they wish it to be, not as it actually is. Assessments of market size, strength of potential competitors, projections of quarterly sales, and prioritization of new product features are but a few of the issues commonly the target of "shading" or outright deception in corporations, often engendering a highly conservative approach to innovation. In successfully innovative companies, leaders always deal in reality, speaking the truth and demanding the same of their subordinates. In scores of surveys conducted throughout the world and over decades, honesty has been selected consistently as the most important leadership characteristic in the leader-constituent relationship (Kouzes and Posner, 2002). Organizations that innovate most effectively are those in which leadership demands reality and develops systems of rewards and penalties that put a premium on realism (Bossidy and Charan, 2004).

For companies to succeed in this remarkably competitive worldwide economic environment, they must formulate and consistently use metrics that are clearly stated, valid, reliable, and expansive (Davila *et al.*, 2006). The traditional rule of thumb is, "what gets measured gets done." If the right metrics and subsequent rewards are not implemented and consistently used, it is unlikely that productive innovation will be achieved (Hamel, 2002; Davila *et al.*, 2006). Non-linear or radical innovation, as opposed to incremental innovation, always begins with "unreasonable" goals (Hamel, 2002; Bennis and Biederman, 1997), and the contention that the only limitation to successful innovation is a lack of focus and imagination (Martin, 2005). While traditional efficiency thinking considers constraints like budgets and quarterly reports to be an undesirable barrier to the generation and implementation of ideas, those who utilize design thinking believe constraints simply serve to increase the challenge and excitement level of the task at hand (Martin, 2005; Boland and Collopy, 2006). These expansive goals, which are nonetheless aligned with the values, vision, strategy, and tactics of the corporation, should be continually monitored using a small number of simple, meaningful, and objective metrics (Taylor *et al.*, 2000). Changing perspectives regarding problems is essential to innovation (May, 2007), and the use of quantum objectives automatically reframes problems so that novel cost-effective solutions to customer needs may be explored (Hamel, 2002). To achieve quantum objectives, organizations often reach beyond inductive and deductive logic, and additionally incorporate abductive logic (Martin, 2004 and 2005). Quantum objectives automatically force thinking that escapes the limits of current processes, discovering new pathways of thought and action (Liedtka and Friedel, 2008). Quantum metrics are not limited to what can be improved, but instead consider what is impeding perfection (May, 2007). They focus on what are referred to as wicked problems (Martin, 2005), featuring incomplete, contradictory, and changing requirements, yielding solutions that are often unclear, and that respond to the question, "What if anything were possible? (Liedtka, 2004 and 2006). Innovation efforts iterate by doing...which involves *suggesting* that something *may be*, and reaching out to explore it. It is important that new metrics not be clouded by legacy strategies (Manu, 2007), that they focus more on outputs than inputs (Hamel, 2002), that all activities of the organization tie back to this small number of measurements (Pfeffer and Sutton, 2000), and that they continue to be the subject of review and internal conversation (Charan, 2007). Most importantly, corporate metrics must accurately measure those innovation efforts tied specifically to how a company makes money (Charan, 2007), and be appropriately translated into individual day-to-day performance requirements that are clear, aggressive, and unconstrained (Bennis and Biederman, 1997). Developing and successfully using innovation metrics that support both creativity and value creation is essential to corporate success (Oster, 2008a).

Encourage experimentation and small failures

To demonstrate fiscal responsibility, companies have traditionally required activities to be eminently measurable, highly predictable, and to promise a specific return on investment. One common method used by innovation antibodies is to push for the absolute elimination of the possibility of failure: before something new is tried, its ultimate success must be proven beyond a shadow of a doubt. For an innovation antibody, corporate risk is the penultimate straw man: they continually encourage peers to seek safety, worrying about the worst that can happen. Unfortunately, their favored innovation antibody terms like "predictability," "perfection," "harmony," and "sameness," are never hallmarks of successful companies having innovative ideas continually bubbling to the surface. To the contrary, a corporate culture must be intentionally developed that consistently encourages unusual ideas and small experiments and prototypes that sometimes fail (Oster, 2008d). Failure to observe real or perceived rules is critical to successful innovation. True innovators consistently disdain, proudly ignore, and often publicly flout virtually every corporate rule. This means it is smart to hire slow learners, to tolerate heretics, eccentrics, and original thinkers, even though they will come up with many ideas that result in dead ends. The cost is worthwhile because they also generate a large pool of ideas — especially innovative ideas (Sutton, 2002). *New* ideas require *more* ideas: *more* ideas require *intellectual freedom*.

Firms must be intentional in creating an environment where appropriate risk is welcome, and corporate incentives must likewise be designed to reduce risk-averse behavior (Wind, 2006). An environment must be cultivated where long-term results are valued (Fraser, 2008) and where taking risks on breakthrough innovations is recognized as valuable to the company (Davila *et al.*, 2006). In order to achieve truly valuable breakthroughs in the long term; it is necessary to accept (and learn from) failures in the short term. Regular and methodical failure is *essential* to eventual innovative success, and yet most corporations brutally sanction failure. Leaders must make sure that employees do not find it difficult or dangerous to try something. The right kinds of failure contain valuable information and should be "listened to" (Schwartz, 2004). An important role for leaders of innovation is to clearly signal the propriety of failure and to distinguish between "good failure" and "bad failure." "Bad failure" is that which is repeated, and nothing new is learned from it. "Good failure" happens often, but the same event is not repeated because something is learned from it, duly recorded, and disseminated to others

(Bennis and Biederman, 1997). Increasing the number of successful innovation "hits" is simply a function of an exponential growth in the right kind of failures.

One important methodology for mitigating risk associated with innovation is the development of a dynamic internal culture of prototyping (Kelley, 2001) requiring regular prototyping in ten specific areas, including the corporation's business model, networking, enabling process, core process, product performance, product system, service, channel, brand, and customer experience (Tekes, 2007). Unlike traditional firms that use a refined model to show a new product to a lead customer or supplier, design thinking utilizes quick, inexpensive, rough prototypes to elicit feedback from current or potential customers (Brown, 2005; Davila *et al.*, 2006). Prototypes should be regularly produced using paper, computer simulations, clay, foamcore, process maps, spreadsheets, bubble charts, videos, digital pictures, or any other inexpensive and malleable material (Peters, 1995; Kawasaki, 1999). A prototype, regardless of its type, is not meant to represent a *final* idea: an explosion of prototypes is utilized to get and refine *many* possible ideas on the path toward a smaller number of useful ideas (Brown, 2008; Conley, 2007; Jones and Samalionis, 2008). Prototypes encourage people to temporarily suspend reality in order to be inspirational and expansive as they consider new insights (Jones and Samalionis, 2008), and to "try on" a multitude of possibilities (Schrage, 2000). Constant prototyping that ignores industry orthodoxies encourages insight into needed organizational capabilities (Jones and Samalionis, 2008), plausible future products and services (Kelley, 2001), and even entirely new areas of expansion for the corporation (Lafley and Charan, 2008).

Expand institutional learning

Markets that do not yet exist cannot be analyzed and the market applications for disruptive technologies are similarly unknowable (Christensen, 2005). A critical antecedent to innovation is therefore broad institutional learning. Learning is how people convert ideas into action (May, 2007), and innovative people and organizations consider transmission of personal knowledge to others to be the central activity of the knowledge-creating company (Nonaka, 1991). Appreciating the value of focused failure to institutional learning and organizational memory is not enough. Appropriate information must be recognized, evaluated, shared, and utilized. Institutional learning is predicated upon a transparent internal market for information and ideas, freely open for all to utilize (Bennis and Biederman, 1997). New information is embraced, not feared, and formal mechanisms have been established for finding new information, ushering it into the organization, and putting it into the hands of the people who can best use it (Gryskiewicz, 1999). Those who have created knowledge must quickly and efficiently come to the attention of those who seek knowledge creation (Von Grogh et al., 2000). Employees must engage in frequent and free dialogue for the necessary connections to occur spontaneously. This, in turn, requires a culture of trust, respect, and curiosity, and the recognition that information sharing is important to corporate success (Day and Schoemaker, 2006). Without this openness, crucial problems might never be discovered and solutions might never be found (Bennis and Biederman, 1997).

Every innovative idea starts and ends with a current or prospective customer in mind. Customer focus certainly is not new to companies, but it has become obvious that standard market research methods continue to yield less and less useful information (Stevens, 1999). Traditional market research methods are inherently incomplete because research subjects are generally imprecise communicators, often using verbal shorthand, metaphors, body language, and facial expressions that can provide ambiguous information (Fournies, 1994). New methods for listening to customers, including electronic, social networking, and empathic research methods, must also be fully employed (Brown, 2005). Primary research such as direct observation of much smaller cohorts and their compensatory behaviors will reveal more useful information than traditionally gained from secondary research (Suri, 2005; Oster, 2008b). This decade has witnessed growth in an area termed "empathic design," based upon the premise that empathy is a tool of design used by observers who can and should enjoy consumer/world interactions and respond to people's need to be unique. Focused, direct observation of customers in their natural settings, technically referred to as "empathic research," yields nuances of human behavior, in addition to clues to the emotion and motivation, context, habits, rituals, priorities, processes, and values of customers (Kelley, 2001; Suri, 2005). Empathic research is derived from the word "empathy," which refers to the ability to recognize and understand a person's state of mind, metaphorically to "live inside someone else's skin." Similar to anthropological studies of people in foreign lands, empathic research is qualitative in nature and based on focused observation (Stevens, 1999; Suri, 2006). Empathic research does not need to be limited to customers. Vendors, employees, and even competitors can provide crucial information on possible improvements to products, services, and ideas. The ultimate goal is to form close partnerships with current and prospective customers to ensure the swift and comprehensive development of products, services, and ideas that perfectly match their realized and unarticulated needs (Brown, 2005; Hagel and Brown, 2005).

Seeing and accurately describing a gap between what customers need and what is available is a substantive challenge, and a sea of data does not automatically equal a spoonful of knowledge. Interpreting and understanding potential answers requires intention and method, and positive organizational change may only occur when guided by timely, relevant, and focused corporate learning (Day and Schoemaker, 2006). Internal barriers to communications must be intentionally disassembled (Von Krogh et al., 2000), the number of voices participating in conversations related to innovation increased (Manu, 2007), formal and informal communications networks developed (Bennis and Biederman, 1997), and incentives for effective sharing of information implemented (Kawasaki, 1999). Regular primary research and wide formal and informal sharing of the resultant information helps the organization and all of the employees to develop exceptional "peripheral vision," the knowledge of where to look more carefully, knowing how to interpret far-off, fuzzy, informational fragments, and knowing how to act when the signals are still incomplete or ambiguous (Davila et al., 2006; Day and Schoemaker, 2006). They detect emergent trends in what they see, stand ready to embrace the odd occurrences that may lead to something big, and fly at a higher imaginative altitude than others (Schwartz, 2004; Charan, 2007). Organizations consciously deciding to tune in to these intermittent signals get critical information faster than those who wait for it to arrive in a neat, orderly bandwidth, and achieve the strategic advantage that can ultimately ensure survival (Gryskiewicz, 1999). In innovative companies, leaders support institutional learning and guide the development of systems that capture appropriate information and disperse it to those who need it (Hagel and Brown, 2005; Davila *et al.*, 2006). Successful leaders know how to discover and learn, and how to manage and inspire discovery and learning in others (Manu, 2007; Bennis and Biederman, 1997). Driving innovation into the business mentality requires continual learning and change (Davila *et al.*, 2006), and leaders constantly remove physical and organizational barriers that hinder information sharing (May, 2007).

Embrace productive friction

The purposeful mixing of people having diverse backgrounds, experiences, and skill sets to solve wicked problems often generates friction — that is, misunderstandings and arguments — before resolution and learning occur (Hagel and Brown, 2005). Highly innovative people are often accompanied by personal idiosyncrasies, a strong will, a touch of hubris and arrogance, and a tendency to ignore or reject the organizational code (Bennis and Biederman, 1997; Sutton, 2002). This is referred to as *productive friction, creative abrasion,* or *dynamic tension* (May, 2007). If it is properly harnessed, this friction can become *very* productive, accelerating learning, generating innovation, and fostering trust between diverse participants. Productive friction often requires difficult negotiations among people with very different skills, experiences, and mind-sets (Hagel and Brown, 2005). The goal of leaders in innovative companies is not to reduce friction by diluting or compromising positions, but instead to develop leadership styles that intentionally identify and incorporate polarized viewpoints (Hirshberg, 1998). At the same time, leaders must prevent that conflict from becoming personal or from going underground where the pressure of resentment can build. Over time, the dysfunctional aspect of diversity can be overcome when (and only when) heterogeneous group members learn to interact with each other (Tsui and Gutek, 1999; Kelley, 2005). In summation, innovative companies must learn to embrace friction, even to seek it out and to encourage it when it promises to provide opportunities for learning and capacity building. Additionally, innovative companies must develop institutional frameworks that can help foster productive friction, encourage team members to be willing to listen to each other and understand different viewpoints, and to question each other's assumptions.

Display leadership courage

Most corporations aid and abet innovation antibodies by rewarding employees for their allegiance to the historical past of the company. Commitment to past decisions signals consistency and persistence, and reaffirms the company's social identity (Pfeffer and Sutton, 2000). Because the familiar is so comfortable and doing things differently from how they have always done them is confusing and threatening, most organizations "lock in" their historical trajectory (Griskiewicz, 1999). Those who engage in innovative practices and step outside the smothering embrace of the corporation are often publically sanctioned (Sutton, 2002), and history is littered with those who endured dismissals, mockeries, and persecutions on their way to changing the world (Berkun, 2007). Virtually every innovative organization has a strong and visionary head, and leaders of innovative organizations must have a steel backbone (Bennis and Biederman, 1997). Courage is *essential* because innovation leaders are often considered pariahs for proactively bucking the status quo, since they routinely move alone, outside of the established business order, and toward uncertainty (Davila *et al.*, 2006). "Chief innovator" is a role often played by the CEO or chairman, especially when the company must make a change from another business strategy, such as cost cutting, merger and acquisition, or geographic expansion (Andrew and Sirkin, 2006). This leadership happens through commitment, example, and solid decisions rather than grand statements (Davila *et al.*, 2006), and it is the intelligent allocation and management of resources which justifies their existence (Kao, 1997). The remarkably complex and difficult innovation choices they make set the course for innovation triumph or failure, and render the position of corporate innovation leader to be so vitally important.

Concluding Thoughts

This chapter has shown that innovation is crucial to enterprise sustainability, which in turn contributes to the success of society. Only innovative ideas are likely to create new wealth for corporations, and the fountain of those innovative ideas is a workforce that is widely diverse. This chapter showed that key attributes of innovative corporations include appropriate metrics, the encouragement of experimentation and small failures, expansive institutional learning, productive friction, and leadership courage. Strong and visionary leadership is necessary to develop systems to overcome impediments to innovative ideas in the enterprise. To positively change customer expectations, up-end industry convention and its basis for competitive advantage, and reap the welcomed financial harvest (Hamel, 2002), corporations must routinely and consistently employ innovation. The development of efficient markets and effective business models through enterprise innovation not only generates a needed economic transformation, but also provides members of society respect, choice, self-esteem, and a welcomed future (Prahalad, 2006).

References

Amabile, T. (1998). How to kill creativity, *Harvard Business Review*, 76(5): 77–87.
Andrew, J. and Sirkin, H. (2006). *Payback: Reaping the Rewards of Innovation*. Boston: Harvard Business School Press.
Bennis, W. and Biederman, P. (1997). *Organizing Genius*. New York: Addison-Wesley.
Berkun, S. (2007). *The Myths of Innovation*. Sebastopol, CA.: O'Reilly Media.
Bossidy, L. and Charan, R. (2004). *Confronting Reality*. New York: Crown Business.
Boland Jr., R. and Collopy, F. (2006). Design matters for management, *Rotman Magazine*, Spring/Summer, p. 52.
Brown, T. (2005). Strategy by design, *Fast Company*, pp. 52–54.
Brown, T. (2008). Design thinking, *Harvard Business Review*, 86(6): 84–92.
Charan, R. (2007). *Know-How*. New York: Crown Business.
Christenson, C. (2005). *The Innovator's Dilemma*. New York: Collins Business Essentials.
Conley, C. (2007). Educating designers for broad roles in organizations, *Design Management Review,* 18(3): 10–17.
Davila, T., Epstein, M. and Shelton, R. (2006). *Making Innovation Work*. Upper Saddle River, NJ: Wharton School Publishing.

Day, G. and Schoemaker, P. (2006). *Peripheral Vision*. Boston: Harvard Business School Press.
DePree, M. (1989). *Leadership is an Art*. New York: Dell.
Dundon, E. (2002). *The Seeds of Innovation*. New York: Amacom.
Dyson, J. (2003). *Against the Odds*. New York: Texere.
Fournies, F. (1994). *Why Customers Don't Do What You Want Them to Do — and What to Do About It*. New York: McGraw-Hill.
Fraser, H. (2008). How design thinking enables personal growth and enterprise success, *Rotman Magazine*, pp. 79–82.
Gryskiewicz, S. (1999). *Positive Turbulence*. San Francisco: Jossey-Bass.
Hagel, J. and Brown, J. (2005). *The Only Sustainable Edge*. Boston: Harvard Business School Press.
Hall, C. (2001). *The Responsible Entrepreneur*. Franklin Lakes, NJ: Career Press.
Hamel, G. (2002). *Leading the Revolution*. New York: Plume.
Hirshberg, J. (1998). *The Creative Priority*. New York: HarperBusiness.
Horibe, F. (2001). *Creating the Innovation Culture*. New York: Wiley.
Jones, M. and Samalionis, F. (2008). From small ideas to radical service innovation, *Design Management Review*, 19(1): 22.
Kanter, R. (1977). *Men and Women of the Corporation*. New York: Basic Books.
Kao, R. (1997). *An Entrepreneurial Approach to Corporate Management*. New York: Prentice Hall.
Kao, R.W.Y., Kao, R.R. and Kao, K.R. (2002). *Entrepreneurism: A Philosophy and a Sensible Alternative for the Market Economy*. London: Imperial College Press.
Kawasaki, G. (1999). *Rules for Revolutionaries*. New York: HarperCollins.
Kelley, T. (2001). *The Art of Innovation*. New York: Currency Doubleday.
Kelley, T. (2005). *The Ten Faces of Innovation*. New York: Currency Doubleday.
Kouzes, J. and Posner, B. (2002). *The Leadership Challenge*. San Francisco: Jossey-Bass.
Lafley, A. and Charan, R. (2008). *The Game Changer: How You Can Drive Revenue and Profit Growth with Innovation*. New York: Crown Business.
Liedtka, J. (2004). Strategy as design, *Rotman Magazine*, Winter, p. 15.
Liedtka, J. (2006). If managers thought like designers, *Rotman Magazine*, Spring/Summer, pp. 14–18.
Liedtka, J. and Friedel, R. (2008). Possibility Thinking, *Rotman Magazine*, Winter, pp. 15–19.
Manu, A. (2007). *The Imagination Challenge*. Berkeley, CA: New Riders.
Martin, R. (2004). The design of business, *Rotman Management*, Winter, p. 10.

Martin, R. (2005). Embedding design into business, *Rotman Magazine*, Fall, pp. 4–7.
May, M. (2007). *The Elegant Solution*. New York: Free Press.
Nonaka, I. (1991). The knowledge-creating company, *Harvard Business Review*, 69(6): 96–104.
Oster, G. (2008a). Derailing design thinking, *International Journal of Leadership Studies*, 4(1): 107–115.
Oster, G. (2008b). Divining the need, *Regent Global Business Review*, 2(2): 14–18.
Oster, G. (2008c). Effective antidotes for innovation antibodies, *Effective Executive*, 11(10): 33–40.
Oster, G. (2008d). Radical innovation: risk mitigation techniques, *Global CEO*, October.
Oster, G. and Gandolfi, F. (2008). Innovation during an era of downsizing, *Review of International Comparative Management*, 9(5): 125–145.
Peters, T. (1995). Do it now, stupid!, *Forbes (ASAP)*, 156(5): 170–172.
Pfeffer, J. and Sutton, R. (2000). *The Knowing-Doing Gap*. Boston: Harvard Business School Press.
Prahalad, C. (2006). *The Fortune at the Bottom of the Pyramid*. Upper Saddle River, NJ: Wharton School Publishing.
Salk, J. (1972). *Man Unfolding*. New York: HarperRow.
Schrage, M. (2000). *Serious Play*. Boston: Harvard Business School Press.
Schramm, C. (2006). *The Entrepreneurial Imperative*. New York: HarperCollins.
Schwartz, E. (2004). *Juice: The Creative Fuel that Drives World-Class Inventors*. Boston: Harvard Business School Press.
Skarzynski, P. and Gibson, R. (2008). *Innovation to the Core*. Boston: Harvard Business Press.
Stevens, T. (1999). Lights, camera, innovation, *Industry Week*, 248(14): 32–34.
Suri, J. (2005). *Thoughtless Acts?* San Francisco: Chronicle Books.
Suri, J. (2006). Informing our intuition: design research for radical innovation, *Rotman Magazine*, Winter, pp. 52–57.
Sutton, R. (2002). *Weird Ideas that Work*. New York: Free Press.
Taylor, J., Wacker, W. and Means, H. (2000). *The Visionary's Handbook*. New York: HarperBusiness.
Tekes (Finnish Funding Agency for Technology and Innovation) (2007). *Seizing the White Space: Innovative Service Concepts in the United States*, Tekes Technology Review 205/2007, Helsinki.

Tsui, A. and Gutek, B. (1999). *Demographic Differences in Organizations.* New York: Lexington Books.

von Krogh, G., Ichijo, K. and Nonaka, I. (2000). *Enabling Knowledge Creation.* Oxford, UK: Oxford Press.

Wind, Y. (2006). Managing creativity, *Rotman Magazine*, Spring/Summer, pp. 20–23.

12
TOWARD SUSTAINABLE ECONOMIC DEVELOPMENT: AN EXPERIMENT IN WEST AFRICA

Leo Paul Dana

This paper uses a naturally occurring event as an experiment; it is almost a controlled experiment in the sense that it compares the current state of affairs in two adjacent economies which used to be one, up to World War I. After the war, German Togoland was split into two territories, one exposed to the policies of French rule (Togo) and the other to that of British Gold Coast administration (Ghana). Both are independent today, Ghana attempting to promote entrepreneurship much more so than Togo. This article examines entrepreneurial activity in both settings, explaining the lack of success of new venture programs in West Africa, and concluding with recommendations for such developing environments.

Introduction

The purpose of this study was to investigate the results of the different approaches of economic policy, where other independent variables have been controlled for over a substantial period of time. Ghana and Togo naturally provide such a setting in West Africa.

Under colonial rule, sub-Saharan Africa was self-sufficient in food production, and much produce was exported from Africa to Europe. Prior to obtaining independence, Ghana (British West African Gold Coast) and

Fig. 1   Train station at Accra; photograph by Leo Paul Dana.

Togo had among the most prosperous economies on the continent (see Fig. 1). Since both obtained independence, however, population growth has not been matched by a growth in agriculture and business activity.

Today, West Africa exhibits most of the symptoms of underdeveloped economies, low manufacturing output, low per capita GNP, low per capita income, and mass poverty, along with large balance of payment deficits, yet a lucrative distribution sector (see Fig. 2) dominated by the small business sector.

The Economist reported some time ago, in an article entitled "Africa Lessons" (March 4, 1989, p. 63):

> "*Remarkably, black Africa has actually become poorer in the 1980s. Factors beyond its control — an adverse external environment usually gets the blame. This is wrong. Africa's problems are largely of its own making, and so must be the solutions.*"

The same is true today. Yet consultants from industrialized countries have been trying to bring their solutions, some of which are ethnocentric or culturally-specific, and not always sensitive to local needs and external environmental variables. Among these imported "solutions" are US-style new venture programs. Despite their success in industrialized

Fig. 2   Ambulant dealers; photograph by Leo Paul Dana.

nations, such programs have different impacts in environments such as found in West Africa. The environment is not necessarily adverse, just different, and new venture programs are only one of many factors affecting entrepreneurship.

Giamartino[1] noted that the effect of external components can influence the entrepreneur's ability to create viable organizations. He listed among such factors: government, taxation, laws, regulations, trade policy, infrastructure, labor force, access to capital, university support, research facilities, partnerships and networking, all of which affect the entrepreneur. He also cited Dana[2] explaining that the existence of a multitude of owner-managed small businesses must not be confused with entrepreneurship, the latter incorporating more innovation and creating more jobs.

---

[1] Giamartino, G.A. (January 1991). Will small business be the answer for developing economies?, *Journal of Small Business Management*, 24(1): 91–93.

[2] Dana, L.P. (July 1998). More small business is not the answer for Peru, *Journal of Small Business Management*, 26(3): 68–70.

Indeed, small business and entrepreneurship serve different roles. Schumpeter[3] stressed the entrepreneur's role in improving society. Nevertheless, for nearly half a century, governments around the world gave little if any support to entrepreneurs and new venture creation; on the contrary, Strinati[4] showed that up to the late 1970s, many nations preferred instead to encourage mergers of existing firms into larger units. Scase[5] found the trend was to evolve away from small independent business; governments believed that a means to facilitate economic growth was to encourage a close partnership between state agencies and the existing large firms in the private sector. Since the 1980s, however, the policy of some governments has shifted from discouraging to encouraging independent business,[6] and recently governments have viewed entrepreneurship as a means of improving output.[7]

Governments in industrialized nations such as Australia, Austria, Canada, Singapore, the United Kingdom and the United States and elsewhere have looked at the formation of new ventures as a solution to national economic stagnation, and consequently funded programs intended to encourage entrepreneurship. However, it should not be assumed that such new venture programs shall necessarily have the same impact in developing economies. Nevertheless, as socialism goes out of fashion in black Africa, even less developed countries such as Nigeria[8] and Ghana, as discussed in this essay, have been pouring funds into new venture programs. What is needed, but lacking, is research into how effective such programs are. Their success, it will be shown, depends on

---

[3] Schumpeter, J.A. (1934). *Change and the Entrepreneur*. Cambridge: Harvard University Press.

[4] Strinati, D. (1982). *Capitalism, the State and Industrial Relations*. London: Croom Helm.

[5] Scase, R. (1980). *The State in Western Europe*. London: Croom Helm.

[6] Scase, R. and Goffee, R. (1987). *The Real World of the Small Business Owner*, London: Croom Helm.

[7] Rainnie, A. and Scott, M. (1986). Industrial relations in the small firm, in Curran, J., Stanworth, J. and Watkins, P. (eds.), *The Survival of the Small Firm*. Adeshot, UK: Gower.

[8] Chi, A.-A. (1987). The role of entrepreneurs in economic development: an analysis of remote and operating environment in Africa, in Wyckham, R.G., Meredith, L.N. and Bushe, G.R. (eds.), *The Spirit of Entrepreneurship*. Vancouver: Simon Fraser University, pp. 31–43.

other factors such as regulation and infrastructure among other external variables.

Ghana and Togo, West Africa

Ghana is the name which its new rulers gave the British colony of the Gold Coast when it became independent in 1957. Ghana is Togo's neighbor to the west, south of Burkina Faso (formerly Upper Volta); to the west of Ghana lies the Ivory Coast. Ghana is 91,690 square miles. The 2000 census suggested a population exceeding 18 million, up 50% from the 1984 census. The nation's capital is Accra, rich with British colonial architecture as featured in Fig. 3.

Togo was administered as part of Afrique occidentale francaise from World War I until its independence in 1960. The Republic of Togo is home to three million people from 40 ethnic groups, making it among the most heterogeneous countries in Africa. It covers 21,623 square miles, with a 35 mile coastline on the Gulf of Guinea (South Atlantic).

Fig. 3 Accra; photograph by Leo Paul Dana.

Fig. 4 Lome; photograph by Leo Paul Dana.

Its neighbors are Benin (formerly Dahomey) to the east, Burkina Faso to the north, and to the west, Ghana. Togo's capital city is Lome, featured in Fig. 4.

A Short History

Late in the 15th century, the Portuguese, soon to be followed by the Dutch, French and English, established themselves in West Africa to buy slaves from the local tribes who were eager to do business. During the 16th century, the Mina tribe of Togo prospered as agents for the slave trade, importing slaves from other tribes inland to the north, and then exporting them abroad. Elmina, shown in Fig. 5, served as hub of the slave trade. In 1807, however, England outlawed the slave trade, putting the merchants (African and European) out of business; these shifted their commerce toward various commodities such as palm oil (see palms in Fig. 6). In 1884, Germany signed a treaty to protect Togoland, in return for German sovereignty. By 1885 German Togoland was undergoing an unprecedented economic miracle. The economy boomed as cocoa, coffee and cotton became leading exports. The colonial government built excellent roads, a brewery, a radio transmitter reaching Germany, etc. Three railroads further facilitated the transportation of goods and services. Togo achieved

Fig. 5 Elmina; photograph by Leo Paul Dana.

Fig. 6 Palm trees are plentiful; photograph by Leo Paul Dana.

the highest level of educational development in Africa; by 1914, 90% of school-age children were in school.

During World War I, German Togoland was occupied by the UK and France. In 1956, the British sector of Togoland voted to integrate with the Gold Coast, soon to become the Republic of Ghana. At the time, Togo and Ghana were among the most prosperous areas in Africa. In 1960 Togo obtained its independence from France. By then, the Mina tribe had come to dominate at the exclusion of northern tribes, whom they treated as savages and excluded from significant government positions. In 1963 Togo had the first post-independence military *coup d'état* in Africa.

To many in both Togo and Ghana, political ideology became more important than food on the table. Colonial mansions were demolished, and statues were shattered as they were viewed to be representative of imperialism. Most expatriates returned to Europe; their departure meant many jobs would disappear. The exodus of Europeans coincided with the flight of substantial capital and expertise, and much entrepreneurial activity vanished; previously, they had served as role models to African entrepreneurs. Per capita GNP plummeted. Until the 1980s, public policy, development plans and budget statements gave priority to public organizations and large firms as entrepreneurship was not recognized as being of any particular use.

During the 1980s, the Republic of Ghana changed its approach in favor of new venture programs, expecting that such would ease economic malaise by stimulating a healthy small business sector with thriving entrepreneurial spirit. In 1983, the Provisional National Defence Council launched the Economic Recovery Program. *Despite the introduction of such new venture creation measures in Ghana, per capita income fell.* In 1986, per capita GNP leveled at US$390,[9] remaining there through the end of the decade.[10]

The Private Sector Development Program is being pursued to promote new ventures in Ghana and the government is trying to encourage entrepreneurship using small business as its flagship. Despite such efforts, Ghana as well as Togo exhibits massive poverty, low per capita

---

[9] Source: World Bank, Washington, D.C.
[10] Source: Statistical Service, Accra, Ghana.

income, high population growth, low manufacturing output, and immense balance of payment deficits. In both countries, markets exist to consume, but there are shortages of virtually every consumer good and markups are high in most distribution channels. In contrast to Gabon where per capita GNP is close to US$5000 or Cameroon where per capita GNP is in excess of US$1000, per capita GNP for Ghana and Togo has been in the US$400 range.

Extent of Entrepreneurial Activity

Microbusiness versus entrepreneurship

A fundamental difference between small business and entrepreneurship must be emphasized. As explained by Schumpeter,[11] the entrepreneur improves his society, doing things in innovative ways by defining new products, new services, new methods of production, new markets, new sources of supply or new forms of organization. The entrepreneur is also a creator of jobs.

The small business owner-manager also contributes to the economy, as he is self-employed, but he provides little wage employment. The small business owner-manager often provides distribution of existing products (often assisting in import substitution) providing a market for locally made goods, and an outlet for local producers, but the sector tends to provide a low manufacturing output. Included here are a chemist (see Fig. 7), a printer (see Fig. 8), a sorcerer (see Fig. 9) and a tailor (see Fig. 10). This is not Schumpeterian entrepreneurship.

Both Togo and Ghana have a multitude of microbusinesses — one-man operations, peddlers, some selling medicines such as crocodile skulls (see Fig. 11), dead parrots, etc. Yet both are lacking entrepreneurship. In both countries, there are numerous self-employed individuals who call themselves entrepreneurs, but whose small business is really small, often with no address: a man from Mali (see Fig. 12) selling camel hides in the street; peddlers from Ghana and Nigeria roaming around Togo; a boy from Togo selling his services to tourists in Ghana. Black Africans complain that the

---

[11] Schumpeter, *op. cit.*

Fig. 7 Chemist; photograph by Leo Paul Dana.

Lebanese control the textile industry and gold trade, preventing new entrants.

A street vendor asks for 250,000 CFA for an imitation Rolex watch, but he'll sell it for 5000 CFA happily. An imitation Ralph Lauren polo shirt costs US$5. A shopkeeper asks 5000 CFA for a wooden elephant, but without discussion, he accepts a note of 1000 CFA instead. At the central bus station, housewives sell snacks through the windows of the bus. A self-ordained priest and witch doctor boards the bus to advertise and sell his medicine. The passengers respond, "Amen". A woman walks off the street, into a restaurant (with which she is not affiliated) and takes a client's order. From the plate she carries on her head, she makes a sandwich for the client and leaves before the establishment's waiter arrives.

Fig. 8   Owner-manager of a printing shop; photograph by Leo Paul Dana.

Environment dampers entrepreneurial spirit

Ghana has traditionally put emphasis on subsidizing large and public organizations which have been operating at a loss. Although the Provisional National Defence Council launched the Economic Recovery Program during the 1980s, reviewing existing programs for small business sector, West Africa has no framework to foster entrepreneurship.

In Togo, government offices are open from 7:00 am to noon, and from 2:30 pm to 5:30 pm. Business hours, when respected, are only between

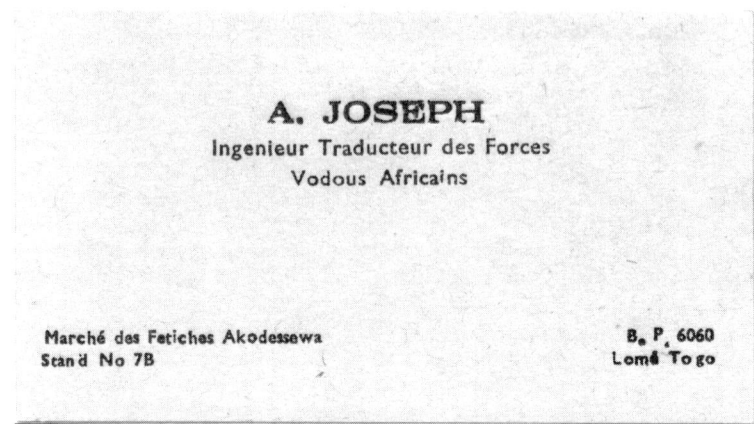

Fig. 9 Engineer in witchcraft; photograph by Leo Paul Dana.

Fig. 10 Tailors; photograph by Leo Paul Dana.

8:30 am and noon, and between 3:30 pm and 6:00 pm. Mondays to Fridays, and 8:30 am to half past noon on Saturdays. Hours are flexible, depending on personal needs. If a merchant is "busy", it is unlikely he will open his shop at all; when the president of Sierra Leone came to Lomé,

Fig. 11 Skulls for sale; photograph by Leo Paul Dana.

the city came to a standstill. The major road was closed at night, so that the visitor would not be disturbed.

The government of Ghana puts up billboards reading: "Export and earn foreign money." However, would-be entrepreneurs in Ghana report a lack of access to foreign markets. Ability to reach the outside world is indeed limited. *The Economist*[12] confirmed, "without decent telephones, no business can be efficient." As for a telex or facsimile machine, businesses in Ghana usually lack the hard currency to purchase one. Currency restrictions

---

[12] Africa's Hard Road (8 July 1989), p. 45.

Fig. 12 Trader from Mali; photograph by Leo Paul Dana.

often cripple numerous potential international transactions unless an official is offered a *gift*; the government is reluctant to allow letters of credit, crucial to international trade. Unpredictable drastic currency devaluations in Ghana are a further hindrance. Ideally, entrepreneurs need an environment reflecting ideology more in harmony with values of enterprise.

The government of Ghana is trying to promote entrepreneurship, using small business as its flagship. However, pouring funds into new venture programs for small business does not necessarily yield entrepreneurship. A policy framework should exist before implementing a program, and policy should include the need for small business to attain *critical size*. Furthermore, the State should ensure the existence of an environment compatible with the values of entrepreneurism; this includes the acceptance of ethics such as accepting law over bribery.

Excessive regulation dampers trade

Cumbersome regulatory procedures constrict commerce in both Togo and Ghana. When the French colonial government left Togo in 1960, perhaps the greatest single contribution it gave to the Togolese was a hard currency, the CFA, the currency of French Africa. Togo uses the West African CFA which is legal tender in the area which was l'Afrique occidentale francaise, specifically in Benin, Burkina Faso, Ivory Coast, Mali, Niger, and Senegal. In theory, when several countries share an identical currency, trade is simplified. At par with the West African CFA is the Central African CFA used in Cameroon, the Central African Republic, Chad, Congo, Equatorial Guinea, and Gabon. The same stable currency throughout eliminates foreign exchange risk when doing business within any of these countries or France. One might expect, then, that trade between Togo and France might be simplified, but there is an immense affinity for bureaucracy and other trade barriers. To import a video cassette, for example, the "Brigade speciale togolaise" imposes five different taxes; plus a stamp duty. (Official stamps are most important in Togo — even a police report requires a 250 CFA stamp, a problem when one has been pickpocketed.)

Ghana has its own regulatory requirements. A foreign businessperson, for example, must register with police. Upon arrival at the police station in downtown Accra, one is informed of the need for a photo. None can be made in the vicinity, but the official might accept a *gift* in lieu.

Ghana has been modifying its tax and tariff structure. It has also legalized foreign exchange dealings recently, now holding weekly foreign exchange auctions. Paperwork involved is nevertheless highly time-consuming, and the cost of importing machinery (see Fig. 13) is still prohibitive, a deterrent to manufacturing industry. According to *The Economist*, mis-regulation ensures that one of the biggest industries in the area is smuggling rather than manufacturing.[13]

Entrepreneurship requires infrastructure

The government of Ghana spends money promoting, "We must grow what we eat and we must eat what we grow." Yet many people cannot read. Illiteracy is 74.5% in agricultural areas, although only 36.7%[14] in the

---

[13] For details, see: Africa, *The Economist* (April 1989), p. 62.
[14] Source: Statistical Service, Accra, Ghana.

Fig. 13   Valuable machine; photograph by Leo Paul Dana.

capital city,[15] and even among those who can read, the low educational background of the people results in gross managerial incompetence. In contrast to Namibia which spends 15% of its budget on education,[16] Ghana spends about half that.[17]

Nevertheless, Ghana spends an unknown amount on the maintenance of billboards promoting self-sufficiency. Yet, as explained by *The Economist*,[18] "without government spending on roads...farmers cannot get their grain to town."

Ghana, especially, has a lack of feeder roads; the result is that raw materials such as wood are available but not accessible; furthermore,

---

[15] For the sake of comparison, Steward, D.W. Best wishes, *Southern Africa Today* (August 1989), p. 1, reports only 27.5% illiteracy in Namibia.

[16] Dana, L.P. (July 1993). An analysis of strategic intervention policy in Namibia, *Journal of Small Business Management*, 31: 90–95.

[17] Source: Statistical Service, Accra, Ghana.

[18] Africa's Hard Road (July 1989), p. 45.

Fig. 14 Aneho; photograph by Leo Paul Dana.

it is difficult to distribute finished goods, especially perishables. Even in downtown Accra, the sewer parallel to the often-broken sidewalk, and holes in the poorly maintained roads make it difficult to get around.

Transportation in Togo has also deteriorated since independence. One might expect that with a common currency Togo and its French neighbors would be actively trading. There are other obstacles: Although the capital of Togo, Lomé, is only 35 miles from the border of Benin, the drive takes several hours on a road which was partially washed away by the tide many years ago. The trains have recently been discontinued while the station in Aneho (last major stop on the Togolese side, see Fig. 14) has become a cement warehouse. Once at the border, crossing it may involve several hours or a few *gifts* to local officials. Trade between Togo and Burkina Faso is also very limited. Air links are few, there is no railroad, and the road is treacherous. Few have enough entrepreneurial spirit to persevere. The train between Togo's major coastal cities, Lomé and Aneho, was discontinued in 1988. One may board a bus destined for Aneho, only to learn that the driver has changed his mind. Such factors do not encourage the would-be entrepreneur.

As for the border with Ghana, it was created by the French and English at the time of World War I, upon the partition of German Togoland. It closes at 6 pm sharp. Individuals identify themselves as import/export entrepreneurs; their operation consists of carrying a basket of coconuts on the head from Ghana. So-called import/export entrepreneurs also walk across the border with bananas on their head.

Suppose a more entrepreneurial individual from Ghana seeks to speak to a prospective client in Togo. To get through by telephone is a major undertaking. Travelling by private bus involves frequent stops by police; the experience of the author suggests five roadblocks per hour, on average. An alternative is to ride the government bus from Accra to Lomé: tickets are available at 1:00 pm for the 2:00 pm departure; at 4:30 pm the bus is still being fueled. At 6:00 pm the border closes before the bus gets there. There are hotels at the border, for example, the "Good God Clinic & My Good God Hotel" owned by entrepreneur Dr. George Grant, MDH India, in Aflao (telephone 0962-264). Bedsheets are less easy to find.

Entrepreneurship requires access to capital

The banking system in Ghana was recently restructured, and rural communities given unprecedented access to banks. There are all types of banks. Around Ghana, one sees many banks, including agriculture development banks and even a "Bank for Housing and Construction." However, high inflation has contributed to a lack of trust in banks. Furthermore, the public tends to believe that bank staff are often improperly trained. Consequently, people believe that money is safer at home than at the bank, and preferably in foreign currency. As people hoard their cash, the banks experience a shortage of banknotes. A great constraint to entrepreneurial activity is lack of credit. As reported by *The Economist*,[19] many banks in West Africa are in trouble, and a modest US$100,000 cannot be found to finance a new venture to turn sawdust into charcoal.

---

[19] Africa (1 April 1989), pp. 61–62.

The Togolese government has capital, and in an attempt to improve a deteriorating economic situation, it recently invested in tourism, hoping that by becoming a beach resort, Lomé would attract foreign money which might help the worsening economic situation. A massive beach resort hotel was built, but several miles from the beach. Its deficit is an annual burden on the government. Meanwhile, the beach is still used as a public lavatory by much of the population.

Recommendation

This essay described the state of small business and entrepreneurship in Ghana, a country offering new venture programs, and that as its neighbor Togo lacking in new venture programs. Research findings reveal that both countries have a multitude of microbusinesses (see Fig. 15). Yet entrepreneurship is lacking, in both Togo and Ghana even though the latter has new venture programs. This suggests that other factors with which the entrepreneur interacts, are *more important* causal variables.

Fig. 15 Micro-firms at bazaar; photograph by Leo Paul Dana.

Fig. 16 Limited access to technology; photograph by Leo Paul Dana.

These environmental uncontrollables, external to the entrepreneur, have a greater impact on entrepreneurial activity than does the existence of new venture programs. As discussed above, numerous factors hinder entrepreneurial activity in West Africa, regardless of new venture programs. Problems include: lack of literacy and other skills among the labor force, lack of managerial skills, lack of access to technology, lack of access to capital, along with poor infrastructure (telephone service, road maintenance, etc.), and excessive regulation among others (see Fig. 16).

In summary, West Africa is characterized by countless microbusinesses, but the lack of entrepreneurship. The attempt to introduce new venture programs in Ghana has not resulted in a noticeable increase in per capita GNP, as both Togo and Ghana export similar figures below the US$400 range.

Indeed, the entrepreneur is in constant interaction with his environment. The lack of telephone service, excessive regulation and particular ethics affect the ability to do business efficiently. The lack of transportation facilities is particularly noticeable as individuals walk around the streets of Lomé with antique Singer sewing machines on their heads.

Yet despite all these problems, individuals conduct their day to day activities, in Togo as well as Ghana, suggesting that the North American style new venture programs introduced in Ghana are of little if any use, in West Africa. These should be replaced by a more environmentally sensitive policy framework which would ensure more efficient use of funds.

As previously suggested by Loucks,[20] this study has provided evidence that new venture programs, despite their success in industrialized societies, may not be effectively translocated to developing nations. Interactive elements, including values, ideology, culture and infrastructure must not be ignored.

Experience has shown that financial grants alone have minimal success, if any. Senegal receives more monetary assistance than any other country in western Africa, yet real growth per capita since independence has been virtually zero. In one entrepreneurship project alone, the US spent US$4.6 million assisting cereal production; increase in output was nil!

How can the absence of entrepreneurial activity be explained? *Societal attitude toward entrepreneurship* as an important causal variable. The development of an entrepreneurial culture is as important to the growth of the small business sector as are specific new venture programs.

This study suggests that before new venture programs can have an effect on a given society, the environment must be at harmony with entrepreneurial values so that an enterprise culture can exist. Rather than spend money on randomly designed and implemented *new venture programs*, a policy framework and infrastructure should be established. A framework should ensure that *entrepreneur development programs* (and resulting entrepreneurial values) precede expenditures on *new venture programs*, contributing to the effectiveness of the latter.

Other areas requiring attention include a need to increase emphasis on education, to increase literacy in general (see Fig. 17), to improve managerial competition, and to develop entrepreneurial potential to identify opportunities.

Specific opportunities for entrepreneurship in Togo include antelope breeding. The numbers of wild antelope, once plentiful in occidental

---

[20] Loucks, K.E. in Peterson, R. Peterson, M.A. and Tieken, N. (1988). *Encouraging Entrepreneurship Internationally*. Dubuque, Iowa: Kendall/Hunt.

374 L. P. Dana

Fig. 17 Who can read this?; photograph by Leo Paul Dana.

Africa, are being rapidly depleted, yet there is a large demand for their meat in local cooking. Breeding would be lucrative as well as contributing to society. Another opportunity is that of importing plantain from Ghana, where it is abundant. In Togo, plaintains grow only inland and on a small scale. However, plantain and cassava are the major ingredients of foufou (see Fig. 18), which is the native staple of Togo. Whereas in Ghana foufou is made of plantain and cassava, in Togo, because of the plantain shortage, foufou is made only from yams. Numerous other entrepreneurial possibilities exist, once the ideology of entrepreneurship is accepted.

The sages taught us that if we only give food and money to the beggars, they will be forced to beg more; if we teach them to be self-sufficient, they will no longer be dependent but rather, they could help others too. Perhaps the role of industrialized powers should include fostering a spirit of entrepreneurship in developing countries, such that their small

Fig. 18 Making Foufou; photograph by Leo Paul Dana.

business sectors can attain the critical size necessary to make more significant contributions to their societies.

In the words of British scientist J.B.S. Haldane in 1928, "for every type of animal there is a most convenient size ... just as there is a best size for every animal, so the same is true for every human institution."

13
LANDSCAPE ENTREPRENEURSHIP: LESSONS FROM THE MONT SAINT HILAIRE NATURE CENTRE

*Emmanuel Raufflet, Maria Tengö,
Marc-André Guertin, Kafui Dansou
and Louis Jacques Filion*

Introduction

Entrepreneurship as a mean to meet social needs

Entrepreneurship is a process that can be applied to all kinds of human activities, not just creating businesses. For example, it can be used to add value to many aspects of our lives and the natural environment. This chapter is very much in line with this way of thinking, which is being put forward by an increasing number of authors in the field (Kao, 1995; Kao *et al.*, 2002 and 2005). The case study discussed here is an example of social entrepreneurship applied to regional conservation and ecology. The analysis of the Nature Centre at Mont Saint Hilaire, south-east of Montreal, Canada, using the perspectives outlined in this chapter, aim to shed light on what we broadly refer to here as "landscape entrepreneurship."

For the purposes of this paper, we define *landscape entrepreneurship* as a set of innovative activities conducted by an actor aimed at sustaining and developing ecological and social processes in a specific region or landscape so as to improve the ecosystem for human well-being. The actor may be an individual or a group of individuals, acting independently of government structures. The organization may be a non-governmental organization (NGO). Landscape entrepreneurship activities may be profit-oriented, or non-profit-oriented. The case presented here involves a non-profit situation. We propose that social-ecological entrepreneurs can play a crucial and innovative role in promoting and navigating ecological change to help save our planet and to improve conditions for human life.

Our definition of the term "landscape" comprises interpretations from cultural geography, a distinct area of study that looks at the combined work of nature and humans,[1] as well as from landscape ecology where landscape denotes a mosaic of landscape elements with ecosystems interacting across space (Forman and Godron, 1986). In this chapter, we focus on the management of ecosystems from two standpoints: (1) recognizing spatial connectivity (connections between spaces) and (2) recognizing the interdependence between ecological and human-related processes.

In addition, our perspective on sustainable development is derived from resilience science. Resilience is the capacity to absorb change without losing the capacity to continue to develop (Holling, 1986; Gunderson and Holling, 2001). Resilience science has its roots in ecology but is developing into a science of how to manage systems where social and ecological processes interact.

Resilience as applied to ecosystems, or to integrated systems of people and the natural environment, has three defining characteristics (Carpenter *et al.*, 2001). The first is the degree of change a system can undergo and still maintain the same level of control over function and structure. The second is the degree to which a system is capable of self-organization. The third characteristic is the ability to build and increase capacity for learning and adaptation. In a resilient system, such as the specific landscape discussed here, disturbance and change have the potential to create opportunity for innovation and development (Folke, 2006). Acting on that potential, however, requires the presence of entrepreneurs — actors who know how to take advantage of opportunity. Ecological activities require more and more innovative capabilities.

---

[1] Cultural landscape was defined by UNESCO (2005), in *Operational Guidelines for the Implementation of the World Heritage Convention*. Paris: UNESCO World Heritage Centre, p. 83.

This chapter comprises four sections. In the first, we distinguish between "classical" and "social" entrepreneurship and situate the notion of landscape entrepreneurship. In the second, we describe the experience of the Mont Saint Hilaire Nature Centre, a biosphere reserve located 40 kilometers south-east of Montreal. In the third section, we propose four perspectives on landscape entrepreneurship based on the experience of the Nature Centre, namely (1) landscape entrepreneurship as social entrepreneurship and organizing; (2) landscape entrepreneurship and the potential and challenges of stakeholder engagement processes; (3) landscape entrepreneurship and the construction of resilience in social/ecological systems; and (4) landscape entrepreneurship as seen from the experience and lessons learned in the implementation of a United Nations (UN) developed framework for conservation. In the fourth section, we identify lessons and insights potentially relevant to our understanding of the role and forms of entrepreneurship in addressing social and environmental concerns. We conclude by pointing out tensions that arise in the complex process of landscape entrepreneurship, and suggesting that landscape entrepreneurship is at the tipping point of an emerging field of study with significant implications for related disciplines and fields of study.

From Classic to Social Entrepreneurship

Entrepreneurship began as a term denoting opportunity detection as a means to innovation. Schumpeter (1934) referred to the effect of entrepreneurial activities as "creative destruction": entrepreneurs develop new products that make those already on the market obsolete (see also McCraw, 2007). Over the last decade, a growing number of researchers have remarked that entrepreneurship occurs not only because an entrepreneur recognizes a business opportunity, but also out of necessity. We observed this phenomenon several times in the course of our research, in particular, in a study of self-employed persons (before it became part of the entrepreneurship literature), where more than 25% of the sample had gone into business simply because they could not find a job (Filion, 1996 and 2004).

If we look closely at the life stories of entrepreneurs, it becomes clear that many launched their businesses in response to a specific social or human need, rather than to pursue what is commonly termed a business opportunity. The trajectory of three recognized "classical" entrepreneurs illustrates this search for the answer to a need.

Alexander Graham Bell (MacKay, 1997) had a relative with impaired hearing, so he worked on a device to amplify sound. It was only later that he started to develop devices to carry sound, which led to the invention of the telephone.

Joseph Armand Bombardier (MacDonald, 2001) ran a small-town garage where he repaired farm machinery. He was a handyman-inventor, developing all kinds of farm equipment. When a close relative died because roads were blocked during a snowstorm, and the person could not be transported to hospital, Bombardier swore this would never happen again, and built a snowmobile. The original idea was for a vehicle that could take sick people to hospital. Word of the new vehicle spread quickly. The Canadian Army asked him to produce snowmobiles for its Second World War operations in northern Europe. The lightweight vehicles could carry six to ten people and gave a tremendous advantage to the Canadian troops operating in northern environments. After the war, people in Canada began to buy snowmobiles as transport during the long winters. Bombardier went on to develop the skidoo, again with the aim of providing a flexible vehicle that could go anywhere across snow.

Yvon Chouinard (2006) was the creator of Chouinard Equipment, which went on to become Black Diamond, a leader in mountaineering equipment in the US Some years later, he founded Patagonia. Chouinard is a mountain climber, and he needed equipment and clothing suited to the kinds of activities he enjoyed.

Examples abound where entrepreneurship occurred as a result of someone wanting to meet a human or social need, rather than simply take advantage of a business opportunity. This is certainly the case for many inventors who became entrepreneurs, and for most social entrepreneurs. Clearly, a business opportunity is usually preceded by need, but the difference with the cases cited above is that the entrepreneurs in question did not regard the opportunity as a means of building a business; they wanted to fulfill the underlying need, and they set up the business to do that. This is not the same thing, and does not lead to the same process. The original purpose and root definition are not in the same category of activity systems, so the learning process will not be geared to the same pattern.

We consider landscape entrepreneurship to be part of *ecopreneurship*, which can be classified in the broader category of social entrepreneurship. Figure 1 below lists some of the differences between classic and social entrepreneurship.

Over the last decade, there has been a surge of interest in the notion of social entrepreneurship. Landscape entrepreneurship is a form of social entrepreneurship that involves a social cause where something needs to be protected. The process involved resembles that used in social entrepreneurship, but one aspect that may be specific to landscape entrepreneurship is the fact that it is *a complex process* with many actors and stakeholders involved, some in conflicting situations, focused on a central issue. In the case of the Mont Saint Hilaire Nature Centre, the central issue was the protection of the natural environment of an exceptional geographic site. In the next section, we describe the trajectory and experience of the Nature Centre.

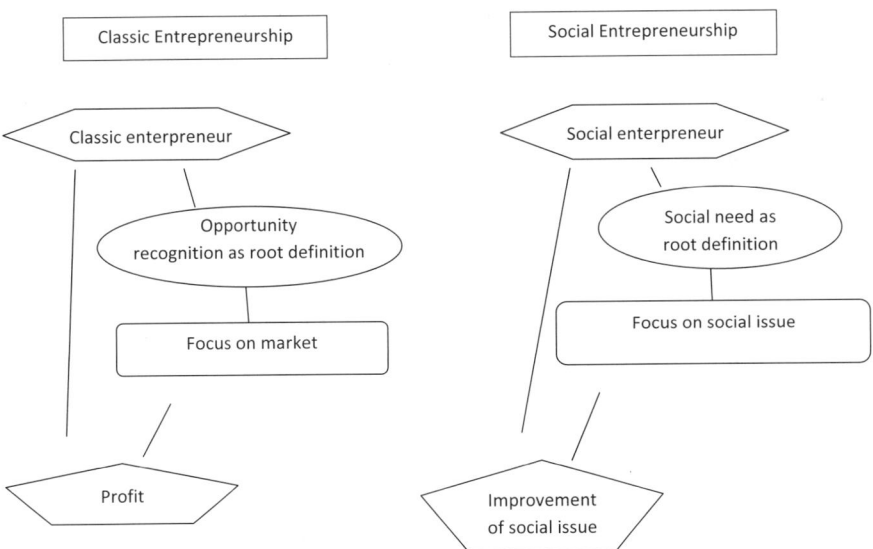

Fig. 1 Differences between classic and social entrepreneurship.

Case Study: The Mont Saint Hilaire Nature Centre

"The problem with the protection of nature is that when the situation is not urgent, people don't think about it, and when the situation becomes urgent, it is often too late. We face this dilemma: when there's a fire we extinguish it, but if there's no fire, why prevent it? In conservation, this has always been the challenge. People wait till it is urgent, and then when it is too late, they have to pay three times the price for something they could have saved with less effort before."

A manager at Mont Saint Hilaire Nature Centre (2008).

The Nature Center

Mont Saint Hilaire is a beautiful mountain, a hiker's paradise and one of the best preserved Monteregian hills in the Montreal area. Located near the Richelieu River about 40 kilometers south-east of Montreal, it is renowned for the diversity of its flora and fauna, as well as for its numerous minerals. Mont Saint Hilaire is also known for its rich human history, which dates back at least 8000 years. Throughout the periods of human settlement in the region, from the period when it was home to Native Americans to the time of European settlements, and subsequent periods of private ownership, this exceptional ecosystem has been preserved more or less intact.[2]

Mont Saint Hilaire covers a geographic area of some 1100 hectares. At its heart is Hertel Lake, covering some 32 hectares. The site boasts one of the last remnants of old growth deciduous forest in Quebec, with trees more than 400 years old, consisting mainly of sugar maple and beech, white ash, bitternut hickory, basswood, red pine, white pine and eastern hemlock. The mountain is also home to nearly 1000 species of plants, mammals, birds, reptiles and amphibians — more than 50 of them rare or endangered. Mont Saint Hilaire is also recognized for the richness of its minerals; at least 16 were first discovered and named here, and it is listed as one of the top ten mineral-collecting sites in the world.

---

[2] McGill website: http://www.mcgill.ca/gault/reserve/history/.

Mont Saint Hilaire is located near a major urban area of some 3.5 million people. Surrounding the site is a greenbelt consisting of a number of privately owned lots with various types of natural growth including forested areas,[3] apple orchards and farmland. The greenbelt offers essential cover and corridors for the local fauna and a protective buffer zone for the mountain. The orchards draw many visitors to the area, contributing to a flourishing industry, and the apple blossoms add to the mountain's natural beauty. These economic activities do, however, make the mountain's ecosystem more vulnerable. The resulting increase in urban development and higher levels of human disturbances are the reasons the Nature Centre developed a regional conservation program to protect the mountain and surrounding areas.[4]

Mont Saint Hilaire holds a storied place in Quebec's artistic and political history, associated with Quebec's intelligentsia in the late 19th and 20th centuries. Paul-Émile Borduas, principal author of the *Refus global* manifesto, was born and went to school there, apprenticing with another legendary local painter, Ozias Leduc, at his studio on the Montée des Trente. Leduc's mystical paintings of the mountain are now iconic, including *L'Heure Mauve* and *Neige Dorée*.[5] Modern dance and experimental film on dance in Quebec were also born here, when Françoise Sullivan, a frequent visitor to painter Jean-Paul Riopelle's country house at Saint-Hilaire (along with other artists in the Automatist movement) and a contributor to the *Refus global*, improvised *Danse dans la neige* in the fields below the mountain to the music of wind and crunching snow. Filmed by Riopelle and photographed by Maurice Perron in 1947, the work was remounted for the 2007 film *Les Saisons Sullivan*.

Evidence also suggests that Mont Saint Hilaire, particularly the *Pain de Sucre* summit, was a sacred site for the Algonquin First Nations. Many local legends relate to the mountain; for instance, the unusual ice patterns found on the northern cliff-face of the mountain where a vaguely

---

[3] The Virtual Museum: http://virtualmuseum.ca/Exhibitions/Hilaire/html-en/index.php?page=nature_locations_perimeter.html.

[4] UNESCO Biosphere Reserve website: http://www.unesco.org/mabdb/br/brdir/directory/biores.asp?mode=all&code=CAN+01.

[5] Musée des beaux arts de Mont Saint-Hilaire: http://www.mbamsh.qc.ca/.

horse-shaped ice formation does not melt until late in the spring, is said to represent the spirit of a local farmer's horse warning farmers against planting their crop as long as the ice formation remains.[6]

The history of the Mont Saint Hilaire Nature Centre

Since 1958, when it became the property of McGill University, the Nature Centre at Mont Saint Hilaire (then known as the Gault Nature Reserve) has gone through several management phases, both in terms of the type of activities developed, and the organizational structure adopted.

The early years (1958–1972)

In 1958, Andrew Hamilton Gault[7] donated his personal estate on the upper slopes of the mountain to McGill University. Surprisingly, during the early years, the University was uncertain as to how the land should be used. Gault specified that he was making the bequest

> *that its beauties and amenities may be preserved for all time to come, not only to the immediate interests of the university itself, but through its corridors of learning, as a great heritage for the benefit and enjoyment of youth of Canada.*[8]

Patrick D. Baird was appointed director of the Gault Estate (1958–1968) and in accordance with the recommendations in a University committee report, introduced plans that made the land available to McGill departments for education and research. In line with past practices, the policy allowed for the continued use of the site for recreational purposes by local residents and the general public.

---

[6] Wikipedia site: http://en.wikipedia.org/wiki/Mont_Saint-Hilaire.
[7] A British army officer and, at some point in his life, a member of Parliament in the UK, the son of a wealthy family, Gault lived in England but spent time at his Mont Saint-Hilaire Estate. See Williams, J. (1995). *First in the Field, Gault of Patricias*. London: Leo Cooper, 278 pp. (ISBN 0-85052-436-9).
[8] McGill website: http://www.mcgill.ca/gault/reserve/.

In 1970, the University and the Estate's Board of Directors commissioned the National (US) Audubon Society to do a complete study of the mountain. The report recommended the creation of a Nature Conservation Centre which would promote the conservation of the mountain's resources, and administer activities to help protect its ecosystems from human overuse and misuse.[9]

On her appointment as the second director of the Gault Estate in December 1970, Alice E. Johannsen set out to develop the Nature Conservation Centre as an essential complement to academic activities on the mountain.

The conservation phase (1972–1995/6)

Alice Johanssen had been the director of the Redpath Museum (a unique interdisciplinary arm's-length institution within the Faculty of Science at McGill University).[10] In 1972, she founded the Nature Conservation Centre at Mont Saint Hilaire. She moved into Gault House, Gault's original home on the mountain, and assumed directorship of both the Gault Estate and the newly created Nature Conservation Centre.

The university supported the creation of the Nature Conservation Centre, and the Board of Directors of the Gault Estate decided to focus the Centre's efforts on three areas: (1) preservation of the Gault Estate; (2) increasing public outreach; and (3) expanding the reach of the Gault Estate's programs through a stewardship program that encouraged collaboration with local residents and private landowners in the protection of the area's unique habitats.

Under Johannsen's leadership, the Gault Estate became recognized internationally as a major draw for recreational activities in the area. Johannsen, thanks to her connections in outdoor recreation and the tourism industry, raised funds to build ski hills and develop recreational programs, as well as build the Nature Centre Pavilion. In 1978, she succeeded in having the Gault Nature Reserve named a biosphere reserve under UNESCO's Man and the Biosphere program, which is aimed at

---

[9] McGill website: http://www.mcgill.ca/files/gault/planang.pdf.
[10] McGill website: http://www.mcgill.ca/redpath/.

protecting representative examples of the world's ecosystems. It was the first Canadian site to be so listed.

Also in the 1970s, Quebec's Ministry of Education launched several programs for environmental education that included guided tours to protected areas. It was a move inspired by the vision of Frère Marie-Victorin, an eminent Quebec botanist who had created the Botanical Gardens in Montreal and promoted natural history and environmental education. Throughout the 1980s, all across Quebec, programs for school visits to protected areas received substantial grants from the Quebec government. At the Nature Centre, school visits reached 70,000 in the 1980s, accounting for the bulk of the Centre's revenues.

Several McGill departments used the Gault Estate for field courses on ecology. A number of research projects were also conducted in the area. Over a mere six years (1986 to 1992), 121 scientific articles in geography, geology, biology, ecology, plant science and entomology[11] were published based on research carried out at the Gault Estate.

In 1979, Michel Drew was appointed to succeed Alice Johannsen on her retirement as Director of the Gault Estate and Director of the Nature Conservation Centre. In the 1990s, he led the Nature Conservation Centre through a severe financial crisis, which threatened the future of the biosphere reserve. In the early 1990s, budget cuts at the Ministry of Education led to a drastic reduction in the number of school trips to the Centre. By 1995, the Nature Conservation Centre was on the verge of financial collapse, with an accumulated debt of US$500,000.

The financial crisis revealed that the Nature Centre needed to clarify its mission, which would encompass both public education and outreach, and scientific research. Until the crisis hit, the Nature Centre had never thought to write a mission statement. It had a charter, developed under Alice Johannsen's directorship, which served it well. With the new challenges to the Centre, the McGill University Board of Directors felt that an unequivocal mission statement was needed, one that would help unify the activities of the director, the staff, and fundraisers.

---

[11] Ecological Monitoring and Assessment Network website: http://www.eman-rese.ca/eman/reports/publications/gault/intro.html.

A mission statement for a dual undertaking

The drafting of a mission statement for the Nature Conservation Centre was also motivated by the need to assert and make visible to all stakeholders the dual nature of the Centre's undertaking. Starting in the 1960s, the Mont Saint Hilaire region had been experiencing significant changes, putting increased pressure on the area's natural resources. The Centre was also facing internal challenges resulting from the tension between stakeholders advocating a greater focus on conservation and research, and those proposing an expansion of interpretive and outreach activities.

At the regional level, the once prosperous apple orchards had become less profitable, and speculators were actively buying up the land for housing projects. Several orchards were transformed into residential areas with evocative names that made reference to the former idyllic surroundings, such as "The Three Apples." An order-in-council (later, the *Act to Preserve Agricultural Land, Bill* 129), which came into effect in 1978, put an end to the sale of the orchards for non-agricultural purposes.

Farmland also underwent significant changes as family-run farms were transformed into niche agricultural operations. Traditional farm allotments included a wooded area to supply the family's needs and wood for the construction of farm buildings. The new agricultural niche operations, however, did not need this wood, and treed areas on farm properties were rapidly disappearing.

The construction of the Trans-Canada Highway beginning in the early 1960s, linking to Highway 116, improved road access to Mont Saint Hilaire from Montreal and other major urban areas. This encouraged residential developments on the sides of the mountain. As a result, the population of Mont St-Hilaire grew from 6000 in 1975 to 16,000 at the end of 2007. This demographic explosion and the increase in housing starts meant that the green belt around the mountain began to shrink. In addition to the obvious pressure on land use for new housing projects, the influx of new residents also posed new challenges for the management of the natural resources of the region.

As a result, tensions developed between the various interests in the region. In 1988, this situation led to the creation of the "Friends of the Mountain," a citizen movement that pressured the local government to slow down construction around the mountain. The town responded favorably, imposing a moratorium on housing development on the southern slope. Further conflict developed in 1997, this time over the construction of residences on a plateau near the Dieppe Cliffs on the western slope. The Cliffs were known as a nesting site for peregrine falcons (designated by the Quebec Government as a protected species). An agreement was finally struck between the town and the owner of the property at the base of the mountain, through which the town acquired the portion of the land adjacent to the Mont Saint Hilaire biosphere reserve.

The beginning of a new era

The recurring civic tension coupled with the economic development of the region, and the Nature Centre's internal struggles led to the development of a new platform. The Nature Centre took up the challenge of incorporating a broader perspective, based on the fact that the protection of the Reserve required promoting the protection of the surrounding area. It was the beginning of a new era that saw the launch of a stewardship program to promote the protection of endangered species at the regional level, thereby maintaining the greenbelt around the mountain. The stewardship program led to six bequests of privately owned lots sheltering endangered species (about 17 hectares), the signing of two conservation agreements with the owners of land occupied by endangered species (between the Municipality of Sainte Madeleine and the Nature Centre), and the inclusion of five lots in a wildlife refuge to protect the nesting habitat of the peregrine falcon.

In addition, for many years, researchers had been gathering data on the mountain's ecosystems and had generated information that had the potential to assist regional decision-makers in developing land use practices that would be respectful of conservation. Using this information, the Centre developed a series of tools to help local administrators manage local resources: among them, atlases, and databases using a Geographical Information System (GIS) to integrate data on the natural environment in support of local planning processes and implementation. The system also facilitated collaboration on data gathering outside the biosphere reserve — information that would prove invaluable in the formulation of the Nature Centre development plan. The Nature Centre also developed closer relationships with municipal and regional authorities during those years, in order to have a voice in future land use and zoning discussions.

These changes in focus and new developments called for the writing of a mission statement that would clearly lay out the mission of the Nature Centre. This was done in 2001. The aim was to improve communication with the different groups involved, and to guide the Centre's actions to address both the conservation objective and the public outreach and regional vision.

The mission of the Nature Centre was then stated as follows:

(1) Assure the short- and long-term integrity of the mountain's natural heritage.
(2) Offer to all groups of society a privileged contact with nature accompanied by a range of educational and cultural activities.
(3) Promote the conservation of natural environments in the region.

In the words of a longstanding member of the Gault Estate Board:[12]

We felt that it wouldn't make sense if the Centre's work didn't go further. Expanding it to the region also fitted nicely with the concept of a biosphere reserve which is not just like a little museum. The biosphere is supposed to be a place of influence. It has to influence a whole region, so although the structure of the biosphere reserve was sort of vague for us, the idea wasn't. And its philosophy resonated with what we were feeling.

In June 1995, for the first time, the directorship of the Gault Estate was separated from that of the Nature Conservation Centre. Martin Lechowicz became the Gault Estate's third director, and Kees Vanderheyden was then chosen as director of the Nature Conservation Centre.

The Nature Centre: Exerting influence on regional ecological issues

The Nature Centre's efforts to protect the areas around the mountain were developed in partnership with numerous private landowners, municipalities

---

[12] Interview with a member of the Gault Estate Board of Directors in February 2008.

and local authorities. The actions of the Centre also included working with the whole community to protect the mountain's immediate surroundings to ensure that they remained natural areas.

Getting organized with new tools: development plan and multimedia tools

A key concern for the Nature Centre is to develop new tools that would help decision-makers manage the natural environment, and assist in the formulation of its own management plan. To this end, in developing these tools it adopted a three-stage approach which consisted of: (1) identifying the geographic priorities through the development of very detailed plans of the area; (2) consulting with local decision-makers on these findings; and (3) presenting proposals to the Municipality on the use of the natural resources surrounding the Mont Saint Hilaire reserve.

This approach was used by the Nature Centre in discussions about land use and zoning decisions affecting new housing developments, as well as when they presented the Centre's Development Plan for 2003–2006, and in subsequent years.[13] The 2003–2006 Plan illustrates the awareness and strategy within the Centre to manage "out," i.e. to nurture and develop its relationships with visitors, local communities, and other actors in the region, and to manage "in" by maintaining a consensus and mutual vision within the organization. The Plan also affirmed that science that was the foundation of the Centre's activities Centre was being conducted properly.

Nature centre partnerships with regional authorities

Partnerships with local decision-makers have included collaboration initiatives with the municipalities, and with the community-at-large including private landowners. In the case of private landowners, partnerships consisted of donations of habitats of endangered species and the signing of agreements for the preservation of vulnerable species. A partnership with the Town of Mont-Hilaire was also established to protect the ecological

---

[13] The Nature Centre website: http://www.centrenature.qc.ca/en/pdf/MasterPlan2004.pdf.

richness of the mountain's surroundings while taking the expectations and concerns of the citizens into account. Finally, to complement other communication activities directed towards the general public, a CD-ROM entitled *Atlas of the Forested Areas of the Richelieu Region: Understanding and Protecting our Heritage* was created with the goal of increasing public awareness about the need to protect forested areas in the region. It included a presentation of the different types of forests in the Richelieu region, and provided general information about the entire region.

The Nature centre's partnering approach: making partnerships work

Working with local landowners, municipalities and community groups was no easy task, however. The Nature Centre had no formal authority over the management of the natural environments surrounding the mountain. One of the Nature Centre leaders equated the role of the Centre with that of an orchestra conductor:

> *"In the orchestra, making sure that everybody plays the same tune in a harmonious way is not a given. Sometimes, to introduce some new activities, it is very weird. People get very strict about it, and you have to make sure that the Nature Centre is not viewed as four different entities melted into one, but rather four parties collaborating together towards a common goal."*[14]

First, in its dealings with municipal and regional actors, the Centre used several approaches to inform and influence them to incorporate conservation objectives into their decision-making processes. The use of the GIS, for instance, allowed the Centre to share information on local ecology in an integrated manner, and to support conservation priorities for the region. This approach aimed to create a more territory-embedded regional planning, which contrasted with more traditional forms of planning that tended to be centered around administrative boundaries, sometimes regardless of ecological natural boundaries.

---

[14] Interview with a Nature Centre senior officer (June 18, 2008).

Second, the Nature Centre worked to build the emblematic value of the mountain in the regional landscape to bring its partners together. The mountain was used to symbolize the link between them; its human history, natural richness and beauty attract much attention. Over the years, the Nature Centre developed several activities related to the promotion of local traditions and cultural heritage. For instance, the Centre organizes an annual event named "Tales of the Fall," an autumn storytelling festival where stories and legends from the Mont Saint Hilaire area are shared. Seasonal activities also include "Christmas at the Mountain," a local song festival, a photography competition among others.

Third, in working with municipalities and regional authorities, members of the Nature Centre are guided by ideas of a sustainably managed region and a way of thinking that recognizes that change does take time. They are only marginally concerned about structures, and in fact, the Nature Centre management structure is very simple. The Nature Centre's managers are motivated by the desire to connect with local partners, to create a sense of shared regional goals, and to work in a non-confrontational manner to identify practical solutions that satisfy all the parties concerned.

The Nature Centre as Landscape Entrepreneur: Four Perspectives

In this section, we propose four perspectives from which to look at the experience of the Nature Centre, centered on the notion of landscape entrepreneurship. These perspectives are (1) landscape entrepreneurship as a component of social entrepreneurship and organizing; (2) landscape entrepreneurship and the challenges of stakeholder engagement in the process; (3) landscape entrepreneurship and the construction of resilience in social/ecological systems; and (4) landscape entrepreneurship as seen through the experience of implementing a UN developed framework for conservation.

Landscape entrepreneurship as a component of social entrepreneurship and organizing

The first perspective builds on social entrepreneurship and focuses on the organizational dimensions of the process of landscape entrepreneurship.

As mentioned in the introduction, social entrepreneurs are motivated by intentions related to addressing a social issue; their root definition consists of "meeting a social need" in the broad sense. In this section, based on the experience of the Nature Centre, we explore how the definition of this "social need" or "intention" has evolved over time, as well as the implications of this change for the organization, based on its mission and its processes. These changes are summarized in Table 1.

The mission of the Nature Centre before the mid-1990s, informed by Gault's and Johannsen's intentions, focused on two dimensions, namely conservation and recreation, that valued scientific thinking and a focus on research: the landscape was viewed as a field station with exceptional value from the scientific and aesthetic perspectives. Defining the mission this way implied the development of internal competencies, as a research station (working for scientists), as a research center (working with scientists), and as a recreational center (providing services by working with individuals trained to manage outdoor recreation programs). The "intention" — defined here as what the Nature Centre intended to accomplish in light of the identified social need, was based on the premise (1) that scientific research would lead to an improved understanding of the mineral, vegetal and animal populations and ecosystems of the reserve, which would in turn lead to better management decisions and (2) that environmental education — learning about and experiencing nature — by school children, weekend visitors, hikers, and others, would lead to their developing more sophisticated perceptions of nature. In turn, these experiences and heightened awareness and knowledge would influence collective perceptions of nature, eventually contributing to better ecosystem management.

The two-part (financial and mission-related) crisis in the mid-1990s led to the inclusion of a third aspect to this mission: a regional scope. This decision was based on the recognition of ecological and social interdependencies. In terms of natural interdependencies, it recognized that the ecological integrity and resilience of the reserve depended on the regional landscapes; in terms of social interdependencies, it recognized the need to embed the reserve in the social, administrative and economic regional consciousness.

Table 1 Transition from a conservation-recreation focus to conversation-building

Intention/Mission	Conservation-Recreation	Conversation
Intention: what are the potential contributions of the organization to a better future?	• Science and Research. • Environmental education and experience. • Learning about and experiencing nature by visitors (children, young people, weekend visitors, hikers, etc.) will have an impact on their perception of nature. In turn, this increased awareness and knowledge will influence collective consideration and care for nature. In turn, this will lead to improved ecosystem management.	• Science and Research. • Environmental education and experience. • Regional influence. • Influence decision-makers, users, land-owners and people who live around the mountain through workshops, conversations, courses, public lectures, presentations, etc. based on scientific knowledge. • Translate into tools (scale models, graphics, (scale models, graphics, maps) useful to existing administrative and and individual decision-making processes.
Organizational mission	• Maintain a natural heritage and protect species. • Educate through visits and education programs.	• Maintain a natural heritage, and protect species. • Educate through visits and general education programs.

(Continued)

Table 1 (*Continued*)

Intention/Mission	Conservation-Recreation	Conversation
	• Provide recreational experiences to improve ecological sensitivity.	• Provide recreational experiences.
What is the reserve about?	• Reserve as living museum, island, protected area.	• Reserve connects to non-reserve areas for ecosystem-services (corridor) and species-habitat. • Flora and fauna do not respect human boundaries. • Reserve ecosystems are interdependent with the future of regional ecosystems.
Who contributes to realizing the mission?	• Scientists, with applied and theoretical research. • Educators, who provide knowledge that helps develop scientific thinking and makes people more sensitive to ecological issues.	• Scientists, communicators, mobilizers, conveners. • Scientific, connection, communication, interpersonal skills, etc.

This broader, three-part mission had implications for the core competency of the organization; individuals capable of embedding the reserve in the regional consciousness had to be recruited. These individuals had to be able to translate scientific research into information designed for local and regional decision-makers. They had to connect the recreational activities to the overall mission of the organization. And they had to be boundary-spanners, connecting inside with outside and reformulating previously formulated intentions (Gault's and Johannsen's) for a new context.

In other words, they needed to become entrepreneurial actors. They could not manage the system in the usual ways. They had to become much more creative, innovative, and entrepreneurial. The new intention of the Nature Centre after the mid-1990s was to influence decision-makers, landowners, local residents and users through training, conversations, education, and presentations based on the scientific knowledge accumulated about the deterioration of the local environment. All this needed to be translated into concrete models. People were dealing with a challenge where there were no past examples from which they could draw a pattern of strategy for action. They had to muddle through, quickly and in such a manner as to get the public support for them to act in a way that would be perceived as unusual. They had to swim against the tide. This landscape entrepreneurship activity involved new ways of thinking and of doing for the long term. The old mental model of how we relate with Mother Nature had to be changed quickly, through an intensive program of information and education about awareness on how to preserve the ecosystems.

Landscape entrepreneurship and the challenges of stakeholder engagement in the process

The second perspective from which we can look at the experience of the Nature Centre focuses on landscape entrepreneurship as a multi-stakeholder partnership. Partnerships in natural resource management are often developed when mounting social, economic and environmental challenges lead concerned stakeholders to promote integrative management schemes. The experience of the Nature Centre at Mont Saint Hilaire provides an interesting illustrative case. Indeed, the partnership of the Nature Centre currently includes the Nature Centre itself, McGill University, private landowners, the surrounding municipalities, and in particular, the Town of Mont Saint Hilaire which has been actively involved, and the community at large.

Economic and social changes that have taken place over the past 40 years have altered the existing balance between the natural resource preservation and the use of both the reserve area (the mountain) and the surrounding land (the lower slopes). More specifically, the presence of a growing number of visitors has led to discussions at the Nature Centre about whether new infrastructure development should be considered in the mountain area. In a similar vein, in the Mont Saint Hilaire vicinity, a wave of urbanization and high-intensity farming have given rise to a civic debate about the region and its future. While some groups have been advocating further development, others have denounced the threat that economic development poses to safeguarding the mountain's unique biodiversity and natural beauty.

The conflicting interests and the search for solutions to shared problems provided a fertile ground for partnership formation. Multi-stakeholder collaboration has been an alternative and more promising approach to managing local resources compared with the endless, and fruitless, confrontation between different stakeholder groups. The creation of partnerships for natural resource protection and management is a deliberate effort, a demanding process, and a risky venture.

Natural resource management partnerships are driven by an entrepreneurial force, which supports the building of constructive and enduring interactions among the various stakeholders. The Nature Centre has been playing a catalyst role in the case of Mont Saint Hilaire. By broadening the geographic scope of its actions to interact with the various groups in the local communities, it has been instrumental in bringing different voices to the table to reflect together on the preservation and use of Mont Saint Hilaire and surrounding areas. Multi-stakeholders were invited to participate in discussions to express and share their values, goals and objectives and to join a process where they could find common ground with others.

The efforts undertaken by the Nature Centre to rally conflicting interests — including extensive urbanization, speculation, economic productivity, preservation, research, education and recreational interests — were built on a recognition of the differing, and often opposing, demands on the resources. This was an essential part of the process for an effective nurturing to build bridges and eventually collaboration among the stakeholders.

The development of partnerships takes into account the forces at play. Different types of interaction may be required depending on the types of stakeholders involved. At the Nature Centre, there is a core group where partnership works in a very positive way. The dialogue with these stakeholders became part of the regular activities. Ideas and propositions are debated in good faith. Other stakeholders who do not participate in this forum are consulted on specific issues of interest to them. This two-pronged approach allows the Nature Centre to involve stakeholders in a meaningful and non-threatening way, and helps build effective collaboration.

Shared values and intentions as the basis for the entrepreneurial dynamic of partnerships

Collaborative arrangements often take shape owing to the values and intentions the partnerships espouse, and their evolution depends on the strength and relevance of these shared values and intentions over time. Indeed, these values serve as the glue, the bonding factor, which symbolizes the aspirations and hopes of the partnership. These values may be developed when the social entrepreneurs involved bring stakeholders together to reflect on and devise new management schemes. In some instances, however, as in the case of the Nature Centre, the values originate with the property owner. Andrew Hamilton Gault bequeathed the land to McGill University in 1958 to enable future generations to use it for recreation purposes, research and education. This intention guided the formulation of strategic planning and management plans over the years. It went from a charter in the 1970s to a mission statement congruent with the partnership development efforts.

The original intention served as the cornerstone of the whole project. It fuelled the development of partnerships and remained critical for the continuous development of the project. It acquired additional substance and meaning when invoked by the social entrepreneurs to clarify the higher goal being pursued and its implications for current stakeholders and the partnership's activities. The vision statement was developed from the original intention. It may evolve over time to take into account changes in the physical environment, economic situation and social setting. The entrepreneurs' ability to give it contemporary meaningfulness in order to mobilize stakeholders remains a key ingredient in the formation of multi-stakeholder partnerships that really work.

These partnerships were developed to contend with differing interests and conflicting demands on the natural resources, but the creation of collaborative arrangements never completely wiped away opposing views. Indeed, the idea that participating in a collective undertaking will homogenize the views of stakeholders seems incongruous (e.g. Berghöfer and Berghöfer, 2006). Rather, partnerships facilitate negotiated agreement on shared values which find roots in the original intention. Over time, if all conditions were to remain unchanged, it is conceivable that differing opinions would gradually converge and that broader and more holistic perspectives could be held by each group of stakeholders.

However, life is often capricious and conditions rarely remain static. It is thus not surprising that when partnerships face natural resource disturbances, economic downturns or changes of actors in stakeholder groups, new tensions may emerge and may challenge the very substance of the existing partnerships. These changes may unsettle the dynamics between stakeholders, the order of priorities that had been agreed to, or the bases of the understanding between stakeholders. The challenge is then to sustain the collaboration in the inevitably changing conditions that characterize integrative natural resource management. The ability to hold the original intention high and to give it meaning in changing conditions lies at the heart of the maintenance of multi-stakeholder partnerships. It is through landscape entrepreneurial action that stakeholders are mobilized to form partnerships. It is also through that process that the original intention continues to guide stakeholders' collaboration.

It is important to note that Gault's original intention serves as a foundational resource not only because it provided meaning that was used for the crafting of a vision statement, but also because it was given substance through the actions undertaken by the partnerships involved. A series of programs organized by the Nature Centre highlight the diverse yet complementary values that characterize the region, such as the aesthetic and cultural values associated to the mountain, the scientific value of its rich biodiversity, the economic value of surrounding orchards and farms, and the community values held by those living in both the rural areas and the surrounding municipalities. The development of an atlas, the frequent use of GIS to ground land use planning exercises, and the organization of social events such as the "Tales of the Fall," are examples of specific activities that epitomize the integrated management intention that the partnerships uphold (Nature Centre website: http://www.centrenature. qc.ca/en/activities/index.html).

Landscape entrepreneurship involving multi-stakeholder partnerships for natural resource management is not without risks: challenges always arise as natural, social and economic conditions evolve and stakeholders' interests may also change as a result. The entrepreneurial endeavor may be viewed as continuous and enduring efforts to give current meaning to the original intention and maintain social mobilization. It proceeds through a series of achievements, when it manages to surmount socio-economic and environmental hurdles. Success may not be linear, as previous achievements may be lost when new challenges arise, but when effective, it offers complementary achievements to previous realizations and supports the advancement of the collaborative arrangements.

Landscape entrepreneurship and the construction of resilience in social-ecological systems

The third perspective focuses on the connections between landscape entrepreneurship and resilience. Our starting point is that ecosystems are not only the home of species threatened by human activities, but also constitute the basis of human life. Ecosystems and the organisms that live there are indispensable for our well-being; they generate food, fibers, and medicines; purify water, recycle nutrients, and pollinate crops, to mention just a few "ecosystem services" we take for granted. Further, ecosystems are essential to our spiritual well-being, as sources of play, inspiration, understanding, physical health and sanity (Millennium Ecosystem Assessment, 2005). Thus, sustaining such ecosystem services, in an era of climate change and increasing human pressure, is essential to securing human well-being in the future.

Obstacles to the resilience of ecosystems arise from the fact that there is a general mismatch between the ecological processes that underlie the generation of ecosystem services and existing ecosystem management regimes. The first obstacle is spatial: critical ecological processes typically occur at a scale that crosses municipal or other administrative boundaries. The second obstacle is temporal: ecological time spans and cycles are often longer than management plans or typical election cycles. The third obstacle concerns focus: authorities focusing on maximizing agricultural yield in the landscape, or protecting single species in specific habitats, have little preparedness for dealing with change occurring across the landscape, especially for dealing with changes that happen abruptly, such as the construction of a road or buildings.

This mismatch is illustrated around Mont Saint Hilaire, where forest remnants are scattered across the landscape between the Monteregian hills. Three Quebec ministries and several municipalities are involved in environmental issues, with very little coordination among them. Hence the need to increase resilience by connecting management across geographic areas, improving the match between ecological and decision-making processes, and across spheres of authority including collaboration among stakeholders.

Numerous recommendations exist as to how ecosystem management should be improved for more sustainable futures, framed by theories on adaptive management and resilience, the ecosystem approach, and others (Holling, 1978; Christensen *et al.*, 1996). A key question that has not been sufficiently addressed is, how do you go from "business as usual" management to innovative and adaptive ways to manage the environment? How do you transform conventional management approaches to ecosystem management that acknowledges integrated social-ecological feedbacks at a landscape scale? We use the case of the Nature Centre at Mont Saint Hilaire to argue that in a specific landscape such as the urbanized area around Mont Saint Hilaire, a landscape entrepreneur such as the Centre has the potential to build resilience and thus enhance the capacity of the system to navigate change. The defining characteristics of resilience, as we have seen, are: (1) the degree of change or disturbance that can be buffered; (2) the capacity for self-organization, or re-organization following disruptive change; and (3) the ability to build and increase the capacity for learning and adaptation. Along with this, we will also revisit the challenges for ecosystem management mentioned above.

Building a buffer: *shifting the focus from the mountain to the landscape*

First, the Nature Centre shifted its focus from protecting a mountain and the endangered species in its biosphere reserve, to managing forest cover with a wider landscape perspective through the mobilization of regional actors for sustainable development. The Centre introduced and promoted the corridor perspective to see wooded areas not as discrete areas but as pathways that connect the Monteregian hills.

Second, the Centre worked intensively to expand the perimeter of the Gault Nature Reserve and to establish stewardship agreements with private landowners to secure these corridors. This increased the potential for animals and seeds to spread in the landscape, colonize or re-colonize disturbed areas, and maintain healthy ecosystems.[15]

Third, the Centre worked to move forest conservation and environmental concerns higher on the agenda of municipal managers and decision-makers at regional and provincial levels. Getting the message from ecology research across contributed to increasing awareness about the importance of forests for human well-being, as did showing how small-scale decisions — for example the protection of key forested areas that improved the corridor pathways — can have an impact on a larger landscape scale.

In addition, the Nature Centre highlighted possible activities and tools to protect ecosystems, and identified how existing rules, such as agricultural zoning, could be applied to protect forests. Stewardship agreements and mobilization of existing rules and norms for forest protection can be seen as enhancing a buffer against forest loss within the social system.

---

[15] Research in ecology shows that maintaining a network of forest ecosystems across the landscape contributes to buffering for disturbance such as conversion of forest to agriculture and infrastructure development.

Providing direction for self-organization: mobilizing local support

The corridor project promoted by the Nature Centre provided a framework for ecosystem management in the region, a project that brought people together and enabled different actors to envision their respective contributions. The project, maps and data were presented in a CD-ROM produced by the Centre as well as in workshops and individual meetings with decision-makers. The Centre works with a wide set of actors and in many partnership projects, thus building a network of actors that can be mobilized as needed. For example, in a neighboring municipality, an area with valuable forest in one of the forest corridors was threatened by illegal logging. The Nature Centre found out, and informed the authorities. After preventing the logging, the Centre was contacted as a potential partner. As the property could not be logged, it lost its interest to the owners, and the Nature Centre could, through its various partners, mobilise the financial resources to acquire it and turn it into a publicly available reserve. That is another example of landscape entrepreneurship.

Trust is essential to make partnerships work. As described in the previous perspectives (see the above sections), the Nature Centre has built credibility and trust in a network of actors that can be mobilized to respond to new events and threats, be they disruptions, such as the logging in the example above, or opportunities, such as new municipal leadership. Further, their work with the CD project had a strong focus, indicating areas and issues with strategic impact for the development of the region, be they ecological, such as how the amount of forest cover increases property value, or social such as how heritage buildings and local businesses contribute to value.

Thus, the Nature Centre contributes to the capacity to organize for regional strategic decision-making, connecting people and bringing key issues to light, presenting them within a framework that provides sense-making and pathways for action.

Building a center for learning

The crisis of urban development that threatened the mountain perimeter in the 1990s taught the managers at the Centre the importance of gathering information proactively. In negotiations with municipalities and developers, existing information about the forest around the Gault Estate and its values could be used to craft a win-win solution for conservation, development interest and to negotiate protection for the most valuable areas.

The Nature Centre is emerging as a center for knowledge on conservation and sustainable development in the region, and municipalities as well as regional authorities turn to them for consultation. They have compiled existing information, and generated new information through research as well as practical experience with the restoration of forest habitat. The Centre is now seen as an asset to the region. As the management of forest and environmental issues is highly fragmented in the region across a wide range of authorities as well as across municipalities, the staff at the Nature Centre have developed excellent databases that help them provide information, continuity, depth of knowledge and understanding that would otherwise be lacking.

The material is also presented and communicated in new and attractive ways. They make extensive use of communicative tools such as maps and GIS. The Centre's "social marketing" approach (i.e. making this information available) tailors or "packages" the information for the different audiences they address, according to their culture and educational levels. For example, when presenting an inventory of forest values to a municipality, they also included information on how the presence of forest affects housing prices.

In short, the Nature Centre's activities as a landscape entrepreneur build capacity to navigate change by (1) enhancing the protection of existing assets, such as remnant old-growth forest in the corridors; (2) increasing social connectivity and awareness to organize for problem solving across fiscal boundaries; and (3) building a platform for acquiring expertise and spreading knowledge. The case illustrates how the need to protect the landscape generated windows of opportunity to transform existing traditional management practices into an entrepreneurial organization.

Landscape entrepreneurship as seen through the experience of implementing a UN framework for conservation

The fourth perspective builds on the experience of "making it happen" in and around the Nature Centre in the biosphere reserve. It focuses on the tensions between the general principles of a UNESCO-based[16] framework for stakeholder engagement and the challenges of making it happen on the ground from the standpoint of an organization. This section focuses on the activities, strategies and tactics of entrepreneurship for conservation.

UNESCO proposes a framework for stakeholder engagement in biosphere reserves (UNESCO, 1996), which can take many forms based on locally relevant geographic and cultural characteristics. However, these structures face several challenges to become reality: they do require investments in time and in financial resources. Their construction often does not fit within the time constraints of local stakeholders. They may be perceived as inefficient and irrelevant. The Nature Centre's experience as the principal manager of the Mont-Saint-Hilaire Biosphere Reserve shows limitations to an institutionalized approach linked to formal structures of forum and stakeholders' consultation as proposed by UNESCO. This section focuses on the Nature Centre's entrepreneurial approach to stakeholder engagement based on three factors: small gains; small but incremental consensus-building; and concrete actions that contribute to building a sense of place.

Framework for biosphere reserve activities: *the limitations of the Seville Strategy*

The UNESCO Seville Strategy proposes a framework for biosphere reserve activities.[17] Its three main objectives are to: (1) use biosphere reserves to conserve natural and cultural diversity; (2) use biosphere reserves as models of land management and approaches to sustainable development; and (3) use biosphere reserves for research, monitoring, education and training. In this light, biosphere reserves are more than just parks or protected areas. They strive to be facilitators and partners, providing both a forum and a helping hand for groups to discuss and understand conservation and sustainability (Francis, 2004). In other words, actors within a biosphere reserve are invited to "think globally and act

---

[16] UNESCO: United Nations Educational, Scientific and Cultural Organization.
[17] UNESCO organized the International Conference on Biosphere Reserves, held in Seville (Spain) in 1995. The conference drew up the Seville Strategy that recommends action to be undertaken for the future development of biosphere reserves in the 21st century.

locally." Both the controversial nature of conservation issues and the necessity to be guided by or to promote sustainable development to maintain cultural and biological diversity within a biosphere reserve make stakeholder and public participation a fundamental component of the Seville Strategy.

The Seville Strategy suggests that to facilitate stakeholder participation, actors should (1) survey the interests of the various stakeholders and fully involve them in planning and decision-making for the management and use of the reserve (II.1.5); (2) develop and establish institutional mechanisms to manage, co-ordinate and integrate the biosphere reserve's programs and activities (II.2.3); and (3) establish a local consultation framework in which the reserve's economic and social stakeholders are represented, including a full range of interests.

The Nature Centre's experience as the principal manager of the Mont-Saint-Hilaire Biosphere Reserve shows the limitations of an institutionalized approach linked to formal structures of forum and stakeholder consultation as proposed by UNESCO. Implementing such a strategy involves overcoming several obstacles.

First, such processes do require time — sometimes months before any consensus or decision is reached. Second, such lengthy processes mobilize many stakeholders and often require a secretariat to coordinate activities, which is costly for small organizations. Third, it may be difficult to facilitate such demanding processes within the various time constraints and agendas of multiple stakeholders.

Fourth, it has also been seen that successful consultation processes have been shelved because of lack of political will. Last, but not least, a compounding factor concerns the absence of official jurisdiction or legal authority for biosphere reserves; informal structures have to continue over a long period of time to gain recognition, which may lead to the demobilization of local stakeholders as they see no return on their time, energy and monetary investment. Sixth, attempts at mobilizing stakeholders are often very problematic. Most individuals are already engaged in an important number of committees or commissions, and those who have the time and knowledge to engage in consultations are often scarce. This can even lead to an over-representation of certain types of actors in consultation structures because they are available and financially more able to participate. For these reasons, traditional fora and consultations have tended to be perceived as inefficient and even irrelevant.

Innovative consultation

Understanding the necessity for effective participation by local communities, the Nature Centre managers decided to work differently. They decided to use three main tactics, namely: (1) a focus on lower-level consensus-building; (2) the promotion of projects that ensure small-scale gains; and (3) the creation of a strong sense of place. Working in this fashion also helped to ward off the kinds of bigger disagreements that often create major drawbacks.

Beyond these tactics, the Nature Centre has developed a broad modus operandi to promote the biosphere reserve. The ingredients of this modus operandi are three.

The first ingredient consists of gathering significant data and knowledge regarding the biosphere reserve and surrounding territory. Information on land use, biodiversity and pollution is scarce, scattered and it often needed a good deal of analysis in order to be turned into policies or management guidelines.

Fortunately, McGill University owns the core area of the biosphere reserve and has been conducting studies over a 40-year period. McGill University also provided software and geographical information to map the territory. Using these data and GIS information through a project approach, many different issues were documented and presented to stakeholders and to the local population in various forms. For example, a regional forest atlas produced by the Nature Centre in CD format was widely distributed. Many articles were published in local newspapers and summaries of these different knowledge-based projects were presented to different audiences. This transfer of knowledge and information often created possibilities for interactions between stakeholders and helped co-generate more information.

The Mont Saint Hilaire Nature Centre thus became a partner of municipal and county officials and conducted further projects that generated more detailed information on a landscape scale, both local and regional. This solid knowledge base and these interactions made the Nature Centre a key local stakeholder and helped create a biosphere reserve perspective on local issues. Overall, producing and co-generating information represents a strategy to accumulate small gains and to demonstrate that it is possible to move forward in building consensus and addressing issues. Quantifiable data, based on reliable methodology and the participation of local actors in generating the new data sets, help to generate a shared understanding of the territory.

The second ingredient deals with using existing fora. Consultation and fora are often used to come to decisions that address issues related to land use, such as water management, agriculture and biodiversity conservation. Realizing municipal and county officials were increasingly becoming bogged down by these issues and that local controversy was often making their work difficult due to tighter deadlines and increased criticism, the Nature Centre often proposed to map the interests of the various stakeholders to fully involve them in planning and decision-making about the management and use of the territory. This was done without taking away the responsibility of local government who have kept the final authority and jurisdiction over these issues.

Local officials were at first reluctant to adopt this approach because of time constraints and because of the difficulty in seeing the benefits of such a participatory approach. At first, the Nature Centre helped them conduct neighborhood consultations on relatively simple issues to illustrate the added value of consultation and stakeholder participation.[18] Over time, issues addressed by the participatory approach and the level of stakeholder engagement have increased and led to several outcomes. One outcome is that, for some municipalities, participation and stakeholder involvement have become routine.

A second outcome has been the development of a local stakeholder engagement ethic to prevent controversy and larger disagreements. A third is the setting up of formal structures, including a Perimeter Committee, an Environment Committee at the municipal level, a Forest Management Committee, and technical committees for public utilities at the county

---

[18] UNESCO has produced an interesting guide that helps to better understand the level of participation needed to solve different issues (Bouamrane, 2006).

level. Nature Centre representatives were invited to sit on each of these committees.

As the scope of consultations and stakeholder engagement increased among municipal and county officials, biosphere reserve issues could be addressed and the information developed could be used for conservation and sustainable development. It became irrelevant, therefore, to create a biosphere reserve structure to survey the interest of the various stakeholders and to fully involve them in planning and decision-making about biosphere reserve management and use, since these new structures could more efficiently address the issues. The institutional mechanism to manage, coordinate and integrate the biosphere reserve's issues is located at the appropriate jurisdictional level, and representation issues were also addressed by including the full range of interests and a locally significant ethic offering an appropriate place to stakeholders representing civil society, as opposed to private stakeholders.

The third ingredient consisted of developing and promoting a sense of place and a sense of pride. The generation of information and the increased involvement of various stakeholders in the planning and decision-making processes have both made the notion of "biosphere reserve" more concrete for all. This has led to a more concrete understanding of such concepts such as "biodiversity," "local sustainable development," "social responsibility," and the "importance of ecosystems."

This concrete understanding of such concepts contributes to the development of a sense of place, or a sense of belonging to a place, which means addressing issues not just in a "rational" perspective but by linking issues and challenges using a communication media such as art, emotions, story or scientific formats. Communicating in a positive perspective, using relevant channels of communication, and using a message that was relevant to the stakeholders about a given area as demonstrated in this case study is vital to developing a sense of place but, even more importantly, to developing a sense of pride about that place and the preserved quality of that place.

Learning from entrepreneurial activities at the Mont St-Hilaire biosphere reserve

How does all this relate to entrepreneurship? By working differently within the Mont Saint Hilaire biosphere reserve, the Nature Centre staff recognized opportunities for action, used available resources, built strong relationships with the community and envisioned the future of the biosphere reserve — all activities and characteristics attributed to entrepreneurs (Filion, 2009). There was a major need, both social and environmental. Somebody had to do something about it. Like Alexander Graham Bell and Joseph-Armand Bombardier, but on a smaller scale, the directors and other people involved in the management of the Nature Centre decided to roll up their sleeves and act entrepreneurially.

This was an innovative approach to biosphere reserve management. It meant designing and implementing a genuinely entrepreneurial way to deal with sustainable development (Francis, 2004). It meant opening up conservation activities to real people and people to conservation. The Nature Centre put forward not only a biosphere reserve management concept but also a spirit of innovation in how that could be done. As some of the managers at the Nature Centre like to say, "We don't just talk about the biosphere reserve, we do something about it!"

These entrepreneurial activities have not just shaped the landscape, conserved it or promoted its sustainable use; they have also motivated people to get involved in concrete action to make their ecological environment better. They have created a landscape entrepreneurship movement. The power of these entrepreneurial activities can be seen in the number of working relationships with the community and the capacity to build a shared view of the future of the territory involved (Pollock, 2004), the commitment to a high quality environment, and the protection of "place."

The experience clearly shows that a sense of pride in the landscape has been built. Landscape entrepreneurship becomes a means to an end. If the Nature Centre people did not act entrepreneurially in the first place, if they had not informed and rallied local people around their project, the project would not have endured. By sharing their understanding of how the natural system works in relation to the social system, the Nature Centre people involved the community in a collective commitment to innovate, to protect and to add value to the ecosystem that surrounds them.

Lessons for Landscape Entrepreneurship

This chapter is based on the experience of the Mont Saint Hilaire Nature Centre. The story of the Nature Centre and its activities have led us to introduce an emerging concept, that of landscape entrepreneurship, which is a form of social entrepreneurship. In this chapter, we have described and discussed the case from different perspectives. In this last section, we present and discuss the entrepreneurial aspect of this case in more detail. To help structure the understanding of the complex process that is landscape entrepreneurship, we have identified some of the lessons learned from this case. These lessons could be used by actors in similar situations. The lessons are presented in Table 2 below.

Table 2 Ten lessons for landscape entrepreneurship practice from the Nature Centre case

Lesson 1: The intentions and embryonic root definition[19] of Andrew Hamilton Gault led the way in the preservation and learning process that followed. He stipulated that the land was to be protected, and made the gift on condition that it not be sold or used for commercial purposes.
Lesson 2: There was a clear main beneficiary mentioned: the young people of Canada. We can expect that Gault focused on the youth as the main beneficiary of the ecological system he wished to see conserved in order to motivate the McGill University management to get involved in the project. Clearly, however, there are many beneficiaries for this donation, especially the people living near the property, the scientists doing research on site, and the general population.
Lesson 3: The official body that would become responsible for preserving this property and developing it for the purpose of generating knowledge was a

(Continued)

---

[19] We suggest Checkland's definition of an issue based root definition: "A root definition describing a notional system chosen for its relevance to what the investigator and/or people in the problem situation perceive as matters of contention" (Checkland, 1999: 317).

Table 2 (*Continued*)

well-established university chosen for its reputation for integrity and social development activities. An intention was expressed as a root definition by the initiator protection system.

Lesson 4: The organization's lack of expertise in this very new field of activity meant that long periods of thought and discussion were needed before activities, decisions and actions were possible. Between 1958 and 1972, few strategic, managerial or entrepreneurial activities took place as people were wondering how to tackle this unusual situation.

Lesson 5: The people who designed the landscape system were acting as representatives of the property owner (the university). Their role was to implement the intention expressed in the root definition. This is where the actors had to become entrepreneurial; they had to be highly resourceful to muddle through a new area of activity. Obtaining Canada's first-ever UNESCO biosphere reserve listing for this project (1978) was an outstanding entrepreneurial achievement.

Lesson 6: The values, intentions and root definitions of founding entrepreneurs often engender effects in organizations that last for decades. Gault's values and goals, and the way those were implemented by management — by Alice Johanssen in particular — had a major impact on the ecological activity system that was designed and implemented over time.

Lesson 7: The survival of any form of social entrepreneurship seems closely bound to its social legitimacy and the public consensus in its support. Landscape entrepreneurship seems to require social mobilization following on from a well-organized communication process about the issue concerned and its evoked relationship with the public good and interest.

Lesson 8: Some forms of social entrepreneurship reflect the commitment of one person; examples include Mother Teresa in India and Abbé Pierre in Paris. However, most forms of social entrepreneurship require the commitment of many people who agree to act as partners entrepreneurially. The stability of the structure created and the non-profit aspect of the phenomenon appear to contribute to the continuity of this type of process.

Lesson 9: People involved in landscape and social entrepreneurship seem to get results not because they know the answers, but because they are so committed that

(*Continued*)

Table 2   (*Continued*)

they become resourceful. They do a lot of thinking and learning about what needs to be done. They have to define guidelines for action in emerging sectors where there are few reference points. Some people call this creativity. This approach leads them to design visionary entrepreneurial activity systems for the long term that are bound to last.

Lesson 10: Although there are some significant differences between the purpose of a classic entrepreneurial activity system and a social entrepreneurial activity system (see Fig. 1), there are also many similarities in terms of process. These include innovation, opportunity identification or fulfillment of a need, action (activity system design and implementation), use of resources and the contribution of added value. One aspect of the process appears to be different, however: the level of risk of the entrepreneurial actors does not appear to be the same. Social entrepreneurs and landscape entrepreneurs appear to deal with a level of risk closer to that of intrapreneurs, since they are not the owners of the property and resources used. Intrapreneurs and social entrepreneurs risk their reputations and their jobs, but not their assets, as is the case for entrepreneurs. On the other hand, they have to deal with more complex social systems that require a much higher level of political ability.

Landscape entrepreneurial system

The Nature Centre case study shows that landscape entrepreneurship can be a lengthy process. Indeed, based on this case, landscape entrepreneurship appears to involve long and complex interactions, going through cycles and involving many stakeholders. The people involved in these projects become entrepreneurial system designers and implementers because they share the basic values of the original social entrepreneur. They use their expertise to advance the cause. Their innovations can be classified as "managerial innovations" rather than product innovations (Hamel, 2007: 32). Figure 2 illustrates the concepts, relationships and complex process involved in designing a successful landscape entrepreneurship project.

Landscape entrepreneurship seems to present characteristics similar to those of social entrepreneurship (Austin *et al.*, 2006; Chell, 2007). Most

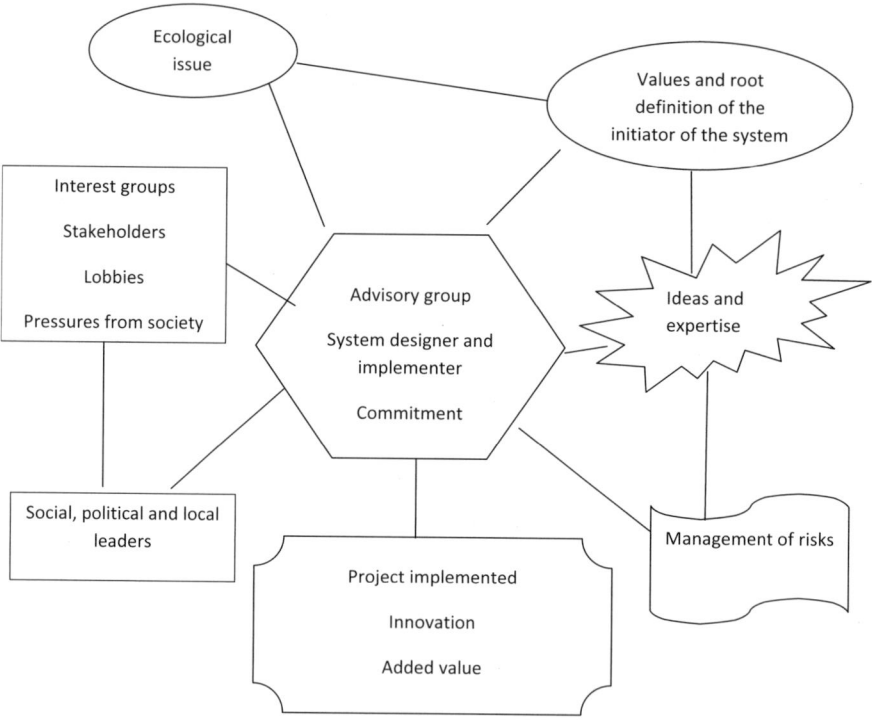

Fig. 2 The design of a landscape entrepreneurial system.

SMEs are short of resources and that seems to be even more true in non-profit sectors. It was and still is the case of the Nature Centre. It could be the case of landscape entrepreneurship when practiced in non-profit activities.

Landscape entrepreneurs develop activity systems that also resemble those of intrapreneurs. Their activities seem to imply capabilities similar to those of intrapreneurs. They have to be innovative, but as non-owners of the property involved negotiating with so many stakeholders, they need good political abilities, as is the case with intrapreneurs (Burns, 2005; Morris and Kuratko, 2002). People who plan to act entrepreneurially in the public landscape and ecology sector certainly need some expertise in the area but they also need to develop good political skills.

Most of the time, acting as intrapreneurs in a non-profit sector implies working in teams. In this case, we noticed that consensus had to be developed as to which innovations should be implemented. People involved in managing the Nature Centre became social intrapreneurs since they had to become innovative to make their organization achieve its real purpose. They had to share ideas, ways to look at problem situations and ways to solve these problems. They had to share their views and design activity programs that were acceptable to the team. So, in many respects, the management approach of the Nature Centre resembles the kinds of shared entrepreneurial management practices that partners use to develop promising high-tech ventures.

Finally, we compared the non-profit landscape entrepreneurs studied in this case with ecopreneurs, as presented in the research literature. We also tried to classify them among the different types of ecopreneurs in the literature. We suggest that the social intrapreneurs who manage the Nature Centre could be compared to the *visionary champions* suggested by Walley and Taylor (2002) in their typology of ecopreneurs. These people are champions fighting for sustainable development: they want to change the world in a way that will save the planet. These social intrapreneurs could also be classified as *alternative actors* in the typology proposed by Schaltegger (2002). They are the ones who provide fertile ground for other types of ecopreneurs who often operate in profit sectors. If we apply Linnanen's (2002) typology of ecopreneurs, they could be classified as *successful idealists*. Whatever the typology or the category used, these social intrapreneurs could also be labeled as social ecopreneurs since they are acting like ecopreneurs — they espouse the same goals — but in a non-profit and distinctly marginal activity.

Conclusion

Tensions in landscape entrepreneurship

Based on an analysis of the case study and the four perspectives presented above (landscape entrepreneurship as organizational change, as a process of multi-stakeholder engagement, as a process of building social/ecological resilience, and as a process of making it happen on the ground), we have identified four tensions in the process of landscape entrepreneurship.

The first tension concerns the sense of relevance. The experience of the Nature Centre offers an example of tension between two conflicting needs, namely, loyalty to the initial intention of the founder (Gault), expressed more than five decades ago in a specific social, economic and ecological context, and doubts about its relevance in a fast-changing institutional, natural, social and economic regional environment. On the one hand, "sticking" to the initial intention (or being zealously (too) loyal) may simply lead to being irrelevant locally in 2009, which may in turn lead to the eventual demise of the organization. On the other hand, omitting or denying the founder's intention may lead to a disconnected relationship between past, present and future memory and sense of place, which may lead to a much more instrumental approach. Building these bridges between past, present and future, between a founder's intention and the present and future relevance of the project is a significant challenge in the landscape entrepreneurship process. It requires landscape entrepreneurs to be able to constantly reinvent themselves while remaining loyal to an initial intention.

The second tension concerns general principles, illustrated here by the UNESCO sponsored framework for stakeholder engagement with a biosphere reserve, and the challenges of making it happen on the ground in a local/regional terrain. This framework, consisting of the fairly generic Seville principles, and more recently, the guiding principles of "corridors" and "belts," has the power to simultaneously spark the imagination, mobilize local residents, and draw attention to the key components and connections within the ecological/social system. Whereas traditional or "classic" business entrepreneurs manage to gather clients and mobilize constituencies to a new product with new features, landscape entrepreneurs mobilize stakeholders with a back-and-forth translation of principles into concrete interactions and actions.

The third tension places the need for short-term results against the long-term construction of resilience in the regional social/economic/ecological system. The experience of the Nature Centre shows that *landscape entrepreneurship* can be a lengthy process. In that respect, it is not dissimilar to more general processes of entrepreneurship and in particular, social entrepreneurship, which seem to be characterized by long and complex trajectories involving numerous stakeholders. These situations appear to go through cycles, initiated when new leaders trigger high-intensity events. Such leaders become entrepreneurial system designers and implementers because they share the basic values of the original social entrepreneur and can use their expertise to advance the cause.

The fourth tension concerns science and practical relevance. Scientific knowledge is the raw material in the process of landscape entrepreneurship; solid research is crucial to keeping local decision-makers informed as to the "right" decisions on local development and zoning plans. The robustness of this data is a necessary condition for inclusion in the decision-making processes. It was certainly necessary to establish the credibility of the Nature Centre as a knowledge center in the region. At the same time, scientific data needs to be translated into discrete, usable, simple data sets that are relevant and user-friendly for local decision-makers. These two interdependent processes, which involve different skills (scientific rigor and the ability to translate and simplify), are both necessary. Managing them simultaneously is an inherent part of landscape entrepreneurship.

The research in landscape entrepreneurial practice in non-profit sectors shows that landscape entrepreneurship involves a process and a pattern of activities similar to those in entrepreneurship; and this is even more true for social entrepreneurship: the importance of identifying a need (opportunity), commitment, sector expertise, innovation, communication, shared values, risk, wise use of resources, action, and added value.

The implications for theory building lead us to look not only at entrepreneurship, social entrepreneurship (Chell, 2007), ecological entrepreneurship (Schaltegger, 2002; Walley and Taylor, 2002) or even environmental entrepreneurship (Linnanen, 2002), but at other fields such as ecology and system design — fields involving activities that also contribute added value. With landscape entrepreneurship, we are reaching the tipping point of an emerging field of study that is a cross-fertilization of the fields mentioned above and is at the crossroads of these fields. The application of entrepreneurship to conservation and social issues provides an illustration of the very essence of the entrepreneurship process. Where is the innovation and the added value, and how is it generated in ecological and landscape systems? In our view, the Nature Centre case makes a contribution to entrepreneurship and presents an interesting canvas illustrating the design and implementation of landscape and ecological entrepreneurship. Landscape entrepreneurs appear to be part of the family of social entrepreneurs. They want to help improve the human condition in the long term. The Nature Centre case is a clear demonstration that landscape entrepreneurship can be used for the common good, and not only for self interest.

References

Austin, J., Stevenson, H. and Wei-Skillern, J. (2006). Social and commercial entrepreneurship: same, different, or both?, *Entrepreneurship Theory and Practice*, 30(1): 1–22.

Berghöfer, U. and Berghöfer, A. (2006). Participation in development thinking — coming to grips with a truism and its critiques, in Stoll-Kleemann, S. and Welp, M. (eds.), *Stakeholder Dialogues in Natural Resources Management: Theory and Practice*. Springer, pp. 79–116.

Bouamrane, M. (ed.) (2006). Biodiversité et acteurs: des itinéraires de concertation. Réserves de biosphère — Notes techniques 1 — 2006.

Burns, P. (2005) *Corporate Entrepreneurship: Building an Entrepreneurial Organisation*. New York: Palgrave MacMillan.

Carpenter, S.R., Walker, B.H., Anderies, J.M. and Abel, N. (2001). From metaphor to measurement: resilience of what to what?, *Ecosystems*, 4: 765–781.

Checkland, P. (1999). *Systems Thinking, Systems Practice*. New York: Wiley.

Chell, E. (2007). Social enterprise and entrepreneurship: towards a convergent theory of the entrepreneurial process, *International Small Business Journal*, 25(1): 5–26.

Chouinard, Y. (2006). *Let My People Go Surfing: The Education of a Reluctant Businessman*. New York: Penguin Books.

Christensen, N.L. *et al.* (1996). The report of the Ecological Society of America Committee on the scientific basis for ecosystem management, *Ecological Applications*, 6: 665–691.

Filion, L.J. (1996). Travail autonome: des volontaires et des involontaires, *13th Annual Conference, 13ᵉ Colloque Annuel du Canadian Council for Small Business and Entrepreneurship-Conseil Canadien de la PME et de l'Entrepreneuriat, CCSBE/CCPME*, Montréal, November, in Filion, L.J. and Lavoie, D. (eds.), *Support Systems for Entrepreneurial Societies — Systèmes de Soutien aux Sociétés Entrepreneuriales, Proceedings/Actes*, Vol. 1, pp. 189–204. Working paper 1996-11-02, Rogers-J.-A.-Bombardier Chair of Entrepreneurship, HEC Montreal.

Filion, L.J. (2004). Two types of self-employed in Canada, in Dana, L.P. (ed.), *Handbook of Research on International Entrepreneurship*. Cheltenham, UK, Northampton, USA: Edward Elgar, Chap. 17, pp. 308–329. Working paper 2004–09, Rogers-J.-A.-Bombardier Chair of Entrepreneurship, HEC Montreal.

Filion, L.J. (2009). Defining the entrepreneur complexity and multi-dimentional systems, some reflections, to be published in Dana, L. (ed.), *Encyclopaedia of Entrepreneurship*. Cheltenham, England: Edward Elgar. Working paper 2008-03, Rogers-J.-A.-Bombardier Chair of Entrepreneurship, HEC Montreal (can be downloaded: www.hec.ca/chaire.entrepreneurship).

Folke, C. (2006). Resilience: the emergence of a perspective for social–ecological systems analyses, *Global Environmental Change*, 16: 253–267.

Forman, R.T.T. and Godron, M. (1986). *Landscape Ecology*. New York: Wiley.

Francis, G. (2004) Biosphere reserves in Canada: ideals and some experiences, *Environments*, 32(3): 11.

Gunderson, L and Holling, C.S. (eds.) (2001). *Panarchy: Understanding Transformations in Human and Natural Systems*. Washington, DC: Island Press.

Hamel, G. (2007). *The Future of Management*. Boston, Massachusetts: Harvard Business School Press.

Holling, C.S. (1986). Resilience of ecosystems, local surprise and global change, in Clark, W.C. and Munn, R.E. (eds.), *Sustainable Development of the Biosphere*. Cambridge (UK): Cambridge University Press, pp. 292–317.

Holling, C.S., Ludwig, D. and Jones, D.D. (1978). Qualitative analysis of insect outbreak systems, *Journal of Animal Ecology*, 47(1): 315–332.

Kao, R.W.Y. (1995). *Entrepreneurship: A Wealth-Creation and Value-Adding Process*. New York: Prentice Hall.

Kao, R.W.Y., Kao, K.R. and Kao, R.R. (2002). *Entrepreneurism: A Philosophy and a Sensible Alternative for the Market Economy*. London: Imperial College Press.

Kao, R.W.Y., Kao, K.R. and Kao, R.R. (2005). *An Entrepreneurial Approach to Stewardship Accountability: Corporate Residual and Global Poverty*. Singapore: World Scientific.

Linnanen, L. (2002). An insider's experiences with environmental entrepreneurship, *Greener Management International*, 38: 71–80.

MacDonald, L. (2001). *The Bombardier Story: Planes, Trains and Snowmobiles*. Etobicoke, Ont: Wiley.

MacKay, J. (1997). *Alexander Graham Bell: A Life*. New York: Wiley.

McCraw, T.K. (2007). *Prophet of Innovation. Joseph Schumpeter and Creative Destruction*. Cambridge, Massachusetts: The Belknap Press of Harvard University Press.

Millennium Ecosystem Assessment (MA) (2005). *Synthesis*. Washington, DC: Island Press. Available on the Internet: http://www.MAweb.org.

Morris, M.H. and Kuratko, D.F. (2002). *Corporate Entrepreneurship: Entrepreneurial Development within Organizations*. USA: South-Western College Publishing.

Pollock, R.M. (2004). Identifying principles for place-based governance in biosphere reserves, *Environments*, 32(3): 25.

Schaltegger, S. (2002). A framework for ecopreneurship: leading bioneers and environmental managers to ecopreneurship, *Greener Management International*, 38: 45–58.

Schumpeter. J.A. (1934). *The Theory of Economic Development*. Cambridge, Massachusetts: Harvard University Press.

UNESCO (1996). *Seville Strategy and Statuary Framework of the World Network*. Paris: UNESCO.

Walley, E.E. and Taylor, D. (2002). Opportunists, champions, mavericks…? A typology of green entrepreneurs, *Greener Management International*, 38: 31–43.

Websites

International Model Forest Network Website: http://www.imfn.net/index.php?q=node/535.

Nature Centre Website: http:// www.centrenature.qc.ca/en/infos/whoweare.html.

14
THE CANDLE OF HOPE*

Raymond W. Y. Kao

Based on our lifetime commitment to serving humanity, our research, teaching, consulting and business experiences have led us to have one hope: The hope that we shall have, and work toward attaining "A Sustainable Economy" to serve us so that humanity as a whole will continue infinitely.

Our group of a little more than a dozen, believes in what was said in a few words by the late US President J.F. Kennedy: "All our problems are human made, and they can be solved by humans." This is exactly the message that we hope will reach everyone — that we can solve the problems we created in the interest of humanity.

Our hope is that:

(1) We shall have a sub-distributive system in the market economy, to recognize all contributions made to generate positive results in corporate operations for redistribution to those who have been long neglected. This includes better process accounting information.
(2) All political leaders and governments will work together to reach a long term economic equilibrium; not just to be re-elected at the end of a four- or five-year period.

---

* *Source*: Kao, R.W.Y. (2007). *Stewardship-Based Economics*. Singapore: World Scientific Publishing Co., pp. 191–192.

(3) We shall eliminate, if at all possible, greedy desires and attempts to collect and waste resources just for the sake of personal satisfaction. The human greed must be gotten out of our system. It is not possible to tell the late behavioral theorist, Maslow, to return from the grave to admit that he should add: "Greed" to the behavioral hierarchy analysis.
(4) To preserve whatever possible resources for future use and eliminate causes that will damage environmental health.
(5) For every able individual to have opportunities to create and innovate for self-interest and common good.

All of the above seem to be next to nothing but a dream, although it is our hope.

Here I shall return to the story from the Introduction, of the candle of Hope that so inspired me, in the card I received from my former MBA student, Catherine Jiong Gu. Along with her season's greetings card included a message entitled: "The Story of Four Candles."

The story of four candles

The four candles burned slowly.

Their ambience was so soft you could hear them speak.

The first candle said, "I am Peace, but these days, nobody keeps me lit."

Then Peace's flame diminished and went out completely.

The second candle said, "I am Faith, but these days, I am no longer indispensable."

The Faith flame slowly diminished and went out completely.

Sadly, the third candle spoke, "I am love, and I haven't the strength to stay lit any longer. People put me aside and don't understand my importance. They even forget to love those who are nearest to them." And waiting no longer, Love went out completely.

A child entered the room and saw the three candles no longer burning. The child began to cry.

"Why are you not burning? You are supposed to stay lit until the end."

Then the fourth candle spoke gently to the little boy,

"Don't be afraid, for I am Hope, and when I still burn, we can re-light the other three candles."

With shining eyes, the child took the Candle of Hope and lit the other three candles.

Never let the Flame of Hope go out.

With hope in your eyes, no matter how bad things may be, Peace, Faith and Love may shine brightly once again.

The end of the story, but not the end of our hope.

Our hope, everyone in the market economy, collectively and individually, is to work for the need of "sustainable economy" for now and the future:

(1) All governments would govern based on the merits of capitalism's idea to create and innovate, and adopt the socialist's doctrine for distribution to intervene market performance where and when necessary.
(2) Every individual in business needs to work for self-interest, although they must also be responsible and considerate for the common good — for a system of residual distribution, conservation of resources and a healthy natural environment.

INDEX

accounting
    bias 13
    convention 13
    income 13, 29
advanced ceramics 154
Africa 353–358, 360, 363, 367, 368, 370, 372–374
anti-poverty strategies 98
atheism 4

bank system 308
behavioral hierarchy 422
Bowater, Abitibi 31
Buddhism 4
business social responsibility 10
business strategies 272, 277

Cantillon 293, 294, 295, 302
capital 355, 357, 358, 360, 368–372
capitalism 4
capitalist process 35, 38, 42
Catholicism 4
cermet 158, 162–168, 170, 223
Chiang, Kai-shek 9, 23
China 3
    corporate social responsibility draft guide 27
clinical trial 118–123, 129

combined micro heat and power generation 201
commercial ethics 24,
communism 4
communist revolutionary 9
community of life 237, 239, 240, 241, 244, 264
compact fluorescent lamp (CFL) 137, 140, 144, 145, 150, 152, 154, 175, 177, 198, 199, 203
conflict 54–56, 58, 64–66
consumption 1, 2
corporate
    charter 10
    crime 15
cost 12–16, 19, 27, 29
cost reduction per kW 202
creative 291–294, 297, 301, 303, 305–308
credit card 17–19

decision making 239, 244, 249–255, 258, 259, 260, 262–264
development aid 101
disenfranchised 3
dispersed power generation 201, 203–205, 207, 234
distribution 1–3
diversity 335, 336, 338, 346
Dunn, Frank 21

earth   4, 237–244, 246–255, 260, 262, 264
earth charter   237–239, 241–244, 246–249, 251
economic
	dynamics 44
	equilibrium 421
	policy 353
empathic research   344, 345
energy consumption   1
energy saving lamp   145, 152
enterprise culture   297, 298
entrepreneur   355, 356, 361, 369, 370–373
	attribute 296, 297
	definition 294
entrepreneurial
	government 305
	thought 302, 303
entrepreneurship   4, 36, 43, 265, 267, 269, 270, 273–277, 280–287, 291–293, 296–304, 306, 309, 310, 353, 355, 356, 360, 361, 363, 366, 367, 370–374
	education 265, 267, 270, 273–276, 285–287
environment   1–5
environmental
	damage 14–16, 29, 135, 136, 173, 200, 201, 235
	health 308
equilibrium   24
ethical reflection   239
ethics   24–26, 240–243
experiment   339, 341, 342, 348
exploitation   13, 23, 26

failure   341–344, 347, 348
family firm   53–67

financial
	income 5
	meltdown 17
Friedman, Milton   9, 10
Fu-Dan University   291
fuel cell   201–223, 225–230, 232–235
fuel flexibility   230

gallium nitride   154, 176, 185, 195, 198, 199, 200
Ghana   353, 356, 357, 358, 360, 361, 363, 365–368, 370–372, 374
Gibb, Allan   297, 298
global economic crisis   16
globalization   107, 108, 111, 117, 118, 123, 125, 268, 285
Gold Notes   22
gold yuan   22
goodwill   20
Great Depression   17
greed   299, 307–309
green house gas (GHG)   136, 153, 234, 235
grid   193, 201, 202, 204–207, 220, 228, 234
Gu, Catherine Jiong   422

health   107–15, 117–126, 128–132
health care   107–109, 118, 120, 125, 131
Hick, J.R.   12
high intensity discharge light source   140, 143, 156, 172
high pressure sodium lamp   140, 159, 162, 165, 168, 172, 177, 193
high temperature and intermediate temperature solid oxide fuel cell   233, 234

home   237, 240, 243, 264
homosocial reproduction   338
Hornaday   296
human
　　research   117, 119, 120
　　sacrifice   13

implications for entrepreneurship education   320
inequality   73–75, 77, 83, 84, 87–89, 98, 99, 101
　　alleviation   80, 81, 95, 97, 105
　　reduction   94, 95, 98, 99, 102, 103
inflation   22, 30
inheritance   56, 60, 63, 64, 66
innovation   269, 272, 275, 277, 279, 280, 286, 333–343, 345–348
　　antibody   338, 342
innovative   292, 293, 296, 297, 301, 303, 305–308
integrated approach   239, 244–246, 249, 264
invisible hand   305, 307, 308
Iraq   3
Iraqi civilian   14

Kennedy, J.F.   421
Keynes, John Maynard   11

landscape   377–379, 381, 392, 393, 395, 396, 399–404, 407, 410–418
leadership courage   347, 348
learning   337, 339, 343–346, 348
Lehmann Brothers   21
libertarianism   4

Manger, Carl   297–299, 303
market
　　economy   1, 4, 5
　　reforms   99
Marxist vs. Schumpeterian "dialectics"   42
Marx, Karl   3
Maslow, Abraham   422
metal halide lamp   140, 142, 155, 157, 163, 165, 167, 168, 170–172, 177
metrics   340, 341, 348
Mill, John Stuart   11
mortgage   17, 19

Namibia   368
Nanyang Technological University of Singapore   291
Nationalist China   9, 23
neo-classical economic thinker   11
Newfoundland and Labrador   30–33
non-economic goals   329
non-renewable resource   14, 16, 28

Olympic Games   23
organ trafficking   116
ownership   56–59, 61–65
ownership-based economics   306

participatory processes   239, 250, 261, 263
pharmaceutical industry   120, 122, 123, 128–131
political leader   421
poverty   2, 3, 73–104
　　absolute   75, 94, 101

causes and effects 74, 92
  extreme 75, 76, 78, 89, 91, 92, 96
  involuntary 74
  moderate 75, 76
  relative 75, 77, 80, 88, 94
  scope and scale 78
  voluntary 101
President Bush 14
productive friction 346–348
profit 1, 2, 5, 9, 11–15, 17–21, 23, 27–30
profit chasing economy 2

quantification 13, 28
  of non-renewable resource 28
quantum objective 341

reduction of carbon dioxide 154
residual 5
resilience 378, 379, 392, 393, 400, 401, 415, 416
resource 1–3, 5
  drain 135, 173, 201
revenue 12, 13, 27, 29
revolving credit 18
risk 337, 342, 343

Schumacher 313–318, 320–323, 325, 328, 330
Schumpeter, Joseph 294, 299
Schumpeterian entrepreneur 37, 41
Second World War 21
self-employed 293, 294, 295, 302, 303
Shanghai 21, 23

small beginnings 317, 329, 330
Smith, Adam 11
social entrepreneurship 276, 277, 281, 283, 284, 286
socialism 295, 304
societal and environmental responsibility 24
solid oxide fuel cell (SOFC) 213, 220
solid state lighting (LED) 138, 154, 173, 192, 194, 195, 197–200, 203
South Sea Bubble 17
stakeholder 15, 16, 20, 21, 30
stewardship 2, 4, 5
stewardship-based economics 291, 306, 309, 310
succession 54–58, 60, 63, 64, 66
sustainability 53, 55–63, 65–67, 107, 110, 125, 129–133, 239, 244, 245, 248–250, 252, 255, 261, 263, 264, 267–272, 275–287, 311, 315, 321, 322, 329
sustainable
  development 246, 252, 253, 255, 259, 260, 378, 402, 404–406, 409, 410, 415
  economy 1, 4, 421, 423
  lighting 136, 138, 141, 154, 173, 200
Suzuki, David 1, 4
systemic perspective 41

tacit knowledge 53, 57, 60
Taiwan 23
territory 391, 407, 408, 410
The Candle of Hope 421–423

The Story of Four Candles   422
Togo   353, 354, 357, 358, 360, 361, 363, 366, 367, 369–374
trade   355, 358, 362, 366, 367, 369
translucent alumina   155–160, 162, 168
trust   57, 59
Tulip mania   16

uncertain return   293–295
unrestricted earnings   11
United States   3

Vatican Council   300

Wall Street   17, 19, 21
white light LED   177, 185, 195, 197, 200